D0079477

Mathematics, Education and Philosophy

Studies in Mathematics Education Series

Series Editor:
Dr Paul Ernest
School of Education
University of Exeter
Exeter, UK.

Studies in Mathematics Education Series: 3

Mathematics, Education and Philosophy:
An International Perspective

Edited by

Paul Ernest

 The Falmer Press

(A member of the Taylor & Francis Group)
London • Washington, D.C.

UK   The Falmer Press, 4 John Street, London WC1N 2ET
USA   The Falmer Press, Taylor & Francis Inc., 1900 Frost Road, Suite 101, Bristol, PA 19007

© Paul Ernest 1994

All rights reserved. No part of this publication may be reproduced, stored in a retrieval system, or transmitted in any form or by any means, electronic, mechanical, photocopying, recording or otherwise, without permission in writing from the Publisher.

First published in 1994

A catalogue record for this book is available from the British Library

Library of Congress Cataloging-in-Publication Data are available on request

ISBN 0 7507 0290 7 cased

Jacket design by Caroline Archer

Typeset in 9.5/11pt Bembo by
Graphicraft Typesetters Ltd., Hong Kong.

Printed in Great Britain by Burgess Science Press, Basingstoke on paper which has a specified pH value on final paper manufacture of not less than 7.5 and is therefore 'acid free'.

510.7
M426e
1994

Contents

v

METHODIST COLLEGE LIBRARY
Fayetteville, N.C.

Contents

List of Figures and Tables

Preface by Series Editor

Mathematics education is established worldwide as a major area of study, with numerous dedicated journals and conferences serving national and international communities of scholars. Research in mathematics education is becoming more theoretically orientated. Vigorous new perspectives are pervading it from disciplines and fields as diverse as psychology, philosophy, logic, sociology, anthropology, history, feminism, cognitive science, semiotics, hermeneutics, post-structuralism and post-modernism. The series *Studies in Mathematics Education* consists of research contributions to the field based on disciplined perspectives that link theory with practice. It is founded on the philosophy that theory is the practitioner's most powerful tool in understanding and changing practice. Whether the practice is mathematics teaching, teacher education, or educational research, the series intends to offer new perspectives to assist in clarifying and posing problems and to stimulate debate. The series *Studies in Mathematics Education* will encourage the development and dissemination of theoretical perspectives in mathematics education as well as their critical scrutiny. It aims to have a major impact on the development of mathematics education as a field of study into the twenty-first century.

Unusually for the series this book and its companion volume are edited collections. Instead of the sharply focused concerns of a research monograph the books offer a panorama of complementary and forward looking perspectives. In the spirit of the series' philosophy, the two volumes illustrate between them the breadth of theoretical and philosophical perspectives that can fruitfully be brought to bear on mathematics and education.

The companion to the present volume is *Constructing Mathematical Knowledge: Epistemology and Mathematics Education*, and its contents are listed overleaf. Its emphasis is on epistemological issues, encompassing multiple perspectives on the learning of mathematics, as well as broader philosophical reflections on the genesis of knowledge. It explores constructivist and social theories of learning, and discusses the role of the computer in the light of these theories. It brings new analyses from psychoanalysis, Hermeneutics and other perspectives to bear on the issues of mathematics and learning. It enquires into the nature of enquiry itself, and an important emergent theme is the role of language. Finally, it relates the history of mathematics to its teaching and learning. Many of the chapters are from leading thinkers in the field, and the result is a definitive contribution to current debate.

The present volume provides a complementary focus. On the one hand, it addresses the central problem of the philosophy of mathematics education: the impact of conceptions of mathematics on educational practice. On the other hand, it embodies a far-reaching interdisciplinary enquiry into philosophical and reflective aspects of mathematics and mathematics education. It combines fallibilist and social philosophies of mathematics with exciting new analyses from post-structuralist and post-modernist theorists, offering both a reconceptualization and a critique of mathematics and mathematics education. The outcome is a set of new perspectives which bring out the human face of mathematics, as well as acknowledging its social responsibility.

Between them, the two volumes set a research agenda for the philosophy of mathematics education, a rapidly developing area of enquiry. Together they survey research and indicate orientations for future work from some of the best known and exciting young researchers in the field. Future volumes in the series will build upon and consolidate some of the perspectives offered by contributors here.

Paul Ernest
University of Exeter
School of Education,
March 1994

Contents to Constructing Mathematical Knowledge: Epistemology and Mathematics Education

Constructivism and the Learning of Mathematics

Psychology, Epistemology and Hermeneutics

Enquiry in Mathematics Education

History, mathematics and education

Introduction

Paul Ernest

All mathematical pedagogy, even if scarcely coherent, rests on a philosophy of mathematics. (René Thom[1])

In one short sentence René Thom articulates the rationale of this book. It is a contribution to the philosophy of mathematics education, that loosely defined cluster of interests at the intersection of mathematics, education and philosophy; whence the title of this volume. This focus represents an attitude of mind, the desire to enquire into philosophical and reflective aspects of mathematics and mathematics education, and to bring the two together. It also embodies the move towards interdisciplinarity that is sweeping the social sciences and humanities, driven by the desire to break down barriers between disparate fields of knowledge, and to apply some of the exciting new methods and perspectives from one field of study to another.

Central to the philosophy of mathematics eduction are two problems. First, there is of course the problem of the nature of mathematics itself. Second, as the quote by Thom suggests, there is the question of how a philosophy affects the teaching and learning of mathematics. Traditionally the first problem belongs to the philosophy of mathematics. But this field is changing, reflecting a new interdisciplinarity. The philosophy of mathematics might be said to be in the midst of a 'Kuhnian revolution'. The Euclidean paradigm of mathematics as an objective, absolute, incorrigible and rigidly hierarchical body of knowledge is increasingly under question. One reason is that the foundations of mathematics are not as secure as was claimed. Technical results such as Gödel's theorems have shown that formal axiomatic systems can never be regarded as ultimate. Another reason is a growing dissatisfaction amongst mathematicians, philosophers, educators and multidisciplinary scholars with the traditional narrow focus of the professional philosophy of mathematics, usually limited to questions of the foundations of pure mathematical knowledge and of the existence of mathematical objects (Kitcher and Aspray, 1988).

A revolutionary new tradition in the philosophy of mathematics has been emerging which has been termed quasi-empiricist (Lakatos, Kitcher, Tymoczko), maverick (Kitcher and Aspray) and post-modernist (Tiles).[2] This is primarily naturalistic, concerned to describe the nature of mathematics and the practices of mathematicians, both current and historical. It is quasi-empiricist and fallibilist in its epistemology, thus displacing mathematics from its place as the secure cornerstone of absolutism. A number of philosophers and mathematicians can be identified as contributing to this new tradition, including Wittgenstein, Lakatos, Putnam, Wang, Davis and Hersh, Kitcher, Tymoczko. These authors have proposed that the task of the philosophy of mathematics is to account for mathematics more fully, including the practices of mathematicians, its history and applications, the place of mathematics in human culture, perhaps even including issues of values and education — in short — describing the human face of mathematics.

This concern with external, social dimensions of mathematics including its applications and uses, has given rise to the desire to see a multidisciplinary account of mathematics drawing inspiration from many currents of thought, including ethnomathematics (Ascher, D'Ambrosio, Zaslavsky), social constructivism and the rhetoric of science (Billig, Knorr-Cetina, Latour), post-structuralism (Foucault, Walkerdine), post-modernism (Derrida, Lyotard), semiotics (Peirce, Eco), social constructionist psychology (Gergen, Harré, Shotter), feminism (Harding, Rose), critical theory (Habermas, Marcuse), externalist philosophy of science (Feyerabend, Hacking, Kuhn, Laudan), social epistemology (Fuller, Toulmin), and philosophy in general (Rorty, Bernstein).

Consequently, a number of researchers are drawing on other disciplines to account for the nature of mathematics, including Bloor and Restivo, from social constructivism in sociology; Wilder and Livingston, from cultural studies and ethnomethodology; Rotman from semiotics, Aspray and Kitcher, Joseph, Kline and Gillies from the history of mathematics.

Thus a growing number of scholars share a common concern with external, social dimensions of mathematics including its history, applications and uses, and often a desire to see a multidisciplinary account of mathematics which accommo-dates ethnomathematics, mathematics education studies, and feminist and multi-cultural critiques. What drives this for many is a sense of the social responsibility of mathematics. For once mathematics is reconceptualized as a social construction, then the social function of mathematics in society must be examined. Its relations with broader issues of power, social structure and values, needs to be considered to see whose interests it serves. The question must be asked: who in the world economy gains by mathematics, and who loses? An ethics of mathematics is called for, once it is seen as both an instrument and product of values and power. For one of the conclusions to be drawn from a radical social view of mathematics is that it plays a key role in the distribution of life chances. For example, there is widespread concern with how mathematics acts as a 'critical filter' in depriving minority and women students equal opportunities in employment. Philosophical and ethical considerations like these thus have important implications for math-ematics and particularly for educational theory and practice.

Within mathematics education there is an increasing awareness of the signi-ficance of epistemological and philosophical issues for important traditional areas of inquiry too. Theories of learning have been epistemologically orientated for some time, with discussions of the philosophical assumptions of constructivism and various forms of social constructivism and socio-cultural cognition wide-spread. Other areas drawing on the philosophy of mathematics and philosophical perspectives in general include mathematical thinking, problem-solving and investigational pedagogy, curriculum theories, teacher education and develop-ment, teacher beliefs, learner conceptions, and applications of the 'Perry Scheme' and 'Women's Ways of Knowing'.[3] Scholars are also reflecting on broader social issues including the culture of mathematics and its politics, its philosophy, its social context, its language, and issues of gender, race and class.

Philosophical considerations are also central to empirical research in mathematics education and its methods of inquiry, with researchers becoming increasingly aware of the epistemological foundations of their methodologies and inquiries, and referring to them explicitly. Multiple research paradigms are now widely used, and proponents of the scientific, interpretative and critical theoretical research paradigms discussing and comparing their philosophical and methodological bases (when not engaged in internecine paradigm war, *à la* Gage, 1989).

Problems of the Philosophy of Mathematics Education

This introduction outlines some of the areas of activity in the philosophy of mathematics education. A more systematic insight into its central questions or 'problematique' arises from considering Schwab's (1978) four 'commonplaces of teaching'. These are the subject (mathematics), the learner of mathematics, the mathematics teacher, and the milieu of teaching, including the relationship of mathematics teaching and learning, and its aims, to society in general. Each area of concern gives rise to a characteristic set of problems and questions, which begins to make up a research agenda for the philosophy of mathematics education.

- **Aims and the social context**
  What are the aims of mathematics education? Are these aims valid? Whose aims are they? For whom? Based on which values? Who gains and who loses? How do the social, cultural and historical contexts relate to mathematics, the aims of teaching, and the teaching and learning of mathematics?
- **The nature of learning**
  What philosophical assumptions, possibly implicit, underpin the learning of mathematics? Are these assumptions valid? Which epistemologies and learning theories are assumed? How can the social context of learning be accommodated?
- **The nature of teaching**
  What philosophical assumptions, possibly implicit, does mathematics teaching rest on? Are these assumptions valid? What means are adopted to achieve the aims of mathematics education? Are the ends and means consistent?
- **The nature of mathematics**
  What is mathematics, and how can its nature be accounted for? What philosophies of mathematics have been developed? Whose? What features of mathematics do they pick out as significant? What is their impact on the teaching and learning of mathematics?

The Nature of Mathematics and Its Relation to Teaching

The issue, then, is not, What is the best way to teach? but, What is mathematics really all about? . . . Controversies about . . . teaching cannot be resolved without confronting problems about the nature of mathematics. (Hersh, 1979, 34)

What might be identified as the central problem of the philosophy of mathematics education is the issue of the relationship between philosophies of mathematics and mathematics education. The question is: what is their impact on the teaching and learning of mathematics? Hersh and Thom claim that different philosophical positions have significantly different educational implications. Steiner elaborates this claim as follows.

> **Thesis 1**. Generally speaking, all more or less elaborated conceptions, epistemologies, methodologies, philosophies of mathematics (in the large or in part) contain — often in an implicit way — ideas, orientations or germs for theories on the teaching and learning of mathematics.
> **Thesis 2**. Concepts for the teaching and learning of mathematics — more specifically: goals and objectives (taxonomies), syllabi, textbooks, curricula, teaching methodologies, didactical principles, learning theories, mathematics education research designs (models, paradigms, theories, etc.), but likewise teachers' conceptions of mathematics and mathematics teaching as well as students' perceptions of mathematics — carry with them or even rest upon (often in an implicit way) particular philosophical and epistemological views of mathematics. (Steiner, 1987, 8)

Thus the claim is that the association is bi-directional. First, that all teaching and learning practices in mathematics rest upon possibly implicit epistemologies or philosophies of mathematics. Second, which I shall stress more here, that any philosophy of mathematics (including personal philosophies) has powerful implications for social and educational issues, and many educational and pedagogical consequences. However such consequences are not in general strictly logical implications of a philosophy, and additional values, aims and other assumptions are required to reach such conclusions (Ernest, 1991, 1994). Because the link is not one of logical implication, it is theoretically possible to consistently associate a philosophy of mathematics with almost any educational practice or approach. Both a neo-behaviourist or cognitivist (such as Ausubel) and a radical constructivist may be concerned to ascertain what a child knows before commencing teaching, despite having diametrically opposite epistemologies. Likewise a traditional purist mathematician and a social constructivist may both favour a multicultural approach to mathematics, but for different reasons (the former perhaps to humanize mathematics, the latter to show it as the social construction of all of humanity for social justice reasons).

Although there is no logical necessity for, e.g., a transmission-style pedagogy to be associated with an absolutist, objectivist epistemology and philosophy of mathematics, such associations often are the case (Ernest, 1988, 1991). This is presumed to be due to the resonances and sympathies between different aspects of a person's philosophy, ideology, values and belief-systems. These form links and associations and become restructured in moves towards maximum coherence and consistency, and ultimately towards integration of the personality.

In particular, the observed consistency between the teachers' professed conceptions of mathematics and the way they typically presented the content strongly suggests that the teachers' views, beliefs and preferences about mathematics do influence their instructional practice. (Thompson, 1984, 125)

Research over the past several years on teachers' beliefs gives strong testimony that teachers' conceptions make a difference in how mathematics is taught. (Cooney, 1988, 356)

Much work in the philosophy of mathematics education pertains to exploring the link between the philosophies of mathematics implicit in teachers' beliefs, in texts and the mathematics curriculum, in systems and practices of mathematical assessment and in mathematics classroom practices and the results with learners. Whilst much progress has been made, much work remains to be done in the area.

The Philosophy of Mathematics Education Network

This burgeoning area of shared interest led to the founding of a philosophy of mathematics education network in 1990. This is a network of interested persons revolving around an organizing group, a newsletter and regular conference symposia and discussion groups.

The 'Philosophy of Mathematics Education Organising Group' is an informal collective of interested and cooperating scholars, who have each made significant contributions to the area in their own personal research. The members are the following: Raffaella Borasi (USA), Stephen I. Brown (USA), Leone Burton (UK), Paul Cobb (USA), Jere Confrey (USA), Thomas S. Cooney (USA), Kathryn Crawford (Australia), Ubiratan D'Ambrosio (Brazil), Philip J. Davis (USA), Sandy Dawson (Canada), Paul Ernest (UK), Group Chair, Ernst von Glasersfeld (USA), David Henderson (USA), Reuben Hersh (USA), Christine Keitel-Kreidt (Germany), Stephen Lerman (UK), John Mason (UK), Marilyn Nickson (UK), David Pimm (UK), Sal Restivo (USA), Leo Rogers (UK), Anna Sfard (Israel), Ole Skovsmose (Denmark), Francesco Speranza (Italy), Leslie P. Steffe (USA), Hans-Georg Steiner (Germany), John Volmink (South Africa), Yuxin Zheng (Peoples Republic of China).

The Philosophy of Mathematics Education Newsletter is edited in rotation by members of this organizing group, including, to date: Sandy Dawson, Paul Ernest, Stephen Lerman, Marilyn Nickson and Leo Rogers. The newsletter is mailed to several hundred subscribers in many countries covering every continent of the globe. Its aims are to foster awareness of philosophical aspects of mathematics and mathematics education, understood broadly and inclusively; to disseminate news of events and new thinking in these topics; and to encourage international cooperation and informal communication and dialogue between teachers, scholars and others engaged in research in the area. The newsletter has carried discussions on many themes, including radical constructivism, ethnomathematics, the popular image of mathematics, post-modernism, revolutions in mathematics and the philosophy of mathematics education itself.

There are also regular Philosophy of Mathematics Education symposia at national and international conferences. The most significant of these was the Philosophy of Mathematics Education Topic Group at the 7th International Congress of Mathematical Education, Québec, August 1992, which played an important part in the genesis of this book. There have also been philosophy of mathematics education symposia and discussion groups at the First British Congress of Mathematics Education (Loughborough, 1991), the British Society for Research into Learning Mathematics (Bath, 1990), and the conferences of the International Group for the Psychology of Mathematics Education numbers 14 (Mexico, 1990), 16 (USA, 1992) and 17 (Japan, 1993).

This Volume

This book represents some of the most interesting aspects of current work in the philosophy of mathematics education, as well as an indication of some of the more exciting new departures. The aim is both to survey the field and to try to predict future areas of fruitful research. A few of the chapters began as contributions to the Philosophy of Mathematics Education symposium at the ICME-7 conference in Québec, 1992, but most have now changed beyond recognition. Almost all of the chapters were specially written for the book, and were solicited from leading figures as well as from promising young researchers in the field. In fact, the response to the invitation to contribute was so overwhelming, that even when all but the very best chapters had been discarded, the remainder was enough to make two good sized volumes. Therefore this book is published at the same time as a sister volume entitled *Constructing Mathematical Knowledge: Epistemology and Mathematics Education*, the contents of which are listed above. Together the two volumes survey current research in the philosophy of mathematics and mathematics education. As editor, one of the most exciting features of putting this collection together, as the discerning reader can tell, is that many of the most important contributors to the field are themselves represented in the collection.

The contents of this volume have been divided into four sections.

- *Reconceptualizing the Philosophy of Mathematics*. This includes contributions on fresh approaches to the philosophy of mathematics from fallibilist perspectives.
- *Post-modernist and Post-structuralist Approaches*. This is the largest section, made up of a number of innovative chapters applying post-structuralist and post-modernist perspectives to both mathematics and mathematics education. This is one of the areas of growth in philosophical research on mathematics and education, and it is expected to bear significant fruits in the future.
- *The Human Face of Mathematics*. In varying ways, this section shows how the human face of mathematics can be revealed by contrasting individual mathematicians, disciplines, or even cultures.
- *The Social Context of Mathematics and Education*. This carries on where the last section left off, but also considers social aspects of mathematics, including the crucial issues of race, gender and values, within the context of education.

The four themes in the other volume are as follows.

- *History, mathematics and education*. This relates the historical development of mathematics to the teaching and learning of mathematics; a vital and growing area of research.
- *Enquiry in Mathematics Education*. This is concerned with both the nature and the outcomes of reflective research that illuminates mathematics in some significant way.
- *Psychology, Epistemology and Hermeneutics*. This section ties in with that on post-modernist and post-structuralist approaches in Volume 1, also bringing new perspectives from psychoanalysis and Hermeneutics to bear on mathematical and educational issues.
- *Constructivism and the Learning of Mathematics*. This is the largest section in the second volume, exploring constructivist and social theories of learning mathematics, and their relationships, viewed from multiple perspectives. This continues to be one of the most central areas of philosophical research in mathematics education, and still has a great deal to yield in the way of insight, not to mention controversy.

There are other themes shared by the chapters too. These include the relationship of mathematics with art, computers, history, gender, race, social critique, language and curriculum. Shared perspectives in the chapters include those of social theory, sociology of knowledge, and various insider, outsider and educational viewpoints. All these recurring themes serve to illustrate the rich complexity of the chapters and their interconnections, together making up an invaluable resource. This book is offered in the hope that readers will be stimulated to pursue and develop some of these perspectives and connections, both enriching the teaching of mathematics and philosophical reflection on it too.

Notes

1. Thom (1973, 204).
2. Details of most of the philosophy of mathematics references are provided at the end of Chapter 3.
3. See Perry (1970) and Belenky *et al.* (1986).

References

COONEY, T.J. (1988) 'The issue of reform', *Mathematics Teacher*, 80, pp. 352–63.
BELENKY, M.F., CLINCHY, B.M., GOLDBERGER, N.R. and TARULE, J.M. (1986) *Women's Ways of Knowing*, New York, Basic Books.
ERNEST, P. (1988) 'The impact of beliefs on the teaching of mathematics', in KEITEL, C., DAMEROW, P., BISHOP, A. and GERDES, P. (Eds) *Mathematics, Education and Society*, Paris, UNESCO, 1989, pp. 99–101.
ERNEST, P. (1991) *The Philosophy of Mathematics Education*, London, The Falmer Press.
ERNEST, P. (1994) 'The philosophy of mathematics and mathematics education', in BIEHLER, R., SCHOLZ, R.W., STRAESSER, R. and WINKELMANN, B. (Eds) (1994) *The Didactics of Mathematics as a Scientific Discipline*, Dordrecht, Kluwer, pp. 335–49.

GAGE, N.L. (1989) 'The paradigm wars and their aftermath: A "hisorical" sketch of research on teaching since 1989', *Teachers College Record*, 91, 2, pp. 135–50.

HERSH, R. (1979) 'Some proposals for reviving the philosophy of mathematics', *Advances in Mathematics*, 31, pp. 31–50.

KITCHER, P. and ASPRAY, W. (1988) 'An opinionated introduction', in ASPRAY, W. and KITCHER, P. (Eds), *History and Philosophy of Modern Mathematics*, Minneapolis, University of Minnesota Press, pp. 3–57.

PERRY, W.G. (1970) *Forms of Intellectual and Ethical Development in the College Years: A scheme*, New York, Holt, Rinehart and Winston.

SCHWAB, J. (1978) *Science, curriculum, and liberal education*, in WESTBURY, I. and WILKOF, N. (Eds) Chicago, University of Chicago Press.

STEINER, H.G. (1987) 'Philosophical and epistemological aspects of mathematics and their interaction with theory and practice in mathematics education', *For the Learning of Mathematics*, 7, 1, pp. 7–13.

THOM, R. (1973) 'Modern mathematics: Does it exist?', in HOWSON, A.G. (Ed) *Developments in Mathematical Education*, Cambridge, Cambridge University Press, pp. 194–209.

THOMPSON, A.G. (1984) 'The relationship between teachers' conceptions of mathematics and mathematics teaching to instructional practice', *Educational Studies in Mathematics*, 15, pp. 105–27.

Part I

Reconceptualizing the Philosophy of Mathematics

> But all that mathematics is still tricked out in, its absolute character and perfect accuracy, its generality and autonomy, in a word, its truth and eternity, *all this* (if I may be forgiven the expression) *all this is pure superstition!* (Mannoury, 1947, in Beth and Piaget, 1966, 58)

Today the philosophy of mathematics is a specialist academic field, with its own literature and community of scholars. It has become professionalized as a branch of philosophy, employing the styles of thought and reasoning acceptable to the philosophical community at large, and publishing in general philosophical journals. Its current concern is largely with issues of the warrants for mathematical knowledge and the status of mathematical objects.[1]

However this 'professionalized' model of the philosophy of mathematics is a recent construction (Kitcher and Aspray, 1988). Earlier this century, in the works of Frege, Russell, Hilbert, Brouwer, Heyting, Weyl, Carnap, Curry, Gödel, and others, the field looked more like a branch of mathematics, and was identified with the foundations of mathematics. Even today the field is not static, and currently there is a growing interest relating individual knowing in mathematics to theories of cognition and empirical findings in psychology (Detlefson, Kitcher). Thus due to internal forces, a broadening of the scope of the philosophy of mathematics is taking place.

In addition to the 'professionalized' philosophy of mathematics, there is also a broader domain of questions, interests, literature, and non-specialist scholars, concerned with reflecting on the nature of mathematics. These include mathematicians, historians, anthropologists, sociologists, and educationists specializing in mathematics, and interested in issues concerning the nature of mathematics. It also includes historians of ideas, and interdisciplinary 'European' (e.g., French and German) philosophers, including Husserl, Enriques, Bachelard, Mannoury, Serres, who have always related the nature of mathematics to the conditions of human experience, or to culture and history.

There is a also a multidisciplinary 'maverick' tradition emerging in the philosophy of mathematics itself, which is broadening the focus to include historical and methodological issues in the philosophy of mathematics (Davis, Hersh, Lakatos, Kitcher, Wang, Tymoczko).

Overall, it can be concluded that academic philosophy of mathematics has not the unity that is sometimes assumed. It is an area of contestation, and its history reveals different perspectives and standpoints on the nature of the field itself.

The authors in this section share the view that mathematical knowledge is fallible and quasi-empirical, and that consequently in mathematics (as in science and other areas of human knowledge), the contexts of discovery and justification interpenetrate. Because of this feature, social and cultural issues cannot be denied legitimacy in the philosophy of mathematics and must instead be admitted as playing an essential and constitutive role in the nature of mathematical knowledge. Just as has happened in the modern philosophy of science, the philosophy of mathematics needs to be broadened and reconceptualized to include 'external' factors related to the historical, methodological and wider cultural and social aspects of mathematics.

One view of what the reconceptualized field should treat is the following:[2]

- epistemology (the nature, genesis and justification of mathematical knowledge, and proof);
- ontology (the nature and origins of mathematical objects and relations with language);
- mathematical theories (constructive and structural, their nature, development, and appraisal);
- the applications of mathematics (and relations with other areas of knowledge and values),
- mathematical practice and methodology (including the practices and methods of mathematicians in the past and present); and
- the learning of mathematics (and its role in knowledge-transmission and creativity).

Three of the researchers whose contributions to the reconceptualization of the philosophy of mathematics have been decisive are David Bloor (1976), Reuben Hersh (1979), and Thomas Tymoczko (1986), so their contributions to this section are especially welcome.

Notes

1. Ironically the only dedicated journal *Philosophia Mathematica* has in its editorial policy explicitly adopted a broader view of the field than the narrow professional focus described here.
2. Adapted from Ernest (in press).

References

BETH, E.W. and PIAGET, J. (1966) *Mathematical Epistemology and Psychology*, Dordrecht, Reidel.

BLOOR, D. (1976) *Knowledge and Social Imagery*, London, Routledge and Kegan Paul (Second revised edition, University of Chicago Press, 1991).

ERNEST, P. (In press) *Social Constructivism as a Philosophy of Mathematics*, Albany, NY, SUNY Press.

HERSH, R. (1979) 'Some proposals for reviving the philosophy of mathematics', *Advances in Mathematics*, 31, pp. 31–50.

KITCHER, P. and ASPRAY, W. (1988) 'An opinionated introduction', in ASPRAY, W. and KITCHER, P. (Eds) *History and Philosophy of Modern Mathematics*, Minneapolis, University of Minnesota Press, 1988, pp. 3–57.

TYMOCZKO, T. (Ed) (1986) *New Directions in the Philosophy of Mathematics*, Boston, Birkhauser.

Chapter 1

Fresh Breezes in the Philosophy of Mathematics

Reuben Hersh

Since the time of Pythagoras, philosophy of mathematics has tried to account for mathematical existence and the nature of mathematical objects.

The mystery is that numbers, circles, analytic functions, n-dimensional manifolds, all seem to be different from everything else we think about. They're neither physical nor mental. Not mental, because the Pythagorean theorem or any other well-established mathematical fact is independent of what you or I think. Whether we know it and believe it or don't know it and don't believe it, the Pythagorean theorem is still true. Yet it's not physical either. Plato and Aristotle explained clearly that the triangles and circles of the geometer are not the same as the carpenter's triangles or circles, but something 'ideal'.

Spiritual, empirical, psychological, formalist, and logicist explanations have been offered. None give a credible account of what we do when we do mathematics. Presently some dozen authors are working to construct a social-historical-cultural answer.

An Israeli mathematics education researcher, Anna Sfard, recently published an interesting insight. In learning a new mathematical concept, children first learn it as an algorithm — a procedure, a method. Later, the algorithm or procedure is transformed into an entity or object. She calls this transformation 'reification'. It's difficult to achieve, often requiring help from the teacher. This story is close to the theory of a Russian psychologist, Lev Vygotsky, who died in the 1930s and has recently become well-known.

For example, subtraction is an algorithm. It isn't hard. It reifies into the negative numbers — very hard. Again, it isn't hard to connect two points by a straight line. It is hard to conceptualize the straight line as an entity in itself, apart from operations. Everyone understands the operation of collecting distinct individuals into a set. The set as an entity in itself, apart from any act of collecting, is subtle.

Is every entity in mathematics just a frozen algorithm? Which are? Which aren't? What about high-level novelties like submartingales, dual functors, kittygories, generalized functions? What is the relationship, the interaction between doing and being, between algorithm and entity? This is an example of a question in the philosophy of mathematics that's based on mathematical practice, on seeing mathematics as a human activity. It's an answer to people who say, 'If philosophy of mathematics isn't foundations of mathematics, then what is it?'

Foundations Lost

In books on philosophy of mathematics (S. Körner, or P. Benacerraf and H. Putnam) one reads of the leading problem, 'foundations'. How to establish mathematical knowledge as certain, indubitable, free of any possible doubt? Three historically important solutions to that problem were offered — logicism (Platonism), formalism, intuitionism. All three proved unsuccessful. For logicism and formalism, as far as I know, no major new idea has been suggested in over half a century. Intuitionism, and its offspring constructivism, did strive to carry out the programme enunciated by Brouwer and streamlined by Bishop. But their goal of replacing classical mathematics is more remote now than sixty or seventy years ago.

Logicism, the doctrine of Gottlob Frege and Bertrand Russell, said 'Build on logic!' In fact, they believed that mathematics is actually a part of logic. This would be a good thing, they thought, because they thought logic was the most indubitable, rock-bottom part of human thought. But in building mathematics out of logic they needed set theoretic axioms such as the axiom of infinity ('There exists an infinite set') which aren't logic in the original sense. Russell's famous paradox exposed unsuspected treachery in set theory. So as an explanation of the nature of mathematics, logicisn died. Some investigators still study the relation between mathematics and logic.

Next came intuitionism, the doctrine of Henri Poincaré, Emile Borel, Henri Lebesgue and above all, L.E.J. Brouwer. The intuitionists said, 'Build on counting — the natural numbers! Only what's obtained constructively from the natural numbers must be allowed in mathematics'. They didn't think it necessary or possible to define 'constructive'. They did say it didn't include indirect proof — proof by contradiction. For the intuitionists, mathematics that depends on indirect proof is not valid.

Errett Bishop produced a streamlined intuitionism called 'constructivism', closer to mathematical practice, not coloured with mysticism as is Brouwer's intuitionism. Groups of Bishop's followers can still be found here and there. But their dream of constructivizing mathematics, of converting the mathematics profession, is dead. The overwhelming majority of mathematicians rejected intuitionism and constructivism years ago.

Formalism is credited to David Hilbert. It's been said that his leap into foundationalism was a reaction to the flirtation of his favourite pupil, Hermann Weyl, with Brouwer's intuitionism. Hilbert was an implacable foe of Brouwer and intuitionism. He said that depriving the mathematician of proof by contradiction was like tying a boxer's hands behind his back.

Hilbert intended to prove that mathematics was *consistent* — not tautologically true as Russell had thought, nor objectively true when stripped of unacceptable reasoning, as Brouwer thought. To do this, he had a brilliant, original idea: work with formulas, not content. Think of axiom and theorem as strings of meaningless symbols. Think of the transformation from axioms to theorem — the *proof* — as a permutation of symbols. Permutations of symbols are elementary mathematical objects, studied in 'combinatorics' or 'combinatorial analysis'. To prove mathematics is consistent, Hilbert had to prove that the permutations allowed in mathematical proof, starting with the axioms, could never yield a falsehood: 0 = 1, for example.

A few years later, Kurt Gödel proved that such a thing could never be proved by the proof methods Hilbert allowed. This incompleteness theorem of Gödel's is commonly cited as the death blow to Hilbert's programme, and to formalism as a philosophy of mathematics.

The surviving remnants of foundationalism have been named 'neo-Fregeanism' by Philip Kitcher. This doctrine today dominates the philosophy of mathematics as done by academic philosophers. It says: 'Philosophical thinking about mathematics need only concern itself with sets, and with set theory's twin sister, logic.' The goal of foundationalism admittedly is hopeless and forgotten, but the assumption persists that 'Foundations of mathematics is the philosophy of mathematics.' But the great majority of researchers, users, teachers, and historians of mathematics aren't primarily concerned with set theory. Consequently, philosophers of mathematics ignore mathematics and mathematicians, and mathematicians find nothing of interest in philosophy of mathematics.

A deplorable situation! The principal problem in philosophy of mathematics left unsolved by all schools, which for over half a century are in paralysis! Mathematicians and philosophers of mathematics virtually ignorant of each other's existence!

A Harvard philosopher Hilary Putnam once published a foundationalist paper titled 'Mathematics Without Foundations'. Is philosophy of mathematics pointless and unnecessary? Or is it time for a new start?

Phil/m and Phil/sci

A weird fact about modern US philosophy is that philosophy of science and philosophy of mathematics are almost disconnected from each other. Authors in philosophy of science rarely refer to philosophy of mathematics, and vice versa. Even an author who writes on both subjects, in any one article sticks to one or the other. It's like baseball and football — play one or the other, but not both at the same time.

I want to compare philosophy of mathematics and philosophy of science, because philosophy of science offers hope to philosophy of mathematics. I'm not looking at a specific problem in mathematics or physics, but comparing the recent histories of the two subjects.

I want to compare philosophy of mathematics today to philosophy of science in the 1930s and 1940s. That subject was dominated by 'logical positivists' or 'logical empiricists': Rudolf Carnap and his friends from the *Wiener Kreis* (Vienna Circle). As a result of taking Bertrand Russell and Alfred North Whitehead's *Principia Mathematica* and Ludwig Wittgenstein's *Tractatus Logico-Philosophicus* too seriously, they believed they had the correct methodology for science: (1) state the axioms; (2) state the correspondence between words and physical observables; (3) derive the theory, as Euclid derived geometry, or Mach derived mechanics.

Some logical positivist work was useful. But it was soon noticed that what logical positivists said science should be had little in common with what scientists actually did or wanted to do. Critics of logical positivism included Karl Popper, Thomas Kuhn, Imre Lakatos, Paul Feyerabend. These radicals disagreed with each other. They weren't a disciplined movement. But they all said philosophy of science could talk about what scientists actually do. It didn't have to provide philosophical presuppositions and instructions for scientists to ignore.

New Day A'Comin'!

Philosophy of mathematics is overdue for its Popper, Kuhn, Lakatos, and Feyerabend. It's overdue for analysis of what mathematicians actually do, and the philosophical issues therein. In fact, this turn is actually taking place.

Wittgenstein made an important contribution by insisting that mathematics is something people do. But he didn't recognize that it's also something people think and something people know. He insisted, or seemed to insist, that since it's just something we do, we could do it any way at all, not only in the way we happen to have chosen. This conventionalism is contrary to experience and necessity, and so his true insight, that mathematics is something people do, has been underestimated.

Lakatos' masterpiece, *Proofs and Refutations*, was an inspiration to many of the people who are now working on social constructivism of mathematics. It was a dissertation written under the influences of Karl Popper and George Polya. In the preface he made a devastating attack on formalism and logicism. The book is a classroom dialogue, showing in brilliant detail how mathematical concepts can grow in a dialectic of proof and refutation, argument and counter-argument — not in a mechanical logic machine working on sacred axioms. Lakatos called his viewpoint quasi-empiricism. He never amplified or explicated his views, to tell us what he thought mathematics really was. I suspect his commitment to Popper's objectivism trapped him in a position where he couldn't escape the Platonism he wanted to repudiate.

In recent years Ray Wilder, Leslie White, Alfred Renyi, Michael Polanyi, George Polya, Greg Chaitin, Phil Davis, Paul Ernest, Nick Goodman, Phil Kitcher, Penelope Maddy, Michael Resnik, Gian-Carlo Rota, Brian Rotman, Gabriel Stolzenberg, Robert Thomas, Tom Tymoczko, Jean Paul van Bendegem, and Hao Wang have contributed.

The temptation is irresistible to quote the 'Introductory Afterthoughts' in the recent collection by Echeverria *et al.*, from a 1990 conference on philosophy of mathematics at the University of the Basque Country in Spain, attended by over 200 people. The editors, whom I have never met or corresponded with, write: 'As is evidenced by a wealth of recent publications the philosophy of mathematics presently is undergoing a rather dramatic transformation and reorientation.' Below is a footnote referring to me, Lakatos, Maddy, Goodman and Tymoczko.

Some ideas some of us hold:

1. Mathematics is human. It's part of and fits into human culture. It's not Frege's timeless, tenseless, objective abstract reality.
2. Mathematical knowledge isn't by nature infallible. Like science, mathematics can advance by making mistakes, correcting them and recorrecting them. This fallibilism is brilliantly argued in Imre Lakatos' *Proofs and Refutations*.

3. There are different versions of proof or rigour, depending on time, place, and other things. The use of computers in proofs is a nontraditional version of rigour.
4. Empirical evidence, numerical experimentation, probabilistic proof all help us decide what to believe in mathematics. Aristotelian logic is not necessarily always the best way of deciding.
5. Mathematical objects are a certain variety of social-cultural-historical objects. They're distinctive. We can tell mathematics from literature or religion. Nevertheless, mathematical objects are shared ideas, part of the culture or a significant subculture — like Moby Dick in literature, or the Immaculate Conception in religion.

What do social constructivists answer to the big question, 'What is the nature of mathematical objects?' If the question seems difficult, it's because of a centuries-old assumption in western philosophy: 'There are two kinds of things in the world. Everything that isn't physical is mental; everything that isn't mental is physical.' When Frege proved that mathematics is neither physical nor mental, he had to account for it by inventing a new kind of entity — 'abstract objects' — about which he could say nothing except that they're neither physical nor mental.

Mental is thought, individual consciousness, subjectivity; lusts, wishes, fears, angers; perceptions, hopes, desires, yearnings; and also private thoughts about science or mathematics before they are communicated to the world. Matter is whatever takes up space, has weight, can be studied by scientific instruments. Mountains, trees, bugs, the Earth, the sun, the stars, sound, light, heat, X-rays, gamma rays, infra-red and ultra-violet rays. Is there anything that's neither mental nor physical? Yes! : sonatas; poems; churches; morality; the profit motive; armies; wars; academies of science.

Does the New York Academy of Science exist? Undoubtedly yes. Is it mental? If the Secretary and the President of the Academy took amnesia, the life of the Academy would continue. The Academy isn't just somebody's thoughts. If the building were blown up and the trustees moved the Academy to Yonkers, it would go on. If the officers, trustees and members died of some dread disease, they would be replaced. The Academy would live on. Its physical and mental embodiments are necessary, but they're not *it*. The Academy isn't just the minds and bodies of anyone. Neither is it just the stones of its building.

What is it then? It's a social institution. The mental and physical are not sufficient to describe the New York Academy of Science, let alone the world. Indeed, most of the things that concern us most closely are not mental or physical but social entities: marriage, divorce, child care; admission to, and graduation from, schools and colleges; advertising, shopping, prices; war, peace, the draft; politics, taxes, salaries, employment; the news, sports and entertainment. All these have mental and physical aspects, but they aren't mental or physical entities. They're social entities.

Sometimes I expand 'social entities' to 'social-cultural-historical entities'. The histories of physical entities don't usually seem crucial. The history of a mental entity might be interesting, but it would be nebulous, hard to know. Social entities are created and evolve in history, knowledge of which is essential to understand them. 'Cultural' is because the study of social artifacts is anthropology, and anthropology says 'cultural' rather than 'social'.

By listing things in Group 3, I've shown that there are at least three kinds of things in the world. Are there still others, a fourth kind, even a fifth? This issue is not relevant for us. I don't know of other kinds. Some people believe in extra-sensory perception, ghosts, messages from previous centuries or from the future. If there are such things, they're neither mental, physical, nor social-cultural-historical. I don't believe there are such things, so I'm satisfied with three. (Karl Popper's World 3, which consists of scientific theories and works of art, is a second cousin to the social-cultural-historical reality I am talking about.)

Now to the point. Since there are mathematical objects — such as numbers — which exist, and since what exists is either mental, physical, or social, which of the three are numbers? We have already seen that numbers aren't mental or physical. By Aristotelian logic (the law of the excluded middle) we could conclude immediately that they must be social. But let's not be peremptory. Let's consider it a hypothesis. Is mathematics social-cultural-historical?

Certainly it is historical. The history of mathematics is a developed subject, and its specialists have studied mathematics back to the Babylonians. We don't know the remote origin of mathematics, nor the remote origin of writing, speech, religion, the family, chiefhood or war. We recognize that these origins were part of the self-creation of the human race. Archeology, linguistics, genetics, ethnology gradually tell us a little more. Counting and talking both had their human beginnings.

Mathematics is a social entity. This may not be apparent to people with no direct acquaintance with mathematics. But mathematicians never did work as isolated hermits. Today they are usually in academic, government or industrial institutions, paid directly or indirectly by the government.

Srinivasa Ramanujan, the self-taught Indian mathematical genius, worked to be recognized by the English mathematics establishment. Once he received an invitation, he left India for England, at great hardship to his family and his religious commitments, and to his ability to find daily food that he could eat. His motive was to work with other mathematicians capable of understanding what he was doing.

In the sixteenth and seventeenth centuries, before today's mathematical institutions were created, Fermat, Huygens, Leibnitz were devoted letter writers, constantly exchanging ideas with colleagues in other cities. Today a new result becomes part of mathematics only after experts read it and pronounce it good, or it's published in a recognized journal, preferably after being refereed. The mathematics profession monitors its product. Acceptance by the profession is essential to be recognized or accepted as a mathematician.

Mathematics is a cultural product, in the sense that its overall content, its direction of movement, respond to the pressures of society. (In saying this, I do not underestimate the insistence of pure mathematicians on autonomy.) The militarization of US mathematics in World War II was a familiar example. Newton's calculus was a tool of his gravitational theory. His gravitational theory was a way to understand the motions of the stars and planets. The motions of the stars and planets were important because England was a maritime nation. Navigational skills better than those of Spain and Portugal had cash value for England.

Taking the Test

To test a philosophy of mathematics confront it with questions:

1. What makes mathematics different?
2. What is mathematics about?
3. How do we acquire knowledge of mathematics, apart from proof?
4. Why does mathematics achieve near-universal consensus? Why are mathematical results independent of time, place, race, nationality and gender, in spite of the social nature of mathematics?
5. Does the infinite exist, and if so, how?
6. Why does pure mathematics so often become useful in physics?
7. What about the axiom of choice?
8. What about the continuum hypothesis?

I dealt with number 6 in (Hersh, 1990) and will not repeat that here. Questions 7 and 8 are fundamentally important. But they are specialized technical problems. They probably will not be touched by social constructivism; but then neither can anybody else touch them.

Questions 1 and 2 have already been discussed thoroughly. The answer is, mathematics is about a special kind of socially shared idea (or notion or concept!), namely, those that demonstrate science-like reproducibility, that yield the same result independent of persons and places.

The social constructivist approach gives better answers to questions 1 through 5 than the neo-Fregean, the intuitionist-constructivists, or any other proposed philosophy I know of.

Question 3 was powerfully taken up by Lakatos and later by Kitcher, both within the social constructivist viewpoint. I don't review their work in this article. Questions 4 and 5 remain to be considered.

I take up question 5 first. Does the infinite exist? It depends on your ontology. It also depends on whether you value mathematics as we know it or are prepared to throw most of it in the garbage.

If you're a Platonist, and you value mathematics, you cannot help maintaining that infinitely many mathematical objects exist, and some of them may justly be described as infinitely large or infinitely small, infinitely far or infinitely near. Such terms and concepts are used in mainstream mathematics. If mainstream mathematics talks about actually existing objective entities, and if as Platonist you believe that mathematical objects exist as real entities, you have no way out. Someone may ask where and how all these infinites are piled up. All you can do is ignore such a rank Philistine.

In today's philosophical literature one rarely meets a formalist or an intuitionist. People who don't accept Platonism are called fictionalists. Their idea is that mathematical objects (finite and infinite) are fictions, not realities.

This is good as far as it goes, but adopting a name 'fictionalist' doesn't conceal the lack of content in this position. It's not enough to reject Platonism and name yourself a fictionalist. If mathematics is about fictions, what sort of fictions are they? Why are they more like scientific concepts than like fictional characters in Dickens or Dumas? Why are they useful in science?

Nevertheless, the fictionalist position does eliminate the platonists' problem about infinity. If in mathematics we are just telling each other stories, then there is no reason why the stories can't be imaginative and fantastic. We tell stories about winged horses and tablets handed down to Moses on Mount Sinai. Why not stories about infinitely large numbers? As long as it's free of contradiction and has some use or amusement value, we can tell the story. This way of dealing with infinity is open to fictionalists, and also to social constructivists.

In conclusion, I want to deal with one of the most popular arrows that opponents like to shoot at social constructivism. In the course of this final argument, I will give my answer to question 4.

2 + 2 = 4, they say, everywhere and always. In fact, 2 + 2 = 4 before there were human societies, or even human beings. When 2 brontosauruses went to the water hole and met two other brontosauruses, there were four brontosauruses at the water hole. The truths of mathematics are universal, independent not only of individual consciousness but of social consciousness.

This, of course, is Platonism, the view that Wittgenstein attacked so fiercely, and the view, let's face it, that nearly all mathematicians accept.

How can a social constructivist answer this attack? It will take a little analysis, a little discussion. First of all, 'two' plays two linguistic roles; it is an adjective and it is a noun. When we talk about two brontosauruses, 'two' is an adjective. When we use 'two' as an adjective, we are using it to talk about objects, usually physical objects. The fact that two brontosauruses plus two brontosauruses equals four brontosauruses is a statement about brontosauruses, not about numbers. Even if you say two discrete, reasonably permanent, non-interacting objects collected together with two others of the same ilk makes four such objects, you are talking about the behaviour of discrete, reasonably permanent non-interacting objects. This is a statement in elementary physics.

The noun 'two', on the other hand, as everybody knows since Pythagoras, is not physically observable. It is some kind of abstract or ideal object. Plato, Descartes, Frege knew that 'two' is an abstract, ideal object. But they did not explain what they meant by an abstract, ideal object, except in negative terms — not mental, not physical. I am pointing out that these abstract ideal objects are social concepts.

2 + 3 = 5, not because of Peano's axioms, but because the words or symbols 2, 3, and 5 have a a shared, common, understood meaning, which is not up to me to choose as I please, but to learn in accordance with an established language and way of thinking. The social meaning of 'two', 'three' and 'five' forces us to agree that 2 + 3 = 5.

But the Platonist says, 'How can you explain the fact that always and everywhere, regardless of time and place, politics or religion, race or sex, 2 + 2 always equals 4? The only way to account for it is to say that it's an objective truth, which we all recognize because it is an objective truth. Otherwise, the universal agreement that 2 + 2 = 4 would be an inexplicable miracle.'

I answer, 'It's bad logic to say something must be true because I can't think of any other explanation.' That's how the phlogiston theory of combustion was justified. The existence of God the Creator was considered to be proved by the fact that we couldn't conceive any other way for the universe to be here except by Creation.

Now you say that because I haven't got an explanation that satisfies you about the objectivity of mathematics, therefore I must believe in abstract entities whose relation to the physical world is totally obscure, which number incredibly remote uncountable infinities, and which are apprehended by our mental or physical faculties in a totally unexplained manner.

I don't believe in that. I think you believe in it only by closing your eyes to the absurdity of it. Then what do I believe? I believe that there are social or intersubjective concepts which have the rigidity, the reproducibility, of physical science. The reproducibility of a mathematical calculation is comparable only to the reproducibility of a physical measurement or experiment.

Anyone who wants to can ask, 'How is it that the physical world has traits and attributes which are so consistent, so reproducible? Why is the gravitational constant the same from one day to the next? Why is the speed of light in vacuum so reliable?'

If anyone asked those questions, he might receive compliments for thinking up ingenious questions. But no one, physicist or philosopher, would feel obliged to answer them. The possibility of a science of physics in this universe we live in is something we accept. We start from there, we don't try to look at the back of it. A similar question of Heidegger's was, 'Why is there a universe?' I don't know what progress he made on that problem. Few physicists or philosophers would consider it a promising investigation.

Now back to mathematics. Just as there is lawfulness and stability in certain parts of the physical world, there is lawfulness and stability in certain parts of the social-conceptual world. Why should this be so? I do not know. I suspect it's as fruitless as the same question about the physical world.

The study of the lawful, predictable parts of the physical world has a name. The name is 'physics'. The study of the lawful, predictable, parts of the social-conceptual world has a name. The name is 'mathematics'.

References

BENACERRAF, P. and PUTNAM, H. (Eds) (1985) *Philosophy of mathematics*, 2nd edition, Cambridge University Press.

BROUWER, L.E.J. (1985) 'Consciousness, philosophy and mathematics', in BENACERRAF, P. and PUTNAM, H. (Eds) *Philosophy of Mathematics*, Cambridge University Press.

BISHOP, E. (1967) *Foundations of Constructive Analysis*, New York, McGraw Hill.

CHIHARA, C. (1973) *Ontology and the Vicious Circle Principle*, Cornell University Press, Ithaca.

CHIHARA, C. (1990) *Constructibility and Mathematical Existence*, Oxford, Clarendon Press.

CURRY, H. (1951) *Outline of a Formalist Philosophy of Mathematics*, Amsterdam, North Holland.

DAVIS, P.J. (1972) 'Fidelity in mathematical discourse: is 1 + 1 really 2?', *American Mathematical Monthly*, 78, pp. 252–63.

DAVIS, P.J. and HERSH, R. (1981) *The Mathematical Experience*, Boston, Houghton Mifflin Company.

DEMILLO, R., LIPTON, R. and PERLIS, A. (1986) 'Social processes and proofs of theorems and programs', in TYMOCZKO, T. *New Directions in the Philosophy of Mathematics*, Boston, Birkhauser.

ECHEVERRIA, J., IBARRA, A. and MORMANN, T. (1992) *The Space of Mathematics*, Berlin, de Gruyter.

ERNEST, P. (1991) *The Philosophy of Mathematics Education*, London, The Falmer Press.
FIELD, H. (1980) *Science Without Numbers*, Oxford, Oxford University Press.
FREGE, G. (1950) *The Foundations of Arithmetic*, Oxford, Basil Blackwell.
GOODMAN, N.D. (1991) 'Modernizing the philosophy of mathematics', *Synthese*, 88, 2 August.
HERSH, R. (1979) 'Some proposals for reviving the philosophy of mathematics', *Advances in Mathematics*, 31, pp. 31–50.
HERSH, R. (1980) 'Introducing Imre Lakatos', *Mathematical Intelligencer*.
HERSH, R. (1990) 'Inner vision, outer truth', in MICKENS, R.E. (Ed) *Mathematics and Science*, Singapore, World Scientific.
HERSH, R. (1991) 'New directions in the philosophy of mathematics', *Synthese*, 88, 2 August.
HERSH, R. (1991) 'Mathematics has a front and a back', *Synthese*, 88, 2.
KITCHER, P. (1983) *The Nature of Mathematical Knowledge*, Oxford, Oxford University Press.
KÖRNER, S. (1980) *The Philosophy of Mathematics*, London, Hutchinson.
KUHN, T. (1970) *The Structure of Scientific Revolutions*, Chicago, University Press.
LAKATOS, J. (1978) 'Proofs, and refutations', in WORRALL, J. and ZAHAR, E. (Eds) Cambridge, Cambridge University Press.
MADDY, P. (1990) *Realism in Mathematics*, Oxford, Oxford University Press.
MADDY, P. (1991) 'Philosophy of Mathematics: Prospects for the 90s' *Synthese*, August.
MACLANE, S. (1986) *Mathematics Form and Function*, New York, Springer.
PIERCE, C.S. (1976) *The New Elements of Mathematics*, 4 volumes, The Hague, Mouton Publishers.
POLANYI, M. (1958) *Personal Knowledge*, London, Routledge and Kegan Paul.
ROTA, G.C. (1991) 'The pernicious influence of mathematics on philosophy', *Synthese*, August.
SFARD, A. (1989) Translation from Operational to Structural Conception: 'The notion of function revisited' in VERGNAUD *et al.*, (1989) *Proceedings of PME 13*, Paris, CNRS, University René Descartes.
STEINER, M. (1975) *Mathematical Knowledge*, Ithaca, Cornell University Press.
TILES, M. (1991) *Mathematics and the Image of Reason*, Routledge, London.
TYMOCZKO, T. (1985) *New Directions in the Philosophy of Mathematics*, Boston, Birkhauser.
TYMOCZKO, T. (1991) 'Mathematics, science and ontology', *Synthese*, 88, 2, pp. 201–28.
WANG, HAO *Beyond Analytic Philosophy*, A Bradford Book, MIT Press.
WHITE, L.A. (1975) *The Concept of Cultural System*, Columbia University Press.
— (1947) 'The locus of mathematical reality', *Philosophy of Science*, 14, pp. 289–303.
WILDER, R. (1975) *Evolution of Mathematical Concepts*, New York, Wiley.
WITTGENSTEIN, L. (1956) *Remarks on the Foundations of Mathematics*, Oxford, Basil Blackwell.

Chapter 2

What Can the Sociologist of Knowledge Say About 2 + 2 = 4?

David Bloor

Zweifle an allem wenigstens einmal, und wäre es auch der Satz: zweimal zwei ist vier. (G.C. Lichtenberg)

Sociologists are professionally concerned with the conventional aspects of knowledge. So I will try to identify the conventional components of the concepts '2' and '4' and 'addition'. Conventions are shared ways of acting that could in principle be otherwise. They are contingent arrangements, not necessary ones. Thus it is conventional that we drive on the side of the road that we do, and (if proof were needed) we could point to others who drive on the other side. Even if everybody, as a matter of fact, drove on the same side, we could easily imagine the alternative. Demonstrating conventionality therefore involves demonstrating alternative possibilities. Although this necessary condition is easy to state it isn't always easy to satisfy in practice. For one thing, our imaginations are limited.[1] Another reason is that candidate alternatives often meet objections. Reasons are found to sideline, trivialize or re-interpret them so that their character as alternatives is disguised.

Since this will be an important feature of the following discussion, let me dwell on it for a moment. Suppose that an anthropologist wished to demonstrate the conventional character of morality. This could be done by exhibiting alternative patterns of accepted behaviour, e.g., societies in which polygamy was taken for granted. I would count this as a successful demonstration. But it could always be met by saying that this isn't an alternative morality, it is sheer immorality. Thus the proposed candidate is sidelined. I doubt if there is anything that the anthropologist could say in reply to absolutism and essentialism of this kind, so it is well to acknowledge this in advance.

Fortunately, not all essentialist strategies are as intractable as moral dogmatism. Suppose it is said that the game of chess is a conventional structure. This could be justified by observing that the rules could have been different. It would not be adequate to resist this on the grounds that then the variant game simply would not be chess. Such a reply to the conventionalist would be rightly dismissed as pedantic. Nevertheless we must be alert to the fact that superficial moves of this form can be made to sound plausible.

Just one more preliminary. It is often said that 2 + 2 = 4 is a 'cultural universal', i.e., something everyone seems to believe. I had better say something in advance about cultural universals. A simple example will help us orient ourselves.

Food is a cultural universal, because everybody has to ___ ⹀⹀ survive. Does this preclude the sociologist having significant things to say about food? Clearly not, because there is still the question of how people eat, who eats what, and when, and with whom. We might say that while 'nutrition' is a biological category, 'the meal' is a sociological category. And *not* eating is also a response to the demands of the natural world. The 'fast' coexists with the 'feast' as a cultural category. Both are institutions developed in the face of biological necessity. We must see if analogous ideas and distinctions apply in the case of 2 + 2 = 4. Can numbers be divided into their physical, biological and social aspects in the way that the ingesting of food can?

Now to the business in hand. Here is a quick and simple argument, one that, if it were adequate, would establish the sociological character of 2 + 2 = 4. It might be argued that arithmetic is a game played with symbols. In this game, symbols are manipulated according to certain rules. These rules have the status of conventions, and have been selected by some form of collective choice. They are socially created and sustained, so arithmetic is, through and through, a social phenomenon. QED.

This is a simple version of what might be called 'formalism'. It reduces arithmetic to the level of a game of chess. There are things that can be said in favour of this position, e.g., it is consistent with the important fact that there are alternative arithmetics. We know alternative games can be played with arithmetical symbols. For example, in some finite arithmetical systems 2 + 2 does *not* equal 4. In arithmetic modulo 4, 2 + 2 = 0, while in arithmetic modulo 3, 2 + 2 = 1. This is just as the simple argument would predict.[2]

Nevertheless there are shortcomings in the argument. Here are three of them:

1. It provides no explanation for how arithmetic is, or can be, about something, whereas chess *isn't* about anything. It makes a puzzle out of the fact that arithmetic can be applied.
2. It says nothing about the role of proof in arithmetic. Surely we can prove that 2 + 2 = 4 — didn't Russell and Whitehead do this? — and that seems to import an element of necessity into the story that is alien to its basic thrust.
3. Doesn't this argument make too much of the possibility of alternatives, e.g., of systems in which 2 + 2 ≠ 4? Ordinary arithmetic, in which 2 + 2 = 4, seems universal, suggesting that it must be anchored in something other than an arbitrary social convention.

Clearly, the quick argument needs supplementing. If we are to stay within a naturalistic framework there seems to be only one way to do justice to the reference of arithmetical terms, to the applicability of arithmetic and to its wide-spread acceptance. We must bring in the empirical world, something common to everyone. Let us therefore look at an empiricist theory of arithmetic, jumping from the 'thesis' of formalism to the 'antithesis' of empiricism. This way of expressing things indicates that the argument won't rest here: we will need to produce a 'synthesis', but we can approach it through empiricism.

An empiricist theory of arithmetic has a lot to recommend it. It is perhaps the most under-rated of the classic approaches.[3] It certainly fits with the fact that if you ask people why they believe 2 + 2 = 4, you will often get a version of

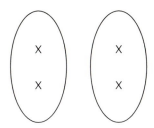

Figure 2.1: Visual Proof of 2 + 2 = 4

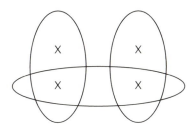

Figure 2.2: Visual Proof of 2 + 2 + 2 = 4

empiricism. People don't usually say, 'it's an arbitrary game I like to play with symbols.' They say, 'Look, here are two apples, one, two'. Then they take another two apples and say, 'one, two'. Then they bring the two pairs together, and conclude by counting them, 'one, two, three, four'.

Most people would take this as an adequate explanation of why they believe that 2 + 2 = 4, of what kind of thing they believe, and as an adequate proof of the truth of that belief. Sophisticated persons, however, often don't accept this proof. They believe that more is required, and that more can be given. All the naïve proof does is to produce a truth about four apples, rather than establishing a timeless necessity about the number 4. It rests, they say, on a confusion of merely inductive procedures with truly mathematical ones. Here, then, is a small but significant sociological fact in its own right: there is a social distribution of belief about what counts as an adequate proof of 2 + 2 = 4. Who is right on this matter — the naïve or the sophisticated? — I will look into it shortly. For the moment let us see what the sociologist of knowledge might say about the general attempt to ground arithmetic simply in our perception and knowledge of material objects.

Here is what one famous, but idiosyncratic, sociologist of knowledge had to say. I am referring to Ludwig Wittgenstein. In his *Remarks on the Foundations of Mathematics* he imagines someone who says: 'you need only look at the figure [see Figure 2.1] to see that 2 + 2 = 4.' Wittgenstein replies: 'Then I only need to look at the figure [see Figure 2.2] to see that 2 + 2 + 2 are 4.' (Wittgenstein, 1978, Part 1, Section 38)

What is Wittgenstein getting at? I detect two basic points. First, he is telling us that simply confronting two objects isn't the same as having the concept of 'two'. Confronting four objects isn't the same as having the concept of 'four', and perceiving two lots of two objects as adjacent to one another isn't the same as having the concept of 'addition'. Second, he is saying that to extract the arithmetical significance of the figure we have to analyse and respond to it in certain ways. For example, we have to draw the envelopes round the crosses in precisely *this* way, not *that* way. To use Wittgenstein's preferred terminology, we must respond to the figure using a specific 'technique'. We must master a technique, and those who have mastered it see the figure in a way that leads them to write '2 + 2', and not '2 + 2 + 2'.[4]

Is Wittgenstein right? It might be objected that we can literally see that there are two lots of two crosses on the page, that the numerical character of the figure is immediately obvious to us. The argument turns, I think, on what we are going to count as concept possession, and Wittgenstein is quite clear on this. His claims about number are exactly like those he makes about colour. We mustn't think, he says, that we have the concept 'red' just because we see a red object. His point is that seeing a red object — and being told it is 'red' — doesn't, in itself, settle how we are going to use the word subsequently. It is the move to new cases, and the subsequent use of the label, that constitutes its meaning; and this is the criterion of our possessing the concept. In short, Wittgenstein brings to bear on number concepts all the considerations that apply to ostensive definition and its use. That is to say, he invites us to appreciate the problematic character of the move from case to case. What counts as the correct application of 'two', just as with the correct application of 'red', derives from its role in a shared language-game, and that takes us beyond the immediate apprehension of the crosses on the page in front of us.

The ostensive learning of number concepts does not, of course, consist solely of being shown samples of two things or three things or four things. It also consists in training in the technique of counting and adding. We are, says Wittgenstein, drilled in these techniques until they have a routine, taken for granted character. Indeed our sense of the inexorability of mathematics is a product of the inexorability of this training (Wittgenstein, 1978, 1, 4; also 1, 118 and 7, 67). Again, we experiment with the numerical properties of groups of objects, or we have these displayed for us. For example, we see four objects split up into two groups of two, which are separated and then combined. These operations impress on us the physiognomy of the number (*idem.*, 1, 78). We retain certain memorable patterns. What begins as an experiment then comes to have a different role, a picture or criterion of correct addition (*idem.*, 1, 80).

Two points deserve emphasizing in this account. First, nothing in it implicitly criticizes the naïve proof of 2 + 2 = 4 using apples. That performance is precisely the exhibition of a technique that can be applied and re-applied: to pebbles, marks on paper, or whatever. In other words, the naïve proof exhibited a paradigm of 2 + 2 = 4 (*idem.*, 1, 8). And that, for Wittgenstein, is bedrock. Second, we must remember the most important feature of Wittgenstein's account of ostensive learning. The learner has to go on from the cases used in training to new cases. The teacher can only furnish a finite number of examples. So how is the next step taken? Not, according to Wittgenstein, by our grasping some essence or by the subsequent usage being in some mysterious way present now, to be apprehended by some form of ultra-perception (*idem.*, 1, 122–6).

The implication is that we must get ourselves from case to case by seeing them as similar to past cases. The terms Wittgenstein uses here are 'analogy' and 'paradigm'. Fortunately, in many cases, we proceed automatically, even blindly.

We experience no problem, but that is not because the correct path is already laid out in advance. Nor must we mistakenly assume that the automatic application of a technique, or the blind rule-following of the individual, itself furnishes a criterion of correct procedure. A standard, Wittgenstein insists, must be something external, i.e., external to the individual: 'But justification consists in appealing to something independent.' (Wittgenstein, 1953, 1, 265). If it were not, the notion of correct rule-following or correct concept application would be at the mercy of individual judgment, with all its idiosyncrasy and variation. For this reason Wittgenstein insists on the collective and conventional character of rules and concepts: he stresses 'custom and use' (Wittgenstein, 1978, 1, 63 and 1, 9) and asserts that 'Mathematics forms a network of norms' (*idem.*, 7, 67).

Let us give Wittgenstein's account a name. Because its essential point is that learning must proceed on the basis of a finite range of examples — e.g., a finite number of cases of a rule — it might be called finitism. No doubt the word has other connotations as well, but I am taking over its use in this connection from Mary Hesse (Hesse, 1974, Chapter 8; see also Barnes, 1982, Chapter 2).

We now have before us all the elements of the 'synthesis' I hinted at earlier. The excessively formalistic approach (the quick argument I began with) has been blended with some down-to-earth considerations drawn from an empiricist approach to arithmetic. Wittgenstein's example and his finitist account of meaning have shown us how to keep the two things in our sights at once. We have now got the basis of a sociological, i.e., a conventionalist, account of 2 + 2 = 4. But if we are to make progress with it we must surmount two obstacles. Here is the first.

Even if we accept that conventionalized techniques for manipulating objects underlie the definition of arithmetical ideas, still it might seem that the subsequent utilization of those ideas cannot be just a matter of convention. Don't we follow out their logical implications? Experience and convention might serve to introduce what is to count as '2' and '4' and 'plus' and 'equals', but once the ideas have been given meaning, surely the mind must follow that meaning. At that point we leave the world and society, far behind. We move into a new realm, the realm of logic and mathematical truth as such. This is a compelling picture, perhaps even a natural one. I cannot prove that it is false, but it is possible to do justice to the facts with the alternative, finitist picture which has just been sketched.

Assume we have just learned to count, and let us reflect on our predicament from a finitist perspective. We are confident in our new skill, so we set off with it into the complicated, empirical world around us. We count all manner of things. Their spatial and temporal distribution, even the nature of the objects, makes little difference to us. We can count events, ideas, feelings, as well as apples and pebbles. We apply our technique in all manner of novel circumstances. We can even count the very things we use for counting, e.g., saying 'there are as many even numbers between 1 and 10 as there are odd numbers.' No one need have told us in advance that this is what we can or should do: we just apply our techniques for ourselves and draw our own conclusions, and mostly find that others agree.

Emboldened, we become more exploratory. We construct a wheel and arrange some numbers around the perimeter, say 0, 1, 2, 3. Then we turn the wheel and watch the numbers go by as we count them. We turn it from one number to the other, and say 'one more'. We let two go by, and say '1, 2'. As we turn the wheel in one direction, we think of ourselves as adding, adding 1 as we turn from one number to the next, and adding 2 as we move along two numbers. As we turn it in the other direction, back from 3 to 2, say, we think of ourselves as subtracting. Just as we felt a naturalness about carrying our counting technique from one empirical circumstance to another in the past, so we feel a naturalness about this. Quite rightly: we are just applying what we have learned to a new case. Nothing in our past exposure to instances of two, nor any past employment of the numeral two, is at odds with what we are doing. The same applies to adding. We have successfully extended the range of concrete operations involved in adding from physically grouping things, to watching them move by us, to merely replaying them through our memory. So why not this too? Then, of course, we make the inevitable discovery: we set the wheel at 2, and then turn it so as to add a further 2, and we get back to zero. $2 + 2 = 0$.

Recall that I mentioned this equation in passing in connection with the 'quick argument'. I said it was arithmetic modulo 4, and characterized it as a different 'game' we could play with symbols. I am now introducing it as a quasi-empirical discovery that might be happened upon by someone who set off into the world equipped with a set of conventional techniques. The change of emphasis is important. I want to get away from the idea that there is some pre-existing set of rules for generating the equation $2 + 2 = 0$ — some pre-existing game or system. I want us to think about it as a possible application of the concepts as they had previously been acquired and utilized. Finitism invites us to make the experiment of discarding one image of concept application and replacing it by another. Don't think of the path ahead of the learner as already mapped out into a set of right and wrong applications of what he has learned, or into this system or that system. Suppose instead that the various concept users just proceed in whatever way seems natural. Once a set of terms, such as '2' and '4' and 'add', have been introduced, the user's mind is not (on this picture) carried along a set of ethereal railway tracks, i.e., tracks laid down by the 'meaning' of the concept (going off, as it were, into infinity). Instead, all we have are the local contingencies that bear on each act of application in turn. We all move, as J.S. Mill put it, from particulars to particulars. All we have are our habits and dispositions, our purposes, our past applications, and our sense of similarity and analogy with the present case. And, of course, our interactions with one another. What will other people make of $2 + 2 = 0$? These are the finite contingencies out of which we must collectively construct our sense of the rightness or wrongness of the next case.

Let me continue the story. In some cases $2 + 2 \neq 4$. What is to be done? A number of responses are possible. The anomalous result could be ignored: viewed as a trivial oddity and left to coexist alongside $2 + 2 = 4$. Alternatively, it could be viewed as an abominable perversion of true and proper counting, and a defensive barrier of definitions erected to exclude it. It could in principle, I suppose, be treated as a refutation of the standard equation, a falsifying instance that brings the entire procedure into discredit. Or it could be deemed to be a different kind of operation from normal counting, a different kind of arithmetic to be studied in its own right. And then there would be the question of defining the relation of the different kinds: do they have equal status, or does one exist on sufferance, having a derivative or parasitical role?[5]

According to finitism, there is no 'correct' response implicit in what went before. It isn't a case of 'discovering' the right status to accord the discovery that $2 + 2$ can add up to something other than 4. It is a case of deciding. The existing

1. $(\exists r)\ (\exists s)\ [r\epsilon K.\ s\epsilon K.\ r \ne s.\ (w)\ \{w\epsilon K \supset (w = r\ v\ w = s)\}]$.

   $(\exists t)\ (\exists u)\ [t\epsilon L.\ u\epsilon L.\ t \ne u.\ (x)\ \{x\epsilon L \supset (x = t\ v\ x = u)\}]$.

   $(y)\ [y\epsilon K \supset \sim y\ \epsilon L].\ (z)[z\epsilon\ M \equiv (z\epsilon K\ v\ z\epsilon L)]$ — supposition.

2. $a\epsilon K.\ b\epsilon K.\ a \ne b.\ (w)\ [w\epsilon K \supset (w = a\ v\ w = b)]$ — from 1, by simplification and E.I.

3. $c\epsilon L.\ d\epsilon L.\ c \ne d.\ (x)\ [x\epsilon L \supset (x = c\ v\ x = d)]$ — from 1, by simplification and E.I.

4. $a\epsilon M.\ b\epsilon M.\ c\epsilon M.\ d\epsilon M$ — from 1, 2, and 3, using U.I. etc.

5. $a \ne b.\ a \ne c.\ a \ne d.\ b \ne c.\ b \ne d$ — from 1, 2, and 3, using U.I., Id., etc.

6. $e\epsilon M$ — supposition.

7. $e\epsilon K\ v\ e\epsilon L$ — from 1 and 6.

8. $e = a\ v\ e = b\ v\ e = c\ v\ e = d$ — from 2, 3, and 7.

9. $(x)\ [x\epsilon M \supset (x = a\ v\ x = b\ v\ x = c\ v\ x = d)]$ — from 6–8 by C.P. and U.G.

10. $a\epsilon M.\ b\epsilon M.\ c\epsilon M.\ d\epsilon M.\ a \ne b.\ a \ne c.\ a \ne d.\ b \ne c.\ b \ne d.\ c \ne d.\ (x)\ [x\epsilon M \supset (x = a\ v\ x = b\ v\ x = c\ v\ x = d)]$ — from 2, 3, 4, 5, and 9.

11. $(\exists r)\ (\exists s)\ (\exists t)\ (\exists u)\ [r\epsilon M.\ s\epsilon M.\ t\epsilon M.\ u\epsilon M.\ r \ne s.\ r \ne t.\ r \ne u.\ s \ne t.\ s \ne u.\ t \ne u.\ (x)\ \{x\epsilon M \supset (x\epsilon M \supset (x = r\ v\ x = s\ vx = t\ v\ x = u)\}]$ — from 10 by E.G.

12. $(K)\ (L)\ (M)\ [(1) \supset (11)]$ — from 1–11 by C.P. and U.G.

Figure 2.3: The Proof of 2 + 2 = 4 Discussed by J.L. Mackie

state of culture, the context around the new result, and the interests that inform our practices, will all impinge on the decision. An act of discretion, not of discovery, is called for. And that discretion will in general be exercised collectively. The decision will itself become a further element of convention in the story. So the conventionalist account has overcome the first obstacle. It doesn't just concern definitions, it also illuminates the so-called 'drawing out' of their implications.

Now for the second obstacle. This concerns proof. Surely if we can prove that 2 + 2 = 4, then all this talk of 'discretion', and 'moving from case to case', as if each step were creative and problematic, *must* be wrong. So let us have a look at a proof; not the naïve proof that involved counting up apples or pebbles, but a rigorous, logical proof. We need to know if proof really does undermine the finitist, sociological account that is emerging.

I am going to reproduce the proof of 2 + 2 = 4 discussed by J.L. Mackie in an article called 'Proof' (1966). What I have to say about it is just an echo of Mackie's astute comments in this fine and thought-provoking paper.[6] The proof is shown in Figure 2.3. The proof uses the definition of number that grew out of the tradition of Frege and Russell. The number 2 is the set of sets with two members. The number 4 is the set of sets with four members, and so on. There are objections to this definition, but they are not central to our concerns (see Benacerraf, 1965).

Let's look at the first few lines of the proof. If we call a set with two members a 'two-group', and a set with four members a 'four-group', then here is what they say. Line one introduces a two-group called K, and line two introduces a two-group called L. The third line introduces a group called M, made up of the members of K and L. You can see how it sets the stage for the proof. More specifically, line one reads: there is an r and there is an s, and r belongs to set K, and s belongs to set K, and r is not the same as s; and for all w, if w belongs to K, either w = r or w = s. The second line repeats this for the two elements t and u of the set L. The third line reads: for all y, if y belongs to K then it does not belong to L, and for all z, if z belongs to M, that is equivalent to z belonging to K or z belonging to L.

Steps 2 and 3 repeat this information in a way that gets rid of the existential quantifiers. Instead of saying that there exists at least one object r, reference is made to a particular object, here called a. Similarly with the letters s, t and u. By so-called 'existential instantiation', we can now talk about objects a, b, c and d. The subsequent steps manœuvre the a, b, c and d until we come to step 10, telling us that M is a group consisting of objects a, b, c and d, and only these. Step 11 puts the quantifiers back, and step 12 tells us that for all sets K, L and M, if K belongs to the set of 2-groups, and L belongs to the set of 2-groups, and they have no members in common, and M is got by bringing the members of these groups together, then M is a 4-group. In the idiom of *Principia Mathematica*, this is taken to mean that 2 + 2 = 4.

You might have some lingering doubts as to whether this proof really tells us that 2 + 2 = 4, since 2 + 2 = 4 is an equation, and the conclusion of the proof is an implication. Implications and equations are, surely, different. This was an objection that Frederick Waismann used to make against the work of the logicist school (Waismann, 1982, pp. 63–71). But I won't dwell on that point because Mackie has some critical observations of more immediate interest. Mackie argues that, for all its show of rigour, the formal proof depends on exactly the same processes of thought as the naïve proof with the apples. The conclusion that issues from it, says Mackie, has exactly the same status as that issuing from the apple proof. That is to say: it depends on an instance of 2 + 2 = 4. We use the result that 2 + 2 = 4 in order to select, order, apprehend and arrange the symbols of the proof. He puts it like this:

> The logical techniques used here to formulate 'K is a two-group' and 'L is a two-group' enable us to introduce 'a' and 'b' as names of the members of K, and 'c' and 'd' as names of the members of L; this ensures that the names of members of M will be 'a', 'b', 'c' and 'd'; and the fact that there are just four names here ensures that M will be described by the expression which is a formulation of 'M is a four-group'. The proof goes through, and it yields the desired results; but it does so precisely because the theorem we are trying to prove is true of the groups of symbols which play a vital role in the proof. (Mackie, 1966, p. 34)

Mackie isn't saying that the proof is circular, that it asserts 2 + 2 = 4 in its premises. But he is saying that the proof 'rests upon the truth of one particular instance of the theorem proved' (p. 35). I take this to mean that if the person producing the proof, or the person reading the proof, weren't already in a position to apply the equation that 2 + 2 = 4 to the symbols of the proof, then they could neither generate nor assimilate it. So the proof in fact leaves us in no better position than we were with the apples. We assemble the 'a' and 'b' in the rigorous proof just as we assemble the first two apples in the naïve proof; and we assemble 'c' and 'd' as we assemble the second lot of apples. We bring 'a, b, c, d' together just as we brought the apples together, except that the physical act of collecting takes the form of the manipulation of symbols.

Mackie's conclusion is that the knowledge derived from the naïve and rigorous proofs has the same empirical character. If the performance with the apples only gives us empirical knowledge, then so will the performance with symbolic tokens. I think Mackie's conclusion is right but, for our purposes, it might be expressed more pointedly. Recall that our analysis of the procedures by which arithmetical operations are impressed upon us suggested that they are not just or purely 'empirical'. They have a quasi-empirical character which involves a normative or conventional component: a socially accepted technique. Mackie's argument has indeed brought us full circle. It shows us that these same conventional procedures or techniques are presupposed by the rigorous proof. Rather than this proof representing some principle of knowing, or some avenue to knowledge, that is superior to the conventionalized procedures of arithmetic, it presupposes them. The rigorous proof, therefore, does not transcend the sociological considerations already advanced: it exemplifies them.

Now let me sum up. I began by saying that to demonstrate conventionality it was necessary to exhibit alternatives, and I have sought to do this by reference to alternative arithmetics where $2 + 2 \neq 4$. I have tried to show how these results could arise naturally from the application of the concepts and techniques by which our ideas of number and counting and adding are first introduced. Of course we now treat these results as belonging to a different system from ordinary arithmetic, one that lives side by side with it. If this seems to trivialize its significance, I suggest that this is only because we are reading the story backwards, and helping ourselves to essentialist ideas about the meaning and scope of the relevant concepts. It is in order to lessen the hold of this style of thinking that I laid so much emphasis on what I called finitism — that is, seeing concept application moving from case to case. The metaphors to use are those of 'construction', not 'unfolding' or 'uncovering'; we make the meaning of our concepts as we go along. Since all our individual, constructive steps have to be coordinated with one another, the result is the construction of conventions.

The stereotype of a sociological discussion of $2 + 2 = 4$ would, I suspect, have the sociologist citing some exotic 'tribe', claiming 'Amongst the X, 2 + 2 *isn't* 4!' There is good reason for this picture. To make the case, something of this form does have to be produced. My argument conforms to this stereotype and meets the necessary condition. The only oddity is that *we* are the exotic tribe in question. It is we who sometimes drive on the opposite side of the mathematical road, and we who sometimes say 2 + 2 makes 4, and sometimes say it doesn't.

Finally, what about the apparently universal use of $2 + 2 = 4$? Recall the example of the biology of nutrition and the sociology of the meal, and the harmonious division of labour between biologist and sociologist that it permitted. Both are needed to tell the full story. How does this map on to the present case? The crucial partition is between 'a thing' and 'the number one', and 'two things' and 'the number two'. We could say things *qua* things belong to 'nature', while numbers belong to us, to society — though we mustn't forget that society is part of nature. Numbers, like meals, are institutions; things are like nutrients voided of their social meaning. I do not deny that our innate ability to perceive in some sense puts us in contact with the numerousness of things. A bird can detect at a glance the difference between two eggs and three eggs in the nest: and so can we. Such innate abilities are obviously vital to our individual and collective lives — just as eating is. It is around such instinctive practices and tendencies that society always weaves a web of more or less elaborate demands and prohibitions. This is where, in Wittgenstein's phrase, there is a deep need for conventions (Wittgenstein, 1978, 1, 74) whether it concerns eating, or counting. They are too important to be left to individuals. Remember the problematic and divergent ways with which an individual might respond to the ostensive definition of number.

A naturalistic, psychological objection to my argument might be as follows: it is wrong to think that we might naturally move from exposure to samples of two, three and four, and training in addition, to an application of the 'wheel' sort (i.e., an embryonic finite arithmetic). That would be a most unnatural move. The normally functioning, intact psychological apparatus of a human being would never deviate in this way; it would keep us on the straight-and-narrow path of normal addition. This objection is a forceful one because I know of no decisive psychological evidence to support my claim — though, of course, neither does the objector have decisive negative evidence. We are just pitting our intuitions about an empirical question against one another. Nevertheless I can reformulate my argument in a way that works, even if my imagined critic is right about our natural dispositions. My reply depends on the fact that dispositions alone do not furnish norms, i.e., standards of right and wrong. It is always open to a social group to decide that the psychological dispositions of its individual members must be overridden, either in the name of truth or morality. To dramatize this point we could imagine a 'sceptic' who took the position that the 'correct' generalization of the ostensive training was to the result that $2 + 2 = 0$. How would those whose dispositions led them to avoid this, and assert that $2 + 2$ was never anything but 4, show that *their* claims were correct? How could they prove that they had responded correctly to the ostensive training? They could not. The argument here is, of course, identical to that of the undefeated and undefeatable sceptic in Kripke's exposition of Wittgenstein (1982).

That there are — from a certain point of view — close similarities between many of our number institutions is not surprising, though that similarity will almost certainly diminish the closer we get to the details.[7] As yet very little empirical work has been done on how people understand their number concepts, or what they take themselves to be doing when they use them. The two proofs of $2 + 2 = 4$ that we have examined serve, however, to make the point that variation is to be expected; they show that widely divergent thoughts and justificatory claims may surround $2 + 2 = 4$, even if in the end they all subserve the same humble purpose. Indeed, one way to sum up Mackie's argument, which makes the connection we have been looking for, is to say that Russell made something of a meal out of $2 + 2 = 4$.

Notes

1. Lichtenberg again: '*Wenn uns ein Engel einmal aus seiner Philosophie erzählte, ich glaube, es müssten wohl manche Sätze so klingen als wie 2 mal 2 ist 13.*' The references for this quotation, and the motto, are G.C. Lichtenberg: *Wie glücklich könnte man leben*, Scherz Verlag, p. 17 and p. 76. I am grateful to Herr and Frau R. Joachimsthaler of Göttingen for the gift of this volume.

2. Here are the tables representing addition in these cases:

+	0	1	2	3
0	0	1	2	3
1	1	2	3	0
2	2	3	0	1
3	3	0	1	2

$2 + 2 = 0$

+	0	1	2
0	0	1	2
1	1	2	0
2	2	0	1

$2 + 2 = 1$

    A good elementary introduction is Sawyer, 1959.

3. Fortunately there are signs that interest is reviving. See, for example, Kitcher, 1984, Chapter 5. For my own defence and sociological extension of J.S. Mill's empiricism, see Bloor, 1976, Chapter 5.
4. Others have made the same point, e.g., the pragmatist John Dewey: 'The whole structure of things, so to speak, seems to abound in twos. But it is not to be supposed that this common experience has given him the number two as expressing order or relation to measuring units.' McLellan and Dewey, 1903.
5. The second of the above strategies could be called 'monster-barring'. In this case Peano's axioms bar the 'monster' because they preclude systems in which 0 is a successor, and on the wheel 0 is the successor of 3 (modulo 4). The list of strategies, such as monster-barring, comes from Lakatos, 1976. For a sociological 'reading', see Bloor, 1978, pp. 245–72.
6. The proof from J.L. Mackie's paper is reproduced by kind permission of the Aristotelian Society.
7. One dimension that has received some emphasis is the distinction between 'abstract' concepts of number and relatively 'concrete' notions, closely tied to the nature of the things counted. It is clear that whether an ostensive demonstration is meant to be taken abstractly or concretely will modify what counts as its proper generalization to new cases. For an early discussion see Wertheimer in Ellis, 1950, section 22.

I should like to thank Barry Barnes, Celia Bloor and Martin Kusch for their valuable criticisms of an earlier draft. They are in no way responsible for the remaining shortcomings.

References

BARNES, B. (1982) *T.S. Kuhn and Social Science*, London, Macmillan.

BENACERRAF, P. (1965) 'What numbers could not be', *Philosophical Review*, 74, pp. 47–73.

BLOOR, D. (1976) *Knowledge and Social Imagery*, London, RKP, 2nd. edition (1991), Chicago, Chicago University Press.

BLOOR, D. (1978) 'Polyhedra and the abominations of Leviticus', *British Journal for the History of Science*, 11, pp. 245–72.

HESSE, M. (1974) *The Structure of Scientific Inference*, London, Macmillan.

KITCHER, P. (1984) *The Nature of Mathematical Knowledge*, Oxford, Oxford University Press.

KRIPKE, S. (1982) *Wittgenstein on Rules and Private Language*, Oxford, Basil Blackwell.

LAKATOS, I. (1976) *Proofs and Refutations*, Cambridge, Cambridge University Press.

LICHTENBERG, G.C. (n.d.) *Wie glücklich könnte man leben*, Scherz Verlag.

MACKIE, J.L. (1966) 'Proof', *Proceedings of the Aristotelean Society*, 40, pp. 23–38.

MCLELLAN, J. and DEWEY, J. (1903) *The Psychology of Number*, New York, Appleton.

David Bloor

SAWYER, W.W. (1959) *A Concrete Approach to Abstract Algebra*, San Francisco, Freeman.
WAISMANN, F. (1982) *Lectures on the Philosophy of Mathematics*, Grassl, W. (Ed) Amsterdam, Rodopi.
WERTHEIMER, M. (1912) 'Numbers and numerical concepts in primitive peoples', in ELLIS, W.D. (Ed) (1950) *A Source Book of Gestalt Psychology*, New York, Humanities Press.
WITTGENSTEIN, L. (1953) *Philosophical Investigations*, Oxford, Basil Blackwell.
WITTGENSTEIN, L. (1978) *Remarks on the Foundations of Mathematics*, 3rd. edition, Oxford, Basil Blackwell.

Chapter 3

The Dialogical Nature of Mathematics

Paul Ernest

This chapter sketches an account of mathematics based on the underlying explanatory metaphor of conversation and dialogue.[1] It suggests that mathematics is dialogical in a number of central defining ways, through the underlying

- textual basis of mathematics, mathematical knowledge and proof;
- nature of a number of central mathematical concepts;
- origins and nature of proof; and
- social processes whereby mathematical knowledge is created, warranted and learnt.

This account is offered as part of a social constructivist philosophy of mathematics (Ernest, in press), which sits at the crossroads of two major currents of modern thought, the recent fallibilist tradition in the philosophy of mathematics, and the multidisciplinary use of conversation as a basic underlying metaphor for human knowing and interaction.

Developments in the Philosophy of Mathematics

Recently there has been a move in some quarters towards a reconceptualization of the philosophy of mathematics. Early twentieth-century philosophy of mathematics was largely focused on a foundationalist project, the quest for absolutely certain foundations for knowledge. The logicist, intuitionist and formalist schools each tried to reconstruct mathematics into an indubitable rational structure of thought based on a logical masterplan, the Euclidean paradigm. However the ultimate failure of each of these prescriptive programmes to achieve this goal is well documented (Davis and Hersh, 1980; Ernest, 1991; Kline, 1980; Lakatos, 1976, 1978; Tiles, 1991).[2] More recently, the philosophy of mathematics has become professionalized, and its dominant interest has moved beyond the foundationalist project. It remains internalist but with ontology and other technical philosophical issues as a major focus of activity instead (Kitcher and Aspray, 1988).

However, a new tradition in the philosophy of mathematics has been emerging which has been termed 'maverick' (Kitcher and Aspray, 1988), 'fallibilist'

(Lakatos, 1976, 1978; Ernest, 1991), and 'empiricist' or 'quasi-empiricist' (Kitcher, 1984; Putnam, 1985; Lakatos, 1976, 1978). This new tradition is primarily naturalistic, concerned to describe the nature of mathematics and the practices of mathematicians, both current and historical, and rejects absolutism in epistemology (Lakatos, 1976; Kitcher, 1984). A number of philosophers and mathematicians can be identified as contributing to this tradition, including, Davis and Hersh (1980), Putnam (1975), Tymoczko (1986), Wang (1974) and Wittgenstein (1956), as well as those cited above. In addition, there is a growing number of researchers drawing on other disciplines to account for the nature of mathematics, especially social studies of science, including Bloor (n.d.), Restivo (1992), Wilder (1981), Livingston (1986), and Rotman (1988, 1993), and the history of mathematics, including Aspray and Kitcher (1988), Crowe (n.d.), Kline (1980), Gillies (1992), and Joseph (1991).

The rejection of the Euclidean paradigm by this newer sceptical tradition in the philosophy of mathematics means that new paradigms and new explanatory metaphors are required. Authors have proposed accounting for mathematics as a culture (Wilder, 1981; Bishop, 1988), as a social system (Restivo, 1992; Livingston, 1986), as a language (Pimm, 1986; Rotman, 1993), in terms of evolutionary epistemology (Rav n.d.; van Bendegem n.d.), and as in the present chapter, as conversation (Ernest, 1991, in press). Most of these approaches are not from professional philosophers, but from scholars in some other cognate discipline who are committed to engaging with the phenomenon of mathematics in some sense *as it is*, rather than with professional philosophizing.[3] What is shared by these and other contributors to the maverick tradition is a view of the essential contribution of the history of mathematics to any acceptable account of mathematics (Davis, Gillies, Hersh, Kitcher, Kline, Lakatos, Tymoczko). There is a shared acceptance of mathematics as an essentially social phenomenon — something long agreed by historians (and sociologists) of mathematics, but long denied by traditional philosophers of mathematics. In particular, what most supporters of the maverick tradition agree on is that the role of proof in mathematics is social: to persuade the appropriate mathematical community to accept the knowledge as warranted. To quote one well-known mathematician:

> A proof becomes a proof after the social act of 'accepting it as a proof'.
> This is as true of mathematics as it is of physics, linguistics and biology.
> (Manin, 1977, p. 48)

Overall, these approaches challenge and attempt to overturn some of the traditional dichotomies presupposed in the philosophy of mathematics, including:

1. the claim that mathematical knowledge is *a priori* as opposed to *a posteriori*, and is justified without any recourse to experience, that it is wholly non-empirical;
2. the claim that mathematical knowledge is analytic as opposed to synthetic in Kant's sense, that is, mathematical knowledge is logical in nature, derived from the law of non-contradiction, and that its theorems add nothing which is not implicitly contained in the premises;[4]
3. the claim that epistemologically, mathematical knowledge concerns the context of justification as opposed to context of discovery: for although

it may be discovered by human, historical and other contingent means, it is justified by logic and mathematical proof alone; and

4. the claim that mathematics is monological as opposed to dialogical, consisting of monological claims and proofs, based on a unique, firm foundation, and that no conversation, dialogue or dialectic is needed.

The first three points are argued elsewhere in the 'maverick' literature cited above, and I merely note them, rather than repeat the arguments made elsewhere.[5] The last point is the focus of this chapter, and a key emphasis of the social constructivist philosophy of mathematics which I have been developing (Ernest, 1991; in press). The claim is that in deep and multiple ways described below, mathematics is at base conversational. However, all of these points are interwoven in the rejection of the absolutist, monological account of mathematical knowledge. For what is rejected is the following four theses:

1. there is a secure and fixed basis of truth on which mathematical knowledge is founded;
2. there are wholly reliable logical deductions of mathematical theorems from explicit premises;
3. absolute mathematical knowledge based on impeccable proofs is an ideal which is attainable;
4. the logical properties of mathematical proof alone suffice to establish mathematical knowledge without reference to human agency or the social domain.

These theses underpin the traditional absolutist views of mathematical knowledge and establish its monological character.[6] They are also central assumptions of Cartesian rationalism and the modernism based on it.

Instead of focusing on the negative task of criticizing these conceptions and assumptions, the aim of this chapter is to develop aspects of a positive alternative: a dialogical and dialectical account of mathematics. However, given the traditional dominance of absolutist monological philosophies of mathematics, and the modes of thought they have engendered, the proposal of conversation as a basic metaphor is perhaps shocking. Is not conversation idle, amiable chatter among friends, unlike the ineluctable progress of impersonal monological proof which warrants mathematical knowledge? I shall argue that conversation permeates mathematics in deep and multiple ways.

The Role of Conversation in Epistemology

Conversation in the form of written dialogue has been used in philosophy and epistemology from the time of the Ancient Greeks. One of Socrates' distinctive contributions is 'the use of dialogue as a means to uncover truth'. (Ferguson, 1970, 15). Some of the best-known philosophers and scientists used dialogue in their work, including: Plato, Boethius, Alcuin, Bruno, Galileo, Fontenelle, Berkeley, Leibniz, Hume, Nietzsche, Renyi, Heyting and Lakatos.[7]

Over and above mere use, conversation has been explicitly adopted as a central epistemological concept by many philosophers and theorists, including:

Paul Ernest

Bakhtin, Collingwood, Gadamer, Gergen, Habermas, Harré, Lakatos, Lorenzen, Mead, Oakshott, Peters, Rorty, Shotter, Volosinov, Vygotsky, and Wittgenstein. For example, the philosopher of history Collingwood (1939) proposes a dialogical 'logic of question and answer' in place of the (mono) logic of propositions. Shotter (1993) argues for a rhetorical-responsive (conversational) view of interpersonal relations and knowledge. Rorty adopts conversation explicitly as his philosophical basis for epistemology and mathematical knowledge.

> If, however, we think of 'rational certainty' as a matter of victory in argument rather than of relation to an object known, we shall look toward our interlocutors rather than to our faculties for the explanation of the phenomenon. If we think of our certainty about the Pythagorean Theorem as our confidence, based on experience with arguments on such matters, that nobody will find an objection to the premises from which we infer it, then we shall not seek to explain it by the relation of reason to triangularity. Our certainty will be a matter of conversation between persons, rather than an interaction with nonhuman reality. (Rorty, 1979, pp. 156–7)

If it is to be adopted as an epistemological basis, a clarification of the nature of conversation is needed. Conversation can be understood on three levels.

First of all, conversation of course originates at the interpersonal level, where persons in one or more shared 'forms of life' engage in direct conversations (based in one or more shared language games', adopting a late-Wittgensteinian perspective). At this level conversation is one of the basic modes of interpersonal human interaction, perhaps the most basic one.

Mediated forms of conversation involving written texts (understood broadly to include all forms of notation, diagram, and materially embodied complexes of signs) represent an important extension of the notion.

> The original form of conversation can also be seen in derivative forms in which the correspondence between question and answer is obscured. Letters, for example, are an interesting transitional phenomenon: a kind of written conversation, that, as it were, stretches out the movement of talking at cross purposes before seeing each other's point. (Gadamer, 1965, p. 332)

The transition from spoken to written textual forms of conversation is a crucial one. It creates a different relationship between author and utterance, and allows the utterance to be objectified and preserved beyond the moment of the illocutionary act. It allows mathematical texts and arguments, proofs in particular, to be construed as monological, with all answers anticipated and incorporated in the text.

Second, there is conversation at the cultural level. For example, for Oakeshott, humanity inhabits a world of ideas, and whose growth and development is the 'conversation of humankind'.[8] This larger-scale conversation is the direct sum of interpersonal conversations in oral cultures. However the rich, complex, symbolic culture of the history of mathematics as we know it is only possible through the extended conversation that Gadamer remarks on, based on the production and use of texts (but not limited to just that).

Third, there is internalized private conversation. Some of the theorists mentioned in the previous section (including Plato, Gergen, Harré, Mead, Shotter, and Vygotsky) argue that thought itself is internalized conversation. Whether or not one accepts this (and I am inclined to), there are patterns of thought that clearly originate in persons, mathematicians for example, having internalized some of the conversational roles and procedures they learnt through conversation of the first (and second) kind. These include, most notably, the role of proponent, in which a line of thinking or a thought experiment (Peirce, Rotman) is followed through sympathetically, for understanding; and the role of critic, in which an argument is examined for weaknesses and flaws.

All three forms of conversation are either actually social in their manifestation (the interpersonal and cultural forms), or are social in origin (the intrapersonal form), which is thus social in a constitutive, originary way. My proposal is to adopt conversation as a basic epistemological notion of a social constructivist philosophy of mathematics. It is both social, and constructed, as are all linguistic and cultural entities and phenomena.

The basis for adopting conversation as epistemologically basic is twofold. First there is the Wittgensteinian (1953) assumption that 'forms of life', that is persons in shared activities situated in the world, is ontologically primitive. This is the *sine qua non* of human life, and subsequently of discourse and of all forms of knowledge. Second, there is the assumption that discourse and language (deployed in Wittgenstein's language games) play an essential role in the genesis, acquisition, communication, formulation and justification of virtually all knowledge, including, in particular, mathematical knowledge.

The underlying form of conversation is dialogical because of its ebb and flow, with its alternation of voices, and its assertion and counter assertion. Dialogical response in conversation is the source of feedback, in the form of acceptance, elaboration, reaction, criticism and correction. The form or underlying 'logic' of conversation might even be termed dialectical, because of the way assertions are met with counter assertions or antitheses, leading to new assertions. However, this is not a strictly Hegelian dialectic, nor the dialectical materialism of Marx.[9]

The Dialogical Nature of Mathematics

According to social constructivism, mathematics is at base conversational and dialogical, and is based on 'dialogic' or a dialectical logic. However, this 'logic' is not intended to challenge or supplant the vital technical role of deductive logic in mathematics and in warranting mathematical proof. As Rosen (1989) argues:

> logic and dialectic are joined together in the texture of everyday modes of reasoning. There is no natural competition between logic and dialectic, and my task is never to reduce one to the other. However . . . dialectic is the broader of the two functions of thought. It is surely uncontroversial to observe that there cannot be a logical justification of logic [on pain of contradiction]. Even such defences as by Aristotle of the principle of noncontradiction are dialectical. (Rosen, 1989, p. 118)

My claim is that the conventional and absolutist accounts of mathematics and mathematical knowledge as purely deductive suppress the dialogical nature of mathematics in two ways. The first is to accept at face value the historical assimilation, absorption, suppression and final denial of the dialogical components within mathematics itself. The second is to locate the remaining dialogical aspects of mathematics in its pragmatic, human and social penumbra, which is regarding them as immaterial to the nature of mathematical knowledge, especially to its context of justification.[10]

In contrast, the social constructivist claim that mathematics is dialogical can be understood in a number of ways, including the following four.

1. understood as a primarily textual or symbolic activity, mathematics is necessarily dialogical in general: this also holds in a special way for mathematics, because of the unique characteristics of mathematical language and the way it is employed (Rotman, 1988, 1993);
2. a substantial class of modern mathematical concepts and content are constitutively dialogical or dialectical;
3. dialectic provides the origins of mathematical proof and logic in Classical Greece, and a philosophical foundation for certain modern conceptions of logic and proof (Lloyd, 1990); and
4. the epistemology and methodology of mathematics can be accounted for in an explicitly and constitutively dialectical way, accommodating both the justification of objective mathematical knowledge (following Lakatos, 1976, 1978, and Wittgenstein, 1953, 1978), and the ratification of personal knowledge.

Mathematical Language

Mathematics is primarily a symbolic activity, which uses written inscription and language to create, record and justify its knowledge (Rotman, 1993). Viewed semiotically as comprising texts, mathematics is inescapably conversational and dialogical in an immediate and overall way, for by its very nature it addresses a reader.[11]

Mathematical proof is a special form of text, which since the time of the ancient Greeks, has been presented in monological form. This reflects the absolutist ideal that total precision, rigour and perfection are attainable in mathematics. Thus the monologicality of the concealed voice uttering a proof itself belies and denies the presence of the silent listener. But as it is an argument intended to convince, a listener is presupposed. The monologicality of proof tries to forestall the listener by anticipating all of his or her possible objections. So the dialectical response is condensed into the ideal perfection of a monologic argument, in which no sign of speaker or listener remain, except for the idealized and perfected utterance, the proof itself.

A detailed analysis of mathematical texts, proofs and algorithms, reveals that the verb forms employed are both in indicative and imperative moods. The declarative case of the indicative mood is used by the writer to make statements, claims and assertions. According to Rotman (1988, 1993), drawing on the work of C.S. Peirce, these are claims describing the future outcomes of thought experiments

Table 3.1: Examples of Dialectical Concepts in Mathematical Topics

Topic	Dialectical Concept
Analysis	ε–δ definitions of the limit
Constructivist logic	Interpretation of quantifiers: $\forall x \exists y \ldots$ 'You choose x, and I show how to construct y'
Recursion theory	Arithmetical Hierarchy – $\forall \exists \forall \exists \forall \exists \ldots$
Set theory	Diagonal argument: for any enumeration, omitted element
Set theory	Game-theoretic version of Axiom of Choice
Game theory	Alternation of moves by opponents
Number theory	J. Conway's game theoretic foundations of number
Statistics	Hypothesis testing (H_0 versus H_A)
Probability	Analysis of wagers, betting games

which the reader can perform, or can simply decide to accept. 'By such a process . . . like mathematical reasoning, we can reach conclusions as to *what would be* true of signs in all cases.' (Peirce, cited in Rotman, 1993, p. 76).

The imperative mood is used for both inclusive and direct imperatives, which are shared injunctions, or orders and instructions issued by the writer to the reader.

> The speaker of a clause which has selected the imperative has selected for himself the role of controller and for his hearer the role of controlled. The speaker expects more than a purely verbal response. He expects some form of action. (Berry, 1975, p. 166)

Thus mathematical texts comprise specific assertions and imperatives directed by the writer to the reader. The reader or addressee of mathematical text is therefore either the agent of the mathematician-author's will, whose response is an imagined or actual action, or a critic seeking to make a dialectical response. In both cases mathematical knowledge and text can be claimed to be dialectical or dialogical (Rotman, 1988, 1993; Ernest, 1993).

Mathematical Concepts

Dialogical and dialectical processes underpin a substantial class of modern mathematical concepts and content, including aspects of analysis (limit definitions), statistics (hypothesis testing), game theory, constructivist logic, number theory (Conway, 1976), set theory (axiom of choice), recursion theory (arithmetical hierarchy). They do so both as a possible interpretation of some mathematical concepts, and as a necessary characteristic of some others. Table 3.1 lists some examples.

Thus it can be said that dialectical interpretations can be given to significant concepts from some of the main branches of mathematics (number, analysis, foundations) and form an essential underpinning of others (game theory, stochastics). Dialectics is also implicated in the roots of deductive logic. For example, the universal and existential quantifiers can be interpreted more or less constructively as designating 'voices' in a dialogue: Thus, $\forall x \exists y Pxy$ (for all x, there is y, such that Pxy) can be interpreted to mean 'whatever value for x you choose, I can find a value of y so that the relation Pxy holds'.

In each of a wide selection of examples the dialogical alternation of voices can be located in (or read into) the structure of the mathematical concept involved.

Origins and Basis of Proof

Mathematical proof, certainly in its axiomatic form, appears to have developed in Classical Greece. Cornford, Kolmogorov, Restivo, Struik and others have argued that the emergence of proof in Ancient Greek mathematics reflected the social, political and cultural circumstances of the time. These included, most notably, the democratic forms of life in which dialectical argument and disputation were valued and widely practised, coupled with scepticism and speculation about hypotheses and ideas, and an idealistic outlook associated with an aristocratic slave society. It seems very probable that the emergence of proof in Ancient Greece, in the fields of mathematics, philosophy, and logic, was in large part due to these widespread and central cultural practices of disputation and dialectical reasoning, which were central to their public democratic institutions.

The word 'dialectic' already had a number of shades of meaning in the time of the ancient Greeks. In its earliest sense 'dialectic' is the name for the method of argument which is characteristic of metaphysics, and is derived from the verb meaning 'to discuss'.

> dialectic means a co-operative inquiry carried out in conversation between two or more minds that are equally bent, not on getting the better of the argument, but on arriving at the truth. A tentative suggestion ('*hypothesis*') put forward by one speaker is corrected and improved until the full meaning is clearly stated. The criticism that follows may end in complete rejection or lead on to another suggestion which (if the examination has been skilfully conducted) ought to approach nearer to the truth. (Cornford, 1935, p. 30)

Szabo (1967, 1978) claims dialectic reasoning as the source of the axiomatic method, following the use of indirect reasoning by the Eleatics, such as Zeno of Elea. He argues that a key development concerns the rejection of empirical evidence as a source for mathematics, and the acceptance of abstract logical reasoning instead. He suggests that axioms were originally a common, basic starting point for two disputants in a dialectical argument.

Fritz (1955) also locates the source of deductive mathematics and logic in dialectical argument and disputation. This fits well with the more general view that the dialogical nature of Greek public life is a crucial source of proof in both philosophy and mathematics. Which actually came first is perhaps immaterial, according to Lloyd (1990). Indeed Knorr (1975) disputes Szabo's account, and argues that philosophy and mathematics developed in parallel. What does seem to be above dispute, though, is the conversational, dialectical origin of proof in mathematics. Although some of the detailed published proposals are conjectural, and there is controversy over the source of the axiomatic method, there is a loose unanimity that disputation and dialectical reasoning play an essential part in the historical origins and the development of logic and mathematics in Classical Greece (Boyer, 1968). Thus the origins of mathematical proof are dialectical and dialogical.

In modern proof theory, some of the main developments treat mathematical proofs as if they are offered in a dialogue. In them a proponent attempts to convince an opponent of his or her claims, whilst the opponent challenges what is asserted, but accepts a number of agreed basic rules of reasoning and facts. Thus these developments have been dialogical, if not always explicitly dialectical.

Heyting (1931) describes how every proposition asserted in intuitionistic mathematics signifies a promise offered to an opponent, namely that of providing an intuitionistic proof of it. Thus such propositions are claims that are only valid if the opponent can be convinced.

Natural deduction techniques likewise allow a mathematician to build up a proof of a theorem by means of inferential schemes. Once sufficient assumptions or hypotheses have been agreed by the proposer and opposer, then a chain of deductive inferences is built up using the schemes, until the theorem is established. (This strikingly resembles Szabo and Cornford's accounts of ancient dialectical proof.)

The method of semantic tableaux is even closer to a dialectical logic of conversation, since it represents an explicit attempt to refute the claim (or story) as put forward by another in dialogue (Bell and Machover, 1977). One of its originators, Hintikka, also proposes a system of game theoretic semantics for tableaux, which emphasizes the strategic, dialogical aspect of the choice of terms in instantiating quantifiers.

The most fully developed dialogical interpretation of proof is that of Lorenzen, for constructive logic. Lorenzen's (1970) method is based on the interaction between two disputants where one tries to maintain a thesis over the other's objections. He suggests a dialogical interpretation of the logical constants incorporating both the proponent's claims and conclusions, and the opponents queries and claims. Lorenzen's proposals represent an explicitly conversational, dialectical basis for logic reasoning and mathematical proof, which he claims is not another arbitrary formal system, but reflects mathematical practice (Roberts, 1992).

What can be concluded overall is that both the beginnings of logic and mathematical proof and their modern developments confirm that mathematical proof is at root, dialectical, based in human dialogue and conversational exchange.

Epistemology and Methodology

In this last and central section, the focus is on the epistemology of mathematics, including the nature and mechanisms of mathematical knowledge genesis and warranting. The central claim is of the key role of conversation and dialectics in these areas. The questions addressed are as follows:

- How is mathematical knowledge invented or discovered?
- What methodology is involved?
- How does mathematical knowledge achieve its status as warranted knowledge?

Table 3.2: *The Cyclic Form of Lakatos' Logic of Mathematical Discovery*

Stage Context	Components of Cycle	
STAGE n (i)	Problem P_n, Informal Theory T_n	Conjecture C_n
(ii)		Informal proof I_n of C_n
(iii)		Informal refutation of C_n
STAGE n + 1	Problem(s) P_{n+1}, Informal Theory T_{n+1}	Conjecture C_{n+1}

- How do individuals acquire mathematical knowledge?
- How is the mathematical knowledge of an individual warranted as such?

A full answer to these questions, even just from one perspective, requires a book-length treatment. So in the present context I am only able to sketch some of the central features of the conversational and dialectical basis of the epistemology and methodology of mathematics.[12]

The social constructivist account of the conversational basis of mathematics is based on primarily on the work of Wittgenstein and Lakatos. Wittgenstein offers the basis of a social theory of meaning, knowledge and mathematics resting on dialogical 'language games' embedded in 'forms of life'. Lakatos offers a multifaceted if incompletely formulated philosophy of mathematics. At the heart of this is his heuristic or logic of mathematical discovery, which is a dialectical theory of the history, methodology and philosophy of mathematics.

Briefly, Lakatos' logic of mathematical discovery can be explicated as a cyclic process in which a conjecture and an informal proof are put forward (in the context of a problem and an assumed informal theory). In reply, an informal refutation of the conjecture and/or proof are given. Given work, this leads to an improved conjecture and/or proof, with a possible change of the assumed problem and informal theory. This process is summarized in Table 3.2.

Lakatos (1976) not only adopted a dialogical form for his major work, but explicitly appropriated the Hegelian dialectic in his early work for his logic of mathematical discovery.[13]

> The proof procedure seems to me to be a remarkable example of the dialectic triad of thesis, antithesis and synthesis. The progress of mathematical thought — in this case — starts with the primitive conjecture. This is the thesis. This thesis produces its antithesis which consists of the tension and struggle of the proof and refutations.
>
> In the antithesis we have on the one hand the proof which is the positive pole of the antithesis and supports the thesis, lifts it onto a higher level; and we have on the other hand the negative pole of the antithesis, the counterexamples, which tend to destroy the positive pole. It is very much in keeping with this dialectic that by strengthening the negative pole (finding ever more counterexamples) the positive pole will also be stronger (the proof will be ever more improved by the better specification of the lemmas corresponding to the counterexamples), and vice versa by strengthening the positive pole (building up a better proof-analysis) the

Table 3.3: *The Dialectical Form of the Generalized Logic of Mathematical Discovery*

Scientific Context for Stage n
Background scientific and epistemological context, including problems, concepts, methods, informal theories, proof criteria and paradigms, and meta-mathematical views.

THESIS (Stage n)
Proposal of new or revised conjecture, proof, problem-solution or theory.

ANTITHESIS (Stage n') Dialectical response to the proposal:

Critical Response	**Acceptance Response**
Counterexample, counter-argument, refutation, criticism of proposal	Acceptance of proposal. Suggested extension of proposal.

SYNTHESIS (Stage n″)
Evaluation and modification of the proposal:

Local Restructuring	**Global Restructuring**
Modified proposals: new conjecture, proof, problem-solution, problems or theory.	Restructured context: changed pool of problems, concepts, methods, informal theories. Changed proof paradigms and criteria, meta-mathematical views.

OUTCOME (Stage n + 1)
Newly accepted or rejected proposal, or revised scientific and epistemological context.

---

negative pole will also be stronger (new counterexamples being suggested by the clearly stated lemmas). Of course the whole of the antithesis — both proof and counterexamples — is produced by the thesis which contains it in embryo. Now the synthesis is the theorem which embodies the respective values of both poles of the antithesis — proof and refutations — on a higher level, without the limitations of both. The theorem negates and preserves both the proof and the counterexamples. And I shall not be surprised, if the synthesis turns into a new thesis and the dialectical process starts again. (Lakatos, 1961, p. 51)

To make the dialectical aspects of the logic of mathematical discovery explicit, and to overcome some of the criticisms directed at Lakatos for offering too limited a scheme, I propose a generalized logic of mathematical discovery, which is summarized in Table 3.3.[14] This scheme is generalized to accommodate a broader range of changes, outcomes and responses than those considered by Lakatos, including 'mathematical revolutions' (Gillies, 1992). As Table 3.3 shows, dialectical process are immediately present in the warranting dialogue of the generalized logic of mathematical discovery. Mathematical proofs or other proposals are offered to the appropriate mathematical community as part of a continuing dialogue. They are addressed to an audience, and they are tendered in the expectation of reply, be it acceptance or critique. Such replies may play a part in the development and formulation of new mathematical knowledge. However, such replies, when given by the gatekeepers of institutionalized mathematical knowledge (e.g., PhD examiners, conference referees, journal editors) play the essential warranting role in the acceptance (or rejection) of candidates presented as new mathematical knowledge. This conversation constitutes the social acceptance mechanism for mathematical knowledge.

Thus mathematical proof has not only evolved from dialogical form, but its very function in the mathematical community as an epistemological warrant for items of mathematical knowledge requires the employment of that form. The underlying logic is dialectical.

Conversation and dialectics also plays an essential role in the teaching and learning of mathematics. Individual learners develop personal knowledge of language, mathematics and logic through prolonged participation in socially situated conversations of varying types. In the context of mathematics education teachers structure mathematical conversations on the basis of texts and their own knowledge in order to communicate mathematical knowledge to learners. However this is necessary but not sufficient for such knowledge to be learned. Sustained two-way participation in such conversations is also necessary to generate, test, correct and validate personal mathematical knowledge. The acquisition and use of subjective knowledge of mathematics by individuals are irrevocably interwoven. For only through utterance and performance are the individual construals made public and confronted with alternatives, extensions, corrections or corroboration.

Thus within the contexts of mathematics education individuals use their personal knowledge of mathematics and mathematics education to direct and control mathematics learning conversation both (a) to present mathematical knowledge to learners directly or indirectly (i.e., teaching), and (b) to participate in the dialectical process of criticism and warranting of others' mathematical knowledge claims (i.e., assessment of learning). The latter serves a social purpose, the certification of learners' personal knowledge of mathematics.

Likewise, within the contexts of professional research mathematics, individuals use their personal knowledge both (a) to construct mathematical knowledge claims (possibly jointly with others), and (b) to participate in the dialectical process of criticism and warranting of others' mathematical knowledge claims. In both cases the individual mathematician's symbolic productions are (or are part of) one of the voices in the warranting conversation.

Figure 3.1 summarizes how collective 'objective' mathematical knowledge and personal knowledge of mathematics recreate each other in a cyclic process that alternates between academic and school contexts. In this cycle what travels is embodied, either as a text, or as a person. Symbolic representations of would-be mathematical knowledge travel in the academic domain, with accepted versions joining the stock of 'objective' mathematical knowledge. Some of these are recontextualized in the school context as symbolic representations of school mathematical knowledge, and are presented to learners in teaching/learning conversations. Interactions in this context give rise to knowledgeable persons (accompanied by textual certifications of their personal mathematical knowledge). These persons can themselves travel and enter the school or academic contexts as either teacher or mathematician, and participate in the respective warranting conversations.

I have offered a view of mathematics suggesting that it has a dialogical nature which encompasses its textual basis, some of its concepts, the origins and nature of proof, and the social processes whereby mathematical knowledge is created, warranted and learnt. Taking conversation as epistemologically basic re-grounds mathematical knowledge in socially situated acts of human knowing and communication. It offers a way of overcoming the Cartesian dualism of mind versus body, and knowledge versus the world. Mind and knowledge are viewed as

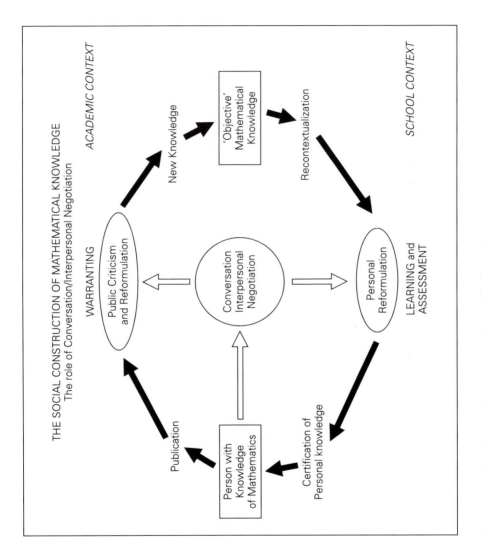

THE SOCIAL CONSTRUCTION OF MATHEMATICAL KNOWLEDGE
The role of Conversation/Interpersonal Negotiation

ACADEMIC CONTEXT

SCHOOL CONTEXT

WARRANTING

LEARNING and ASSESSMENT

New Knowledge

'Objective' Mathematical Knowledge

Recontextualization

Public Criticism and Reformulation

Conversation Interpersonal Negotiation

Personal Reformulation

Publication

Person with Knowledge of Mathematics

Certification of Personal knowledge

Figure 3.1: The Creative/Reproductive Cycle of Mathematics

45

physically embodied, and a part of the same world in which the learning and teaching of mathematics take place.

Notes

1. This is based on the paper 'Dialectics in Mathematics: A Historico-Philosophical study', presented at the 19th International Congress of the History of Science, Symposium 15 — Analysis and Synthesis in Mathematics, Organisers M. Otte and M. Panza, Zaragoza, Spain, 22–29 August 1993.
2. Of course each of these programmes, each in its own way had notable successes too. The point that matters here is that they failed as foundationalist epistemological projects.
3. For philosophers this raises the question: are these concerns philosophy? Although elsewhere I have hazarded my opinion on this issues (Ernest, 1991, in press), here I will get on with the business of describing a dialogical view of mathematics.
4. Ironically, unlike the positivists who made this claim, Kant regarded mathematical knowledge as 'synthetic a priori'.
5. Of course I should acknowledge that these points are very controversial, and that many mathematicians and philosophers of mathematics would strenuously reject them.
6. Note that intuitionists such as Brouwer and Heyting would accept theses 1–3 but reject thesis 4. Elsewhere for this and other reasons I have classified them as 'progressive absolutists' (Ernest, 1991).
7. In modern times Bateson and Hofstadter have also used dialogues philosophically.
8. Conversation at this level was adopted as the underpinning metaphor for the *Britannica Great Books of the Western World* series, as the introductory volume's title *The Great Conversation* shows (Hutchins, 1959).
9. These theories impose an absolute, perhaps metaphysical logical order on the world and thought which are inconsistent with fallibilism and social constructivism.
10. The denial and suppression of its dialogical aspect is perhaps an inevitable part of the ascendancy of the formal and deductive mathematics in modern times. This undeniably represents one of the great human cultural achievements, the articulation of mathematics as a collections of formal, abstract and largely structural systems. However a re-evaluation of the dialogical aspects of mathematics is no threat to this achievement, and perhaps offers philosophical support to a further advance: computer-driven post-modern mathematics.
11. All texts are regarded by theorists such as Bakhtin, Gergen, Halliday, Lotman, Volosinov as dialogical. For example, Volosinov (1973, p. 85) says, in all cases 'The word is orientated towards an addressee.'
12. A sketch of social constructivism is provided in Ernest (1991), and a fuller account is in Ernest (forthcoming).
13. This is under-recognized in the literature for a number of complex reasons. Under the sway of Popper and his followers at LSE in the 1960s Lakatos increasingly repudiated the Hegelian origins of his work. When former colleagues posthumously edited his works they removed further traces of Hegelian dialectics and also undermined Lakatos' fallibilism (most notably in Lakatos, 1976). See Ernest (in press) for a substantiation of this perspective (and a re-evaluation of Lakatos' contribution).
14. See, e.g., Anapolitanos (1989).

References

ANAPOLITANOS, D.A. (1989) 'Proofs and refutations: A reassessment,' in GAVROGLU, K., GOUDAROULIS, Y. and NICOLACOPOULOS, P. (Eds) (1989) *Imre Lakatos and Theories of Scientific Change*, Dordrecht, Kluwer, pp. 337–45.

ASPRAY, W. and KITCHER, P. (Eds) (1988) *History and Philosophy of Modern Mathematics*, Minneapolis, University of Minnesota Press.

BELL, J.L. and MACHOVER, M. (1977) *A Course in Mathematical Logic*, Amsterdam, North Holland.

BENECERRAF, P. and PUTNAM, H. (Eds) (1964) *Philosophy of Mathematics*, Oxford, Basil Blackwell.

BERRY, J. (1975) *Introduction to Systemic Linguistics I*, London, Batsford Books.

BISHOP, A.J. (1988) *Mathematical Enculturation*, Dordrecht, North Holland, Kluwer.

BOYER, C.B. (1968) *A History of Mathematics*, New York, Wiley.

COLLINGWOOD, R.G. (1939) *An Autobiography*, Reprinted 1944, London, Penguin Books.

CONWAY, J.H. (1976) *On Numbers and Games*, London, Academic Press.

CORNFORD, F.M. (1935) *Plato's Theory of Knowledge*, London, Routledge and Kegan Paul.

DAVIS, P.J. and HERSH, R. (1980) *The Mathematical Experience*, Boston, Birkhauser.

ERNEST, P. (1991) *The Philosophy of Mathematics Education*, London, The Falmer Press.

ERNEST, P. (1993) 'Mathematical activity and rhetoric: Towards a social constructivist account', in HIRABAYASHI, I., NOHDA, N., SHIGEMATSU, K. and LIN, F.L. (Eds) *Proceedings of PME-17 Conference*, Tsukuba, Japan, University of Tsukuba, 2, pp. 238–45.

ERNEST, P. (in press) *Social Constructivism as a Philosophy of Mathematics*, Albany, NY, SUNY Press.

FERGUSON, J. (1970) *Socrates*, London, Macmillan.

FRITZ, K. VON (1955) 'Die APXAI in der grieschischen Mathematik', *Archiv fur Begriffsgeschichte*, 1, Bonn (cited in Szabo, 1966).

GADAMER, H.G. (1965) *Truth and Method* (Translation by W. Glen-Doepler), London, Sheed and Ward (1979).

GILLIES, D.A. (Ed) (1992) *Revolutions in Mathematics*, Oxford, Clarendon Press.

HEYTING, A. (1931) 'The intuitionist foundations of mathematics', *Erkenntnis*, pp. 91–121, (translation in Benecerraf, P. and Putnam, H., 1964, pp. 42–9).

KITCHER, P. (1984) *The Nature of Mathematical Knowledge*, New York, Oxford University Press.

JOSEPH, G.G. (1991) *The Crest of the Peacock: Non European Roots of Mathematics*, London, I.B. Taurus.

KITCHER, P. and ASPRAY, W. (1988) 'An opinionated introduction', in ASPARY, W. and KITCHER, P. (1988) *History and Philosophy of Modern Mathematics*, Minneapolis, University of Minnesota Press. pp. 3–57.

KLINE, M. (1980) *Mathematics and Loss of Certainty*, Oxford, Oxford University Press.

KNORR, W. (1975) *The Evolution of the Euclidean Elements*, Dordrecht, Reidel.

LAKATOS, I. (1961) 'Essays in the Logic of Mathematical Discovery', Unpublished PhD thesis, Cambridge, King's College, University of Cambridge.

LAKATOS, I. (Ed) (1967) *Problems in the Philosophy of Mathematics*, Amsterdam, North Holland.

LAKATOS, I. (1976) *Proofs and Refutations*, Cambridge, Cambridge University Press.

LAKATOS, I. (1978) *Philosophical Papers* (2 vols), Cambridge, Cambridge University Press.

LIVINGSTON, E. (1986) *The Ethnomethodological Foundations of Mathematics*, London, Routledge and Kegan Paul.

LLOYD, G.E.R. (1990) *Demystifying Mentalities*, Cambridge, Cambridge University Press.

LORENZEN, P. (1970), 'Scientismus versus Dialektik', in *Hermeneutik und Dialektik*, BAND, I.R., BUBNER, R., CRAMER, K. and WIEHL, R. (Eds) Tübingen, (Cited in Roberts, 1992).

MANIN, Y.I. (1977) *A Course in Mathematical Logic*, New York, Springer.

PIMM, D. (1986) *Speaking Mathematically*, Oxford, Basil Blackwell.

PUTNAM, H. (1975) *Mathematics, Matter and Method*, Cambridge, Cambridge University Press.

PUTNAM, H. (1985) *Mathematics, Matter and Method*, Cambridge, Cambridge University Press.

RESTIVO (1992) *Mathematics in Society and History*, Dordrecht, Kluwer.

ROBERTS, J. (1992) *The Logic of Reflection*, New Haven and London, Yale University Press.

RORTY, R. (1979) *Philosophy and the Mirror of Nature*, Princeton, New Jersey, Princeton University Press.

ROSEN, S. (1989) *The Ancients and the Moderns: Rethinking Modernity*, New Haven, Yale University Press.

ROTMAN, B. (1988) 'Toward a semiotics of mathematics', *Semiotica 72 (1/2)*, pp. 1–35.

ROTMAN, B. (1993) *Ad Infinitum The Ghost in Turing's Machine: Taking God Out of Mathematics and Putting the Body Back in*, Stanford California, Stanford University Press.

SHOTTER, J. (1993) *Conversational Realities: Constructing Life through Language*, London, Sage.

SZABO, A. (1966) *The Origins of Euclidean Axiomatics* (mimeo, edited by B. BURGOYNE), London, LSE.

SZABO, A. (1967) 'Greek Dialectic and Euclid's Axiomatics', In Lakatos (1967) *Problems in the Philosophy of Mathematics*, Amsterdam, North Holland, pp. 1–27.

SZABO, A. (1978) *The Beginnings of Greek Mathematics*, Dordrecht, Reidel.

TILES, M. (1991) *Mathematics and the Image of Reason*, London, Routledge.

TYMOCZKO, T. (Ed) (1986) *New Directions in the Philosophy of Mathematics*, Boston, Birkhauser.

VOLOSINOV, V.N. (1973) *Marxism and the Philosophy of Language*, New York, Seminar Press.

WANG, H. (1974) *From Mathematics to Philosophy*, London, Routledge.

WILDER, R.L. (1981) *Mathematics as a Cultural System*, Oxford, Pergamon Press.

WITTGENSTEIN, L. (1953) *Philosophical Investigations* (translation G.E.M. ANSCOMBE), Oxford, Basil Blackwell.

WITTGENSTEIN, L. (1956) *Remarks on the Foundations of Mathematics* (Revised edition 1978), Cambridge, Massachusetts, MIT Press.

Chapter 4

Structuralism and Post-modernism in the Philosophy of Mathematics

Thomas Tymoczko

Quasi-empiricism is less a philosophical theory about mathematics than it is an approach to the philosophy of mathematics, an approach that stresses both mathematical practice and the natural connection between mathematics and natural science (see Tymoczko, 1986, for discussions of quasi-empiricism). This chapter describes a particular variant of quasi-empiricism called 'structuralism' and explains how structuralism solves the main problems of traditional philosophy of mathematics. Nevertheless, structuralism does not end the philosophy of mathematics — far from it. Instead it leaves us with a profound challenge to our understanding of mathematics.

In order the explain the gap between the success of structuralism and the ongoing problems of philosophy of mathematics, I will appeal to an analogy between mathematics and art. In the philosophy of art something like structuralism (formalism, internalism, new criticism) was called upon to explain the 'modern' in art. Structuralism was one of the explanations of the term 'modernism'. Alas, even modernism is disappearing from the modern scene. Most critics of contemporary art now recognize a new stage of art called 'post-modern' — art constructed after the illusions of modernism are abandoned. Post-modern art not only challenges our aesthetic sensibilities, it challenges our very idea of art. The problem left by structuralism is an analogous challenge to our idea of mathematics. It is the central problem of post-modern philosophy of mathematics.

One of the foremost contemporary advocates of structuralism is Michael Resnik:

> In mathematics . . . we do not have objects with an 'internal' composition arranged in structures, we have only structures. The objects of mathematics, that is, the entities which our mathematical constants and quantifiers denote, are structureless points or positions in structures. As positions in structures, they have no identity or features outside of a structure. (Resnik, 1981, pp. 529–50)

Structuralism emphasizes the importance of pattern in mathematics, and it is partly this emphasis on pattern that brings structuralism into the quasi-empirical fold — we can *perceive* patterns after all (Resnik, 1975, pp. 25–39). Thus structuralism de-emphasizes the individual objects in the pattern and so tries to avoid awkward questions about the nature of mathematical existents — e.g., how can we perceive individual numbers?

Structuralism makes intuitive sense with regard to abstract structures such as groups. There it seems that when we consider, for example, an abelian group of order six we are considering only a single abstract structure; it makes no sense to wonder about the internal composition of the group's elements. Of course, this is so in part because we have lots of examples of this group (e.g., Z(6)) and so lots of individuals to fill in this structure. It is more problematic to claim that all of mathematics is composed of such structures; don't some of the structures need some individuals to start with? Otherwise, it might seem as if we're trying to pull ourselves up by our bootstraps.

This criticism can be answered, I think, if we replace the mathematical structuralism of Resnik with the more general philosophical structuralism of W.V.O. Quine. For some time now, Quine has argued the structuralist case for mathematics: 'Arithmetic is, in this sense, all there is to number: there is no saying absolutely what the numbers are; there is only arithmetic.' (Quine, 1969, p. 45) The crucial difference between Quine and contemporary structuralists in the philosophy of mathematics is that Quine argues the case for structuralism across all of ontology, physical and mental as well as mathematical. Ultimately for Quine, whatever exists are the objects of our theories. 'We do not learn first what to talk about and then what to say about it.' (Quine, 1960, p. 16) That is, we don't first learn to refer to objects with an 'internal' composition arranged in structures. Instead, we learn a theory about a structure, we learn a network of interrelated objects. For an object to exist is just for it to exist in a network of interrelated objects, that is, to exist as a posit of our theories. 'Everything to which we concede existence is a posit from the standpoint of a description of the theory-building process, and simultaneously real from the standpoint of the theory that is being built.' (*ibid.*, p. 22)

The posits of mathematical theories are on par with the posits of physical theories. In both cases we concede existence to things — numbers, functions, forces and particles — because our favoured theories, the best at predicting and the best evidenced, quantify over numbers and functions, forces and particles. Existence, for Quine, is only existence in a structure. Distinguishing between objects is an intra-theoretical task, a task that can be accomplished only within a theory or only relative to a structure. So we distinguish between three and four, between rabbits and the total mass of rabbitiness in the universe. But it simply makes no sense to ask what 'three' really is apart from the position of three in the structure of arithmetic (this much Quine shares with mathematical structuralists such as Resnik), nor does it make sense to ask what 'rabbit' really refers to apart from the theoretical framework encapsulated by English (in this, Quine identifies mathematical structuralism with a fundamental fact about ontology) (Tymoczko, 1991, pp. 201–28). Sometimes Quine calls this point the thesis of ontological relativity, referring explicitly to Einstein (implicitly to Whorf).

Quine's structuralism is especially relevant to quasi-empiricism in the philosophy of mathematics. In effect, Quine blends mathematics and physics: virtually the same evidence supports our high-level theorizing about the structure of the world and the mathematics necessary to talk about this structure. The evidence accrues to our theories as wholes, not directly to individual propositions in them. From a historical perspective, Quine's assimilation of mathematics and physics is well-grounded. Descartes, Newton or Kant did not sharply distinguish between the mathematics of space (geometry) and the mathematics of motions in space (eventually, calculus and Newtonian physics). In just the same way we might say that the same general experience that convinces us that there are decks of playing cards in the world convinces us that there are things like shuffles, hence permutations of playing cards. Accelerations, derivatives and permutations are equally real.

Let me summarize. There is a way of looking at mathematics, the way is Quinean structuralism, that assimilates mathematics to natural science. (In fact, Quine's structuralism extends to the objects of ordinary life, like dogs, tables, and fellow humans. I ignore this extension here.) We have brute phenomena that we're trying to deal with (reality, experience), and certain theories (arithmetic, geometry, calculus, physics) are the best available candidates for dealing with that phenomena (the best evidenced according to our theories of evidence). So we are committed to saying that the objects posited by our theories are real. Forces and masses exist, as do real numbers, functions and derivatives.

Readers sometimes find it difficult to balance what almost seems like convention on Quine's part (we posit things) with the way that objects often seem to force themselves upon us (so Samuel Johnson thought that he could establish that physical objects exist by kicking a stone). But of course there is no real contradiction — good theories force themselves upon us too. Moreover, the forcing, I suggest, is primarily psychological in nature and not part of the argument for existence. Perhaps an example from the cinema could clarify this point. Most of us when watching a film, naturally interpret it in terms of a theory or structure that posits various characters and interactions, like conversations, among them. Cinematic objects, like ones encountered in daily life, force themselves upon us. But one and the same character might be portrayed now by the star, next by a stuntman, then by a body double. And the conversations we 'see' happening between characters are rarely films of actual conversations (or else the cameras would keep appearing on the film), but carefully edited soliloquies. Yet no matter how aware we are of the various tricks of the cinema, it is very difficult to avoid the impression that we are really seeing the same characters throughout the movie and scenes of real conversations.

The analogy between the posits of our filmic theories and those of our more serious theories is limited. Its only point is to reconcile our natural sense of the reality of objects ('they're just there in an undeniable way') with the conventional aspect of our higher-level theorizing (a point Descartes made with reference to a piece of wax). Where the analogy fails is that in the case of a movie character we are tempted to believe that the theoretical posit might be 'stitched together' out of more basic elements, such as the various actors who portray him. Indeed, traditional empiricists would take this comparison to heart and insist that all of our higher-level objects — from tables to stars to atoms — be 'stitched together' from more elementary parts, such as sense data or sensory impressions. But Quinean structuralism will have none of this sort of reduction. The objects it posits exist in and of themselves — in the network of prescribed theoretical interrelations. They have no 'internal' composition apart from what is dictated by theory.

If we accept this view of mathematics, certain traditional philosophical worries about mathematics would no longer bother us. The question of mathematical existence, for example, gets an easy answer. We know that natural numbers exist for pretty much the same kind reason that we know that atoms exist, because we know that number theory and atomic theory are true. And we know these are true because they force themselves on us as the best (best? are there even alternatives?) accounts of what's happening around us. Traditional philosophical worries about the ontology, epistemology and semantics of mathematics get dissolved, or at least reduced to similar worries about science (or about 'material objects'). This is a significant advance for it virtually dissolves traditional philosophy of mathematics. There might be problems about existence, knowledge and meaning left open on Quine's account. But there are no special problems accruing to mathematic *per se*.[1]

Quine's student (and my teacher), Burton Dreben, often described Quine's philosophy as 'deflationary'. By this I think Dreben meant that insofar as Quinean structuralism can be said to answer certain questions — do mathematical entities exist? — it does so in a very unspectacular way. The correct answer is much less profound than we might have thought or hoped.

All in all, a Quinean structuralism seems especially appealing as a quasi-empiricist approach to the philosophy of mathematics. Indeed, what could be wrong with it?

As I see it, the major difficulty of this structuralism approach is that it might actually *lose* mathematics in natural science. What is left of mathematics to single out as a special discipline of human knowledge? Is there any unity to a field called mathematics? What has happened to pure mathematics?

Mathematicians have occasionally suggested that mathematics just is a branch of natural science. While not going quite so far, von Neuman said that

> As a mathematical discipline travels far from its empirical sources, or still more, if it is second and third generation only indirectly inspired by ideas coming from 'reality', it is beset with very grave dangers. It becomes more and more purely aestheticizing, more and more purely '*l'art pour l'art*' . . . there is a great danger that the subject will develop along the line of least resistance . . . will separate into a multitude of insignificant branches . . . In any event . . . the only remedy seems to be the rejuvenating return to the sourse: the reinjection of more or less directly empirical ideas. (von Neuman, quoted in Borel, 1983, pp. 9–17)

When von Neuman warns mathematicians by using the fate of modern art, he is not being philistine. As sympathetic a critic of art as Arthur Danto has analysed the story of western art in a similarly pessimistic fashion. Let me briefly summarize Danto's provocative position, interspersing it with a tentative parallel to mathematics (Danto, 1986).

From the Renaissance to the impressionists — nearly four centuries — European painting could be seen as developing painterly equivalents of actual (or possible) visual perceptions. The most dramatic step was the discovery of perspective but the progress towards painterly perceptual equivalents of hypothetical scenes included many ingredients from more colours to a wider range of scenes (not to mention getting the image of clouds right). Even the impressionists only extended this search in the direction of rendering the play of light and momentary impressions. Throughout this period, paintings were judged with reference to an unpainted reality. It is this fact that allowed the discipline of painting to be seen as a model of a progressive discipline whose products gradually became better and more accurate. (There is a profound fact here, buried from most viewers of paintings, which is that impressionistic paintings are much closer to Renaissance realism than the post-impressionistic paintings that come after. Impressionist paintings aspire to realism of the moment.)

In parallel to the story of art, the story of mathematics from the Renaissance to the mid-nineteenth century can be seen as the search for ever more accurate representations of reality, only now the structures are to be represented conceptually not perceptually, these structures of physical space and time, motion and quantity. And in much the same way that painting did, mathematics and mathematical physics made spectacular progress.

For apparently different reasons both painting and mathematics went through significant crises beginning in the later part of the the nineteenth century. In each case the crises manifested themselves by a proliferation of substantially new methods in the fields, new kinds of mathematics and new kinds of painting. But while the mathematical crises were more or less internal to the field of mathematics — the traditional attempt to prove the parallel postulate led to alternative geometries and the related dissatisfaction with the geometric basis for the calculus, among others — in the case of painting, or so I'm led to believe, the crises were caused in part by developments external to the field. The development of photography and the coming development of cinema were to wrest the search for perceptual equivalents from painting and furthermore, were to take over many of the documentary and pedagogic functions of painting. Painting would lose its *raison d'être* (*ibid.*).

Thus in both cases the steady, but unreflective progress in the representation of reality — the ordinary reality of science and common sense — came to an end and the period modernism was born in both fields — modern mathematics and modern art. If modernism means anything, it means a period of intense self-reflection, a self-conscious concern for the essence of the discipline. In art, this was exhibited by a proliferation of new theories and of artists' manifestos trying to capture the essence of art — from Clive Bell's discovery of 'significant form' (which he thought art shared with mathematics) to Clement Greenburg's claim that the essence of painting was flatness. The corresponding movements in mathematics were the great foundational programmes that sought the essence of mathematics most prominently in logic, set theory, formal systems and mental construction. (Pre-modernists — both in painting and mathematics — did not worry about the nature of their discipline. They took what they were doing to be obvious.)

A.W. Moore's comments on set theory are especially insightful in this regard. It is easy to take each foundational programme at face value as an attempt to 'ground' mathematics in some deep metaphysical way. But with regard to set theory at least, Moore recommends seeing it as extremely self-conscious mathematics (Moore, 1990, p. 147). I think this same point applies to all the foundational disciplines. Just as painters were searching for the essence of painting in two-dimensional flatness, or colour tones, so mathematicians were searching for the essence of mathematics in abstract structures, formal systems or constructions. In painting, new paintings could not be and were not assimilated without a philosophy corresponding to them. In mathematics, the development of new fields was justified in terms of foundational programmes — 'it's just another formal system', 'it's all reducible to talk of sets', and so on.

But modernism, whether in mathematics or in painting, can be maintained only if we believe that someone will eventually get it right, only if we believe in the possibility that some self-conscious assessment can reveal to all and be recognized by all as revealing the essence of its subject matter. In the field of painting, the modern era is now widely regarded as over. It is not just that we still do not know what the essence of painting is; we can no longer believe that painting has an essence. In place of modernism, we now have the post-modern age of pluralism; anything goes. Without a recognized essence to painting, no one can legitimately criticize painting for overstepping its boundaries. At least in art, this has been the slow, painful movement from modern art to post-modern art. According to Danto, the very practice of art is slowly disappearing into the philosophical-critical justifications of it (e.g., conceptual art). Physical art evaporates leaving only philosophical statements and wall decorations.

In the case of mathematics, I think, we are all coming to the recognition that the age of foundationalism is dead. 'Foundations' have acquired such a bad reputation recently, that most of us are likely to regard their passing with unalloyed enthusiasm. But if the modern search for foundations was mathematics' attempt to articulate its own autonomous essence, then the passing of foundations is the failure of mathematics' attempt to articulate its own autonomous essence. We must face the possibility that mathematics has no essence or that it is not autonomous.

This then, is the problem indirectly bequeathed to us by structuralism in mathematics. Quine's structuralism does not provide the essence of mathematics, but only a very simple, general account of theories and things. It leaves us with the post-modern problem of saying what mathematics is without saying what its essence is: a formidable problem indeed.

Prima facie, the situation in mathematics is not as bleak as the situation in art. Mathematics has not abandoned (nor been denied) its basis in natural science, nor have mathematicians abandoned the details of their craft to preach visionary philosophy. Still, there is some cause for concern. Painters were dethroned from their role of capturing perceptual reality by the new technology of the camera. Could it be that the new technology of computers will eventually provide science with all the mathematics it needs? Suppose that hand-held calculators rendered calculus courses irrelevant to scientists and engineers; what then would happen to mathematics departments and the research of mathematicians? Could mathematics, as a discipline, survive these kinds of challenges? It's not clear that it could on von Neuman's view, any more than the practice of oil painting could survive the challenge from the camera and motion pictures.

In any case this is the problem that I end with: what is it about mathematics that unites its diverse practices and theories into an autonomous, worthwhile discipline. Is it a common methodology (proof?), a common history (humanistic mathematics?), or just a common university education (sociology of mathematics?).[2] Another alternative, both more frightening and more thrilling, is that the answer to my problem is not yet determined. It is still open, not to be discovered by the theorizing of philosophers but to be forged in mathematicians' souls, constructed by the hitherto uncreated practices of mathematicians.

Notes

1. See Tymoczko (1991) for an elaborate defense of this claim with regard to epistemology.
2. Tymoczko, 'Humanistic and Utilitarian Aspects Mathematics,' Proceedings of ICME-7, (forthcoming) hazards an anwer to this question.

References

BOREL, A. (1983) 'Mathematics: Art and science', *The Mathematical Intelligencer*, 5, 4.

DANTO, A. (1986) 'The end of art', *The Philosophical Disenfranchisement of Art*, New York, Columbia University Press.

MOORE, A.W. (1990) *The Infinite*, London, Routledge.

QUINE, W.V.O. (1960) *Word and Object*, Cambridge, MIT Press.

QUINE, W.V.O. (1969) *Ontological Relativity and Other Essays*, New York, Columbia University Press.

RESNIK, M. (1975) 'Mathematical knowledge and pattern recognition', *Canadian Journal of Philosophy*, 5.

RESNIK, M. (1981) 'Mathematics as a science of patterns: Ontology and reference', *Nous*, 15.

TYMOCZKO, T. (1986) *New Directions in the Philosophy of Mathematics*, Boston, Birkhauser.

TYMOCZKO, T. (1991) 'Science, mathematics and ontology', *Synthese*, 88.

Part 2

Post-modernist and Post-structuralist Approaches

> There foam'd rebellious *Logic* gagg'd and bound,
> There, stript, fair *Rhet'ric* languish'd on the ground;
> Mad *Mathesis* alone was unconfined,
> Too mad for mere material chains to bind. (Pope, 1742, p. 142)

The intellectual community has a love–hate relationship with post-structuralism and post-modernism. On the one hand, these areas embody an outrageous and decadent theoretical self-absorption, proclaiming that all is text, all is simulacrum. When faced with the environmental, social and political problems of today, who but an alienated late-twentieth century academic could claim that all is text? Yet consider the universe of sets that we generate from ∅ with Zermelo-Fraenkel set theory. What is it but an unending efflorescence of bubbles grown from an empty bubble? The signs create their own substanceless structure of forms, which becomes its own substance. Is belief in this so different from the world of simulacra?

On the other hand, relinquishing the assumptions of Cartesian rationalism and becoming aware of how we are each constructed through our positions in discursive practices wakes us up, as if from a dream, in a new intellectual landscape. This is a universe of texts and meanings held in place by (and constituting) power-relations, rather than a universe of physical objects in space controlled by gravity. But again, is this not merely adopting a sociological worldview?

As these controversies suggest, there are important insights for mathematics and education to be gained from post-structuralist and post-modernist perspectives. Consider first the latter.

Descartes has been said to have ushered in modernism with his 'dream of reason' (Davis and Hersh, 1988). This envisaged the building of indubitable structures of thought based on a logical masterplan, the Euclidean paradigm. Twentieth-century philosophy of mathematics re-appropriated this model for mathematics in the quest for absolutely certain foundations for knowledge. However the failure of this modernist project is well known (Ernest, 1991; Tiles, 1991).

After modernism came post-modernism, which its prophet Lyotard (1979) defines to mean 'incredulity towards meta-narratives'. Post-modernism signals a vision of knowledge which repudiates the centrality of any master narrative, be it philosophy, logic, or reason itself. From this perspective, no static system of logic and rationality underpins mathematics, or any discipline. They rest instead on narratives and language games, which shift with the organic changes of culture. The traditional objective criteria of knowledge and truth within the disciplines are but internal myths, which attempt to deny the social basis of all knowing. Instead, each disciplined narrative has its own internal legitimation criteria, which develop to overcome or engulf contradictions. Lyotard describes how mathematics overcame the crises in the foundations of axiomatics arising from paradoxes and Gödel theorems by incorporating meta-mathematics into its enlarged research paradigm. He also notes that continuous differentiable functions are losing their pre-eminence as paradigms of knowledge and prediction, as mathematics incorporates undecidability, incompleteness, catastrophe theory and chaos.

Certainly the history of mathematics bears out his reading. Mathematics has been defusing uncertainty by colonializing it since its beginnings. Incommensurability, Zeno's paradoxes, Delian problems, zero, negative and imaginary numbers, infinitesimals, transcendentals, probability, statistics, infinite sets, Peano curves, logical paradoxes, and non-standard logics, for example, have all been incorporated as technical advances, and not as challenges to the underlying paradigm of rational control and scientific certainty.

In the philosophy of mathematics the maverick tradition described earlier is termed post-modernist because of its rejection of foundationalism and the associated logical meta-narratives of certainty (Tiles, 1991). This title is also apt because of its concern to accommodate greater plurality and diversity, and to acknowledge its constitutive link with its historical and cultural traditions.

Overall, the post-modernist vision is a powerful one, linking developments in mathematics with grand currents of thought sweeping across the whole of western culture. In it, room is made for human beings amidst the monolithic towers of modernism. Thus there is also a clear link with structuralism, whose rigid determining structures, be they architectural, conceptual or mathematical, with their potential denial of the human presence, are also being challenged and eroded.

Structuralism is a movement that proposes structural theories in fields as disparate as psychology (Piaget), anthropology (Levi-Strauss), linguistics (Jakobson), social theory (Marx), and mathematics (Bourbaki). Post-structuralism offers the critique that such theories overstress static deterministic structures, and ignore both their contingent and the historically shifting natures, as well as the vital place of personal agency. Foucault's (1972) concept of discursive practice has played a central role here, by interrelating social context, power, positioning, knowledge and the human subject with the overarching constitutive role of discourse. Foucault argues that the divisions of knowledge accepted today are discursive formations: modern constructs, defined from certain social perspectives. Their objects, concepts, accepted rules for thinking and aims have all evolved and changed, sometimes dramatically, representing ruptures in the fabric of human ideas.

In the past few years a small but growing number of researchers in mathematics education have adopted or utilized post-structuralist approaches. Perhaps best known is Valerie Walkerdine who helped lay the foundations of a post-structuralist psychology (Henriques *et al.*, 1984) before applying them in her decisive contributions to mathematics education on language, reason and gender (Walkerdine, 1988, 1989). As yet, few philosophers of mathematics have explicitly applied the theoretical concepts of post-modernist and post-structuralist thinkers such as Baudrillard, Derrida, Foucault, Lyotard, or Rorty, in their analyses of mathematics, but a notable exception is Brian Rotman (1987, 1993). It is thus an especial pleasure to have contributions from both of these seminal thinkers in this section, as well as those of a whole host of exciting young researchers.

References

DAVIS, P.J. and HERSH, R. (1988) *Descartes' Dream*, London, Penguin Books.

ERNEST, P. (1991) *The Philosophy of Mathematics Education*, London, The Falmer Press.

FOUCAULT, M. (1972) *The Archaeology of Knowledge*, London, Tavistock.

HENRIQUES, J., HOLLOWAY, W., URWIN, C., VENN, C. and WALKERDINE, V. (1984) *Changing the Subject*, London, Methuen.

LYOTARD, J.F. (1979) *The Postmodern Condition: A Report on Knowledge*, Manchester, Manchester University Press (Reprinted 1984).

POPE, A. (1742) 'The Dunciad', Excerpt reprinted in POPE, A. (1962) *Selected Poems and Letters*, London, Chatto and Windus.

TILES, M. (1991) *Mathematics and the Image of Reason*, London, Routledge.

ROTMAN, B. (1987) *Signifying Nothing: The Semiotics of Zero*, London, Routledge.

ROTMAN, B. (1993) *Ad Infinitum The Ghost in Turing's Machine: Taking God Out of Mathematics and Putting the Body Back in*, Stanford, California, Stanford University Press.

WALKERDINE, V. (1988) *The Mastery of Reason*, London, Routledge.

WALKERDINE, V. (1989) 'Femininity as performance', *Oxford Review of Education*, 15, 3, pp. 267–79.

WALKERDINE, V. AND THE GIRLS AND MATHEMATICS UNIT (1989) *Counting Girls Out*, London, Virago.

METHODIST COLLEGE LIBRARY
Fayetteville, N.C.

Chapter 5

Reasoning in a Post-modern Age

Valerie Walkerdine

Introduction

When I was a little girl at primary school, my headteacher called me a 'plodder'. Many years later I still remembered this designation and I didn't like it very much. A plodder is somebody who gets there in the end, is terribly slow — has no flair, genius or creativity. A snail or a tortoise. I wanted instead to race like the wind, to soar like a bird. When I was at grammar school, I learnt some humiliating lessons, quickly. I learnt that my parents didn't 'know' any of the things that they were supposed to know and that there was right-knowing and wrong-knowing. I learnt that if I opened my mouth to relate a piece of knowledge from home, I was ridiculed: we read the wrong kind of newspaper, listened to the wrong kind of music. I also learnt very quickly that I had to work hard — I got my mother to test me on whatever subject until I could recite my notes in a word-perfect way. I passed all my 'O' levels this way, but still thought that I lacked 'brains', especially in relation to the boys, who I saw as a different species. It never occurred to me to think that actually I had learnt some very valuable things that helped me to survive in that context. I had learnt how to succeed, what the rules were, when to open my mouth and when it was better to say nothing.

When I was in higher education, I suddenly became aware one day in the library, that I felt as though I understood how to construct an argument — what the rules were and what you had to do. I realized that it was easy and that once I'd got hold of the way, I could succeed in academic work. It seems to me, looking back, that image of myself as a plodder, the learning how to do new things in contexts that I didn't understand, turning a poor self-image and bewilderment into success, is something that concerns many of us.

As I will discuss later in the chapter, the headteacher's idea of me as a 'plodder' is not an uncommon kind of designation for girls. But, what I am interested in here, is to understand how I, and other oppressed and exploited peoples come to see themselves as unable to think. As is no doubt well-known, there have been many attempts to help those who do not do well in education to think and reason, be independent and autonomous. I want to think about the ways that this has been approached. There have been attempts to help girls, who are assumed to be weak, passive and dependent, to be independent, creative thinkers. There have been attempts to show the flaws in 'masculine' logic by demonstrating the way in which women's thinking and knowing is different. Both of these have been important, but what I want to point particularly to the flaws in the argument that

METHODIST COLLEGE LIBRARY
Fayetteville, N.C.

girls and other oppressed groups have to be made autonomous and independent, that there is something they lack, be it understood as a fault of oppression, deprivation, faulty socialization, depending on the model, something which could be put right by teaching. I object to this, because of the assumed lack and absence.

In this chapter, I want to examine how it is not so much a question of lacking something, not being able to break rules or failure to be autonomous, but that these explanations have to be understood as part of attempts to produce scientific ideas about exploited and oppressed peoples that are central to their regulation. In other words, I want to question ideas about why certain groups are said to lack certain intellectual powers and examine how these ideas have become part not only of the way we have thought about thinking, but also the way in which this knowledge forms a central component of aspects of government. On the basis of this discussion, I want to go on to talk about how we might think about thinking differently.

Children's Reasoning

Twentieth-century ideas about children's reasoning form one of the 'grand meta-narratives of science'. They tell us a story about development and thinking which claims to be true for all times, peoples, places, which sees all children as progressing towards 'abstract thinking', which is taken to be the pinnacle of civilized being. At a point in our history in which such goals and meta-narratives are being questioned, and in which 'abstracted' reasoning fails to take on board the production of thinking in actual practices, I wish not only to question this model, but also the very idea of development itself. Do not get me wrong, I don't mean to imply that I want to do away with accounts of children's change and transformation as they move towards adulthood, but I do want to question developmental theory as the basis for understanding such change.

The reasoning child is a relatively new invention. Indeed, according to the historian Philippe Aries (1967), among others, childhood itself is a modern invention. That this is so, is easily supported by the wealth of evidence which demonstrates not only that childhood is a concept which arrives with modernity, but that the idea of childhood as a distinct condition and object of a scientific gaze arrives at the same time as the emergence of popular and compulsory schooling. Indeed, it seems as if aristocratic children are treated as little adults and that, according to Aries, adults and children alike from all sections of society, played as well as worked together. The idea of playing was not specific to children. My particular argument here is that the new scientific approach to childhood was inaugurated at a particular historical conjuncture: one at which there were important changes in the mode of government of, especially urban, populations. In this analysis, the designation of childhood as a distinct, scientifically observable, state was one of the most important aspects of government which became centred on the 'scientific' management of populations. This management has been described by Michel Foucault (1976) as part of modern forms of power which place government as part of a minute and detailed (often invisible) surveillance of the population, so that the population to be governed had, in a sense, to come to govern itself, as I will demonstrate. Foucault shows the way in which the 'sciences of the social' (psychology, sociology, for example) become incorporated into 'technologies' for regulating populations. In this way, we can see the human sciences, and developmental psychology in particular, as part of the production of a 'truth' about a child population in order to understand how that population might be effectively regulated and governed.

Such a view of science takes us a long way from the idea of an incontrovertible proof or truth produced in ivory towers by neutral academics. Rather, Foucault suggests that scientific theories and 'discoveries' emerge in historical circumstances which need such approaches because they can be used in practices of government and regulation. In this view therefore, scientific conceptions of 'the child' become not simple descriptions but part of strategies designed to 'know' the child all the better to regulate 'him'. In this sense then, strategies of regulation which claim to tell us the 'truth' of children are far different from a science which claims to present us a 'liberated' view of the child, whose 'natural' characteristics and propensities have been uncovered.

The model of child development as an uncovering of a 'liberating truth' about children, one which frees them from the tyrannies of the 'loss of childhood' contained, for example, in the exploitation of children through work, is a very common story. However, the view that I am putting forward criticizes this story by suggesting that such a model of liberation is founded upon a western conception of Rationality, deeply caught up with the 'Enlightenment', which has been used to claim European civilizations as advanced and rational, while placing the primitive and childlike in one box, as less rational, civilized and evolved. Such a difference of perspective becomes crucial when we are considering issues of the development and education of those who have been considered 'at risk' when it comes to childhood and reason: the proletariat, colonial peoples, women. One way of understanding their position of course is to see them as less liberated and less advanced, lacking in reason, autonomy and independence. Thus, struggles for liberation can concentrate on making good the 'lack': rationality, independence and autonomy are lacking through faulty socialization — socialization for dependency, which can be put right by means of specific teaching and so forth. It is this model that I wish to seriously criticize even though it seems politically progressive.

I want to argue that modern accounts of childhood progression towards rationality actually produce difference from a norm of a reasoning child as a pathology and that this is a central part of a modern strategy of management in which the compliant and law-abiding governable citizen is to be produced by techniques which do not necessarily resemble direct suppression, but then turn the desired characteristic into the normal and natural. All deviations from this norm then appear as medicalized pathologies to be corrected. Hence, in this manner, a regulation can be ensured in a way which actually means the production of a type of subject which regulates or polices itself. In this analysis therefore, childhood reasoning, independence and autonomy have to be looked at in a different light. They become means through which power is organized through the self-regulation and pathologization of the oppressed themselves.

Although in this chapter I cannot go into the necessary historical detail. I want to point to certain conditions pertaining to the first two decades of this century. Popular and then compulsory schooling was introduced in England at the end of the nineteenth century. It was felt that, as well as the philanthropic attempts to get rid of child labour, schooling was also introduced to attempt to produce a 'docile workforce', one with the correct habits of industriousness, thrift and so forth and would thus not become the burden on the government that was envisaged in the way in which crime and poverty were viewed. Crime and poverty were understood as characteristics in the population which were the result of bad habits. Monitorialism was one example of such a practice. However, it was discovered that although children in these schools were learning their lessons, their tendency was to recite the lessons, the Lord's Prayer, for example, for anybody who would give them a little money. Hence, the correct lesson had not been learnt! In this instance, experiments using a more 'natural' form of education, partly after Rousseau and French revolutionary ideas, were tried in various schools, the most famous of which being Robert Owen's school for mill workers' children in New Lanark. Here, education according to 'nature' became the mode and 'love' became a central part of the pedagogy. It is at this point then that educational practices and those of an emerging psychology of children, joined forces. The scientific study of children is also said to have taken off at the end of the nineteenth century. Charles Darwin made a study of his infant son using a translation of evolutionary biology that argued that ontogeny, the development of one species-being towards maturity recapitulates phylogeny, the evolutionary path of the species as a whole. Soon, child-study societies were very common in England and the idea of stages of development soon adopted. Indeed, by the time that Piaget published his first paper in 1918 such ideas were commonplace. What is important about an application of evolutionary theory to childhood is that the evolution of the species and the idea of the most evolutionarily advanced state of the human being get mixed up with the idea of western rationality, European civilization as an evolutionary pinnacle (as in social Darwinism). Hence, the mapping of stages of transformation towards the achievement of western rationality became seen as a naturally occurring evolutionary process which could not be taught, but could be fostered through the medium of love and the provision of a nurturant environment. I want therefore to stress several problems and fallacies here:

1. Education is not organized for liberation but for the production of the appropriate kind of subject for the modern order. This is done by means of producing a theory of the 'nature' of that subject and the pathologizing deviation from it.
2. Evolutionary approaches to development see it as a fixed sequence moving towards a naturally occurring goal of advanced abstract reasoning. There is nothing natural about this progression and nothing inevitable about it.
3. However, it becomes what Foucault calls a 'fiction which functions in truth', that is, because such ideas become incorporated into the way in which educational practices work, it actually produces the very thing it claims to describe through the truths which are presented in the classroom. For example, the idea of stages has become a truism: we 'find' stages everywhere, the curriculum is structured according to stages everywhere because it is precisely what is sought.

The idea of stages and development were incorporated into the way that the curriculum was organized, to the extent that the architecture, the seating arrangements and the timetable all changed. (In 'Changing the Subject' Henriques *et al.*, 1984, I give an example of the transformation suggested to primary-school teachers in the late 1960s in which teachers are encouraged to change their classroom from one with rows to groups of tables. The new classroom contains a space not present in the first, that is, a space for the 'sudden unpredictable interest that requires space'. This space exemplifies the way in which the new ideas about 'the child' are created in the organization of time and space in the transformation of the practices themselves. In the same paper, I also examine the way in which in the same historical period, records about children begin to note developmental accomplishments, such that what counts as evidence of attainment and success begins to change. So, for example, getting the right answer is no longer sufficient. What matters is the developmental cause of and route to an answer, (which may not even have to be right, as we shall see later).

My argument therefore is that theories of the development of reasoning when incorporated into education become 'truths' which actually serve to produce the desired kinds of subjects as normal and pathologizes differences. It attempts to create subjects who will 'fit' the moral and political order and, because, especially their education has been through the medium of 'free will', will indeed police and regulate themselves. The 'love' which I mentioned earlier is supposed to be part of the 'facilitating environment'. And it is no coincidence at all that elementary teacher training was opened to women in the early decades of this century on the grounds that such training would 'amplify their capacities for maternal nurturance' (Hadow Report, 1926). Such women were to become part of the environment which was needed to foster natural child development. What I want to concentrate on next is the way in which the subjectification of women as teachers is said to relate to their exclusion from reason, thus providing evidence for the pathologization of everything which does not fit into the definition of the 'natural child'.

'The reasoning woman is a monster' said one Victorian commentator. For a considerable period of European and western history women have represented the 'other' to 'reason': they have contained the irrational. It is my contention that the naturalization of reason as the end-point of a stage-wise progression of development, places 'Woman' as constantly threatening this goal. She is constantly harangued for not reasoning, while equally being targeted if she does so. Her reasoning is seen to constitute a threat to reasoning masculinity.

If masculinity is understood in terms of a set of base instincts (primitive, animal) to be kept in place only through the civilizing influence of reason, 'Woman' must also be tamed — her animal powers, her sexuality must be subsumed to a model of natural nurturance which protects reason. Yet women are systematically positioned, governed and regulated in two ways. As mothers who must prop up the developing and autonomous child and who are blamed for any failure both of autonomy and in the social body (e.g., criminality or antisocial behaviour in accounts which assume that criminals are produced through inadequate bonding or through a mother's extended absence or failure in infancy: see Walkerdine and Lucey, 1989, for a review). But while girls and women are accused of being dependent and lacking autonomy and independence, there are massive threats posed by the possibility that they might reason.

In the nineteenth century, middle and upper-class women were struggling to enter the academy. But, attempts to prohibit them centred around theories which argued that intellectual work would dry up the reproductive capacities of women, making them unwilling or unable to mother. This, at a time when there were great fears about degeneracy and the future of the right kind of stock, later 'the imperial race'. The race that was to be born to rule had to be ensured of children and that necessitated keeping women away from the contagion of reason.

It might be argued that such ideas no longer hold any sway and that we have moved into an era in which strenuous scientific and pedagogic attempts have been made to help girls and women reach reason and autonomy. However, I wish to argue that the continual research which reveals a 'lack' in girls when it comes to mathematical and scientific reasoning, persists in the idea that girls lack something and yet wants them to contain and nurture the very reason that they are accused of not possessing. I am suggesting that girls are put in a double-bind which follows directly from the danger and threat once posed by their reasoning. The danger and threat persist in that while the mother may no longer be held responsible for the 'imperial race', she is certainly held responsible for producing proper subjects — independent and autonomous children, who will become free and law-abiding citizens, not pathological, mentally ill or criminal.

The research that I conducted into girls and mathematics (Walkerdine *et al.*, 1989) revealed clearly the ways in which it was not a simple matter of girls failing and boys succeeding in mathematics, but that girls might actually do well and boys badly. However, teacher and pupil explanations of this performance were extremely interesting. There appeared to be tremendous investment in the idea that classroom performance did not indicate true worth or potential where boys were concerned, though the opposite was true of girls.

In short, girls were accused of doing well because they worked hard, followed rules, behaved well. Indicators of this were their demeanour and behaviour in the classroom. Think about the way in which 'the child' came to be defined through stages of cognitive development as a playful subject (play being natural to children) who developed through action upon an object world. If this child was understood as 'natural', it also represented the normal, the democratic and the free as against the repressed, authoritarian and fascist. 'Work' in the classroom held other meanings in its shadow: authoritarianism, linked to the fascism of the world wars, to child labour and to the proletariat. In other words, girls working signalled a number of dangers, references to the past, all of which suggested something wrong, unchildlike, irrational, lurking. Boys, on the other hand, could be doing really badly but if their behaviour could be read as active, playful, all was well with the world.

The following quotations from teachers of 10-year-old children are typical of the distinctions that I want to convey.

> About a girl who was top of the class:
> very, very hard worker. Not a particularly bright girl . . . her hard work gets her to her standards.
> About a boy:
> he can just about write his own name. . . . not because he's not clever, because he's not capable, but he just can't sit still, he's got no concentration. . . . very disruptive, but quite bright.

What is going on here? How is it that a girl can be top of her class in terms of attainment and still not be considered bright and a boy can have such poor performance that he can just about write his own name and yet be deemed quite bright. Indeed, my analysis of teachers' reports about their pupils in twenty-six schools, in which such distinctions as this were very common, led me to conclude that it was almost harder for a camel to go through the eye of a needle than for a girl to be called 'bright' (Walkerdine *et al.*, 1989).

Another characteristic which teachers described boys as having, but was never once used to describe a girl, was 'potential'. This is particularly interesting because it is something which is assumed to be present and yet cannot be seen: a hidden cause. Remember, I argued that the correct answer is no longer understood as sufficient any more and may indeed be seen as a danger, because the real cause is taken to be underlying and conceptual, not a surface competence. In the case of girls, it seems to be assumed that what is visible on the surface is all that there is and that only boys have hidden depths. I am trying therefore to show why this explanation has been foisted onto women (like the designation 'plodder' onto me) and how we have taken this on board, believing that we can make good workers, secretaries, research assistants, but never great thinkers or geniuses. I am saying therefore that the problem does not lie in the essence of femininity but in the way in which these fictions, fears and fantasies have entered into the stories told about girls and women and the way that these have been used in our regulation.

The Black British literary critic, Homi Bhabha (1984) argues that the colonial subject, the subject of colonial government, was created through the production of stories about that subject which were turned into 'truths', through which the subject was subjugated and governed. The 'lazy Black' was a story endlessly repeated as if to make it true and it became the basis for strategies of regulation. We could also add here the story of the 'cultureless Aussie'. Edward Said (1979) argued in his book *Orientalism*, that the Orient is a fiction constructed in the fantasies of the West. What people like, Said and Bhabha are trying to argue, is that the 'lazy Black' or 'cultureless Aussie' become fictions, objects of fantasy, referred to as 'fear, phobia and fetish' because as fantasies they are created in the threatened imaginary of the 'colonizer', or the West, and come to operate as though they were true. In this way, they have profound effects upon the lives of colonized and oppressed peoples, while not being constructed out of 'real' characteristics at all. What then are the fears, phobias and fetishes in which the girls are inscribed, what are the stories about girls that have to be endlessly repeated as if to make them true? Perhaps we could find beneath what Foucault calls this 'will to truth' about girls a desire to keep on proving girls' difference and inferiority, because of the threat that their success represents to civilization, as I set out earlier in the chapter.

But, to develop a different point (which I treated in more detail in Walkerdine, 1988), why should we think that hard work and rule-following are bad? Girls are accused of not being great or creative thinkers because they do not break the rules, so naughty boys get validated, while women as mothers get castigated for producing delinquents. Poor old conformist girls — moral guardians of the rules — no breaking rules for them! Yet, the idea that 'real thinking' results from propositional knowledge and not from effective procedures or the following of rules is something which it is quite important to examine. Why is girls' success, announced as low-level rule following, in a pejorative way, linked with conformity the moment it is announced at all? I came to call this the 'just or only phenomenon', because as soon as it was acknowledged that girls might be good it was usually followed by a statement downgrading the success as 'just or only' something or other (such as rule-following), that is, something that amounts to nothing.

My argument therefore is that it is *not* simply the case that girls are poor at mathematics, reasoning and so forth, but that the 'truth' of child development pathologizes and defines their performance in such a way as to read it as bad. To suggest therefore that girls and women are poorer at reasoning is to beg serious questions. There are such threats posed by this position for girls and women and it is embedded so deeply in the regulation of the social world, that it is not so much the issue that girls are poor at reasoning, but that they are caught up inside a series of fictions and fantasies which are about keeping them safe as mothers, while rendering as dangerous and exciting the feminine sexuality which stands outside of that view.

Girls are often positioned as hard-working little women, not children at all. Indeed, if they display those characteristics associated with independence and autonomy, all is not considered well in the classroom. Their behaviour is often castigated as threatening and unfeminine. For example, one teacher referred to the way that one girl was rather active, naughty and troublesome, as her being a 'madam'. We all know the suppressed connotations of that term and its reference to female sexuality. What is interesting here is the way in which the girl simply cannot be judged in the same terms as the boy. Her actions are understood within a framework that is replete with the myth and fantasy surrounding sexual difference.

It is as nurturers of knowers that girls are said to be best suited. Hardly surprising then that as mothers, women are needed to produce the right kind of democratic citizens, by providing the kind of nurturance and development which will allow their children to become the required rational, autonomous, free, but law-abiding citizens.

In this sense, mothers have been positioned as extremely important in modern literature about the production of the right kind of citizen, the one who is free of antisocial and criminal tendencies. Literature targeting women as the relay point in the production of this citizen began early this century with the social hygiene movement (Rose, 1985), but reached its nadir in the 1960s and 1970s with concern about the rise of black power in the American ghettos. Programmes like 'Headstart' placed the blame for urban decay and poor educational standards onto the mothers. Earlier studies of maternal deprivation were invoked and new research on mother–infant interaction blossomed. The minute details of mothers' interactions with their small babies in the laboratory were observed using the new video technology. The idea became common that there was an observable truth of correct mothering, a type of care and interaction which was normal in that it could ensure the production of normal children, that is, ones who would not grow up to be antisocial. As part of this mothers were assumed to be able to be sensitive to the cognitive needs of their children, their need to produce meaning and to be understood and to become rational. Empirical studies monitored success in sensitivity and attempted to use it as a predictor of school performance. The mother was to be the first and best educator. A huge burden was laid at her door, and the danger remained therefore that children who did badly at school may be the product of her faulty nurturance and education. It will come as no surprise that it was white and black working-class mothers who were felt to be in most danger of doing things wrong. It was they who had to become the target of parent-guides and so forth. The normal mother was assumed to be able to offer the correct education through her nurturance of natural development towards reason. She would teach through her love, her play and not attempt any overt lessons, and yet one-to-one correspondence could emerge as natural through the medium of laying the table or sorting. These could become a game played when making the muesli or putting the washing on the line. Mothers who could not achieve this were designated insensitive; they seemed to work when they should be playing with their children or engage in stupid activities like teaching them explicitly. Such explicit teaching has been frowned upon in educational texts, for example

> You are probably helping your child get ready for mathematics in many ways, maybe without realizing it! Here are some of the many activities that you can do for your child which may help: Laying the table — counting, getting the knives in the right place etc. Going shopping — handling money, counting items in basket . . . Spotting shapes, colours, comparing sizes, whether at home or on walks. No doubt you can think of many more. The important thing is that you help your child get hold of the basic ideas of Maths, such as sorting, matching and comparing. But don't turn it into a lesson. All these things can be done incidentally a part of everyday events. (*Early Mathematical Experiences, General Guide*, 1978, p. 11)

In all of this there were some huge silences within the discourse, some mammoth denials. The mother should be achieving all this naturally, but in all of the literature it is difficult to find any reference to domestic work that mothers must do except that they make it play. There is simply no discourse of domestic work in this literature. It is as though mothers could naturally love and play all the time and then correct child development must follow. What a burden of guilt this places on women. Normal mothers then, do not work, are not tired, have enough space and so on. In a study that Helen Lucey and I conducted (Walkerdine and Lucey, 1989) we looked at the ways in which mothering was regulated and the ways in which ideas about normal mothering had been used to differently regulate working and middle-class mothers. The working-class mothers tended to be targeted as pathological by educational and social-work agencies, but middle-class mothers had to endure a stifling normality, which really was not any less oppressive. Indeed, such mothers were often used in voluntary agencies and so forth, to present norms and examples through which the working-class women could be pathologized and regulated. Professional middle-class mothers appeared to fit this norm and had more centrally incorporated it into their consciousness, such that they felt guilty if they should do anything other than this important task. Working-class mothers by comparison were much more likely to tell their child that they had to work and could not play and more. They also did something which some developmental psychologists had roundly criticized: they made power visible.

John and Elizabeth Newson (1976) wrote that children should be given certain illusions, illusions of their own power and autonomy, as an equal person with rights, a reasoning being. They admit that to achieve this the child has to be fed an illusion, an illusion which hides the power the parent has over the child.

> Some conflict between parent and child is inevitable. It arises because parents require children to do things, and this interferes with the child's autonomy as a person, with wishes and feelings of his own. In disciplinary conflicts, by definition, we have a situation where certain individuals excercise their rights as people of superior status (in age, power and presumed wisdom) to determine what younger and less experienced people, of inferior status, may or may not do. If the child complies willingly of course, even if his willingness has been engineered by offering him the illusion of choice, his self-esteem can be kept intact: but whenever he is forced into an unwilling compliance by threat of sanctions, whether these be pain inflicted or approval withdrawn, he will inevitably suffer in some degree feelings of powerlessness and humiliation. (Newson and Newson, 1976, pp. 331–2)

This is to be achieved partly by reasoning with the child. Children have to understand that they can be told that something is unreasonable or they can gain their own power by reasoning. Thus, reasoning and its development play a central part in the production of what I want to call an illusion of democracy and freedom. The child's power is an illusion, but it is now to be maintained. Independence and autonomy are an illusion within our modern social and political order but they have to be maintained as powerful illusions to allow us to believe that we are free enough to accept our place and not become rebellious or criminal. The mother therefore who does not subscribe to this illusion, who makes her power explicit, is revealing something very dangerous and threatening: power and oppression. No wonder then that the idea of normal motherhood is pushed at us everywhere and the injunctions against 'pathology' so strong. As Nikolas Rose (1985) has argued, the production of these practices, these forms of regulation of the modern subject, are produced through desire. We actually want to be those mothers and feel bad when we are not. In this view, thinking, or more particularly reasoning, is something which is to be understood as historically and socially located and intimately associated with the production and regulation of a certain kind of subject.

I am trying to show therefore that the dominance of the grand meta-narratives of science is deeply caught up with a European bourgeois project about power and dominance and has nothing to do with nature, but that the idea of nature was itself manufactured and intimately connected with the deep and minute processes of government. I am suggesting therefore that we need to move beyond such meta-narratives, towards a model of thinking as produced within practices that are themselves historically and culturally located. If the idea of a stagewise progression of reasoning to a pinnacle of abstracted logic is itself not universal and natural at all, but Eurocentric and bourgeois, then it follows that the very idea of a universal progression needs to be abandoned. I contend that we need to view thinking as a socially and historically produced practice, not an abstract and disembodied entity.

To introduce the idea of thinking in practices we need to look at what is referred to in developmental psychology as the context and transfer debate. The idea that cognition is something which is fixed in the head and can be applied in, or transferred to, a variety of contexts is something that I have been criticizing

(Walkerdine, 1988). The Cartesian Cogito is understood as having central human processes through which the world is perceived and understood.

Calculating As If Your Life Depended on It

In order to explore what this approach might look like I want to make a brief reference to approaches to non-European and informal practices. There is now a considerable literature on the cognitive practices of non-European peoples. The early literature is steeped in the view that non-western thinking is primitive and childlike and indeed much work concentrated on applying a stage-wise analysis to the thinking of non-European adults. Important work, such as that of Michael Cole and Sylvia Scribner (1974) highlighted the way in which African and Latin American adults produced sophisticated thinking in specific practices which were important in their daily lives, but could not even attempt logical problems such as syllogisms, because they would not accept the premises as abstract. When engaging in problems about John being taller than Fred, for example, they would typically say that John was short and therefore the problem had no sense. What they refused to do was to separate reasoning from the meanings in which thinking was produced. Western logical reasoning demands a certain discourse in which reference is actively suppressed. I will discuss the consequences of this later in this chapter. When such issues have been discussed in relation to children, it has usually been around the theme that non-European, black and white working-class and peasant children tend to perform very well on certain tasks connected with the world outside school, such as selling in a street market, calculating betting odds, and very poorly on logically equivalent tasks at school. One of the problems is the idea of logical equivalence. What it does is to read all problems as though they were exemplars of a logical type. This leads onto the common educational idea that, for example, 'mathematics is everywhere' because many different activities can be read through the same logico-mathematical framework. This view is common in Piagetian inspired curricula in which children are assumed to approach all tasks as examples of logico-mathematical principles and if the tasks have any meaning the task of the child is to learn to ignore and 'forget' the meaning, as in Margaret Donaldson's (1978) approach to disembedding. However, such an approach does in my view teach a very crucial 'forgetting'. It is the forgetting of which post-structuralist theorists have spoken in relation to an understanding of the constructed nature of consciousness. When we treat the world as abstract in this way we forget the practices which form us, the meanings in which we are produced, we forget history, power and oppression. This universalizing and abstracting approach forgets colonization, patriarchy, the forces of 'Unreason', as Foucault called them. When children on the street corner in any Latin American city (or, more recently at the traffic lights on busy London intersections) sell things and deftly make calculations which western psychologists assume are too advanced and complex for them, they are engaging in an activity in which that calculation is crucial. The family's survival may depend on it. Giving the wrong change in this case is no mere mistake, it could mean the difference between eating and going hungry. This calculation is part of a whole body of intersecting practices in which the thinking itself is produced, embodied, emotionally loaded. Yet, in school discourses, calculation is considered to be part of the very rule-following, low-level activity that I discussed earlier.

One day I watched a man and his young son sitting in a park café. The father asked his son to imagine what two cups of tea and cakes would cost. The game was fun. There was no danger that the cakes could not be bought or eaten. I also observed another family in the café of a bus station. Here the mother stopped her two sons buying cans of coke because they were too expensive. They had to buy 'warming cups of tea'. When a 4-year-old girl in one of the pieces of research I conducted talked to her mother one day, a man was cleaning their windows. The family was middle-class and comfortably off. They also employed a cleaner. The girl struggled to understand why the window cleaner should be paid for his work. In analysing this example Tizard and Hughes (1984) called this struggling 'the power of a puzzling mind'. By doing this, they generalize the idea of the 'puzzling mind of the 4-year-old'. This seems then to be a story about all 4-year-olds who must puzzle because of a property of their minds. There are, of course, 4-year-olds who don't puzzle. Does that mean that there is something wrong with the 4-year-old or with the generalized and universalized story of the puzzling mind? Another 4-year-old, this time a working-class girl did not puzzle. When her mother told her that she could not have any slippers until her father got paid she recognized the exchange relation immediately, a relation that Williams and Shuard (1976), authors of a best-selling teachers' guide on mathematics, saw as an abstract concept well beyond the grasp of young children.

> Money is used only for buying and he pays in coins for what he is asked for, two pence, four pence etc. The idea of money as meaning the exchange value of goods will be beyond him for a long time to come. (Williams and Shuard, 1976, p. 51)

Is it then that so-called abstraction is a forgetting by those who believe themselves autonomous, free and who have enough money and power to treat the world as a logical game, not a matter of survival. What does this removal of meanings do?

When I analysed a corpus of recordings of mothers and their 4-year-old daughters at home, I looked at the production of 'mathematical meanings'. As part of this I took the signifier 'more'. More in these practices was not used to designate a comparison of quantity, but by the mothers in their regulation of their daughters' consumption, as in 'no, you can't have any more pudding until you've eaten what's on your plate'. The lower down the socio-economic scale, the more the mother used 'more' in a negative way. Such daughters are likely to have associated the term both with prohibition and a depriving mother, and to experience their mothers as the source of the prohibition and deprivation, although they are only in fact positioned in that way by the social construction of their mothering. My mother had a phrase which she used to use when I had left home and gone to college, having more than she had ever dared dream about and still wanted more. She called it 'much wants more' and she used it as an injunction against greed, against a wanting that meant that you were dissatisfied with your place. I give this example to point in a shorthand way to the profound way in which thinking is produced in specific practices with specific relations of signification, meaning, emotion. What schools try to teach children to do is to forget and suppress these meanings in an effort to universalize logical reasoning.

In this approach, practices produce and position participants in them (the bad mother, the lazy Black, the cultureless Aussie, the hard-working girl) and meanings are produced in practices, such that there are no 'actions on objects' in the Piagetian sense, but, actions, objects, words in practices. These meanings and practices in which they are inscribed are deeply emotional and replete with fantasy. My view is that we need to analyse these practices as discursive and specific, to understand the production of subjects within them, rather than seeing 'contexts' as something peripheral.

I want to end with two more examples, this time from schools. In the first classroom, a group of top infant children are playing a game that the teacher has given them; she calls it a 'shopping game'. In this game they have to take a card from a pack. Each card has a picture of an item to be bought and then an amount of money, such as a yacht for 2p. The aim of the game is for the children to work out change for each purchase from 10p using plastic coins and record the sum on paper. The children found the game highly amusing because of the disjunction between the expensive items and the cheap prices. So these working-class children acted out fantasies of being middle-class shoppers to the hilt. They pretended to buy expensive goods and take them back because they were dissatisfied. They put on posh accents. Yet they also made mistakes with their calculations. One boy spent all his money, not realizing that he was supposed to have a fresh 10p each turn. The problem is that although the teacher thought of the game as embodying concrete practice of subtraction with small amounts of money, the ignoring of the meanings and practices in which those relations are produced, led to an inability to see either the reason for the children's mirth or for their problems. This task was, in my view, *ersatz* shopping. There was no exchange, the goods were unrealistically cheap, they talked about change and then had to translate to taking away and then, the goal of the task was a calculation on paper not any item bought at all. In short the practices were different and the ignoring of this aspect as well as that of the practices of school discursive production meant that the children had many problems. The main thing that they had to learn was that such tasks were eventually not supposed to mean anything and this would introduce them to the idea of a logical discourse which could apply to anything. The introduction to such a discourse has to get over the idea that a logico-mathematical string has no reference contained within the statement at all. For example, the statement 'A is greater than B' only retains any reference at all through the use of the word greater. If we substitute the symbol, $>$, referential meaning is only conveyed in the spoken form of the discourse. Or, in the example $2 + 3 = 5$, reference outside the string of mathematical signifiers can only be made in the spoken version. The use of terms such as 'makes' or 'equals' shifts the meaning of the string and locates it in something outside the string itself, but the whole point here is to produce a discursive form that has no referential meaning and can therefore refer to anything.

In another classroom in which I observed, this time a nursery classroom, the teacher gave the children a task in which they had to understand addition as the union of sets. They began by putting wooden blocks in two circles drawn on a piece of paper. The circles were connected by two lines to a third circle forming the base of a triangle. The teacher got the children to move the blocks into that circle while making statements of the form 'three and four makes seven'. What she did was to draw around the blocks, making iconic signifiers and repeat the same statement and then eventually replace the drawings by written numerals. In this way, she replaced one signifier by another until she had produced a logico-mathematical statement with no external reference. It is this type of statement that children have to learn and it is difficult because in it all metaphoric relations are suppressed and it is the metaphoric axis which carries the meanings through which our deepest senses of ourselves as subjects are constructed. (see *The Mastery of Reason*, Walkerdine, 1988, for more detail).

In this analysis, abstract reasoning is not the ultimate pinnacle of the intellectual power to abstract, a power essential to the rule of science in the modern world, but a massive forgetting which props up a fantasy of omnipotence of scientific discourses that can control the world, itself a huge fantasy given the present state of the world's ecosystem. In other words, forgetting, meanings, practices and the constructed character of the subject, produce a very special form of power and it is this power, the power of 'western rationality', which has understood nature as something to be controlled, known, mastered.

The mathematician Brian Rotman (1980) called this fantasy 'Reason's Dream', a dream of an ordered universe, where things once proved stay proved forever. The idea that mathematical proof, with all its criteria of elegance and so forth actually provides us with a way of dominating and controlling life itself. Such a fantasy is omnipotent because it is unfulfillable. The earth, like life, is finite. This kind of thinking, to put it starkly is destroying our planet and perpetuating domination and oppression. It is not a universal truth, the pinnacle of civilization, but an enormous and dangerous fantasy. Thinking for a post-modern age needs to dismantle such fantasies and recognize that thinking is produced in practices, replete with meaning and complex emotions, that thinking about thinking is deeply connected to the way that power and regulation work in our present social order. We therefore need to construct new and different narratives which recognize specific practices, which see the place of those stories in the construction of us all. After all, if I can move from being a 'plodder' to being a 'professor', there have to be some different stories to tell, stories which do not universalize one thing only to pathologize the majority of the world's population.

References

ARIES, P. (1967) *Centuries of Childhood*, Harmondsworth, Penguin.
BHABHA, H. (1984) 'The other question: The stereotype and colonial discourse', *Screen*.
COLE, M. and Scribner, S. (1974) *Culture and Thought: A Psychological Perspective*, London, Wiley.
DONALDSON, M. (1978) *Children's Minds*, London, Fontana.
EARLY MATHEMATICAL EXPERIENCES (1978) *General Guide*, London, Schools Council.
FOUCAULT, M. (1976) *Discipline and Punish*, London, Penguin.
HADOW REPORT (1926) *Report of the Consultative Committee on the Primary School*, London, Board of Education, HMSO.
HENRIQUES, J. et al. (1984) *Changing the Subject*, Routledge, London.
NEWSON, J. and NEWSON, E. (1976) *Seven Years Old in the Home Environment*, Allen and Unwin, London.
ROSE, N. (1985) *The Psychological Complex*, London, Routledge.
ROTMAN, B. (1980) 'Mathematics: An essay in semiotics', Unpublished manuscript, University of Bristol.

SAID, E. (1979) *Orientatism*, Cambridge, MA, Harvard.

TIZARD, B. and HUGHES, M. (1984) *Young Children Learning*, London, Fontana.

WALKERDINE, V. (1988) *The Mastery of Reason*, London, Routledge.

WALKERDINE, V. *et al*. (1989) *Counting Girls Out*, Virago, London.

WALKERDINE, V. and LUCEY, H. (1989) *Democracy in the kitchen*, Virago, London.

WILLIAMS, E.M. and SHUARD, H. (1976) *Primary mathematics today*, Harlow, Longman.

Chapter 6

Mathematical Writing, Thinking, and Virtual Reality

Brian Rotman

In the epilogue to his essay on the origin and development of writing systems, Roy Harris declares: 'It says a great deal about Western culture that the question of the origin of writing could be posed clearly for the first time only after the traditional dogmas about the relationship between speech and writing had been subjected both to the brash counterpropaganda of a McLuhan and to the inquisitorial scepticism of a Derrida. But it says even more that the question could not be posed clearly until writing itself had dwindled to microchip dimensions. Only with this . . . did it become obvious that the origin of writing must be linked to the future of writing in ways which bypass speech altogether. (Harris, 1986, p. 158)[1]

Pre-eminent among such dogmas is alphabeticism: the insistence the we interpret all writing — understood for the moment as any mode of graphic activity that creates sites of interpretation and facilitates communication and sense making — along the lines of alphabetic writing, as if it were the inscription of prior speech. Prior in an ontogenetic sense as well as the more immediate sense of speech written down and recorded. Many — Harris' own writings in linguistics, Derrida's programme of deconstruction, McLuhan's efforts to dramatize the cultural imprisonments of typography, Walter Ong's long-standing theorization of the orality/writing disjunction in relation to consciousness, and others — have demonstrated the distorting and reductive effects of the subordination of graphics to phonetics and made it their business to move beyond this dogma. Whether, as Harris intimates, the future of writing will one day find a speechless characterization of itself is impossible to know, but already these displacements of the alphabet's hegemony have resulted in a open-ended and more complex articulation of the writing/speech couple, especially in relation to human consciousness, than was thinkable before the microchip.

Now, a written symbol long recognized as operating non-alphabetically — even by those deeply and quite unconsciously immersed in alphabeticism — is that of number. The familiar and simple other half, as it were, of the alphanumeric keyboard. But, despite this recognition, there has been no sustained attention to mathematical writing that even remotely matches the enormous outpouring of analysis, philosophizing and deconstructive opening up of what those in the humanities have come simply to call 'texts'.

One can ask why this should be so. Why the sign system long acknowledged as the paradigm of abstract rational thought and the without-which-nothing of western technoscience should have been so unexamined, let alone analysed, theorized or deconstructed, as a mode of writing.

One answer might be a second-order version of Harris's point about the dwindling of writing after the microchip, since the emergence of the microchip itself is inseparable from mathematical writing. This, not only in that the entire computer revolution would have been impossible without mathematics as the enabling conceptual technology (the same could be said of almost the whole of technoscience), but in the more telling, crucial sense that hinges on the computer's mathematical lineage and intended application as a calculating/reasoning machine, on its autological relation, in other words, to mathematical practice. This autology would mean that mathematics would presumably be the last to reveal itself and declare its origins in writing. I shall return to this later.

A quite different answer stems from the difficulties put in the way of any proper examination of mathematical writing by the mathematical community itself. Throughout its history mathematics has been characterized in terms of the opposition between a valorized and elevated thought (pure reason, rationality, logic) and a denigrated writing (mere symbols, cyphering, figures, notations). In the twentieth century this denigration has assumed the form of an extreme and universally embraced dogmatism. In the name of a programme of 'rigour' that has dominated mathematics since the late nineteenth century, mathematicians have insisted that mathematical objects are purely abstract entities: mentally apprehensible and yet owing nothing to human psychology, objectively existing and yet without any material, empirical, embodied or sensory dimension. A major consequence of this has been to divorce mathematical practice from its motivations, applications, and physical origins and downplay or entirely occlude the status of mathematical writing as the means by which communication, significance and most importantly the creation of meaning are brought about. An extreme form of this refusal of any exteriority to the objects of mathematics can be found in Brouwer's intuitionism which, despite its opposition to the Platonic metaphysics so central to the legitimation of current versions of 'rigour', managed to deny writing any but a purely marginal and eliminable role in the creation of mathematics. (Analogous, though more complicated, remarks would apply to Husserl's insistence on understanding mathematics in terms of a pre-linguistic 'primal intuition'.) The overall result of this pursuit of rigour and insistence on formal and formalizable mathematics is that the interplay of imagination and writing, familiar on an everyday basis to mathematicians, goes unseen.

Elsewhere, I've given a semiotic account of this interplay by developing a model of mathematical activity — what it means to make the signs and think the thoughts of mathematics — intended to be recognizable to its practitioners. Based on a suggestion of Charles Peirce, the model theorizes mathematical reasoning and persuasion in terms of the performing of thought experiments or waking dreams: one does mathematics by propelling an imago — an idealized version of oneself that Peirce called one's 'skeleton self' — around an imagined landscape of signs.[2]

For the present purposes, the salient features of the model are, in very brief summary, as follows. All mathematical activity is characterized in relation to three interlinked aspects or complementary facets of mathematical discourse and takes place via the users — semiotic abstractions or linguistic actors that I call 'Subject', 'Person', 'Agent' — associated with these aspects (see Figure 6.1).

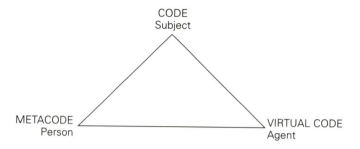

Figure 6.1: The Model of Mathematical Discourse and its Users

The Code represents the total of all rigorous sign practices — definitions, derivations, notational systems — sanctioned by the mathematical community. Its user, the mathematical Subject, the one who reads/writes mathematical texts, has access to no linguistic means other than those allowed by the Code. The metaCode stands for the entire matrix of informal, unrigorous mathematical procedures normally thought of as preparatory and merely epiphenomenal to the real — proper, rigorous — business of doing mathematics. Included in it would be the diagrams and other so-called heuristics which explain, motivate, legitimate and clarify the notations and logical moves that control operations of the Code. The one who speaks the metaCode, the Person, is envisaged as being immersed in natural language with access to its metasigns and constituted thereby as a self-conscious subjectivity in history and culture. The virtual Code is the domain of all legitimately imaginable operations, that is to say idealized activities that represent the signifying possibilities available to an idealization of the Subject. The one who executes these activities, the Agent, is envisaged as a surrogate or proxy of the Subject, imagined into being precisely in order to act on the purely formal, mechanically specifiable correlates — signifiers — of what for the Subject is meaningful via signs. In unison these three agencies make up what we ordinarily call 'the mathematician'.

In relation to this scheme, mathematical reasoning is an irreducibly tripartite activity in which the Person (Dreamer awake) observes the Subject (Dreamer) imagining a proxy — the Agent (Imago) — of him/herself, and on the basis of the likeness between Subject and Agent comes to be persuaded that what the Agent experiences is what the Subject *would* experience were he or she to carry out the unidealized versions of the activities in question. Observe in passing that the three-way process at work here is the logico-mathematical correlate of a more general and originating triangularity inherent in the very notion of self-consciousness: the self-as-object giving rise to to the Agent, the self-as-subject appearing in the guise of the Subject, and the socio-cultural Other, through which any such circuit of selves passes, corresponding to the Person.[3]

Several consequences of this way of understanding mathematical activity are relevant to the discussion I wish to present here: (i) mathematical assertions are to be seen as essentially *predictions* made by the Person about the Subject's future engagement with signs, (ii) mathematical thinking and writing are inseparable, since the Agent's activities only exist and make narrative logical sense (for the Subject) in relation to the Subject's manipulation of signs in the Code, (iii) mathematical persuasion is impossible — to achieve in practice and hence to theorize — if the role of the Person as observer of the Subject/Agent relation is omitted.

I shall enlarge on (ii) and the theme of writing below. Observe first that both (i) and (iii) impinge directly on the meaning of pursuing mathematical rigour, on how the orthodox justification for it rests on a spurious ranking. Thus, though the metaCode–Code difference on which the model rests coincides essentially with that drawn by the mathematical community between unrigorous and rigorous mathematics, the *status* of this difference becomes here inverted and displaced. Thus, once the Person's role is acknowledged as vital to the mathematical activities of making assertions and proving them it becomes no longer possible to see the metaCode as a supplement to the Code, a domain of mere psychological/motivational affect, to be jettisoned once the real, proper, rigorous mathematics of the Code has been formulated. Note that neither the Person nor Subject is to be identified with any private, psychologically defined subjectivity. Thus, though the model here is antagonistic to the Frege-inspired century of logicist rigour that has prevented any understanding of how mathematical signs and their users *constitute* mathematical objects, it in no sense signals a return to 'psychologism'. The account of mathematics as thought experiment excludes from the beginning the kind of 'thought' that Frege fulminated against. This is because like the Subject and Agent, the Person is a semiotic construct, a discursive position made available by, and quite inseparable from, language. In particular, this means that the Person's subjectivity — the capacities that spring from the 'I' of natural language — is already an intersubjectivity.[4] Or, to put it more in the terms Peirce might have used, there is nothing here but signs whose explication will always rest upon and call forth more signs: 'Man himself is a sign.'

But is not advocating Peirce's thought-experimental model of mathematical reasoning a retrograde step? Doesn't opposing the mainstream logicist/Platonist insistence on formalizable exact mathematics and its accompanying programme of foundations and rigour, embrace an approach made obsolete — or at least irrelevant — by the work of Frege and the tradition he initiated? The answer is no on two counts.

Firstly, it's possible to see this tradition and the preoccupation that fueled it as a massive detour, a journey into a new kind of mathematics and away from the examination of mathematics that it claimed to be providing. Of course, this journey through first-order systems and the structuralist programme of giving a set-theoretical formulation of mathematics has been enormously influential and impressively rich in technical results as the meta-mathematical work of Skolem, Godel and Turing, among many others, testifies. But the price has been high. Not only has this work been carried out within, and in relation to, a quite uncritically embraced infinitistic notion of 'number', but it has resulted in what is generally acknowledged to be a barren and uniformative philosophy of mathematics and (not independently of this) a sustained blindness to the importance of understanding mathematics as a culturally and historically produced signifying practice.

Secondly, thought experiments in general, and not just those that mathematicians might make, though they have been central to scientific persuasion and explication from Galileo to the present (figuring decisively in this century, for example, in the original explanation of relativity theory as well as in the Einstein-Bohr debate about the nature of quantum physics) have only recently started to get the sort of sustained attention they deserve. Again there's the question of a

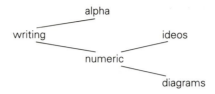

Figure 6.2: Types of inscription and their Relations

detour: in this case the return would be to (a suitably modified version of) Ernst Mach's insistence on the fundamental nature, in relation to a general economy of cognition, of forward-directed reasoning that thought experiments, at least in their scientific and everyday versions, enshrine. No doubt, part of the explanation for this comparative neglect of experimental reasoning lies in the systematizing, mathematics-inspired approach to the philosophy of science that has foregrounded questions of rigour (certitude, epistemological hygiene, foundations, exact knowledge, formal systems, and so on) at the expense of everything else, and in particular at the expense of any account of the all-important persuasive, rhetorical and semiotic aspects of scientific practice.

In any event, as I've indicated, the legacy of pursuing rigour has been to marginalize the metaCode, denying its role in the creation and ongoing understanding of mathematics in favour of the formal texts of the Code. To say more we need to open up the sense in which mathematical symbols are opposed to non-mathematical ones. Crucial to such an opening is the recognition that the Code/metaCode distinction operates within as well as against the term 'symbol'. Thus, the opposition between formally conceived ideograms (+, x, 0, 1, 2, 3, =, >, $\sin t$, . . . , dy/dx, $\log(z)$, and so on) which correspond to signs in their Coded, proper — one might call it literal — manifestation, and mathematical diagrams (points, lines, circles, angles, maps, curves, triangles, graphs, figures, arrows, charts, and so on) which constitute the field of metaCoded, that is to say informal — what might be called metaphorical — mathematical discourse. This has meant that diagrams, as so-called 'merely' explanatory, motivational and heuristic devices, have been excluded from what officially counts as mathematical sense at the same time as linear symbol strings presented as logically normalized sequences of ideograms, have been elevated to mathematics proper. One can see in this phenomenon a kind of transposed alphabeticism in Figure 6.2.

Just as the alphabetic dogma mistakes lettered transcription to be the mode of all writing (at the expense of non-alphabetic numerical forms), so within the construction and justification of mathematical rigour the dogma reappears in the guise of mistaking linear, ideogrammatic symbolization to be the mode of all legitimate mathematical writing (at the expense of non-linearized diagrammatic forms). The alphabeticism transposed in this way to mathematical signs amounts to more than a parallel at the level of inscription. And this in two senses. One, which I'll not elaborate here, relates to wider interpretations of the ideos/diagrams split in which it appears in one direction on the level of mathematical content as the privileging of arithmetic over geometry as well as, in a different direction, in the way the oppositions digital–analogue, discrete–continuous are theorized.[5] Two, on the level of ontology. Thus, whilst it is certainly the case that texts of the Code are linearly laid out and similar to alphabetically written speech in a way that diagrammatic usage isn't, a more important and telling point concerns the *secondarity* inherent in the alphabetic dogma. The dogma in its original form achieves its effects by insisting that writing is essentially the transcription of another, prior scene — speech, in fact. What is of interest is how this insistence on a prior scene is replayed within current — Platonist — interpretations of mathematical signs, according to which signs are always *of* or *about* something, some domain of objects that exists and precedes the signs themselves. Thus the time-honoured distinction between numerals and numbers rests on just such an insistence that numerals are mere notations — names — subsequent and posterior to numbers which exist prior and independent of them. According to this understanding of signs it becomes an easy admission to agree that numerals are historically invented, changeable, epiphenomenal, eliminable, and very much a human product, whilst maintaining a total and well-defended refusal to allow any of these characteristics to apply to numbers. And what goes for numbers goes for all mathematical objects. In short, contemporary Platonism, relying on, and indeed constituted by, this secondarity is precisely the ontological mindset that one would expect to accompany and indeed underpin the pursuit of rigour. Of course, the roots of this secondarity inherent in alphabetically conceived writing are much deeper than twentieth-century rigourization, as the conception of the Bible (book) — scripture, written word of a prior God — and of the universe — a book written, according to Galileo and many after him, by God in the language of mathematics — testify.

One effect of identifying this less literal but no less compelling manifestation of alphabeticism is to appreciate how the case of mathematics raises certain questions about the nature of language and more particularly writing *per se*, about 'writing *as writing*' as Harris puts it. On the one hand, identifying the diagrammatic devices of the metaCode as tropes and insisting on the uneliminable role played by these devices opens up mathematics to the sort of critical activity familiar in the humanities, where discussions of metaphor, for example, have revealed a complex reflexivity (it being impossible to find a trope-free meta-language in which to discuss tropes). So that, appearances and much special pleading to the contrary, mathematical discourse cannot but help inherit the shifting semiosis of ordinary, natural-language, discourse. On the other hand, it by no means follows from this that mathematics' ways of making sense, communicating, signifying and allowing interpretations to be multiplied can be assimilated to those of conventionally written texts in the humanities. For there remains the central question: Why are mathematical symbols — ideograms no less than diagrams — used at all? What purposes do they serve? Cannot the semiotic work they do be achieved, perhaps at greater length and/or textual cost, by words alone? In other words, can we not always speak ideograms — 'one' for '1' — and parse the use of diagrams by describing them? What, in short, is unsayable (in fact, unthinkable, unwritable) except via mathematical symbols? Hardly a new question, but one that surely has had to wait for mathematics to be formulated as a mode of writing/thinking before it can begin to be answered.[6]

But perhaps such a formulation, though it points in the right direction, is already inadequate. Might not the very seeing of mathematics in terms of a writing/thinking couple have become possible because writing is now — post-microchip — no longer what it was? I suggested above that the reflexivity of the relation between computing and mathematics — whereby the computer, having issued from mathematics, impinges on, and looks to ultimately transform its own originating matrix — might be the crux of the explanation for our late recognition of mathematics' status as writing. To open up the point here, I turn to a contemporary development within the ongoing microchip revolution, seemingly remote from the nature and practice of mathematics[7], namely, the construction of what has come to be known as virtual reality.

An extrapolation of current practices, more heralded, projected and promised than as yet realized, virtual reality is the rubric under which a range of effects and projects has been grouped. In these certain themes and elements recur. Thus, one always starts from the given world, the shared, intersubjective, everyday reality each of us inhabits. Within this reality there is constructed a subworld, a virtual space or virtual reality that we — or rather certain cyberneticized versions of ourselves — can, in some sense, enter and interact with. The construction of this virtuality — how it is realized, its parameters, limits, possibilities and manifestations — varies greatly from case to case. Likewise, what is entailed by a 'version' of ourselves and hence the sense in which 'we' can be said to be in such virtual arenas varies, since it will depend on what counts, for the purposes in hand, as physical immersion and interaction, and how these are connected and eventually implemented. In all cases, however, virtual arenas exist inside computers and are entered and interacted with through appropriate interface devices and prosthetic extensions such as specially adapted pointers, goggles, gloves, helmets, body sensors and the like. Perhaps the most familiar example is dipping a single finger into a computer environment via the point-and-click operation of a computer mouse. But this is a minimal interpretation, both in what the internalized finger can achieve as a finger and because it is, after all, only a metonym of a full body: all current proposals call for more comprehensive prosthetic extensions, and correspondingly richer, more fully integrated modes of interaction with/within these realities once they are entered.

Let's call the self in the world the *real-I*; the cyberneticized self we propel around a virtual world the surrogate or *virtual-I*; and the self mediating between these, as the enabling site and means of their difference, the jacked-in or *goggled-I*. Operating a virtually real environment involves an interplay or circulation between these three agencies which ultimately changes the nature of the original, default reality, of what it means to be a real-I inhabiting a/the given world.

This circulation and its transformation of the given world motivates a great deal of virtual-reality thinking. To fix the point I'll mention two very differently conceived recent proposals: *Mirror Worlds*, a blueprint for a series of vast public software projects, by computer scientist David Gelernter, and *Snowcrash*, a science fiction epic by the writer Neal Stephenson of the near — cybered — future. The first maps out a path in terms, more or less, of existing technology for virtualizing a public entity such as a hospital or university or an entire city (more ambitiously a country, ultimately the world). Its aim is to create a virtual space, a computer simulation of say the city — the 'agent space' — which each citizen could enter through various interface tools and engage in activities — shopping, information gathering, witnessing townhall proceedings, monitoring and participating in cultural events, meeting other citizens . . . — in virtual form. The idea being that the results of such virtual-I activities would effect changes in society, of what it means to be a citizen and social actor within a community, to be a real-I;

changes in previously unattainable and — given Gelernter's take on contemporary fragmentation and anomie — sorely needed ways. In *Snowcrash* the writer posits an America whose computer savvy denizens move between a distopic reality (panoptic surveillance and mafia-franchised suburban enclaves) and a freely created, almost utopian computer space — the 'metaverse' — where their virtual-I's — 'avatars' — can access the information net and converse and interact with each other in various virtual ways. Crucial to the plotting and thematics of Stephenson's narrative is the interplay between the inside of the metaverse and the all-too-real outside — the circulation of affect and effects between virtual-I's and real-I's — as the characters put on and take off their goggles.

A certain homology between virtual reality and mathematical thought, each organized around an analogous triangle of agencies, should by now be evident. The virtual-I maps onto the mathematical Agent, the real-I to the Person, and the goggled-I to the mathematical Subject. In accordance with this mapping, both involve phenomenologically based narratives of propelling a puppet of oneself — agent, simulacrum, surrogate, avatar, doppelganger, proxy (Peirce's 'skeleton self') — around a virtual space. Both require a technology which gives real-I's access to this space and which controls the capabilities and characteristics of the agent. In both, this technology is structured and defined in terms of an operator, a figure with particular features, distinct from the puppet it controls and from the figure occupying the default reality — the Person, the real-I — able to put on goggles and operate in this way. And, crucially, both are interactive. In this they are different from the practices made available by literature, which (like mathematics) conjures invisible proxies and identificatory surrogates of ourselves out of writing, and different from theatre, film and TV where (like virtual reality) proxies have a visual presence, since though these media allow and require their recipients/participants an active *interpretive* role, this doesn't and cannot extend to any real — materially effective — participation in the virtual spaces in question.

Mathematics, then, appears not only as an enabling technology but as a template and precursor, perhaps the oldest there is, of the current scenarios of virtual reality. But then what, since something new is evidently enabled here, distinguishes them? Many features, but in the present context a principal difference lies in the technologies available to the operator-participants: the mathematical Subject's reliance on ink and chalk inscriptions as against the prosthetic extensions available to the virtual reality operator. So that what separates them is the degree of palpability they facilitate: the gap between the virtuality of a proxy whose repertoire (in the more ambitious projections) spans the entire sensori-motor range of modalities — ambulatory, auditory, proprioceptive, tactile, kinetic — and the invisible, seemingly disembodied Agent of mathematics. The virtual space entered by mathematicians' proxies is, in other words, entirely imagined, and the objects, points, functions, numbers, etc. in it, are without sensible form. Of course, the journeys that mathematical Agents perform, the narratives that can be told about them, the objects they encounter, are strictly controlled by mathematical signs. Connecting these orders of signification, recreating the writing/thinking nexus, through the manipulation — interactive handling — of visible diagrams and ideograms in the metaCode and Code and the imagined, invisible states of affairs they signify and answer to, determines what it means to be able to *do* mathematics.

We are thus led to the question: What if writing is no longer confined to inscriptions on paper and chalk boards, but becomes instead the creation of pixel arrangements on a computer screen? Wouldn't such a mutation in the material medium of mathematical writing effect a fundamental shift in thinking, adding to and altering what it means to do, mathematics? One has only to bear in mind the enormous changes in consciousness brought into play by the introduction of printing — surely a lesser innovation than the shift from paper to screen — to think that indeed it would.[8] Already new types of mathematics — ways of thinking mathematically — have come into existence precisely within the field of this mutation. Witness chaos theory and fractal geometry with their essential reliance on computer-generated images (attractors in phase space, self-similar sets in the complex plane, and so on) which are nothing less than new, previously undrawable, kinds of diagrams. And, somewhat differently, witness proofs (the four-color problem, classification of finite groups) that exist only as computer-generated entities. Moreover, there's no reason to suppose that this feedback of computer-created imagery and cognitive representations — in effect a vector from an imagination-based technology to an image-based one — on the conceptual technology of mathematics will stop at the creation of new modes of drawing diagrams and notating arguments. More radically, why should such a process be confined to the *visual* mode, to the creation of graphics and imagery, and not to the other sense modalities? What is to stop mathematics appropriating the various computer-created ambulatory, kinesthetic and tactile features made freely available within the currently proposed schemas for virtual reality. Is it unnatural, for example, to suggest that immersion in a virtually realized mathematical structure — walking round it, listening to it, moving and rearranging its parts, altering its shape, feeling it, and so on — be the basis for mathematical proofs? Proofs which by using virtual experience as the basis for persuasion would add to, and go far beyond, the presently accepted practice of manipulating ideograms and diagrams in relation to an always invisible and impalpable structure?[9]

Evidently, natural or unnatural, such a transformation of mathematical practice would have a revolutionary impact on how we conceptualize mathematics, on what we imagine a mathematical object to be, on what we consider ourselves to be doing when we carry out mathematical investigations and persuade ourselves that certain assertions, certain properties and features of mathematical objects, are to be accepted as 'true'. Indeed, the very ground rules would undergo a sea change. An assertion would no longer have to be something capturable in a sentence-like piece of — presently conceived — writing but could be a configuration only expressible within a specifically presented virtual reality. Correspondingly, a proof would no longer have to be an argument organized around a written — as presently conceived — sequence of logically connected symbols but could take on the character of an external, empirical verification. Mathematics would thus become what it has long denied being: an experimental subject; one which though quite different from biology or physics in ways yet to be formulated would nonetheless be organized around an independently existing, computer-created and represented, empirical reality.

This union, or rather mutually reactive merging, of mathematics and virtual reality — a coming together of a still rudimentary and yet to be consummated technology with its ancient, highly developed precursor — would take the form of a double-sided process. As we've seen, from outside and independently of mathematics the goal of this technology is to achieve nothing less than bring into being a *virtualization of the real*, a process which will engender irreversible changes in what for us constitutes the given world, the domain of the real-I. From the other direction, in relation to a mathematics whose objects and structures have already a wholly virtual, non-material existence, the process appears as the reverse, as in effect a *realization of the virtual*, whereby mathematical objects, by being constructed inside a computer, become for the first time materially presented and embodied; a process that will likewise cause radical, irreversible and quite unexpected changes in what constitutes for us the immaterial, the ideal and the purely virtual. To give a more specific content to this last point, one could look at what is surely the most disembodied, idealized and virtual of all the concepts of contemporary mathematics — that of infinity. An idea so inherently spectral, transcendental and unphysical as to make it impossible to render inside any kind of real — that is to say realizable in this universe — computer. Or so I have argued at length elsewhere.[10]

Notes

1. The passage continues with a programmatic injunction not to 're-plough McLuhan's field, or Derrida's either' but to sow them, so as to produce eventually 'a history of writing *as writing*'.
2. For the original presentation of the model, see Rotman (1988). A more elaborated version, particularly in relation to the way the various semiotic agencies involved are abstractions — idealizations and truncations — of each other, is given in Rotman (1993, pp. 63–113).
3. For an indication of how the general form of a self-reflective consciousness, described in terms of a 'second-order observer', might be related to the institution of writing, see Luhmann (1992, p. 40).
4. In terms of rigour, of which more below, it's clear why Frege and his Platonist successors need to confine mathematical meaning to (alphabetically arranged) ideograms: to do otherwise, to include pictures, figures, shapes, and so on, within mathematical reasoning would have opened logic up to the body and its subjectivities; an opening fatal to the idea of objective, unchanging truths of logic so fundamental to this tradition. For a more extended comment on what Frege meant and could not avoid meaning, given the matrix he operated within, by 'a thought', see Rotman (1988, pp. 26–9).
5. The continuous–discrete opposition has been the focus of diverse efforts within physics during the last fifteen years as part of that subject's 'turn to computation'. See Rotman (1994) for a description of some of the attempts by physicists to repudiate the continuum and for related criticism within computer science's attempt to map the ultimate physical limits of computation.
6. The distinction between the writable, sayable and thinkable is never that of an absolute division: mathematical symbols allow one to think certain things which can *then* be spoken in natural, non-mathematical language where they appear (falsely) to have been sayable all along. See, for example, Harris (1986, pp. 149–52). This also applies *within* mathematical writing, to the parsing of diagrams in terms of ideograms. Related to this (though not framed in the present terms) see Harris (1987, pp. 163–71) for a witty discussion of a diagram used by Saussure to concretize his model of speech and thought, a model which itself promulgates a version of the error in question here.
7. But not, it seems, *that* remote. In addition to many implicit connections to mathematical ideas and syntax via computer programming there are explicit links:

e.g. Michael Benedikt's introductory survey of the historical and conceptual context of virtual reality includes mathematics and its notations as an important thread running through the concept (1991: 18–22).

8. See Lenoir and Lecuyer (1994) for an account of the radical impact of screen-based visualization techniques on scientific research and on the status of the theory–experiment opposition as this has been traditionally formulated in the philosophy and history of science. Though concerned with certain aspects of the recent computerization and mathematization of biology, Lenoir's and Lecuyer's narrative and their conclusion that 'visualization *is* the theory' is suggestive far outside this domain.

9. The understanding of writing appropriate to this conception of mathematics, what one might call *virtual writing*, would break out of the matrix prescribed for writing — what he calls 'archewriting' — set out in Derrida (1976) since it would be no longer thinkable in terms of the 'gram' without wrenching that term out of all continuity with itself.

10. Principally in Rotman (1993) but again, in a different context, in Rotman (1994).

References

BENEDIKT, M. (1992) (Ed) *Cyberspace: First Steps*, Cambridge, Massachusetts, MIT Press.

DERRIDA, J. (1976) *Of Grammatology*, Baltimore, The Johns Hopkins Press.

HARRIS, R. (1986) *The Origin of Writing*, London, Duckworth.

HARRIS, R. (1987) *The Language Machine*, Ithaca, Cornell University Press.

LENOIR, T. and LECUYER, C. (in press) 'Visions of Theory'.

LUHMANN, N. (1992) 'The form of writing', *Stanford Literature Review*, 9, pp. 25–42.

ROTMAN, B. (1988) 'Toward a semiotics of mathematics', *Semiotica*, 72, pp. 1–35.

ROTMAN, B. (1993) *Ad Infinitum . . . the Ghost in Turing's Machine*, Stanford, Stanford University Press.

ROTMAN, B. (In press) *The Rise and Fall of Infinity*.

Chapter 7

Mathematics: The Problematical Notion of Closure

Anna Tsatsaroni and Jeff Evans

Posing the Question

The questions we would like to discuss in this chapter are: What is mathematics? — and by implication — What is special about mathematics?

Three qualifications, a *theoretical*, a *methodological* and a *pragmatic* one, must be added from the beginning. First, this question has to be asked not in a general way as if we believed that we needed to clarify the regional ontology of a discipline, thereby repeating the classical move of traditional ontology.[1] Rather, we believe, it is the 'end of philosophy' in 'our present times' which necessitates such a rethinking. For Heidegger (1978), this means that all the essential possibilities of metaphysics are exhausted.[2] Metaphysics dissolves into the empirical and technologized sciences. These sciences continue the metaphysical project and carry it to its global domination. Derrida, on the other hand, defines the end of metaphysical epoch in terms of 'closure'. As will be shown, the unity of a discipline such as mathematics is covertly determined by the idea of *closure*. The questioning of such unity, with the implication of conceiving of mathematics as an open system, will continue to be determined by the same idea. Hence the need for its deconstruction.[3]

Second, at a *methodological* level, we would like this question about mathematics to be asked against the background of ongoing research and theorizing within mathematics education. This is because, beyond our personal interest in the area of mathematics education, we believe, for reasons alluded to in this chapter, that any novel response to a fundamental (i.e., ontological) question such as 'what is mathematics' has not merely to repeat — but also to interrupt — the answer already included in the question. This question, always historically situated, is posed within an already formed discourse. In addition — it is our contention — in the discourse of mathematics education this question has lately become especially acute.

This formulation of course begs the question of what a discourse is, and whether mathematics education has formed itself as such a discourse. But let us sidestep the question for the time being, making only two brief remarks.[4] First, we might perhaps accept at a very general level that the field of mathematics education rather than being a discourse, is instead structured by all sorts of discourses: philosophical discourses, scientific discourses, pedagogical discourses, social discourses etc. More importantly, however, this position is based on, and serves to reproduce, metaphysical assumptions and concepts whose deconstruction, ultimately, must be the target of any research or thinking which claims to be critical.

Finally, at a *pragmatic* level, the need to ask our question about whether mathematics can be linked to two current trends: the most recent shifts in research and theorizing in mathematics education — shifts which call for a response and which we would like to address at a fundamental level, viz. as 'shifts' (see below); and the pervasive climate in which (education or social) research, finds itself, what we can call the debate on modernity/post-modernity. The latter, going on for some time now in philosophy and social theory, has most recently being intensified across all social sciences. This, fundamentally, by questioning the nature of reason and rationality, problematizes our received ideas about the production and the nature of knowledge, including, if not centred on, the nature of scientific knowledge. And if mathematical knowledge (with its applications, the natural sciences) since the beginning of modernity was taken to be the exemplar of formal rationality, exemplifying what knowledge is and what it can do — that is, demonstrating its power both at the theoretical and the practical level — the revealing, as an implication of the debate, for example, of the essential connection between knowledge and power, has done much to discredit it. Rather than being the most pure and perfect form of rational (modern) knowledge, it is intertwined with power; it is power that institutes it (knowledge) as a regime of truth.[5]

An outcome of debates on the modern discourse on knowledge is the so-called constructivist paradigm, and social constructionism more generally: the awareness that what we understand as 'modern' forms of knowledge are, *precisely*, modern.[6] That is, they are not universal and timeless, but the products of a specific historical and social conjuncture, what we happen to call modernity.

In the case of mathematical forms of knowledge, these arguments lead to positions such as for example Ashley and Betebenner (1993); the view that there are transformations in mathematical reasoning which might 'reflect and express' — in ways parallel to other forms of knowledge — 'broader shifts in civilizational orientations'. Independently of our stance as to whether or not we are now entering a new, post-modern era, and therefore of whether we need to deal with a different, post-modern notion of mathematics (as Ashley and Betebenner's paper implies), arguments deriving from social constructionism and/or the modernity/post-modernity problematic have had two broad implications. First, in the existence of such widely accepted insights, the image of mathematical knowledge as universal and timeless — and of mathematical language as a universal language — cannot remain intact.[7] A second and more important implication is that mathematics as a discipline and form of knowledge is *essentially* open to the 'social'.

The latter position, exhaustively debated over the last twenty or thirty years in the neighbourhood of mathematics, since the publication of T. Kuhn's *The Structure of Scientific Revolutions* (1960), should alert us to the difficulty. For this debate has resulted in an impasse of never being able to draw the line between science and society, and a consequent realization that the move or opening to the social can easily leave intact the opposition between the scientific and the social.

Let us briefly rehearse a segment of this debate. Dealing with the issue of whether we need to answer the question of 'what is science' Woolgar (1988) points to the problem:

Not only have philosophers disagreed about the characteristics which distinguish science from other activities, but the character of science has been shown to be historically variable. (Woolgar, 1988, p. 20)

Woolgar distinguishes two positions in the reactions to this variation, namely the essentialist and the relativist one. The former asserts that this variability results from the complexity of science itself. Science is still conceived as an object, a coherent entity or method, although its definitions and descriptions are difficult. This, as Woolgar correctly points out, rather than modifying or abandoning the question, merely postpones a definitive answer. Nominalism asserts that the quest for a definition is futile, because attempts to specify criteria to demarcation ignore a fundamental characteristic of science, namely that it is constantly open to rene- gotiation and reclassification. From this point of view there is no such thing as 'science' or the 'scientific method' except that which is attributed to various prac- tices and behaviours. 'What counts as science varies according to the particular textual purposes for which this is an issue' (p. 21). He then summarizes as follows:

Whereas essentialism tends to the view that definitions of science are, at least in part, a reflection of the characteristics of an actual (transcendental) object called 'science', nominalism suggests that features proposed as characteristic of science stem from the definitional practices of the partici- pants (philosophers, historians and sociologists) themselves. (*ibid.*)

As Woolgar rightly observes, those who adopt a relativistic position — i.e., rejecting essentialism and therefore rejecting the notion of science as an ideal and closed system — have to face the dilemma:

to what extent do the features, characteristics and definitions of phenom- ena reflect the defining practices (constructional work) of the people in- volved rather than the 'actual character' of the phenomena? (*ibid.*)

Woolgar basically accepts the nominalist position, which he finds fruitful because it opens the way to studying how the term 'science' is attributed to, or withheld from, various practices and claims.[8] At the same time, he chooses to work out what he sees as the basic shortcoming of this position: the implications for one's own research.[9]

Refusing to quickly reject the transcendental in favour of the empirical, Tiles (1991) phrases the problem in such a way as to link it to a modern scepticism concerning the nature and power of reason, and the possibility of knowledge: The enlightenment tradition high in its hopes of transcendent reason has been disillu- sioned.[10] Reason, imprisoned in formal chains, has been reduced to instrumental and technological calculation. She succintly formulates this problematic for the case of mathematics, in the following terms:

A striking feature of mathematics is that it has two distinct faces — its number-crunching, calculatory face, revealed in applications, and its almost number- and calculation-free face, revealed in the pure mathema- ticians' study of abstract structures. Somehow these are related; some- how the non-worldly, abstract study where theorems are proved with an exactness and certitude unparalleled in other branches of knowledge yields powerful methods and techniques for dealing with the physical world. Reason delivers, with apparent certainty, knowledge of an abstract, non-empirical realm, knowledge which is nonetheless of immense practical utility in the empirical world.[11] Is it then any wonder that this should be treated as the paradigmatic manifestation of the *power* of reason? But at the same time this very power presents a puzzle and a philosophical challenge — how is it *possible*? [my italics] (Tiles, 1991, pp. 1–2)

This puzzle, this modern paradox, of reason being unable to ground and justify itself has led to one of two situations. Either:

mathematics is then reduced to its applications; it is a source only of convenient representational and calculatory devices. The number crunching involved in applied mathematics, which predominates in technological thinking, spawns a calculatory image of reason. (*ibid.*, p. 2)

Or,

It is by focusing on mathematics that the story of the capture of reason within formal, computational chains is revealed to be a myth, albeit one with an origin in logicist and formalist programmes for the foundations of mathematics, which were formulated toward the end of the nineteenth century and were dedicated to the abolition of reliance on intuition in mathematics . . . But these programmes were not successfully completed; they were decisively demonstrated not to be completable as originally proposed . . . (*ibid.*, p. 3)

Therefore,

it remains the case . . . that any account of mathematics must address itself to the characterization and the relation of the two aspects of mathematics, resisting either a reduction to a single aspect or a mystificatory unification via a metaphysical postulation. (*ibid.*, p. 2)

Hence, Mary Tiles' study is an attempt to show that

. . . mathematics is neither an exemplification of transcendent reason, nor mere calculation of logical consequences, but human knowledge of structures gained by *employing reason beyond the bounds of logic* [my italics] (*ibid.*, p. 4)

For Tiles, then, the production of mathematical knowledge is consequent upon the employment of reason 'beyond the bounds of logic'. Both words 'bounds' and 'beyond' point to the fundamental figure of closure animating this essentially Kantian position. Mathematics, as defined by modernity, is to be understood neither as a sum of representational and calculatory devices; nor as a simple system like logic. On the contrary, it is the act or movement by which and through which reason exceeds and overcomes such boundaries that mathematical knowledge is produced.

In the penultimate section of this chapter we will briefly but specifically address the metaphysical figure of closure and show how it covertly determines the field not only of mathematics but of all the exact — to employ the Husserlian term — sciences as closed systems or totalities. We will also argue that the simple abandonment of this figure — with the implied notion of mathematics as a closed system — is not in itself capable of interrupting the metaphysical determinations (conceptual or linguistic) of the discipline. On the contrary, as an *empiricism*, it blindly repeats and continues the assumptions about mathematics as given by metaphysics. Before this, we would like to show how recent shifts in mathematics education research are falling into a relativist position, similar to that in the area often called social studies of science, a position which has the effect of reinforcing the characterization of mathematics as calculative thinking.

Shifts in Mathematics Education

A long tradition of research into the teaching of mathematics had been based on an assumption that mathematics is a *closed system*: that its empirical repeatability is guaranteed by its character as an ideal objectivity. This assumption is, for example, theoretically and practically put to work in the idea(l) and expectation of transfer: mathematical knowledge, because it is the most pure and rational form of knowledge, has the power to repeat itself, to apply itself to all and every practical context.

Within research in mathematics education the first questioning of this basic assumption took the form of quantitative or qualitative analysis of factors which are social (e.g., Evans and Tsatsaroni, 1993), thus *external* to the subject (both to mathematics, and to the cognitive subject): social factors are supposed to explain the observed failures of this ideal model to work. Gender, class, the pupil's cultural background; these are but empirical inconveniences which inhibit the system from functioning properly — and which inhibit cognition from applying the rational rules and properties of the system correctly.

Most recent thinking realizes the narrow but also futile basis of this questioning move which proliferates possible social factors. If the latter is problematical, it is because it operates under the illusory assumption that transfer is in principle possible: the ideal nature of mathematics guarantees this certainty. The failure to transfer can be explained by reference to the empirical, accidental constraints. These constraints are outside the system. If only we could master these constraints! And this leaves unchallenged the transcendental illusion of a system whose perfection is only postponed for the future; of a division between a cognitive structure and a social reality; of an opposition between inside and outside, necessity and accident; and of an education process which is regulated by transferability as an ideal.

Another generation of research realized the problem that these factors can never be fully enumerated. Some of these research projects/theoretical views went even further in order to question the normativity of transfer, and with it the illegitimacy of mathematics in its claim to possess the truth for every conceivable practical problem. Unlike mathematical/calculative (precise, coherent etc.) thinking, practical activities, the argument goes, exhibit a different, informal, yet rational, thinking (see Lave, 1988; Scribner, 1984; Voss *et al.*, 1991). In these views mathematics becomes a resource for a practical subject — with purposes, desires, intentions etc. — to 'freely' draw on for all practical purposes.

These shifts — to the social and to the practical — however, can only bypass the problem of the hierarchical oppositions already in place from the 'beginning': between transcendental and empirical, theory and practice, formal and informal reasoning, cognitive subject and practical agent. If this perspective is limited, it is, above all, because it leaves open the whole question of 'what is mathematics' and 'truth' in mathematics. That is, the proliferation of mathematics in use creates the problem of its dispersion, of the lack of unity in the field. The multiplicity thus assumed is then contained by reference to institutional decisions: the specific practices which operate in a particular community, which is what makes relevant particular kinds of mathematical knowledge. But, in this apparent levelling down of traditional hierarchical oppositions, there is a form of empiricism slipping in.

It is not only that mathematics is reduced to the empirical-calculative knowledge against which Tiles is warning us. In addition, because of the fear of dispersion of mathematics as a discipline, and as a domain of knowledge, there is a covert replacement of an *essential* identity (totality or closed system) with a *technically imposed* identity. Here, for example, 'institutional decisions' (see second quotation of Woolgar, above) assume the role of a bare and self-evident fact which needs no further questioning. This methodological technicity is characteristic of our modern world view — i.e., knowledge as technological representation, truth as measurable — which defines the cognitivist paradigm (see below). It is also characteristic of our inability to effectively challenge it (see Tsatsaroni, 1991).

To repeat, we would like to claim that the shifts and turns, only roughly sketched above, which characterize the recent developments in the discipline of mathematics education can be seen as exemplifying what we have called methodological technicity. Furthermore, we claim that these shifts to the social and to the practical are but outcomes of the move from an absolute system (essentialism) to the relative nature of all knowledge. The relativization of knowledge, however, is very difficult to contain, hence the series of shifts generated: to the social, to the practical, and as we shall see shortly, the turn to the linguistic. Furthermore, this incapacity to define the limit — essentially because that limit is what remains unthought in these turns — partly results from an uncritical abandoning — though not an erasing of its effects — of that which guaranteed the certainty of a system of knowledge: the cognitivist paradigm of research and theorizing, or the paradigm of perception. The basic presuppositions of this paradigm support conceptual (metaphysical) distinctions that form hierarchical oppositions: transcendental –empirical, identity–difference, form–content, necessity–freedom, essence–accident.[12] It can be summed up as:

- a subject–object dichotomy, where a consciously or unconsciously *knowing* subject is opposed to a world of objects, the latter referring to the 'given' and the 'situation';
- the subject acts as a consequence of, or is determined by, codes/rules — inside the mind as mental/formal *representations/images*, or outside the mind as *social rules/conventions* — and by pre-constituted *meanings* either explicit or implicit; it is assumed that the latter can be analysed and made explicit;
- a concept of *reflection* on rules or mental images as a grounding for action,

and as a grounding and unification of subjectivity; so that clarity about the rules or images clarifies and constitutes the mind of the subject and the quality of the action;

- the epistemological problematic of reflection, object representation and the assumption of a *transparent self* are combined with a conception of a theoretical statement as an infinitely repeatable and demonstrable truth. And this presupposes the ideality of the 'object' of inquiry, which is supposed to confirm the ideality–rationality of a 'subject' and its ability to transcend its temporality;
- truth is understood as a total representation or a revelation of a fully present external reality or original event according to an adequation model; and finally,
- a model of communication which treats language either as a transparent medium transmitting literal meaning or as an intersubjective tool.

Shifting attention from consciousness (intentions, purposes etc.) to semiotics, from a pre-constituted subject representing a world of (ideal) objects (e.g., mathematics) to *signs*, the last few years have witnessed an opening up in educational/ social research. The question posed then is what happens *within* this opening. What happens when there are no metaphysical guarantees, i.e., of an intentional subject, of an external and/or ideal reality, of language as representing or expressing the outside or an inner reality? In other words, is the *linguistic turn* in social and education research capable of 'overcoming' cognitivism or the paradigm of perception? Is this possible? Because implicated in this problematic is a challenging of what Paul de Man has called the assumption of the 'organic continuity of perceptual, cognitive and linguistic structures' (Norris, 1988, p. 116).

It is striking that the latter assumption is so often ironized in everyday jokes. Consider the following:

Teacher: Keith, if I had seven apples in my right hand and ten apples in my left hand, what would I have?

Keith: Huge hands, sir! (Joke in Christmas Cracker, 1991)

What is this joke supposed to mean? In a first commonsensical reading we hear a child playing with language, instead of doing serious maths. Against all expectations, mathematical meaning is being shown to have failed to hegemonize everyday meaning. These expectations are grounded on the assumption that '10 + 7' is repeated, and that its inscription into different contexts cannot essentially affect it: it is always *conceptually* recuperable. But the meaning of '10 + 7' as a mathematical concept is subject to the metaphorics of language, here indicated by the word 'huge'.

In addition, while it is obvious that in using an example with apples the teacher intends the child to see an empirical object, still there are discontinuities between the word 'apple' referring to an empirical object (the referential function of language), and 'apple' within a system of language (the signifying function).

The problem is that, the linguistic signifier 'a-p-p-l-e' gives the illusion of immediacy; it gives the impression of continuity and symmetry between the empirical object, the perception of it, its concept and its linguistic and arithmetic expression, thus concealing that 'a-p-p-l-e' is simply a device. The use of a linguistic device would raise the question of the relation between mathematics and language. By eradicating reference, mathematics is defined as a purely conceptual system.

Now one can argue that a mathematics teacher takes into account this difference between literal and metaphorical meaning. At some point in his or her teaching he or she introduces a metaphor, either because he or she thinks it is necessary because of the indeterminate nature of all theoretical knowledge or because he or she believes it to be difficult for him or her to explain and for the child to comprehend mathematical meaning. For the maths researcher the problem of why mathematics needs fiction, metaphorics and analogies — in other words, why it intrinsically needs the literary — is covered up by the perception object presupposed in research, teaching and learning. An 'aesthetic closure' (based on 'aesthesis'/ perception) is the result. The assumption of the 'thing' as full presence is an empiricism, an *ideology* because it does not let us go further (see Lukacher, 1989, pp. 130–3).[13] But if the whole purpose of rethinking mathematics education is to focus on the students' experience, the question is how far research can go against this ideology. For a mathematics-aesthetics, i.e., a mathematics based on this ideology, might radically close off its investigation.

Thus we believe that the interruption of the continuity assumed between the perceptual (aesthesis), cognitive (conceptual) and linguistic (as material mark) orders, is the interruption of the aesthetic ideology which, we would argue, shapes at present the field of mathematics education, and education research and practice more generally. This is the irony that the joke expresses: the universal, rational, context-free, and intelligent thinking that mathematics is supposed to represent hides from view the ideology of mathematics-aesthesis.

At one level the relation between language and mathematics has been assumed in the tendency of several researchers to inform their research by post-structuralist (and as we shall see, psychoanalytic) perspectives.[14] In the section which follows, using a case-study from Evans' empirical research, we will trace this linguistic/psychoanalytic path.

Let us therefore conclude this section by saying that we understand the linguistic turn in mathematics as both: a necessary consequence — inscribed in the general economy which has also generated the shifts to the social and to the practical; and a more or less conscious decision on the part of the researcher in an attempt to displace the cognitivist model outlined above. In this latter model, the repeatability of mathematics is guaranteed without failure. But in this brief indication of the problematic we have caught a glimpse of an abyss, apparently impossible to bridge. We only point to it: what is the relationship between mathematics and language? In other words, do we use language simply in order to communicate and transmit mathematical knowledge? Or is it that maths cannot constitute itself (its identity) without the work of the linguistic sign?

Error or Repression

Evans' research (1993) was focused on the differences of 'mathematical' thinking within different (discursive) practices, and on the attendant feelings, in particular 'mathematics anxiety'. His empirical work included 'problem-solving' interviews

The London Gold Price — 23 January 1980

This graph shows how the price of gold (in dollars per fine ounce) varied during one day's trading in London. Which part of the graph shows where the price was rising fastest? What was the lowest price that day?

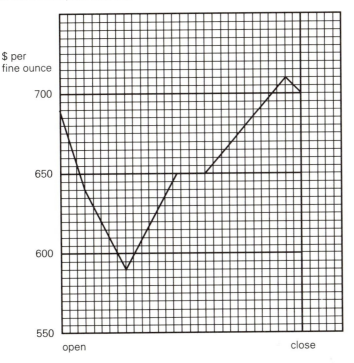

Figure 7.1: Question 3 in the Interview
Source: Evans, 1993; based on Sewell, 1981

with a sample of first-year social-science students. All these students were doing a mathematics course as part of their studies.

'Fiona', aged 26 at entry, was middle-class by family background and on the basis of her own earlier work. Her qualifications in mathematics were 'a very poor CSE grade and a very poor (O-level) grade'.

For question 3 in the interview (see Figure 7.1), Fiona appears to get lost in the detail of the gold price changes, for reasons which emerge:

JE: ... which part of the graph shows where the price was rising fastest?
S: (. . .) there doesn't actually seem to be any time specification along the bottom which I find quite confusing (. . .) my father's a stockbroker, so I *do* understand a little about opening and closing ... [6 lines] ... I mean there actually appear to be two peaks here, but I should say maybe when gold is at 650, it seems to rise very rapidly in the afternoon until close, and afternoon business, you know, afternoon trading ... (Interview transcript, p. 8)

She then confirms that she considers the price to be rising faster in the afternoon (rather than the morning) — which is wrong. It appears that she refuses the terms of the question, and draws on information from an 'outside' discourse to answer. She then goes on to read the lowest price of the day as $580 rather than $590. Thus, for this question, she seems to call up what might be called 'money maths', from the position of a stockbroker's daughter who 'wouldn't understand':

> S: ... my father dealt with money all the time, um, because he was a stockbroker and therefore it was the essence to him and his making a living, um, but (. . .) we were always told we wouldn't understand [10 lines].
> ... because as a stockbroker, your home and your material valuables are on the line all the time (. . .) on a couple of occasions the family home was under great threat (. . .). It wasn't something that family and children discuss . . . [2 lines] . . . he was the man of the household and he could deal with it [. . .] . . . most of the time, it was like living under a time bomb (JE: mmm, mmm, I can appreciate that) especially if you don't quite know how the time bomb's made up or when it's going to explode . . . (Interview transcript, pp. 9–10)

Thus, a first reading of this episode might be that Fiona has made errors on both parts of problem 3, perhaps precipitated by the substantial amount of feeling expressed and exhibited in this passage (and in others, not quoted here). First of all, she seems *angry* at being positioned as a child who is deprived of information about her father and his work because she 'wouldn't understand': this is shown by the range of sometimes ambivalent, but basically negative words she uses to describe his work. This lack of knowledge is linked to the anxiety she exhibits — perhaps most graphically in her comment that growing up with a stockbroker as father was 'like living under (sic) a time bomb . . .'. And being positioned as a child who 'wouldn't understand' is likely to have contributed to the lack of confidence in school subjects including mathematics.

But a second reading is within the researcher's horizon. Consider the following:

> S: ... I had a very, very good maths teacher. She was very, very aware of people's problems (. . .) she used to work through step by step . . . and then she left a few months before I actually sat both my, the CSE and O level, and I went downhill very rapidly. I don't know whether it was a question of confidence, or inability [2 lines] . . . I just felt that once she'd left, it became — it sounds funny — but it became very, very *mathematical* . . . (. . .) Nothing, after she left, nothing was explained. We were just given the formulas and told to get on with it . . . (Interview transcript, pp. 2–3; Evans' emphasis)

Fiona rejects mathematics from an early stage in her studies. This rejection is premised upon a loss or lack: that of the teacher with a good ear for 'social problems'. The bond which is supposed to hold the chain of identifications — mathematics–teacher–student — is broken. The crisis and crack reverberates in the student's mentioning the timing of the incident, that of exams, a period of crisis and of judgment. Mathematics declines into dry formulas. Mathematics and the teacher becomes 'other' to her: 'everything becomes very mathematical.'

Is this not the moment for a researcher to step into the psychoanalytic terrain? This premonition of the researcher is reinforced, the more s/he looks at the case. For example is there a desire for her father *repressed* — but impossible to contain — in the series of epithets she uses to describe her father's work?

> capitalist, corrupt, business-like, . . . um, mathematical, calculating, devious, unemotional . . . (Interview transcript, p. 11)

This chain of signifiers describes the father's activities and (her perception of) his relationships with others in the family, including her.

In this second reading then we consider the chain of signifiers produced in response to Evans' request 'to pick words, adjectives to describe his (i.e., Fiona's father's) work'. Here we draw on theories of signification to analyse the elements and structures of discursive practices — in particular signifier–signified relations and devices such as metaphor (linked with condensation) and metonymy (linked with displacement), see Henriques *et al.* (1984, Sec.3). Here we ask whether there is 'something more', whether there is something in her feelings that is unstated, even *repressed.*

The overall chain of thinking begins of course with the graph showing the changes in the price of gold, including one substantial fall at the start of the day (see Figure 7.1). She associates this with her father and his work several times; there may be a defensive displacement from the father to his work. In this chain, we can expect the affective charge, based on desire for her father, to flow between signifiers. Perhaps the central signifier in this chain is 'calculating': it is located at the intersection of the family discourses about the father/his work, and the mathematical discourses. In the former, it exhibits or signifies disappointment and anger (and anxiety), which is suppressed; in the latter of course it signifies a central activity of the discourse — and this may explain her resistance to getting clear how to calculate, in school mathematics at least.[15]

In this example, the term 'mathematics' shows up in unexpected ways, and what seem to be terms of mathematics are sometimes shared, at intersections with other discourses. The consequences are that what appears to be 'mathematical' activity, or 'mathematics anxiety', may be read quite differently.

This second reading suggests that a 'mistake' cannot with certainty be attributed to a mathematical (conceptual) error. By following, as we indicated, post-structuralist and psychoanalytic insights (signification, chain of signifiers in meaning constitution, condensation and displacement) we have showed that this question can only be answered by saying that what we call error can be seen as the effect of repression and defence.

We have arrived at the theoretical space of post-structuralism and of psycho-analysis where the error/repression problematic as a research problem, echoes and repeats the conceptual distinction between the cognitive and the affective which Evans' research has set out to investigate. While it has gone some way towards upsetting either the cognitive subject of psychology or the subject of sociology, determined by social and/or linguistic structures, Evans' research relies on a notion of subject as defined by psychoanalysis (desire).

What is this subject of psychoanalysis? Nancy and Lacoue-Labarthe (1992) in one of their readings of the Lacanian psychoanalytic theory identify three registers articulated in the theory (see 'Translators' Preface', pp. *vii–xxv*). First, Lacan's linguistic theory articulates itself with the psychoanalytic discourse through 'a certain relation between the signifier and truth, insofar as desire is implicated therein' (*ibid.*, *ix*). This results in Lacan's reading psychoanalysis through linguistics — i.e., a literal translation of Freud's concepts — and linguistics through psychoanalysis — i.e., interpretation of the bar separating the well-known Saussurean distinction between the signifier and the signified as the symbolic bar of repression.[16] In this way he disturbs any neat and systematic relationship between the two disciplines. But, secondly, the Lacanian theory articulates itself with another register, that of the philosophical. Here Lacoue-Labarthe and Nancy reveal a philosophical system which is determined by, and which reinscribes, a number of classical philosophical presuppositions such as systematicity and subjectivity.

This tacit restoration of subjectivity in an otherwise novel and challenging theory results in what we have earlier identified as methodological technicity: a closing off of the opening created in the intersection of the three registers. In a similar manner, our problematic of error or repression revealed in our case study can be covered up by a reading which would be a form of empiricism: a reliance upon the fact of 'lived experience' of the student. Is this repressed experience what repeats itself as error? Following Freud's problematic of 'trauma' (Caruth, 1991a, 1991b), can we read this 'error' according to the model of a *traumatic experience* whose memory produces a response which can neither be a simple error nor a pure repression? Furthermore, can we consider the possibility that

> (c)oncerning the *mémoire involontaire*: its images do not only come without being called up: rather, they are images which we have never seen before we remember them. (Benjamin, quoted in Cadava, 1992, p. 106)

There is no space in this chapter to address the psychoanalytic register in those terms. Yet suspending the possible temptation to try to produce a final and totalizing reading (which would read the case study according to the either/or of error/repression) we will focus instead, in our final section, on the philosophical register which (to pre-empt the argument) reveals a more fundamental 'trauma' or scar at the heart of mathematics itself.

Fractured Mathematics: Metaphysical Closure and Its Deconstructive Representation[17]

In his essay 'Genesis and Structure' Derrida (1978a, p. 154) notes Husserl's aversion to the philosopher's wish to close the question by offering a conclusion, a solution or a decision. A decision implies that a choice has been made, and this closes down the continuous process of faithful description phenomenology aspires to. Here Husserl rejects the idea of speculative 'closure' which would be produced by postulating a closed system or structure. Derrida introduces the idea that the denial, in principle, of closure implies that the opening is structural.

We see this Derridian problematic at work in his 'introduction' to Husserl's

'Origin of Geometry' (1978b). In the 'Origin of Geometry' Husserl seeks to address the problem of how the objective ideality of geometry — and the ideality of the sciences, more generally — arose from the consciousness of its first inventor. For Husserl, this question cannot be addressed scientifically because geometry arose in a pre-scientific lifeworld. Questions like this have the character of a closure within a limited, finite domain.

Derrida describes the Husserlian institution of geometry as a philosophical act. Philosophy is conceived as an infinite task, the idea in the Kantian sense, the telos of reason. The originary infinitization exemplified by Euclidean geometry permitted the overcoming of finite knowledge based upon sense data or facts. For Husserl this originary infinitization constitutes a totality and is bound within a finite closure (finite infinity). In Modernity — for Husserl in the work of Galileo — there is a new infinitization which comes to overturn the originary one. It arises from within the closure of originary infinity, but it differs from the latter in that it overcomes that closure and opens it to the infinite task of scientific knowledge (Critchley, 1992a, p. 8).[18]

In the 'introduction' Derrida poses the problem of intra-mathematical closure: the question of whether there is a closure of the mathematical domain, that is whether mathematical idealization and infinitization take place within a field that is finite and closed. Accepting Hilbert's 'axiom of completeness' Husserl called such systems as mathematics and geometry capable of enclosing mathematical infinitization within a finite domain a 'definite system' or 'delimited closure': 'an infinite yet self-enclosed world of ideal objectivities as a field for study' (quoted in Critchley, 1992a, p. 9 from Husserl's *Krisis*). It is therefore precisely the possibility of closure that characterizes science like mathematics and geometry.[19]

Using the resources of phenomenology, Derrida attacks in a covert way both the notion of finite totality and of structure. Husserl's description of phenomenology partly relies on the distinction between rigorous and exact science. For Husserl, exact science is characterized by the possibility of closure; the completion of a finite totality within which all the propositions, hypotheses and concepts of that science are contained 'so that in *principle . . . nothing further remains open* within it' (Derrida, 1978a, p. 322, n. 14). On the other hand a rigorous science like phenomenology possesses the principled, essential and structural impossibility of closure (p. 162); philosophy as phenomenology is the infinite opening (of the lived experience) beyond the closure. Philosophy is the irruption of infinity into the finite totality of exact science or into finite consciousness. For Derrida, the presence of infinity within finite closure — this transcendentality of the opening — is at once the condition of possibility and *a certain impossibility* of every structure or finite totality.

Let us note here our *first remark*: Derrida's reading of the Husserlian texts reveals a certain structural impossibility of any closed system, structure or totality. This, above all, is an attack on the metaphysical notion of closure.

Critchley (1992a, pp. 5–6) makes a distinction between two senses of closure:

(a)   a spatial closure is that which encompasses and encloses all the coordinates or constituent parts appertaining to a given and finite territory; and

(b)   a temporal closure is the activity or process of bringing something to its end — which must be distinguished from the concept of end as the completion of the act.[20]

Anna Tsatsaroni and Jeff Evans

Understood temporally or spatially, closure is associated with limit, a moment in time or points in space which delimit a given area and seek to circumscribe it. Once the limit is drawn one does not only see the inside but also the outside. Thus Critchley writes:

> . . . the event of closure is a delimitation which shows the *double appartenance of an inside* and an outside. . . . it is precisely the failure of complete delimitation or circumscription that will be of interest, and I shall pay special attention to the *opening* or breakthrough that occurs within the closure, violating its vows and breaching its barriers, offering the *promise* of a new begining. (Critchley, 1992a, p. 6)

Here, we can draw our *second remark*: What is of interest in this problematic of closure is on the one hand the desire to draw a limit; and, on the other, the failure of complete delimitation. But far from being a problem or a deficit, this is the condition and the promise of any new beginning. Critchley shows how closure functions in Derrida's early tests. 'It is a *technical* term designating a finite totality, which the infinitist gesture of phenomenology continually exceeds' (*ibid.*, p. 10). The articulation of a position which constitutes a continuation and a break with phenomenology takes place through a crucial displacement of the concept of closure. The word closure shifts from being part of a technical vocabulary to becoming a key term in the conceptual terminology with which Derrida will engage in the deconstruction of the metaphysics of presence or logocentrism. We can see this shift from technical to terminological usage in 'Violence and metaphysics' (1978c). There the problem of closure, is the problem of belonging and the breakthrough. The contradiction that is at work in every philosopher is that he has to employ the resources of the tradition, the language of metaphysics, in order to overcome it/rupture it (see Derrida, 1981; Tsatsaroni, 1991, pp. 312–14). But if the transgression of closure can only proceed by employing the metaphysical language and conceptuality, this very employment, however, is what restores metaphysics to itself. This adds a new dimension to the problem of closure: It is no longer simply a technical term designating a finite totality; it is the terminological name of a problematic that describes the relations between logocentrism and its other (Critchley, 1992a, p. 11). If Husserl's work implies the challenging of the notion of structural closure, Derrida's reading of phenomenology locates the latter at the point (and as the play) of belonging and non-belonging to the metaphysical tradition.

Third remark, then: The notion of closure describes the paradoxical relationship of logocentrism to its other: We are caught in a double bind between belonging to a tradition and achieving a breakthrough beyond this tradition.[21] Derrida uses the Husserlian project to exemplify the concept of metaphysical closure as the play of transgression and restoration. Husserl's motto to return to the things themselves is itself metaphysical insofar as phenomenology seeks to rediscover the first principles of philosophy, natural sciences and the humanities which have been perverted by degenerate metaphysics. Transcendental phenomenology is caught in the tension between a descriptively authentic metaphysics and a speculatively degenerate metaphysics. Phenomenology appears as both a transgression or breakthrough from metaphysics and a restoration of that tradition.

Derrida in many cases demonstrates the way in which the act whereby the closure is transgressed and accompanied by the restoration of the closure, leaving each text on the limit between belonging and non-belonging to the tradition. We might ask: *what is the form of this limit? What is the representation of closure?* The form that this precarious limit takes, the representation of closure, as Critchley remarks, cannot be represented as a circle with a linear, unbroken boundary surrounding a homogeneous space (1992a, p. 14). And Derrida writes:

> I have put forward the proposition according to which there would never be 'metaphysics', 'closure' not being here a circular limit bordering a homogeneous field but a more twisted structure which today, according to another figure, I would be tempted to call: 'invaginated'. Representation of a linear and circular closure surrounding a homogenous space is, precisely, the theme of my greatest emphasis, an auto-representation of philosophy in its onto-encyclopedic logic. (Derrida, 1978d, p. 14)

Fourth remark: In its deconstructive representation closure is not an unbroken boundary or circle which encloses all the coordinates or constituent parts of a finite totality or homogeneous territory. The closure of metaphysics has a more twisted and devious limit that is 'invaginated' — folded back upon itself. Derrida's displacement of the figure of closure by the figure of an 'invaginated' limit has had two implications: First, deconstructively read, logocentric philosophy — defined as the mastery of the limit, the territorial desire for totality and closure where the inside–outside can be rigorously maintained — is being left as a scarred and flawed body which is unable to draw the limit between the inside–outside and which is divided within itself between belonging and non-belonging to the tradition. Within the texts of the metaphysical tradition, such as for example the text of phenomenology there are the scars/traces of an irreducible alterity which denies the construction of a unitary closure or totality. Secondly, the displacement of the figure of metaphysical closure defines also the task of deconstruction. Deferring any attempt to present such an approach, we would only say that it is the act of reading which produces a dislocation within a text, where the latter is divided between belonging and non-belonging to the metaphysical (logocentric) tradition.[22]

For Derrida, philosophy uses the image of closure as a linear and circular body in order to represent and justify itself as a body of knowledge to be learned, which can be mastered. How does this image affect, say, mathematics? if we take the Hegelian moment as an example, we read:

> . . . the whole or the organic totality of philosophy is the coronet or crown *within whose sphere revolve the circles* of the various disciplines . . . [my emphasis] (quoted in Critchley, 1992a, p. 4)

This is the reason why Derrida declares, as quoted in the introduction to this chapter, that the unity derived from the concepts of science is covertly but continually determined by a historical-metaphysical epoch.

Conclusion

We started off this chapter with a naïve question: 'What is mathematics?' We continued with the further question of whether it is worth asking the question.

Behind the question lurks the image of mathematics as a closed system. Our first and second remarks in the previous section suggest that the metaphysical desire of every scientific project to present its object as a well-rounded totality comes up against a 'structural' opening which is both the condition of possibility and a certain impossibility of any structure. Thus the figure of closure points to a paradox: the fulfilment of the desire to completely master and de-limit an object of knowledge would, in principle, imply the latter's stagnation and demise.

Here we have dealt with the spatial notion of closure. We would need more space to show that the will of the metaphysics of presence, i.e., the will to delimit a discipline, also implies a certain view of temporality of the present. Husserl's inquiries, again, should be the starting point. Because while problematizing the model of temporality assumed in the delimitation of an object of inquiry, Husserl restores closure by a temporal determination of the presence of an object as present now (see Tsatsaroni, 1991, pp. 232–5). Thus the displacement of the question of 'what is' requires the deconstruction of metaphysical closure in both its spatial and temporal sense. This, for example, would apply to Tiles' position briefly referred to above. In the remarks concluding her book *Lack of Closure and the Power of Reason* she writes:

> The capacity to develop new representational forms whose application brings in its wake new ways of thinking and reasoning illustrates the sense in which mathematical reason does not form a closed and fixed system, but is something which has always the potential for development in new directions. The lack of closure of classical analysis is a precondition of the possibility of finding new ways of investigating old forms, such as the equation for a parabola. This does require re-interpreting the equation, linking it to computation in new ways, but not in such a way as to break with, or lose sight of, older interpretations. (Tiles, 1991, pp. 170–1)

While Tiles defines mathematics as a system open to re-interpretation, this system is regulated by a rational ideal.[23] The regulative ideal of rationality is what in Tiles produces closure: a temporal determination of the presence of an object albeit not here and now but postponed for the future.

We can indicate the importance of this point as follows. From an epistemological point of view the question of (re)interpretation of a formalism is indeed the issue. What we have learned from Kuhn is that inquiry into the nature of scientific knowledge has to have a model as to the production of new knowledge. Such is, for example, Kuhn's idea of scientific revolutions which poses the problem of whether the new paradigm relates in a rational way to the existing knowledge or is a break from it. To think the same kind of problematic, Derrida uses the idea of an invention which he characterizes as an undecidable. It is therefore the notion of invention as an undecidable which needs to be carefully considered. For it asks the question of 'What is . . . mathematics?' in a way which refuses to obey an either/or dichotomy, by engaging with the deconstruction of metaphysical closure in its temporal and spatial sense.

This is, in fact, what our third remark in the previous section suggested. That is, that the metaphysical notion of closure in its Derridian usage names a second paradox: Any simple opposition to the metaphysical tradition-logocentrism (its conceptual dichotomies, its oppositions and its language) will reinscribe logocentrism. We cannot simply ignore the figure of closure with an act of choice (e.g., mathematics *either* as a closed *or* an open system); a figure whose baggage will continue to haunt research the more forcefully we reject or oppose it.

Our fourth remark helps us challenge the dominant image of mathematics: the representation of the mathematical field as a linear, circular limit surrounding a homogeneous space, which, as the inside, can be rigorously separated from the outside. In its deconstructive representation — at the philosophical register, with the displacement of the figure of closure — the irreducible presence of 'an outside' prevents mathematics from being a simple and full presence. A scar or irreducible trace of alterity is at the core of mathematics.

We left out — for subsequent analysis — the linguistic register we have identified above. Derrida's deconstruction — again with reference to Husserl — of the relationship between sign and mathematical truth could perhaps show in a more forceful way how mathematics differs from itself: how mathematics cannot constitute its identity because it has to rely on the sign, an irreducible other. This could bring forth the question of the relation between mathematics and language, the structural inability to draw a rigorous distinction between the mathematical concept and its linguistic expression. We believe that such a problematic can open up a very fecund area of research in mathematics education — such as, for example, why it is that mathematics needs fiction. (For one approach to this issue see Walkerdine (1988); and Walkerdine *et al.* (1989)).

We have also left out the psychoanalytic register. At the concrete level of research we have avoided the claim of a totalizing reading. At the analytical level we posed the question of the difference between lived and traumatic experience only programmatically. By opening up this space we hope to rework both the concept of experience and the associated concepts, notably the concept of memory which, at present, is completely defined by the metaphysically dominated discipline of psychology. This, we believe, will have important implications for school practice and for mathematics education research on differences in students' experience.

Notes

1. As will become apparent later, the traditional image of philosophy is that of a sphere. The various disciplines are then represented as regions or circles whose essence can be investigated by asking the question one asks for philosophy: e.g., 'what is the essence of mathematics?.'
2. The term refers to the system of interpretation and of foundation of meaning which has been specific to western philosophy. See Frank (1989).
3. As Derrida himself admits (1988, pp. 1–5), his notion of deconstruction is difficult to define. We can say that it is a gesture of departure which takes seriously, in order to displace, metaphysical oppositions such as for example the distinction between a subject and an object of inquiry. This paper is our third in a series which begins to introduce this term and specify it for the field of mathematics education. See Evans and Tsatsaroni (1993) and Evans and Tsatsaroni (1994).
4. Discourse has become an ubiquitous and therefore an ambiguous notion, which reverberates and marks the difficulties with operating with — and staying with — a basically Foucaultian critique of knowledge, as, for example, in the argument

below, in the text. On the other hand, in another equally crude sense, to talk about discourse is an indication of our commitment to the belief that a programme of research can start only from where it finds itself, with no absolute justification of the starting point being possible. This peculiar kind of empiricism has been addressed by Derrida in 'The Exorbitant Question of Method' (1976, pp. 157–64).

5.   Within mathematics education, see the work of Walkerdine (1988, 1989); Brown (1990); Dowling (1990); and Taylor (1990).

6.   We understand the difference between the two as follows: constructivism tends to be individualistic, originating in psychology. It emphasizes the individual's active participation in the construction of knowledge. Social constructionism emphasizes the social dimension in the construction of knowledge; see also Ernest (1991) and Lerman (1989, 1993). Social constructionism, therefore, is a more direct consequence of the modernity/post-modernity debate, and, as a move, more aware of this problematic.

7.   In the field of mathematics education this is echoed, for example, in the recent conference on 'The Culture of the Mathematics Classroom' (Osnabruck, October, 1993). The universality of mathematics — it is argued in the paper announcing the conference — can be challenged by research 'into the forms mathematical knowledge takes in different cultures and cultural situations'; 'not only between cultures at large but also between the multitude of everyday practical situations within one singular culture'.

8.   Mary Harris (1991), in mathematics education can be seen as having similar concerns, namely about claims that such-and-such is or isn't mathematics; also, Dowling (1991); Evans (1988, 1993); and Taylor (1990).

9.   Woolgar at times calls his work deconstructive, because it is concerned with challenging fundamental assumptions of research, and hierarchical dichotomies which shape our everyday practices and thinking of science and technology. But the fact that, as his work implies (e.g., 1988, p. 27; also Cooper, Hine, Low and Woolgar, 1993), his commitment to a critique and destabilization of the taken-for-granted is a consequence of an act of choice, differentiates this work from deconstructive reading in the Derridian sense (see Critchley, 1992a and 1992b). Deconstruction, in the strong sense, denotes the suspension of choice, decision and critical judgment through the undecidability of an act of reading. The deconstructive reading maintains an interruption or alterity irreducible to critique. At the same time, this programme of, say, 'weak deconstruction', as is currently practised by Woolgar and his associates at the Centre for Research into Innovation, Culture and Technology — Brunel University — pursues our question of what is special about science (or technology) in a distinctive way, namely, how it becomes special. What is of interest for this group of researchers is the processes through which the scientific (technical)/social divide is produced, and their implications. For example, in a recent paper, 'Managing the Social-Technical Divide' (forthcoming), Low and Woolgar write: '. . . what makes it [the technical] distinctive from other types of social accomplishment is the special accomplishment of a private space; a restricted, perhaps even secret space.' Bruno Latour also orients his research towards deconstructing the dichotomy between nature and society or culture (e.g., 1993), and the technical and social (e.g., 1988).

10. While the distinction between essentialism and relativism, and transcendental and empirical cannot be equated, it is obvious that, for example, relativism would tend to accept that the impossibility of specifying an *a priori* object of inquiry is because of the interferences caused by the empirical world.

11. There are parallels between this distinction and the distinction between mathematical psychology — where the theories of psychology are expressed and developed in mathematical terms — and psychometrics — where psychological

theories are tested statistically. See also the distinction between mathematical economics and econometrics.

12. For an analysis of the presuppositions of the cognitive paradigm, and for examples of research projects which attempt to 'overcome' it see Tsatsaroni (1991). For a brief but insightful assessment of the sociological attacks on cognitivism — similar to those which currently take place in mathematics education — as well as for some of the reasons for their restricted success, see Woolgar (1987).

13. The other side of the coin is the figure of 'human' which, for Paul de Man, functions as a pragmatic, conceptually arbitrary principle of closure. For an assessment of the hidden costs of humanism as ideology, as a principle of closure see Redfield (1989).

14. Besides the references in note 5, see, for example, Dowling (1993, Chapter 4); a thesis which aspires to restructure the research concerns of mathematics education according to structuralist and post-structuralist principles.

15. This is evidenced by the description of her actions in the 1st year mathematics course, in Evans' (1993) reflexive account: 'She was a bright but sometimes difficult student, on occasion arriving late, fidgeting, dropping jokey asides in class.'

16. Lacan's view can be represented as follows:

signifier S^1 signifier S^2
------------ ---> ------------
signified s^1 signifier S^1 See Thom (1981)

17. In this section we rely heavily on Critchley's excellent two-part presentation of 'The problem of closure in Derrida' (1992a, 1992b).

18. For a detailed sociological/historical discussion of these developments, including the differences between pre-modern and modern forms of mathematics, see Ashley and Betebenner (1993).

19. Derrida points out that subsequent developments in axiom theory such as Godel's theorem have serious consequences for Husserl's conception of definite axiom systems. Godel showed that metalogical statements concerning the completeness or closure of axiom systems can neither be demonstrated nor refuted within those axiom systems.

20. Critchley also summarizes the meanings of the French word *cloture* that inform Derrida's work: In French *cloture* has several particular usages (spatial and temporal): (a) It means a surrounding wall or fence which produces an area of enclosed space. To erect a closure is to build an enclosing wall which acts as a barrier which divides the inside of a circumscribed territory from the outside and which would often function in the defence of a property etc. (b) One can speak of a religious obligation to keep a closure. One can speak of a vow of closure deriving from Canonical law which forbids/limits the comings and goings in a monastery/convent. To violate the closure is to enter unlawfully and breach its totality. By extension one can speak of closure as a complete obedience or withdrawal within a severe self-imposed discipline. Also the desire to become enclosed within a retreat. (c), closure, in French is an act of terminating a process, of ending a state of affairs (the closure of a meeting or session, of a debate, of an account), that is associated with the activity or process of completion.

21. Derrida (1982, Introduction, p. x) defines logocentrism as the desire to attain a unitary closure where the distinction between inside and outside, of philosophy and non-philosophy can be rigorously maintained.

22. See Critchley (1992b, pp. 135ff) for an attempt to connect the notion of closure with what he calls clotural reading. For an example of deconstructive reading see Tsatsaroni (1991).

23. See, also: 'It was Kant who displaced metaphysics, turning its totalizations into

Anna Tsatsaroni and Jeff Evans

regulative ideals of human practice. To ignore the shift toward method, toward construction and the practical, the shift away from the verbal and discursive . . . [m]akes it appear that the only alternative to the closed, computational reason of logicists and formalists is a wholesale rejection of the tradition of rational inquiry.' (p. 172).

References

ASHLEY, D. and BETEBENNER, D. (1993) 'Mathematics, Post-Modernism and the Loss of Certainty', Paper Produced by Department of Sociology, University of Wyoming and presented at *Research Imaginations*, Annual Conference of the British Sociological Association, University of Essex (April).

BROWN, A. (1990) 'Schools, homes and mathematical activity: Time for critical analysis', in Noss *et al*. (Eds) pp. 46–50.

CADAVA, E. (1992) 'Words of light: Theses on the photography of history', *Diacritics*, 22, 3–4, pp. 84–114.

CARUTH, C. (1991a) 'Introduction', *American Imago: Studies in Psychoanalysis and Culture*, 48, 1, Spring, pp. 1–12.

CARUTH, C. (1991b) 'Introduction', *American Imago: Studies in Psychoanalysis and Culture*, 48, 4, pp. 417–24.

COOPER, G., HINE, C., LOW, J. and WOOLGAR, S. (1993) 'Ethnography and human computer interaction', CRICT Discussion Paper, 39 (September) to appear in THOMAS, P. (Ed) *The Social and Interactional Dimensions of Human-Computer Interfaces*, Cambridge, Cambridge University Press.

CRITCHLEY, S. (1992a) 'The problem of closure in Derrida (Part One)', *Journal of the British Society for Phenomenology*, 23, 1, January, pp. 3–19.

CRITCHLEY, S. (1992b) 'The problem of closure in Derrida (Part Two)', *Journal of the British Society for Phenomenology*, 23, 2, May, pp. 127–45.

DERRIDA, J. (1976) *Of Grammatology*, Translation Gayatri Chakravorty Spivak, London, The Johns Hopkins University Press.

DERRIDA, J. (1978a) 'Genesis and structure and phenomenology', in *Writing and Difference*, translation by A. BASS, London, Routledge and Kegan Paul.

DERRIDA, J. (1978b) *Edmund Husserl's Origin of Geometry: An Introduction*, translation by J. LEAVEY, Lincoln and London, University of Nebraska Press.

DERRIDA, J. (1978c) 'Violence and metaphysics: An essay on the thought of Emmanuel Levinas', in *Writing and Difference*, translation by A. BASS, London, Routledge and Kegan Paul.

DERRIDA, J. (1978d) 'The retreat of metaphor', *Enclitic*, 2, 2, pp. 5–33.

DERRIDA, J. (1981) *Positions*, Translation A. BASS. Chicago, The University of Chicago Press.

DERRIDA, J. (1982) *Margins of Philosophy*, translation A. BASS, Brighton, The Harvester Press.

DERRIDA, J. (1988) 'Letter to a Japanese friend', in WOOD, D. and BERNASCONI, R. (Eds) *Derrida and Difference*, Evanston, Northwestern University Press.

DOWLING, P. (1990) 'Some notes towards a theoretical model for reproduction, action and critique', in Noss *et al*. (Eds) pp. 76–84.

DOWLING, P. (1991) 'The contextualizing of mathematics: Towards a theoretical map', in HARRIS, M. (Ed) *Schools, Mathematics and Work*, London, The Falmer Press, Chapter 11.

DOWLING. P. (1993) *A Language for the Sociological Description of Pedagogic texts with particular Reference to the Secondary School mathematics Scheme SMP 11–16*, Ph.D Thesis, Institute of Education, University of London.

ERNEST, P. (1991) *The Philosophy of Mathematics Education*, London, The Falmer Press.

EVANS, J. (1988) 'Context and performance in numerical activity among adults', in BORBAS, A. (Ed) *Psychology of Mathematics Education Conference XII*, Vezsprem, Hungary, 20–25 July, OOK Printing House, pp. 296–303.

EVANS, J. (1993) *Adults and Numeracy*, PhD Thesis, University of London Library.

EVANS, J. and TSATSARONI, A. (1993) 'Linking the cognitive and the affective: A comparison of models for research', In HIRABAYASHI *et al.* (Eds) PME-17, 17th Conference of the International Group for Psychology of Mathematics Education, Tsukuba, Japan, 19–23 July, 3, pp. 210–17.

EVANS, J. and TSATSARONI, A. (1994) 'Language and "Subjectivity" in the Mathematics Classroom', In LERMAN, S. (Ed) *The Culture of The Mathematics Classroom*, Dordrecht, NL, Kluwer.

FRANK, M. (1989) *What is Neostructuralism?* translation by S. WILKE and R. GRAY, *Theory and History of Literature*, 45. Minneapolis, University of Minnesota Press.

HARRIS, M. (Ed) (1991) *Schools, Mathematics and Work*, London, The Falmer Press.

HARRIS, M. (1991) 'Looking for the maths in work', in HARRIS, M. (Ed) *Schools, Mathematics and Work*, London, The Falmer Press, Chapter 13.

HEIDEGGER, M. (1978) 'The end of philosophy and the task of thinking', in HEIDEGGER, M. and KRELL, D. (Ed) *Basic Writings*, London, Routledge and Kegan Paul.

HENRIQUES, J., HOLLWAY, W., URWIN, C., VENN, C. and WALKERDINE, V. (1984) *Changing the Subject: Psychology, Social Regulation and Subjectivity*, London, Methuen.

KUHN, T. (1970) *The Structure of Scientific Revolutions*, 2nd edition, Chicago, The University of Chicago Press.

LATOUR, B. (1988) 'Mixing humans and nonhumans together: The sociology of a door-closer', *Social Problems*, 35, 3, June.

LATOUR, B. (1993) *We Have Never Been Modern*, translation by C. PORTER, Hemel Hempstead, Harvester Wheatsheaf.

LAVE, J. (1988) *Cognition in Practice: Mind, mathematics and culture in everyday life*, Cambridge, Cambridge University Press.

LERMAN, S. (1989) 'Constructivism, mathematics and mathematics education', *Educational Studies in Mathematics*, 20, pp. 211–23.

LERMAN, S. (1993) 'The "Problem" of Intersubjectivity in Mathematics Learning: Expansion or Rejection of the Constructivist Paradigm?', Paper submitted to *Journal for Research in Mathematics Education*.

LOW, J. and WOOLGAR, S. (forthcoming) 'Managing the social-technical divide: Some aspects of the discursive structure of information systems development', in QUINTAS, P. (Ed) *Social Dimensions of Systems Engineering*, Chichester, Ellis Horwood.

LUKACHER, N. (1989) 'Writing on ashes: Heidegger fort Derrida', *Diacritics*, 19, 3–4, pp. 128–48.

NANCY, J.L. and LACOUE-LABARTHE, P. (1992) *The Title of the Letter: A Reading of Lacan*, translation and preface by F. RAFFOUL and D. PETTIGREW, New York, State University of New York Press.

NORRIS, C. (1988) *Paul de Man: Deconstruction and the Critique of Aesthetic Ideology*, New York, Routledge.

NOSS, R. *et al.* (1990) *PDME. 1: Political Dimensions of Mathematics Education: Action and Critique*, Proceedings of the First International Conference, London April 1–4, Department of MSC, Institute of Education, University of London.

REDFIELD, M.W. (1989) 'Humanizing de man', *Diacritics*, 19, 2, pp. 35–53.

SCRIBNER, S. (1984) 'Studying working intelligence', In ROGOFF, B. and LAVE, J. (Eds) *Everyday Cognition: Its development in social context*, Cambridge, Massachusetts, Harvard University Press.

SEWELL, B. (1981) *Use of Mathematics by Adults in Everyday Life*, ACACE.

TAYLOR, N. (1990) 'Picking up the pieces: Mathematics education in a fragmented world', in Noss *et al*. (Eds) revised version *Educational Studies in Mathematics* (1991), pp. 235–42.

Thom, M. (1981) 'The unconscious structured as a language', in MacCabe, C. (Ed) *The Talking Cure: Essays in psychoanalysis and Language*, London, Macmillan.

Tiles, M. (1991) *Mathematics and the Image of Reason*, London, Routledge.

Tsatsaroni, A. (1991) *Re-writing Professional Discourse*, PhD Thesis, University of London Library.

Voss, J.F., Perkins, D.N. and Segal, J.W. (Eds) (1991) *Informal Reasoning and Education*, LEB.

Walkerdine, V. (1988) *The Mastery of Reason: Cognitive development and the production of rationality*, RKP.

Walkerdine, V. and Girls and Mathematics Unit (1989) *Counting Girls Out*, Virago.

Woolgar, S. (1987) 'Reconstructing man and machine: A note on sociological critiques of cognitivism', in Bijker, W.E., Hughes, T.P. and Pinch, T.F. (Eds) *The Social Construction of Technological Systems*, London, The MIT Press.

Woolgar, S. (1988) *Science: The very Idea*. Chichester and London, Ellis Horwood and Tavistock Publications.

Chapter 8

On the Ecologies of Mathematical Language and the Rhythms of the Earth[1]

David W. Jardine

Introduction: On the Ecologies of Mathematical Language

> Thinking is not a means to gain knowledge. Thinking cuts furrows in the soil of Being. About 1875, Nietzsche once wrote (Grossoktav WW XI, 20): 'Our thinking should have a vigorous fragrance, like a wheatfield on a summer's night.' How many of us today still have the senses for that fragrance? (Heidegger, 1971, p. 70)

How peculiar it seems to consider this passage as offering images of the thinking and language of mathematics. Mathematical language is language at its most civilized, full of explicit rules of order and clear, unambiguous procedures on how to conduct oneself properly. It appears as an unearthly language, borne of what Alfred North Whitehead called the 'celibacy of the intellect' (cited in Fox, 1983, p. 24). It is fully severed from the messes that moisten our lives and give them an unruly fragrance — 'the juice and the mystery' (Adler, 1989).

Mathematics is considered a serious and exact science, a strict discipline, and such images of seriousness, exactness and strictness often inform how it is taught and how it is understood. It requires silence and neat rows and ramrod postures that imitate its exactitudes. It requires neither joy nor sadness, but a mood of detached inevitability: *anyone* could be here in my place and things would proceed identically.

Finally, mathematics, in its very exactitude, conjures images of a mute and exacting authority and consequent punishments — 'lonely school rooms, where only the sometimes tearful wicked sat over undone sums'. (Thomas, 1967, p. 13)

In the face of such persistent images, mathematics has become simply meaningless for some teachers and some children. It often produces little more than anxiety, apprehension and the unvoiced belief that mathematics is a matter for someone else, for some 'expert' who has abilities and understanding which are 'beyond me', someone better able to 'climb up into their heads' (Le Guin, 1987, p. 10) into this 'closed operational system' (Piaget and Inhelder, 1972, p. 278). For many of us, mathematics has become inhuman, lacking *humus*, lacking any sense of direct presence in, or relevance to, our lives as they are actually lived. It seems that it still is, as it was for the ancient Greeks, a divine science that knows no humility, no place in the moist darkness of the Earth. Hence Dylan Thomas' peculiarly apt pairing of undone sums and wickedness.

In these ecologically desperate times, we are being forced to fundamentally re-think the course we have taken in our understanding of ourselves and our relation to the Earth. We are being forced, in turn, to re-think curriculum in a way that considers, not simply its idealized possibilities as a 'closed operational system', but the real, Earthly conditions under which pursuing such ideals and sustaining such closure are possible. We are faced, here, with a strange paradox: we can do the impossible. We can pursue a vision of our course which in fact works against the ecological conditions of the continuance of that pursuit. We can speak with great aspirations about mathematics curriculum and yet that aspiration, in its ecological assumptions and consequences, can unwittingly work against the actual breath needed to utter it.

Mathematics and mathematics education (not unlike education generally) have dovetailed with Enlightenment visions of human life and human Reason which begin with the (ecologically unsustainable) assumption that humanity is somehow separate from the Earth and that, in acts of understanding, we simply give order(s) to an otherwise unorderly Earth. This is an assumption that cascades down from Immanuel Kant (1767/1964) ('the order and regularity in [what] we call nature, we ourselves introduce' [p. 147]), through the neo-Kantianisms of Piagetian theory (Piaget 1971, p. 57; Jardine 1992b) (where the developing child imposes cosmos on the chaos of experience [Piaget, 1971a, p. 10]) down through some contemporary forms of constructivism.

Contrary to the hubris that suggests, in its most degenerate and bewildering form, that '[we] make all the patterns' (Berry, 1987, p. 5), ecology suggests this: prior to our deliberate interventions and actions (actions which admittedly make patterns), the Earth and our Earthly lives are *already* full of patterns and rhythms of interdependency and kinship. Human action and human understanding (of which the makings of mathematics are a part) do not *make* these Earthly relations — mathematics does not *make* one's heart beat rhythmically, nor does it *make* the patterns of a blue jay's call, nor does it *make* the cycles of breath and day and season. Rather, the makings of mathematics are threaded within a fabric of makings that are always already at work. The makings of mathematics are threaded, in fact in a fabric of makings the integrity of which must be maintained for mathematics to actually be possible for us to do *at all* — we rely, for example, on the convoluted intersections of the rhythms of our blood and the rhythms of day and night and the complex rhythms of oxygen-producing ecosystems. Mathematics cannot simply impose its own makings on this fabric of relations *as if* the Earth can or must live up to the clarity and distinctness that mathematics demands *of itself* (this is, in part, the beginnings of an ecological critique of quantitative research; see Jardine 1992).

The Earth and our Earthly lives — including human understanding and human language and the makings of mathematics — are bound together by an 'anciently perceived likeness between all creatures and the earth of which they are made', where 'like *speaks* to like' (Berry, 1983, p. 76). Even in the pursuit of mathematics, we are deeply and inevitably *of* this Earth. Rather than envisaging it as giving the world order or imposing cosmos on chaos, and ecologically sane understanding of mathematics sees it as participating in, and bespeaking, an order that goes beyond human wanting and willing — an order to which human wanting and willing must be attentive if it is not to overstep the bounds of its Earthly possibilities. Unambiguous mathematical formulations of symmetrical relations, for example, are *akin* to the patterns of these spruce tree branches and needles.[2] These mathematical formulations don't *make* these trees 'symmetrical'.

I realize that it is all too easy, at this juncture, to allow this point to devolve into epistemological and linguistic quarrels — for example, ' "symmetry" is not a feature of the Earth but rather is a concept that we impose on our experience.' Rather than enter into these quarrels, I agree with Thomas Berry (1988) when he suggests that ecological insight requires a type of 'post-critical *naïveté*' — I live here, in the foothills of the Rocky Mountains, and all of my experience, and all of the wisdoms of the peoples who have lived here for thousands of years, tell me beyond any reasonable doubt that this precious place has *its own* integrities and rhythms and patterns which I did not author or impose and to which I must become attentive if my life here and the patterns that my living imposes are to be sustainable. Through such attentiveness, my living bears a deep non-epistemological and non-linguistic kinship to the patterns and integrities of this place. I will admit that it is difficult, in our urbane age of hyper-reflectivity, to experience this kinship and these integrities and rhythms and patterns (the eco-logical traumas we have created certainly attest to this difficulty). We get caught too easily in worlds of our own making. I will admit as well that, in experiencing the Earth — not just talking about it and understanding it, but walking it and breathing it — we do impose our expectations and constructions and conceptions upon it. But a clarification and developmental sequencing of these impositions does not describe a sustainable ecological starting point for our curricular reflec-tions as much as it describes a profound *problem* we face in respecting what comes to meet us in our experience as having *its own* life and integrity. Saying that this leaf or the life of this animal (or the cadences between my heaving breath and the pitch of this hill I am climbing) has no pattern/order of its own and that all we can understand of the Earth are the patterns/constructions we impose on it — this might make a sort of epistemological or philosophical sense. But it points to *a way of life* that is becoming no longer sustainable. In the area of academia — here, in this chapter — the ecological task is to explore how to take up issues of human knowledge and language (and the inevitabilities of human imposition) in a way that preserves and honours our kinship with the Earth and that resists replacing this anciently perceived sense of kinship and alikeness with quarrels of our own invention.

Ecologically speaking, then, re-thinking mathematics and mathematics edu-cation requires, in part, that we seek out the language that allows like to speak to like in generous and sustainable ways, in ways different that the patriarchal rela-tions of mastery and dominance and imposition that haunt our Enlightenment legacy.[3] It requires re-embodying mathematical discourse into a more Earthly discourse — a discourse full of pungent dependencies and ambiguities and relation of likeness and kin and kind, a discourse which is bodily, generative, and 'incur-ably figurative and polysemous'. (Clifford, 1986, p. 5). Mathematics has often understood itself as the *cure* for such figurativity and polysemy — a replacement of relations of ambiguous likeness (or, playfully put, relations of 'kindness' and [to cite the parallel Sanskrit root to 'kin'], 'generosity') with unambiguous relations of univocal identity/difference. Ecology is telling us that the envisaging of eco-logical interdependencies and kinships as problems to be cured simply because of their ambiguities and mysteries is *itself* the source of our ecological despair.

Such a curative response assumes that entities in the world are 'in reality' separate and distinct 'substances' ('a substance is that which requires nothing except itself in order to exist' [Descartes, 1955, p. 255]) and that a language that properly names such a reality is itself full of separate and distinct univocal desig-nations (Jardine, 1990). Ecology is showing us that this is not the case, and that the consequences are dual. Not only does the Earth consist of interdependent nests of kinships and relations and not separate substances which require nothing but themselves in order to exist. The language proper to designating such an inter-dependent Earth is *itself* full of kinships and relations that resist univocal, unam-biguous designation.[4] The desire to overcome such resistance (which some feminist writers [e.g., LeGuin, 1989; Bordo, 1987] link up with the dominance of, and violence towards, women — see note 3) spells ecological disaster. In fact, resist-ance to such 'unambiguous designation' (Gadamer, 1989, p. 434) is precisely a sign of the resilience and life of a living system.

A similar set of moves away from our Enlightenment legacy can be found in Edmund Husserl's phenomenology, albeit in a rather more 'epistemologized' version. Phenomenology wishes to describe the deep embeddedness of the 'exact' sciences in the life-world, in life as it is actually lived. Husserl maintained that we cannot understand the discourse of the sciences by beginning with the 'surrepti-tious substitution of [a] mathematically substructured world of idealities for the only real world . . . our everyday life-world'. (Husserl, 1970, pp. 48–9) If we begin with such a substitution, the resonances of mathematical discourse that echo down through the 'living metaphoricity' (Gadamer, 1989, p. 432) of language, and through the deep ecological rhythms and patterns of bone and breath and flesh end up being formulated as simply a blurring of what is in fact clear, a concretizing of what is in fact abstract, a making profane of the sacred, humiliation. Hence the humiliation felt by a Grade 2 child who believes that these undone sums *have* answers already, without his intervention, and that his intervention has only made things worse. Hence, too, the aura of wickedness that surrounds such worsening — a linking of mathematics to sacredness and purity and a linking of the humili-ation of undone sums to the sins of the flesh.[5]

Phenomenologically, the reverse is the case. The idealizations of mathemati-cal discourse appear in the midst of the world of everyday life and they are not despoiled by such appearance, but enlivened by being connected back to their living sources — 'these are *human* formations, essentially related to *human* actuali-ties and potentialities, and thus belong to this concrete unity of the life-world.' (Husserl, 1979, p. 170) Mathematical discourse resonates deeply with our human-ity understood in its full, fleshy, embodied sense — with our *humus* and the anciently perceived likenesses that tie the entrails of our humanity out into the Earth in ambiguous relations of kinship and kind.[6] And again, this does not de-spoil the idealized exactness of mathematics. Rather, it makes such exactness a *real achievement* that erupts out of life as it is actually lived, rather than seeing such exactness as graciously bestowed 'from above'.[7] Mathematics is not something we have to look up to. It is right in front of us, at our fingertips, caught in the whorl patterns of skin, in the symmetries of the hands, and the rhythms of blood and breath.

Giving and Drawing Boundaries: A Class in Early Childhood Curriculum

> To undergo an experience with language . . . means to let ourselves be properly concerned by the claim of language by entering into and submitting to it. If it is true that [we] find the proper abode of [our] existence in language — whether [we are] aware of it or not — then an experience we undergo with language will touch the innermost nexus of our existence. (Heidegger, 1971, p. 57)
>
> If we may talk of playing games at all, it is not we who play with words, but the nature of language plays with us, long since and always. For language plays with our speech — it likes to let our speech drift away in the more obvious meanings of words. It is as though [we] had to make an effort to live properly in language. It is as though such a dwelling were especially prone to succumb to the danger of commonness. Floundering in commonness is part of the the dangerous game in which, by the nature of language, we are the stakes. (Heidegger, 1968, pp. 18–19)

In a recent undergraduate class in 'Early Childhood Curriculum', I asked the students the following question: in precisely what sense is 198 a *higher* number than 56? The initial reaction to this question was silence, followed by scattered bewilderment and confusion. Although the students were becoming accustomed to this sort of question, the precise intent in asking it was not clear. Some students took the question as an indirect form of accusation — 198 isn't 'really' higher than 56, so the fact that they may have been using this language is an error to be corrected. Others simply struggled to make explicit what would be meant by 'higher'. They found themselves caught up in a swirl of interweaving and interconnecting meanings which seemed to resist being 'straightened out' in any definitive manner. One student slipped into the language, common to young children, of numbers being 'big' and 'little'. Far from remedying our situation, it simply multiplied the problem, so to speak.

The question then arose: if we don't know precisely what we mean when we use such language, how is it that we can feel confident when we attempt to teach such aspects of mathematics to young children? Implicit here is the equation of the ability to teach something with knowing what it is that you are teaching. This equation is one which I tend to encourage. However, there is a deeper supposition here that must be addressed.

Implicit here is the equation of 'knowing what it is you are teaching' with being able to be precise, to be exact and fully explicit, to provide foreclosed, literal definitions and the like. One of the points I hoped to educe with my question was that we *do* know what it means to say that 198 is 'higher' than 56, but that this knowing is not definitional, literal, univocal or clear. It interweaves in unanticipated ways with the young child building a higher and higher tower of wooden blocks, with the fact that we can speak meaningfully of 'counting *up* to ten', or with the fact that growing older means growing 'up', and growing up means becoming taller, and that the 'higher' one's chronological age, the 'bigger' one is, and that, for children, importance bears a resemblance to height and age, and so on.

The initial difficulty with such interweavings is precisely this 'and so on'.

Although reflecting on our language can bring forth unanticipated, playful interweavings of experience, it is never quite clear, in following such interweavings, if one has gone too far. After all, is it too much to say that the progression of higher and higher numbers orients to infinity, i.e., to God, the most High, and that numbers which fall below the 'ground' (below where we stand, below '[ground] zero') have a dark and negative character? Or is it too much to say that when counting higher and higher quantities, we must keep track of them by consistently bringing them back to Earth, back to base, so that we use 'base ten' as a way of preventing the pile from spiralling upward out of sight, a way of keeping them at our fingertips (our digits)? that we therefore organize higher and higher quantities into groups we can manage or handle, into 'handfuls'?

Clearly these examples 'go too far', but they are not altogether meaningless simply because they cannot be resolved once and for all into some univocal 'definition' would bind them all together in relations of unambiguous identity. These examples are not *identical* to each other, but neither are they simply *different*. Rather, they all describe the same *kind* of thing. They are *like* each other:

> As in spinning a thread, we twist fibre on fibre. And the strength of the thread does not reside in the fact that some one fibre runs through its whole length, but in the overlapping of many fibres. (Wittgenstein, 1968, p. 32) Don't say: There *must* be something common . . . but *look and see* whether there is anything common to all. — For if you look at them you will not see something that is common to *all*, but similarities, relationships, and a whole series of them at that. To repeat: don't think, but look! [p. 31] We see a complicated network of similarities, overlapping and criss-crossing: sometimes overall similarities, sometimes similarities of detail. I can think of no better expression to characterize these similarities than 'family resemblances'. (*Familienähnlichkeiten*) (p. 32)

Such relations of likeness and kind-ness/kinship and family resemblance are, as these metaphors suggest, full of generativity and life — it seems that new possibilities, new relations, new likenesses simply keep coming (in a way akin to how new children, with new ideas and formulations and experiences, keep arriving in the mathematics classroom). It is never quite clear just what the para-meters are for this kind of phenomenon — each new example, each new interweaving thread or fibre, re-opens the 'kind' to new permutations and possibilities and each new permutation has a cascade effect, rattling through each instantiation, giving it new relations. For example, when I used this phenomenon as an example in a graduate class, a colleague suggested that this whole array of relations becomes inverted if we consider ordinal instead of cardinal numbers. This suggestion is not simply additive to the list given above (like some discrete substance which needs nothing except itself in order to exist). This suggestion arrives *already bearing relations*. It moves indiscretely through this list, bearing/generating relations as it proceeds. It inverts the bodily metaphor and ushers in images of 'ground' and 'grounding/foundation', where 'what comes first' is now visible as 'the lowest' (God, the most High, is also 'number one').[8]

Not only does this new suggestion re-generate the living character of the whole list cited above. It lets us see that there is something incorrect about speaking about the *whole* list without hesitation and caution. 'The whole', in this case, is never simply given (Gadamer, 1989, p. 33) as something that can simply be univocally designated independently of the interdependent nest of threads that make it up. The inherent ambiguity of the list is thus not an accident that must needs be fixed. Rather:

> There is quite a bit of 'give', 'flexibility', indeterminacy or vagueness *right within the concept itself*, with the result that the meaning remains *essentially* incomplete, so underdetermined that it cannot be clearly understood until further reference is made to some mode or modes of realization [my emphasis]. (Norris-Clarke, 1976, p. 67)

The meaning of 'higher and lower numbers' is not separate from its instances, like some ghostly 'idea' that could be univocally named independently of those instances. If we recall Wittgenstein's threads of family resemblances, the 'kind' being named here *is* its diverse instances, and there is no independent, over-arching 'family member' that can fully speak for the rich diversity of all the rest of the family members and thus render them silent. To fully understand the kind, we cannot revert to some foreclosing, overarching pattern (some patri-archal voice which can simply impose itself on the rest of the members of the kind without heeding the generative difference that each member makes). Rather, understanding requires 'running up and down the known *range* of cases to which it applies, actually calling up the spectrum of different exemplifications, and then *catching the point*'. (Norris-Clarke, 1976, p. 68).

This is not to say that abstraction is impossible. We *can* produce and name an 'overarching pattern' which binds all these cases together and which names what we anticipate 'the whole' to be. However, there is another sense in which 'the whole list' is never given. Not only are we always in the midst of working through the diversity of exemplifications in order to 'catch the point'. *There is always another instance just about to arrive.* The full meaning of 'higher and lower numbers' is always in a state of generative suspense. Its full and final meaning is *always* 'yet to be decided' (Gadamer, 1989, p. 333). We cannot say once and for all what the relation of kind are in an embodied sense of number, because we can never know what might come of it in the future as new cases arrive and require us to run down the range of cases anew. The young child who stretches out his arms and says 'I have a *miiiiiilion* stickers at home!' shows us, in the raising of his voice, in the strectching of his arms and the word, that the issue of an embodied sense of number is not a closed, given issue, but an open, yet-to-be-given one. In order to understand 'the kind', we must proceed, not with foreclosing impositions of our constructions upon it, but with 'a consciousness that must leave the door ajar' (Hillman, 1987, p. 154), open to the arrival of that which outstrips our constructions and goes beyond our anticipations.

The strength of Wittgenstein's thread of family resemblance is not simply in the *overlapped* fibres, but in the *overlapping* of fibres. As with relations of kinship and family resemblance, the 'kind' *exists* only if new kin keep coming. Put differently, it only exists if the kind remains open to the arrival of the new which will renew and transform it and open it again. The kind exists, therefore, only if it resists *precisely that sort of foreclosure demanded of unambiguous designation*: the kind *needs* the next case to remain living and vital and to avoid closure and calcification. Thus, 'the kind' does not simply *apply* to the case and represent it. Rather, the case fecundly enters into the flesh of the kind and makes 'waver and tremble' (Caputo, 1987, p. 6) what we have heretofore understood the kind to be. 'Kinds' are therefore *always* and *necessarily* 'yet to be decided' — 'the whole list' is never simply a given to be univocally named.

Suggesting that the whole is never simply given suggests an image of education itself: that our already established understanding of the world is never established and fixed once and for all, but is necessarily *open to the arrival of the young*. More strongly put, it suggests that such re-generative arrival is somehow *essential* to our understanding of the world if that understanding is to remain vital.

This suggests an ecologically delicate matter: it is not only that children need the already established curriculum in order to understand their course. This is certainly the case. As with a vibrant ecological system, already established, 'old growth' protects the young by protecting the living conditions under which such new growth can be nurtured — this is the strength of the ties that bind and the reliability and integrity and strength of the 'kind'. However, to pursue this ecological metaphor, *our already established course needs children in order for it to remain alive and invigorated*. An ecosystem which forecloses against the re-generative arrival of the young is unsustainable. Once the curriculum becomes calcified into static rules and regulations — univocal, unambiguous designations — it becomes closed to the arrival of the new. It becomes *ungenerous* and *un-kind*. In such a 'closed operational system', the next child will, in fact, make no real difference — like those undone sums, where anyone could be here in my place and where my doing of these sums leaves them untouched and untransformed. Worse yet, the next child can be nothing but an annoyance — like so many classrooms where the boundaries of the curriculum and the objectives of the lesson plans are already set and the arrival of the child can only replicate this curriculum and meet these objectives exactly (identity) or despoil them (difference). Ecologically speaking, both of these extremities are unsustainable.

It is precisely the sense of security that comes from the fixing of boundaries that many teachers desire. As Wendell Berry (1987) notes, such boundaries can at once provide a sense of security and be profoundly disruptive: just as they bring under control what falls *inside* the boundary, what is left *outside* the boundary is henceforth understood to be simply *out of control*. From the point of view of univocal designation, the ambiguous, 'living metaphoricity' of language begins to appear as simply meaningless or chaotic. We can, from such a premise, falsely believe that our task in teaching is to somehow 'conquer' the 'wilderness' by imposing order on it. As Alice Miller (1989) has noted, the multivocity and ambiguity that children bring to the classroom can become envisaged as nothing more than wild(er)ness and unruliness. No longer are children understood as our kin or our kind, and no longer is the task to bring out these relations of kind between us and with the Earth. We need not listen to the unvoiced experiences they have already undergone *before* our concerted efforts at 'taming' them. They are not envisaged as ecological beings who are caught, with us, in an already working nest of relations. Rather, they become simply separate objects to be controlled and manipulated in *imposed* relations of dominance and mastery, since they are little more than threats to the security of the boundaries we have set. Teaching thus becomes a 'monstrous state of seige' (Smith, 1988) between the old and the young. Once the bonds of kinship and relations of kind are broken, both the old and the young become understood only in their worst aspects. Out of relation to the nurturing and protecting usherance of the young into the world, the old becomes harsh, static, foreclosing, and unforgiving: the senatorial aspect of age as the passing on of wisdoms becomes mere senility. Out of relationship to the established world that protects and nurtures them, the young no longer provide generativity and renewal, but become simply puerile, cut loose, abandoned.

The telling point in this class demonstration is that even in the use of terms like 'higher' and 'lower', we *already* understood what each other was talking about without aspiring to the boundaries and securities of univocity and exactness: the kinships that bound us together were visible as *already at work 'before we knew it'*. As Ludwig Wittgenstein (1968) noted, we can *draw* a boundary around these concepts, 'but I can also use [them] so that the extension of the concept is *not* closed by a frontier' (p. 33) Regarding the desire we may have to define the term 'higher', to draw a boundary or frontier, Wittgenstein rather playfully says 'that never troubled you before when you used the word'. (p. 33) The attempt to bind discourse to a central, singular, unambiguous designation reflects *only* our need for practical exigency and we become troubled only when explicitly *called upon* to produce a boundary around such a centre

> If someone were to draw a sharp boundary I could not acknowledge it as the one that I too always wanted to draw, or had drawn in my mind. For I did not want to draw one at all. His concept can then be said to be not *the same* as mine, but akin to it. The kinship is just as undeniable as the difference. (Wittgenstein, 1968, p. 36)

And, as Wittgenstein further notes, I can *draw* boundaries or frontiers in such matters, but I can never *give* such matters a boundary. (p. 33) In its lived, lively usage as a mathematical term, the term 'higher' resonates in an untroublesome way, beyond the idealized frontiers that we *can* draw, but *cannot* give. We were not compelled, in this ECE class, to declare in the end that either 198 'really' *is* higher than 56, or that it *is not*, even though such declarations might have made us feel more secure and more in control. Perhaps this is why a student-teacher said recently, when she realized that the topic of her lesson might be one with which the children were already vaguely familiar, 'Wait, I'm not ready!' This is the beginning of a recognition that life goes on beyond our earnest intentions and actions as teachers and that this familiarity/family resemblance that the child brings has its own reliances and securities and strengths which we share with them (not identically, but in relations of kind). These family resemblances describe an ecological strength that we share with them: a common fortitude in which we can both take comfort. It is the first glimmerings of a precious realization so essential for student teachers to undergo — that understanding erupts out of life itself, and not simply as a response to an act of teaching and therefore, that teaching must first and foremost attune itself to what is *already at work* in our lives and the lives of the children we teach. And this, in turn, is the beginning of a precious ecological realization that the Earth and our Earthly lives have an integrity to which our acts and intentions must become attentive so as not to violate this integrity in the name of univocally designated lesson objectives and the like.

Part of the purpose in asking this question to these student-teachers, then, was to help them see that what goes beyond their control and mastery is not simply *chaos* and that they can rely upon these already working relations in which they dwell with children in relations of 'kind-ness'. In a peculiar way, mathematics in its fleshed out sense, is something that 'happens to us beyond our wanting and willing' (Gadamer, 1989, p. 18) — in walking down the stairs, the 2 year-old child's life is already pacing out mathematics in the rhythms of his steps, in the cadences of his breath, and in the recurring patterns of his mother's laughter.

Conclusion

> Every word breaks forth as if from a centre and is related to a whole through which alone it is a word. Every word causes the whole of the language to which it belongs to resonate and the whole world-view that underlies it to appear. Thus, every word carries with it the unsaid. The occasionality of human speech is not a causal imperfection; it is, rather, the logical expression of the living virtuality of speech that brings a totality of meaning into play, without being able to express it totally. (Gadamer, 1989, p. 458)

> The rhythm of a song or a poem rises, no doubt, in reference to the pulse and breath of the poet. But that is too specialized an accounting; it rises also in reference to daily and seasonal — and surely even longer — rhythms in the life of the poet and in the life that surrounds him. The rhythm of a poem resonates with these larger rhythms that surround it; it fills its environment with sympathetic vibrations. Rhyme, which is a function of rhythm, may suggest this sort of resonance; it marks the coincidences of smaller structures with larger ones, as when the day, the month, and the year all end at the same moment. Song, then, is a force opposed to speciality and to isolation. It is the testimony of the singer's inescapable relation to the earth, to the human community, and also to tradition. (Berry, 1983, p. 17)

> Rhyme leads one no doubt to hear in language a very ancient cosmology. Rhyme is not only an echo from word to word. Arrangement for arrangement, the order of language evokes and mimes a cosmic order. In realizing itself, rhyme is tuned in to [this cosmology]. Rhyme and meter are praise. An indirect theology. (Meschonnic, 1988, p. 93)

A 7-year-old friend of my son came to visit us, and I told him about the huge pond in our neighbour's field. The spring runoff had created a slough about eight feet deep. After discussing that it would be over his head if he fell in, over my son's head, and even over *my* head, he asked, 'If a hundred year old man stepped in it, would it be over *his* head too?' I answered, 'Yes, it's *that* deep.'

I told this tale to a mathematics colleague and he said 'Isn't it cute when kids get things so mixed up?'

If we lose a sense of interweaving kinships inherent in this tale, the ways that its relations of bodily height and importance and age and depth 'rhyme analogically' (Berry, 1983, p. 75), the way that this tale has a deep 'analogical integrity' (Berry, 1988, p. 138), we not only lose a sense of our kinship with this child. We also lose a sense of kinship *with ourselves*. We become cut off from our own bodily being and mathematics becomes a disembodied, inhuman discipline, full of my colleague's harsh condescensions of 'cuteness'.

One of the purposes of the class described above was to begin to re-invest these students in the reliabilities of their own fleshy, mathematical being such that they can finally *hear*, not only children, but their own breath and bearing of kinship with children and with the Earth. This child's tale carries with it is own reliable patterns which do not need our constructions and impositions, but simply our openness and care and attention to what is *already at work beyond our wanting and willing*. We need to become obedient: *ab audire*, to heed, to listen.[9] As Ursula LeGuin (1987) has put it, 'Civilized Man has gone deaf,' (p. 13) and the mathematics curriculum has become, for so many of us, language at its most civilized.

Allowing ourselves the freedom to explore the generativity and living metaphoricity of language is at once endangering ourselves and the tranquillity that our boundaries provide. After our exploration of mathematical language in this class, some students said that they have *more* difficulty with language than before, *more* difficulty in finding comfort in the flat, univocal, familiar surfaces of things. The work they did in this class was not meant to make their lives *easier*, but to begin to free them for the real difficulty, the real claim that language makes on us. Some have described how this experience has made them more careful in their language, more attentive to the lessons and themes that our language and the language of children have to offer. For some, however, it induced a sort of temporary paralysis, rendering them silent, speechless, fearful, in some sense, of the unvoiced and unintended implications of meaning that issue with every word. In the long run, this silence might be a good sign. Out from under the noisy clatter of tricks and techniques they have mastered, they may have come upon their silent kinship with children.

If the discipline of mathematics were as unEarthly and pristine and virginal and self-enclosed as it often announces itself to be (if it could *give* itself a boundary, and not merely *draw* one), there could never be any 'new ones' among us. It is precisely a loving attention to these 'new ones' (an act in attunement to the openness and generosity of 'the kind') that defines our special task as teachers.

How peculiar it still seems to consider all this as offering images of the thinking and language of mathematics. But when the 3-year-old child announces that he or she is going to 'count all the way up to ten', literal and disciplined and exacting mathematicians will *already* understand what has been said, even though such understanding belies the unambiguous designations to which they may be professionally accustomed.

Notes

1. Portions of this chapter originally appeared in *Educational Theory* under the title 'On the Humility of Mathematical Language'. (see references under Jardine 1990a).
2. These kinships are not *themselves* unambiguous and therefore, if they are to be generously understood, mere mathematical imposition (which demands unambiguous designation) will not do. This would simply allow the domination of the kinship by one member of it. Put differently, if we are to understand mathematics in its relationships of kinship and kin, we must go beyond its indigenous demands

as an unambiguous, 'closed operational system'. We must find a way that mathematics can become conversant with its kin.

3. The parallels between this legacy and the legacies of colonialism — imposing order on an uncivilized, unruly world — are telling and unavoidable (see Jardine, 1992b for an exploration of the inherent colonialism of Kantian and Piagetian visions of human understanding). Equally telling is an emerging critique of representational knowledge — i.e., a form of knowledge which suggests that a singular, univocal voice is able to stand in for, and represent, a multiplicity of voices:

> The critique of colonialism in the postwar period — an undermining of The West's ability to represent other societies — has been reinforced by an important process of theorizing about the limits of representation itself. (Clifford, 1986, p. 10)
>
> Once dialogism and polyphony are recognized . . . monophonic authority is questioned and revealed to be characteristic of a science that has claimed to *represent* cultures. (p. 15)

And this has been precisely the claim of science in general and mathematics in particular in the guise of quantitative research: that the rich diversity and multiplicity of the Earth can be subjected without qualms to quantification and that the unambiguous monophonic results can claim to *represent* that diversity. Resisting this tendency, Clifford (1986a) suggests that we must move from a vision of knowledge as representational (where one claims that 'this stands in for that', 'this is (or is not) that' — a reduction to relations of identity and difference) to a vision of knowledge as allegorical or metaphorical (where one claims that 'this is a story about that', 'this is *like* that' — an expansion to relations of likeness and 'kind'). In such a case, to understand, say, the 'puddle story' cited in this chapter, I cannot proceed to say in a foreclosing way what it means. Rather, to understand it requires that I enter into the tale it tells and *tell another story* which adds to it, moves it forward in relations of kind. This generative, re-telling work describes the character of interpretive research (Jardine, 1992a).

This critique of representationalism is at once an ecological critique in the sense that it speaks on behalf of the richness and diversity of living systems and against the replacement of living kinship systems with the imposition and dominance of any one member of that system. It is also an implicit feminist critique of the 'monophonic' character of patriarchal forms of knowledge which silence the rich diversity of 'our kin' in favour of a singular, foreclosing, declarative voice.

4. There is a fascinating parallel here to the work of Ludwig Wittgenstein, where, in his *Tractatus Logico-Philosophicus* (1961), he maintained that 'the world is all that is the case' (p. 7) and that 'each item can be the case or not the case while everything else remains the same'. (p. 7) Operative here is the (ecologically disastrous) assumption that all entities are in fact separate, and that language operates best when it univocally designates such separate entities. In his later work, the *Philosophical Investigations* (1968) he showed how our everyday language operates in terms of nests of family resemblance which are not bound to a single univocal meaning but which work in generative, multivocal ways. One can read here a certain ecological consequence by reading this move of Wittgenstein's back into our image of the Earth: it is *not* composed of separate and distinct entities which are what they are independent of everything else. If one member of a 'family resemblance' changes, it has a cascading effect on *every* member. Wittgenstein's later theory suggests that the world is bound together in relations of kind. It is fascinating, then, to understand this transformation of Wittgenstein's work in his own terms: as he suggested

in his later work, forms of language constitute forms of life. The notions of 'family resemblance' and 'kinship' from the *Philosophical Investigations* thereby suggest not only a different epistemological and linguistic theory, but a different way of understanding, of *living* one's life.

5. Victor Turner (1987), citing the work of Mary Douglas, suggests that there is an archaic linkage between *unclarity* and *uncleanness*: that the purifications of knowledge found, for example, in the work of Descartes are precisely that — purification rituals aimed at eliminating the ambiguities/sins of the flesh. Mathematics thus becomes envisaged as a 'pure' discipline in the sense that it has shed the unclarity/uncleanness of the body (one need only think of how Piaget's developmental stages end with formal operations which have shed their bodily inheritances). Hence the metaphors of 'despoiled results' or 'contaminated results' found in quantitative research (see Jardine, 1992).

6. Of course, Edmund Husserl's particular vision of phenomenology linked inevitably with a notion of 'essence' which he conceives as able to be 'fixed once and for all in a way equally accessible to all'. (1970, p. 110) There thus remains in phenomenology the legacy of clarity/purity/cleanness and unambiguous designation found in Enlightenment visions of rationality. See Jardine (1992) for a further exploration of the essentialism of Husserlian phenomenology and its pedagogical and ecological consequences.

7. This is the fundamental gesture of Jean Piaget's genetic epistemology — to understand the 'continuity between life and intelligence' (1952, p. 352) by formulating logico-mathematical operations as a *real achievement of development*. What is missing from Piaget's account is the living inter-relationships with children which we still bear in our language, in our experiences, in our hearts. His formulation of the stages of development as sequential reconstructions offer us little recourse for understanding children except to turn them into an object of scientific discourse. The claim implicit in a focus on analogical language is that, prior to such reconstructions, we are already in relation to children as 'kin'. A network of interweaving relationships is *already at play* (see Jardine and Morgan, 1988; and Jardine, 1988). It is this territory of interweaving relationships that are already at play 'underneath' the reconstructions of scientific discourse that is the domain of phenomenology. However, as noted in note 6, phenomenology itself falls prey to a form of reconstructive essentialism which belies the generosity and ambiguity of 'kinds'.

8. There is a wonderful, convoluted link here between the vision of God as 'one' — the visions of monotheism — and the claims of univocity and representational knowledge (see note 3). (There is another convoluted link between the legacies of constructivism, where the child imposes cosmos on chaos, and the images of Jewish and Christian creation — God's face over the formless waters). Mathematics can be seen as a version of monotheism and monophonic authority, where the 'I am' of God (which imposed cosmos on chaos) is replaced with the 'I am' of Cartesian doubt (which, through Kant and Piaget, imposes cosmos on chaos through the articulations of mathematics). For a further exploration of this point, see Jardine, 1992.

9. This does not mean that the curriculum should be child-centered. In paying careful attention to this child's tale, it is not *the child* that is at the centre, but rather the relations and family resemblances that are at work in the tale itself. This is not child-centeredness, but neither is it simply its opposite, teacher-centeredness. Both of these options lead to little more than monstrous states of siege. Both of these options spell ecological disaster, because both turn away from those relations that house us all.

David W. Jardine

References

ADLER, M. (1989) 'The juice and the mystery', in PLANT, J. (1989) *Healing the Wounds: The Promise of Ecofeminism*, Toronto, Between the Lines Press.
ARENDT, H. (1969) *Between Past and Future*, New York, Penguin Books.
BERRY, T. (1988) *The Dream of the Earth*, San Francisco, Sierra Club Books.
BERRY, W. (1983) *Standing By Words*, San Francisco, North Point Press.
BERRY, W. (1987) *Home Economics*, San Francisco, North Point Press.
BERRY, W. (1988) 'The profit in work's pleasure', *Harper's Magazine*, March.
BOHM, D. (1985) *Wholeness and Implicate Order*, New York, Arc Books.
BORDO, S. (1987) *The Flight to Objectivity*, Albany, State University of New York Press.
CAPUTO, J. (1987) *Radical Hermeneutics: Repetition, Deconstruction and the Hermeneutic Project*, Bloomington, Indiana State University Press.
CLIFFORD, J. (1986) 'Introduction: Partial truths', in CLIFFORD, J. and MARCUS, G. (1986) *Writing Culture: The Poetics and Politics of Ethnography*, Berkeley, University of California Press.
CLIFFORD, J. (1986a) 'On ethnographic allegory', in CLIFFORD, J. and MARCUS, G. (1986) *Writing Culture: The Poetics and Politics of Ethnography*, Berkeley, University of California Press.
DESCARTES, R. (1955) *Descartes Selections*, New York, Charles Scribners' Sons.
FOX, M. (1983) *Original Blessing*, Santa Fe, Bear and Co.
GADAMER, H.G. (1989) *Truth and Method*, New York, Continuum Books.
HEIDEGGER, M. (1968) *What is Called Thinking?*, New York, Harper and Row.
HEIDEGGER, M. (1971) 'The nature of language', *On the Way to Language*, New York, Harper and Row.
HEIDEGGER, M. (1977) 'Modern science, metaphysics and mathematics', *Basic Writings*, New York, Harper and Row.
HILLMAN, J. (1987) 'Notes on Opportunism', in HILLMAN, J. *Puer Papers*, Dallas, Spring Publications.
HUSSERL, E. (1970) *Crisis of European Sciences*, Evanston, Northwestern University Press.
JARDINE, D. (1988) 'There are children all around us', *Journal of Educational Thought*, 22A, 2.
JARDINE, D. (1990) 'Awakening from Descartes' nightmare: On the love of ambiguity in phenomenological approaches to education', *Studies in Philosophy and Education*, 10, 1.
JARDINE, D. (1990a) 'On the humility of mathematical language', *Educational Theory*, 40, 2.
JARDINE, D. (1992) *Speaking with a Boneless Tongue*, Bragg Creek, Makyo Press.
JARDINE, D. (1992a) 'The fecundity of the individual case: Considerations of the pedagogic heart of interpretive work', *British Journal of Philosophy and Education*, 26, 1, pp. 51–61.
JARDINE, D. (1992b) 'Immanuel Kant, Jean Piaget and the rage for order: Hints of the colonial spirit in pedagogy', *Educational Philosophy and Theory*, 23, 1, pp. 28–43.
JARDINE, D. and MORGAN, C.A.V. (1988) 'Analogy as a model for the development of representational abilities in children', *Educational Theory*, 37, 3, Summer.
KANT, I. (1767/1964) *Critique of Pure Reason*, London, Macmillan.
LE GUIN, U. (1987) *Buffalo Gals and Other Animal Presences*, Santa Barbara, Capra Press.
LE GUIN, U. (1989) 'Women/wilderness', in PLANT, J. *Healing the Wounds: The Promise of Ecofeminism*, Toronto, Between the Lines Press.
MESCHONNIC, H. (1988) 'Rhyme and life', *Critical Inquiry*, 15, Autumn.

MILLER, A. (1989) *For Your Own Good: Hidden Cruelty in Child-Rearing and the Roots of Violence*, Toronto, Collins Books.

NORRIS-CLARKE, W. (1976) 'Analogy and the meaningfulness of language about God: A reply to Kai Nielsen', *The Thomist*, 40.

PIAGET, J. (1952) *Origins of Intelligence in Children*, New York, International Universities Press.

PIAGET, J. (1971) *Insights and Illusions of Philosophy*, New York, New American Library.

PIAGET, J. (1971a) *The Construction of Reality in the Child*, New York, Ballantine Books.

PIAGET, J. and INHELDER, B. (1972) *The Child's Construction of Number*, London, Routledge and Kegan Paul.

SMITH, D. (1988) 'Children and the Gods of war', *Journal of Educational Thought*, 22, 2A.

THOMAS, D. (1967) 'Reminiscences of childhood', *Quite Early one Morning*, London, Aldine Press.

TURNER, V. (1987) 'Betwixt and between: The liminal period in rites of passage', in MAHDI, L., FOSTER, S. and LITTLE, M. (Eds) *Betwixt and Between: Patterns of Masculine and Feminine Initiation*, LaSalle, Open Court Books.

WITTGENSTEIN, L. (1961) *Tractatus Logico-Philosophicus*, London, Routledge and Kegan Paul.

WITTGENSTEIN, L. (1968) *Philosophical Investigations*, Oxford, Basil Blackwell.

Chapter 9

Discursive Saturation and School Mathematics Texts: A Strand from a Language of Description

Paul Dowling

My intention, in this chapter, is to provide a theoretical and empirical representation of a project in which I have attempted to generate a theoretical framework — a language of description — for the sociological analysis of pedagogic texts (Dowling, 1993a). The project is empirically concerned with the secondary school mathematics scheme, *SMP 11–16*[1] and also entails a reading of textbooks within the scheme. I shall begin the chapter with an introduction to the idea of a language of description. Following this introduction, I shall pick up a particular strand within the general theoretical orientation of my own project and follow this through to the production of data. It will be necessary to give some introduction to the language more generally. However, this will necessarily be partial and, to a certain extent, elliptical. The tearing out of a particular strand will, unfortunately, give rise to a methodological lesion and to the associated unstaunched haemorrhaging of connotations and unexplored references.

The Idea of a Language of Description

The idea of a language of description is explicitly proposed by Bernstein in his 'Introduction' to *Class, Codes and Control*, Volume 5 (in press). However, the notion is implicit (at least) in all of his work and much of that with which he has been directly associated since the 1960s. Essentially, a language of description is concerned with the move from theory to the production of empirical data out of information, that is, with translating from one language (the observed world) to another (the theory). In his introduction, Bernstein provides a *post hoc* summary of his methodology in a form which I have interpreted (with some minor alterations to terminology)[2] in Figure 9.1.

The topmost term in Figure 9.1, the 'theoretical referents', refers to the general theoretical orientation of the language. Included within this category would be work which has generated, in the author of the language, predispositions to view the world in particular ways. In my own case, this would certainly include the work of Bernstein, himself, also Louis Althusser, Pierre Bourdieu, Umberto Eco and Michel Foucault, among others. The 'theoretical propositions' — the second term in Figure 9.1 — are more explicit and consistent statements which

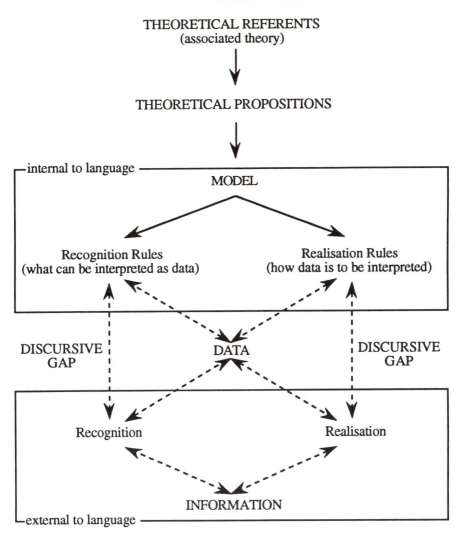

THEORETICAL REFERENTS
(associated theory)

THEORETICAL PROPOSITIONS

internal to language

MODEL

Recognition Rules
(what can be interpreted as data)

Realisation Rules
(how data is to be interpreted)

DISCURSIVE
GAP

DATA

DISCURSIVE
GAP

Recognition

Realisation

INFORMATION

external to language

Figure 9.1:   *Structure and Application of a Language of Description*

have arisen out of a critical engagement with the theoretical referents. They comprise what might be referred to as a theoretical manifesto for the more detailed work which is to follow.

The language of description, itself, comprises, firstly, a consistent theoretical model which has been derived from the theoretical propositions. Secondly, the language must specify what is to count as its empirical object — recognition rules. Thirdly, it must include 'realization rules' which specify how information is to be read as data. The solid lines with single arrows, in Figure 9.1, indicate lines of deductive argument.

Since the language specifies what can count as its empirical object and how that object is to be interpreted, there is a danger that the model itself will not come under scrutiny, that sociology will be reduced to the projection of armchair theorizings onto the world on the other side of the front room window. Thus, in Figure 9.1, there is a 'discursive gap' 'between' that which is internal to the language of description and that which is external to it. Data is shown within this gap. Data can be understood as the product of the recognition and realization rules of the language, but there will always be an excess in terms of possible interpretation. The 'discursive gap' is the region of the 'yet-to-be-described', which concerns the need for an explicit recognition of the possibility of transformations in the language arising out of specific empirical engagements with the world.

This reflexive possibility has not been ignored in the project to which this chapter refers. Certainly, the exposition given above and in that which follows represents an essentially deductive structure. However, in their production, the language of description, and, indeed, the theoretical propositions and referents, were also shaped in and by an immersion in the informational. The process, then, comprised a dialogue between the theoretical and the empirical, the deductive and the inductive. The product is a tactical conclusion, or cadence, which of necessity elides its own history.

I shall now move on to a brief consideration of a specific theme within the general theoretical orientation of my particular language of description, that is, the distinction between abstract and concrete practice.

Abstract and Concrete Practice

A distinction between the abstract and the concrete has been made in a variety of ways within the social sciences in the twentieth century. Vygotsky (1986), for example, distinguishes between complex and conceptual thinking as levels in respect of both individual and societal development. In the work of his colleague, Alexander Luria (1976), this distinction is realized as situational and abstract thinking. Subjects employing the latter are exploiting the higher capacities of language associated with literacy, classifying objects according to abstract categories which are or can be relatively independent of the practical situations in which the objects are encountered. By contrast:

> Subjects who gravitate towards [concrete or situational thinking] do not sort objects into logical categories but incorporate them into graphic-functional situations drawn from life and reproduced from memory. These subjects group together objects such as a table, a tablecloth, a plate, a knife, a fork, bread, meat, and an apple, thereby reconstructing a 'meal' situation in which these objects have some use. (Luria, 1976, p. 49)

The marxist epistemology of Vygotsky and Luria constitutes consciousness as a product of the social. However, the constitution of the social itself is very much undertheorized in this work. The association of conceptual thinking with literacy, for example, hardly specifies a mode of production. Basil Bernstein (1990), on the other hand, establishes a distinction which is similar to the Vygotsky/Luria dichotomy via a description of the social in terms of a Durkheimian model of the division of labour:

The simpler the social division of labour, and the more specific and local the relation between an agent and its material base, the more direct the relation between meanings and a specific material base, and the greater the probability of a restricted coding orientation. The more complex the social division of labour, and the less specific and local the relation between an agent and its material base, the more indirect the relation between meanings and a specific material base, and the greater the probability of an elaborated coding orientation. (Bernstein, 1990, p. 20)

'Restricted coding orientation' refers to the propensity to generate meanings which are highly context dependent; 'elaborated coding orientation' represents an inclination to context independence. This clearly resonates with situational/abstract thinking, but Bernstein has associated his modality of speech codes with Durkheim's (1984) distinction between mechanical and organic solidarity in his classification of the division of labour in society. Furthermore, Bernstein uses the Durkheimian opposition, not to distinguish between societies or their stages of development, but to establish the specificity of the division of labour in different class locations within a society. Speech code orientation is thus distributed (but not determined) by social class.

In both the Vygotsky/Luria and Bernstein conceptions, the concrete/abstract or local/general opposition is a modality of the discursive, that is, it concerns language. In distinguishing between his sensori-motor and pre-operational stages, Jean Piaget (1972) points to the importance of the occurrence of language in facilitating the development between the stages. Piaget thus conceptualizes a pre-linguistic mode of thinking which is thereby outside of discourse. Vygotsky also conceives of pre-linguistic thought, but fails to theorize it, being concerned only with the development of thought through speech. Michel Foucault intends to avoid linguistic reductionism through his introduction of the term 'apparatus' (*dispositif*), which incorporates discursive and non-discursive elements. However, when pressed, in an interview, on how he might be 'getting at' a non-discursive domain, Foucault capitulates:

> . . . it doesn't much matter for my notion of the apparatus to be able to say that this is discursive and that isn't. If you take Gabriel's architectural plan for the Military School together with the actual construction of the School, how is one to say what is discursive and what institutional? That would only interest me if the building didn't conform with the plan. But I don't think it's very important to be able to make that distinction, given that my problem isn't a linguistic one. (Foucault, 1980, pp. 197–8)

Such nonchalance is, perhaps, to be expected in one who rarely makes explicit the principles of his descriptions. Descriptions which would thereby lay claim to a certain transparency of data, were it not for their stunning originality. Foucault clearly needs to index a discursive/non-discursive differentiation, because therein lies the inevitability of the 'failure' of 'programmes' which are realized in purely discursive terms. These programmes are associated with 'technologies' which extend beyond the discursive and, therefore, beyond its control. The result is the subjectless 'strategies' discussed by Foucault in the interview cited above.[3] Foucault's originality lies precisely in his use of such terms. The breadth of these concepts, however, of necessity allows a great deal of scope for idiosyncratic interpretation. Foucault's originality resides in his organizing strategies rather than in the precision of his histories. His ultimate refusal to establish a clear distinction between the discursive and the non-discursive is, possibly, a consequence of his recognition of a paradox: were he to provide such a distinction, then he would either have defined the limits of the discursive within discourse itself[4], or he would have rendered the non-discursive discursive[5]. Jacques Lacan understands the problem in his indexing of the unconscious:

> The unconscious is that part of the concrete discourse, insofar as it is transindividual, that is not at the disposal of the subject in re-establishing the continuity of his [sic] conscious discourse. (Lacan, 1977, p. 49)

The definition invokes a sense of an excess of human practices over that which can be realized within what I am referring to as the discursive, that which can be reduced to the linguistic. This excess corresponds to Lacan's 'unconscious' (in the paper cited) and to Heidegger's (1962) 'background'. The excess can never be fully realized in language, although its extent will vary between different aspects and instances of practice. The importance of this heuristic proposition is that it enables me to differentiate between different modes of practice within the discursive in terms of the extensiveness of the non-discursive excess. Thus, practices which minimize the non-discursive excess are, by definition, those which are most fully realizable within language. Such practices must tend to make explicit the principles of their regulation in order to minimize reliance upon the unsayable. On the other hand, practices which exhibit a comparatively high degree of non-discursive excess are less capable of making explicit their regulating principles; they are, substantially, non-discursively regulated. These modes of practice will be described as exhibiting high and low *discursive saturation* respectively.

Thus, situational thinking and restricted coding orientation may be associated with low discursive saturation and abstract thinking and elaborated coding orientation with high discursive saturation. Practices associated with the former exhibit context dependency or localization; practices associated with the latter display a degree of context independency or generalization.

Mathematics is clearly a case of high discursive saturation, an activity which is highly organized at the level of discourse and so produces generalized utterances. The development of such activities is, as Bernstein suggests, indicative of a complex division of labour. Domestic and manual activities are examples of low discursive saturation, because they are not generally highly organized at the level of discourse and so they produce localized utterances.[6] These activities exhibit a simple division of labour. Of necessity, no activity can be fully realized within discourse. If there really were nothing but discourse, it would not be possible for the pre-linguistic child ever to enter the domain of the linguistic. Even higher mathematics is dependent upon what I might refer to as a mathematical component of *habitus*, as Livingston (1986) has illustrated.[7] This *habitus* consists of the 'yet-to-be-discursive'. However, Livingston's discursive indexing of the tacit assumptions in Gödel's inconsistency theorem still cannot exhaust the practice; there is always an excess of the material over the discursive.[8] The distinction is one of relative saturation of a material activity by discourse.

In the previous paragraph, I have used the expression 'activity' to index a region of the social which is established by the division of labour within any given conjuncture. This is a fundamental term in my language of description. Both as signifier and as signified, 'activity' has its own theoretical referents: in the former case, Leont'ev is important; in the latter, Bernstein, Eco and Foucault are particularly important.[9] The discussion of discursive saturation, above, generates two theoretical propositions which enable a distinction to be made between activities and between realizations of a given activity. These propositions are given below, after which I shall give a brief introduction to the main elements of the language of description.

- Theoretical Proposition 1
  Activity, in general, is the product of any division of labour. Activity, in particular, is the contextualizing basis of all social practice. All activities are material. Activities vary internally and one-from-another according to the extent of the saturation of material practice by discourse, that is, their *discursive saturation* may be high (DS$^+$) or low (DS$^-$). Discursive saturation can never be total.
- Theoretical Proposition 2
  All activities are cultural arbitraries.[10] They are to be understood as particular articulations of a notional Global Semantic Universe[11] comprising forms of expression and contents (signifiers and signifieds[12]). That is, an activity is a relational totality which exhibits principles, discursively and/ or non-discursively (depending upon the level of discursive saturation). In discursive terms: activities exhibiting DS$^+$ can give rise to relatively generalizable utterances; DS$^-$ activities can generate only localized utterances.

Elements of the Language of Description

I have introduced 'activity', in general, as the contextualizing basis of all social practice. Thus, activity is the level of social structure which regulates, within a particular location in the division of labour, who can say or do what. Activity thus constitutes subject positions — generally in a hierarchical relationship of some kind — and practices which are distributed over those subject positions. School mathematics, for example, constitutes mathematics teachers and students (of various categories) and distributes mathematical and pedagogic practices between them. Teachers and 'high ability' students are associated with more dominant subject positions and 'low ability' students with the most subordinate subject positions. The practices of an activity may be distinguished in terms of their level of discursive saturation, as I have indicated in the previous section and to which I shall return later. Practices may also be differentiated in terms of their degree of specialization. This latter differentiation needs a little more elaboration before I can proceed.

All activities constitute a domain of practice which is specialized, that is, it is comparatively strongly classified (Bernstein, 1990) with respect to the practices of other activities. This domain of practice is referred to as the 'esoteric domain'. The esoteric domain is comprised of and by the regulative principles of the activity which, in a DS$^+$ activity, such as school mathematics, will be discursively explicit. However, no activity is entirely cut off from other activities. The esoteric domain is the context within which the practices of the activity are to be interpreted, but it is also the context with reference to which the activity interprets the practices of other activities. The esoteric domain may be represented as a viewpoint, in this respect. It casts a 'gaze' beyond its own practices onto the practices of other activities which it must interpret in its own terms and which are, thereby, 'recontextualized'. This action of the gaze constitutes another, less specialized domain of practice which is referred to as the 'public domain'. With respect to school mathematics, the esoteric domain comprises the specialized forms of expression and content which are unambiguously mathematics, the public domain will incorporate various mathematizings of the world which have been constituted for pedagogic purposes.

The esoteric and public domains constitute one modality of an activity.[13] The other is that which is the principle focus of this chapter, which is the level of discursive saturation. The crucial distinction between practices exhibiting high and low discursive saturation is the extent to which their regulating principles are realizable within discourse. This entails that practices exhibiting DS$^+$ are, at the level of discourse, highly complex and exhibit comparatively complete articulation. They are, furthermore, highly organized: discursive objects (signs) are always defined more or less formally and within discourse.[14] That is, any sign may be objectified within discourse, so that it is always possible to produce generalizations.

The high degree of discursive organization of the esoteric domain of a DS$^+$ activity facilitates the generation, by such an activity, of languages of description having highly explicit realization principles. This concerns the application of the gaze. The descriptive power of the esoteric domain preconceptualizes practices which are recontextualized, so that these are easily subordinated to the grammar of the recontextualizing esoteric domain. Indeed, such subordination is to a large extent necessary, because of the relative inflexibility of the grammar of the recontextualizing esoteric domain. Such activities are, therefore, capable of producing highly generalizable descriptions both within and outside of the esoteric domain. School mathematics provides an obvious example of such an activity. I have discussed the colonizing effects of the recontextualizing power of mathematics elsewhere (Dowling, 1989, 1992a, 1992b, 1993a, 1993b, 1993c; Brown and Dowling, 1989, 1992, 1993).

Where the practices of an activity exhibit low discursive saturation (DS$^-$), they are characterized by implicit regulating principles. That is, specialization is at the level of the non-discursive, but not, to any great extent, at the level of the discursive. These activities are characterized by what Bourdieu terms 'polythetic' thinking. Thus utterances within these activities are, of necessity, highly localized or context-dependent (Bernstein, 1990). This latter term requires a little elaboration. All utterances are context-specific, in the sense that they must be interpreted within the context of a particular activity. However, an utterance within a DS$^-$ activity is also context-*dependent*, to the extent that it cannot be unambiguously interpreted outside of the context of its immediate production. Activities that are characterized by DS$^-$ are those that are commonly (although not necessarily) referred to as 'manual' activities.

An activity thus constitutes a (generally hierarchical) structure of subject positions by the distribution of its practices in terms of domain and discursive saturation. Clearly, relatively dominant subject positions will be associated with DS$^+$ esoteric domain practices, whilst comparatively subordinate subject positions will be confined to public domain and/or DS⁻ practices. Activity, defined in this way, is the structural level of the language of description.

Activities are realized in subjectivities and in texts; school mathematics, for example, is realized in actual teachers and students and in school mathematics texts (textbooks and schemes etc). In this chapter, I shall be concerned only with textual realizations of activities. We can say that a specific text stands in a similar relationship to an activity as speech (*parole*) does to language (*langue*): a text may be construed as an 'utterance' of an activity. In this dialectical scheme, activity is the structure which enables the textual event. The latter, in its production, reproduces the structure of the activity. However, I do not intend to suggest a purely deterministic relationship between the two, because no concrete text can be fully generated by a single activity. There are always contingencies which involve other activities to a greater or lesser extent, so that there is always a sense in which the text is recursively productive of the activity. I therefore use the expression '(re)production' to indicate the relationship between activity and text: the text (re)produces the activity.

Nevertheless, the extent to which (re)production constitutes reproduction must, in the case of significant texts, be quite high, otherwise it would not be possible to speak of an activity in any positive sense. Thus the practices and subject positions of an activity are instantiated in texts. Because these instantiations may be partial and may exhibit contingent variation, however, I use different terms at the textual level. The practices of the activity are instantiated as *message* and the subject positions as *voices*. At the level of activity, practices are distributed over the structure of subject positions; at the level of text, message is distributed across the voice structure. Message and voice are constituted in and by 'textual strategies'. Message is constituted in and by 'message (re)producing strategies', their textual distribution is achieved by 'distributing strategies'.¹⁵ With reference to the SMP mathematics texts, for example, there is a tendency — as is predicted by the model — for esoteric domain message to be distributed to the 'high ability' student and public domain message to be distributed to the 'low ability' student. In this way, the SMP texts construct ideal student readers as dominant and subordinate voices.¹⁶

In order to achieve the distribution of message, textual strategies must recruit 'textual resources'. In distributing public domain message to the subordinate voice, the SMP texts, for example, implicate resources from domestic practices, such as shopping. There is no *a priori* limitation on what can count as a textual resource. Nor is there a predetermination on how they are implicated into the various textual strategies, so that such implication may be close to what Lévi-Strauss (1972) has called *bricolage*, or it may consist of a more engineered approach. There is, then, a theoretical arbitrariness about textual resources which does not obtain with respect to textual strategies. The relationship between these two levels is thus similar in form to the relation between 'action' and 'operation' in Leont'ev's 'activity theory' (1978, 1979). In Leont'ev's conception, 'actions' are goal-oriented, whilst 'operations' are concerned with means. The latter are therefore comparatively contingent rather than necessary. This resonance between Leont'ev's scheme and my model is the principle reason for the choice of the term 'activity', although my use of it is clearly different from Leont'ev's. It should be emphasized that the arbitrariness of textual resources is purely a theoretical arbitrariness. Empirically, there must always be a selection from a notional reservoir of resources to constitute the repertoire(s) of resources which makes up a particular text.

As I have indicated, the most dominant subject position is associated, primarily, with the esoteric domain of the activity and its gaze and with the highest available level of discursive saturation. With respect to the latter, the textual construction of the most dominant voice must entail generalization, that is, the text must move towards relative context independence. Specifically, the text must prioritize principles over procedures and must minimize local specificities. On the other hand, the textual construction of the subordinate voice will prioritize procedures over principles and will tend to maximize local specificities. This is because subordination is achieved by the denial of access to the principles which regulate the activity and which enable the recontextualizing power of the gaze. Thus there are two categories of distributing strategy: 'generalizing strategies' construct comparatively dominant voices and 'localizing strategies' construct comparatively subordinate voices.

Having given a brief introduction to the language of description, I shall now give an illustration of the textual analysis relating to generalizing and localizing textual strategies.

Generalizing and Localizing Strategies

Figure 9.2 shows the first two pages of *SMP 11–16 Book G2*, Chapter 4, for which the teacher's guide gives the following 'aims':

- To give practical experience of drawing regular polygons, and to become familiar with their names.
- Making 'patterns' is, we hope, an enjoyable way of practising drawing skills, and pupils should be encouraged to invent their own patterns.
- Simple ideas of angle are also called upon. (G2TG, p. 12)

The chapter concerns the repetition (practising) of practical, manual skills and of a lexicon within an 'enjoyable' context: 'It might be nice to display particularly pleasing patterns' (*ibid.*). Students are to be 'encouraged to invent their own patterns'. This is a creativity which is doubly spurious in that it is neither mathematically structured, nor is it pedagogically valued. There are no explicit criteria regulating what is to count as a 'particularly pleasing pattern', the patterns are simply vehicles for manual work: a sugaring of the pill. It is noteworthy that 'simple ideas of angle' are only to be 'called upon'. The mathematics, in this respect, constitutes a resource in the rehearsal of manual skills.

Task A4 presents an *algorithm* (a linear sequence of instructions) for the production of a hexagon. It is a sequence of symbolic and iconic instructions which facilitates the drawing and nothing else. The 'angle measurer' is an example of what I refer to as an *operational matrix*, that is, it structurally delimits possibilities other than in a linear sequence. The measurer defines uniquely the circle and therefore the size of the hexagon and locates the vertices. The teacher's guide notes that the 'use of an angle measurer may need revising' (*ibid.*). The ruler is also an operational matrix, defining the sides of the hexagons as straight lines. Nowhere is a hexagon defined in terms of straight lines, it is fixed only by the explicit

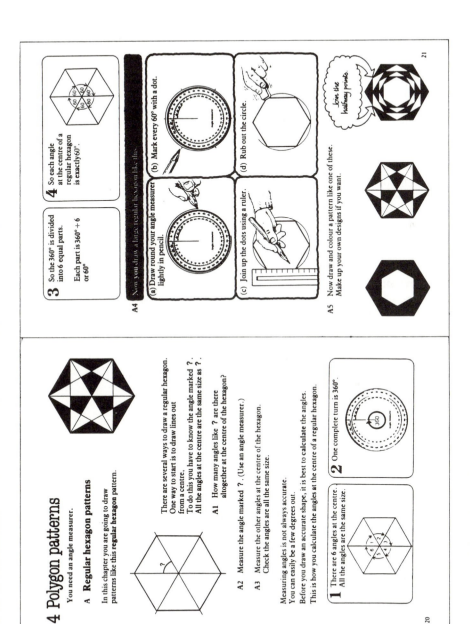

Figure 9.2: SMP Book G2, pp. 20–1
Source: *School Mathematics Project*, 1985, CUP.

133

deictic, '*this* **regular hexagon**', and by the indexical representations of hexagons.[17] Algorithms and operational matrices are examples of *procedures*. Procedures are localizing strategies, because their interpretation is heavily contingent upon local specificities at the expense of general principles. In this case, the contingent action involves drawing a pattern.

Another algorithm is summarized by the contents of the indexical box on page 21 labelled 3. Boxes 1 and 2, on the previous page, offer some background to the algorithm.[18] There are six angles which are all the same and which make 360° altogether, 'So . . .'. This background enables the recognition of the features of the algorithm, facilitating its extension to other polygons. The '360°' is associated with the angle measurer that is to be used in the drawing, and the number of angles represents the specificity of hexagons, pentagons and other polygons (the names of which the student reader is to 'become familiar with').

The chapter repeats these two algorithms for octagons and for decagons and a review section — 'Review: Chapters 4 and 5' — invokes the algorithms in the production of a nonagon pattern. Although these later tasks are reduced to a single page each — denoting a degree of internalizing of the algorithms by the student reader — there has been no other progression in the trajectory defined by the chapter and review tasks. Furthermore, the G2 chapter and the 'review' tasks are unconnected, in explicit terms, with anything else in the G series. There are no more polygons and almost no reference to angular measure.[19] There are clocks and dials and other circular scales in every G book and pie charts appear in G2 and G5, but pie charts are produced using a centigrade scale and without other reference to angular measure.[20] The procedural text relating to 'polygon patterns' is thus almost entirely isolated from the rest of the G series content.

The development of the geometric ratio, π, in *SMP 11–16 Book Y1*, Chapter 7, incorporates a rather different strategy. The teacher's guide describes the chapter as follows:

The idea of ratio, as developed in chapter 6, plays an important part in this chapter. The ratio $\dfrac{\text{circumference}}{\text{diameter}}$ in a circle is approached as a limiting case of the ratio $\dfrac{\text{perimeter}}{\text{diameter}}$ in a regular polygon. (YITG, p. 30)

Unlike the G texts, the Y series is multiply and often explicitly recursive, so it is not generally possible to mark out the beginning of a particular topic in an unambiguous way. However, we can pick up the developing discourse on geometry at the start of section C of Chapter 6, which introduces (albeit, within a public domain setting) the specialized expressions, 'scale factor' and 'enlargement'. Section E, in the same chapter, introduces the terms 'similarity' and 'ratio' in a esoteric domain setting. What is being established, mathematically, is a relationship between the geometrical transformation, 'enlargement', the comparative term, 'similar', and geometrical ratios. This sets the basis for the following chapter, the opening of which is shown in Figure 9.3.

Chapter 7 opens with a formal definition of terms, that is, a definition in terms of esoteric domain objects. The exposition also articulates with 'enlargement' and 'similarity' and with geometric ratios from the previous chapter. The

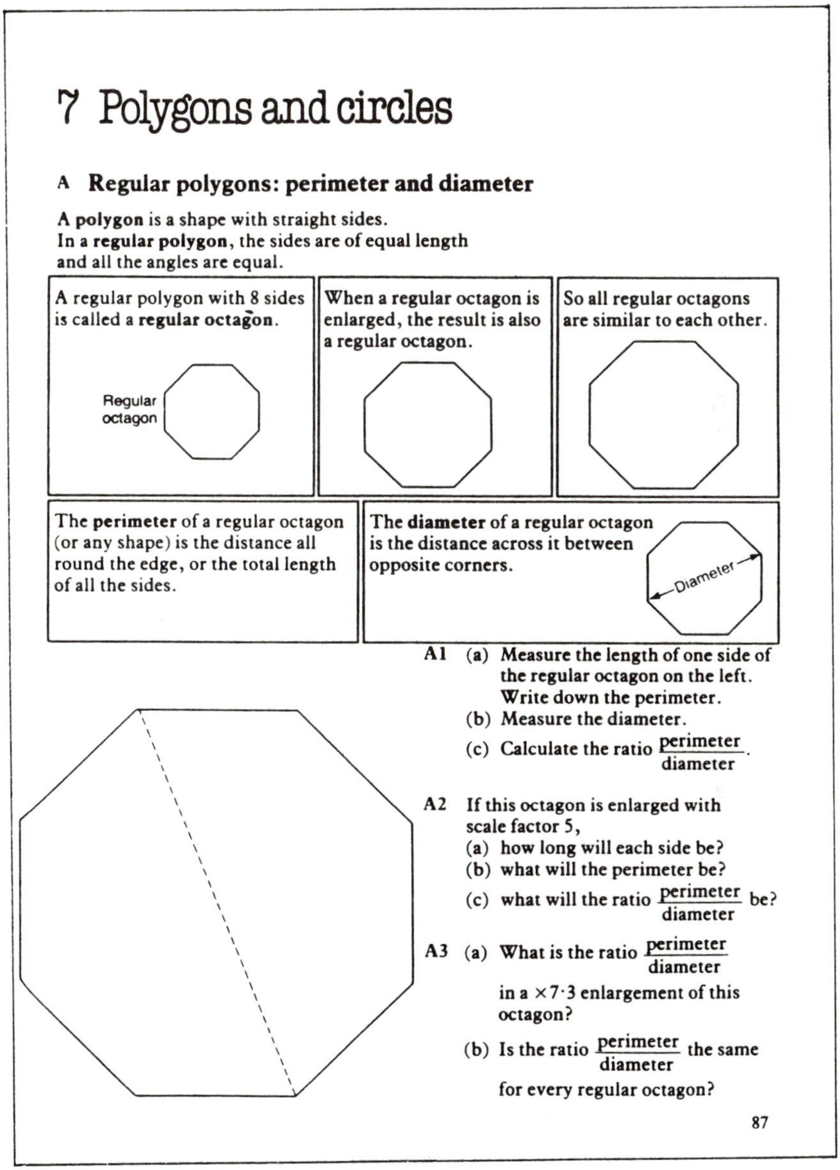

7 Polygons and circles

A Regular polygons: perimeter and diameter

A polygon is a shape with straight sides.
In a **regular polygon**, the sides are of equal length
and all the angles are equal.

A regular polygon with 8 sides is called a **regular octagon**.	When a regular octagon is enlarged, the result is also a regular octagon.	So all regular octagons are similar to each other.
Regular octagon		

The **perimeter** of a regular octagon (or any shape) is the distance all round the edge, or the total length of all the sides.	The **diameter** of a regular octagon is the distance across it between opposite corners. Diameter

A1 (a) Measure the length of one side of the regular octagon on the left. Write down the perimeter.

(b) Measure the diameter.

(c) Calculate the ratio $\dfrac{\text{perimeter}}{\text{diameter}}$.

A2 If this octagon is enlarged with scale factor 5,

(a) how long will each side be?

(b) what will the perimeter be?

(c) what will the ratio $\dfrac{\text{perimeter}}{\text{diameter}}$ be?

A3 (a) What is the ratio $\dfrac{\text{perimeter}}{\text{diameter}}$ in a ×7·3 enlargement of this octagon?

(b) Is the ratio $\dfrac{\text{perimeter}}{\text{diameter}}$ the same for every regular octagon?

87

Figure 9.3: SMP Book YI, p. 87
Source: School Mathematics Project, 1985, CUP.

ratio, $\dfrac{\text{perimeter}}{\text{diameter}}$, is initially referred to as the 'p-number' of a polygon and
sections A and B of the chapter tabulate and graph p-numbers against number of sides up to 48; the graph is followed by an exposition:

> As the number of sides increases, the polygon looks more and more like a circle. The p-number gets closer and closer to the p-number of a circle, which is just over 3.14.
> [...]
> The p-number of a circle is denoted by the Greek letter p, which is written π and pronounced 'pi'. The value of π, correct to 5 decimal places, is 3.14159. The perimeter of a circle is called the **circumference** of the circle. So the ratio $\dfrac{\text{circumference}}{\text{diameter}}$ is π. Or, in other words, π is the multiplier from diameter to circumference. (Y1, pp. 90–1; indexical diagrams omitted)

The exposition gives a new conception of a circle as the limit of a series of polygons having increasing numbers of sides (the circle appeared earlier in the book as a locus). It also introduces the term 'circumference' and the expression π, which is described as both a ratio and as a multiplier. At the end of the chapter, several approximations to π are given including its decimal expansion to thirty-five decimal places.[21] The strategy employed in the Y text is a generalizing strategy in which mathematical signs (esoteric domain) are articulated so that the general principles of mathematical practice are rendered more visible. The signifier 'circle' here denotes a mathematical object which is defined, within the esoteric domain, as the limiting value of a polygon as the number of sides increases. An extensive array of connotated metonyms has been attached to 'circle'. This array includes: polygon, perimeter, side, circumference, radius, diameter, 3.14159, π, ratio, graph, $\dfrac{\text{circumference}}{\text{diameter}}$, multiplier, and ⊸▷➤ the 'labelled arrow' icon (which is also implicated in the exposition). The G text, by contrast, does no more than present algorithms and operational matrices which facilitate the completion of the immediate task in hand. The algorithm for the calculation of the angle subtended at the centre by the sides of regular hexagons, pentagons, octagons and decagons is not even generalized.[22]

The relationship between the circumference and diameter of a circle is introduced in the G series in Book G7 (the last but one book in the G series), Chapter 3. This chapter remains almost entirely outside of the esoteric domain (as does the G series generally), but there are three instances of esoteric domain exposition.[23] The first gives an algorithm for the calculation of radius from diameter, or vice versa, using the expression, 'of', in preference to the mathematically more usual, '×':

> The diameter is the width of a circle. The distance from the centre of a circle to the edge is half the diameter. We call this distance the **radius**.
> *radius* = $\frac{1}{2}$ **of** *diameter* (G7, p. 15; graphical index omitted; bold text in red in original)

The second provides an algorithm for the calculation of circumference, incorporating the equality symbol, even though the algorithm represents an approximation:

> The distance round the edge of a circle has a special name. It is called the **circumference** of the circle. The circumference is a bit longer than 3 times the diameter. If you only want a rough answer for the circumference of a circle you can use *circumference* **= 3** × *diameter* (G7, p. 16; bold text in red in original)

The final section of esoteric domain exposition gives another algorithm:

> The rule *circumference* **= 3** × *diameter* gives a rough answer for the circumference, but it is always too short. To be on the safe side, you can **add 10% to the rough answer.** (G7, p. 18; bold text in red in original)

The only deviation from the immediate mathematical object and its defined features occurs with the implication of the percentage algorithm in the final extract. This is invoked as a routine and not incorporated into a principled articulation such as does occur in the Y text. In fact, adding on 10 per cent is tantamount to using the algorithm: circumference ≈ 3.3 × diameter. This algorithm gives an approximate error of +5.0 per cent, whilst the original algorithm generates an approximate error of −4.5 per cent, so the new algorithm, whilst avoiding an underestimate, is actually less accurate. Furthermore, there will be cases in which the 'safe side' is an underestimate rather than an overestimate.[24] The failure to declare the principles behind the algorithm will, in such cases, result in inappropriate computations.

The two textbook extracts that I have discussed differ not so much in their respective degree of mathematical specialization — they are both substantially esoteric domain texts — as in the ways in which they (re)produce the discursive qualities of mathematical message. The Y text constructs a complex articulation of signs, thereby reducing the dependency of the text upon the immediate setting. Generalizing becomes possible as the specialized mathematical sings are referred to each other, constituting general mathematical interpretants. This text is organizing mathematics on the basis of explicit principles. The G text, on the other hand, isolates its topic from other topics in the scheme. Furthermore, its signs are organized in procedures which are heavily dependent upon the setting which constitutes a localized interpretant. The generalizing strategies of the Y text tend to (re)produce the DS⁺ of mathematical practice, whereas the localizing, G strategies disarticulate these practices, (re)producing them as DS⁻.

Generalizing strategies are almost entirely absent from the G series. The 'rough answers' obtained using the circle algorithms, cited above, are not even marked as instances of 'approximation'. This, despite the fact that 'approximation' appears as a topic elsewhere in the G series. The resulting disarticulation of message is redolent of Fordist techniques in the labour process (see Braverman, 1974; Matthews, 1989) and of the context-specific 'preconceptualization' described by Hales (1980). There is no determinism, here. The actions of the G readers are not predetermined or preconceptualized. Rather, a textually wilful substitution of procedures for principles delimits their access to mathematical practices. The discursive structure of the practices which constitutes the dominant subject position of the activity is invisible in the G texts.

The textual strategies that I have described are message (re)producing strategies — they constitute, in part, the message of the text and so (re)produce the practices of school mathematics. However, the Y and G series are, as might easily be guessed, directed at high and low 'ability' students, respectively. By targeting their readers via the labels Y and G, these message strategies also distribute the esoteric domain, they are thereby implicated in distributing strategies. Thus, the message which is organized in terms of principles is confined to those texts (Y) associated with the dominant voice; the texts associated with the subordinate voice (G) incorporate only procedural message. At the level of activity, DS^+ is exclusive to the dominant subject position; DS^- is constitutive of the subordinate subject position.

Conclusion

There is a tendency for research within the field of mathematics education not to be about anything at all. Expressions such as 'the cognitive', 'the mathematical', 'the social' are frequently employed in pointing to arenas of activity. However, we should ask, just what is being said about the cognitive, or the mathematical, or the social; how are these being conceptualized; how are such concepts as there are being operationalized empirically? My project is, firstly, an attempt to organize conceptually my principle arena of interest, that is, the social — patterns of relationships between individuals and groups which are (re)produced in their cultural practices. Secondly, I have attempted to generate a language of description which enables the systematic reading of empirical cultural products — in this case, pedagogic texts — in terms of this social structure. Thirdly, I have applied the language to a particular instance, the *SMP 11–16* scheme, and produced empirical results.

In representing this project, my approach, in this chapter, has been to take a particular strand of the language of description — that relating to the ubiquitous abstract/concrete opposition — and follow it through from general methodological orientation, via theoretical principles, to its participation in the language of description and its operationalization in empirical texts. The resulting discourse is inchoate in every department and can do no more than suggest the possibility of high discursive saturation in such a language of description.

Empirically, I may speculate that a principal strategy in the construction of subordinate subject positions in mathematics education is the disarticulation of mathematical complexity, a prioritizing of procedures over principles. My more extensive analysis of the *SMP 11–16* materials (Dowling, 1993a) suggests that this is, indeed, the case. Theoretically, I can relate this to the intellectual/manual opposition and, so to social class. This would associate the dominant and subordinate subject positions to middle and working class positions, respectively. Again, this is borne out by my broader empirical analysis, which reveals additional strategies contributing to this association.

Methodologically, I must assert that my readings are biased as, indeed, are all readings. My theoretical propositions are testable only in the sense that there is a recognition of the discursive gap between the language of description and that which it seeks to describe. The recognition of the discursive gap is tantamount to an insistence upon the vitality of the empirical. This space, in relation to the language of description is the location of that which places a limit on discursive saturation in all activity. It is the analogue of Lacan's 'unconscious'. Without coherent theory, sociological and philosophical writing leaves untrammelled the libidinal forces of prejudice. But it is, ultimately, only the unexpected in the empirical that forestalls the discursive closure of thanatos.

Notes

1. Published by Cambridge University Press.
2. The expression 'language of description' is Bernstein's. However, he tends more frequently to refer to 'principles of description' which, in the introduction cited here, encompass the recognition and realization rules derived from the model (and not the model itself). Bernstein's 'theory' would correspond to my 'theoretical propositions'. I have also included, in Figure 9.1, the theoretical referents (contextualizing work) out of which these propositions arise.
3. See Gordon's discussion in the afterword to the same volume (Gordon, 1980).
4. An impossibility also recognized by Wittgenstein (1961).
5. An eventuality which seems not to have bothered Piaget unduly.
6. Other examples of comparatively low saturation in a discursive practice are to be found in spectator sports. In cricket, for example, even apparently technical terms such as 'wicket' and even 'bat' and 'ball' have no unambiguous meaning.
7. After Bourdieu (1977, 1990).
8. In his introduction, Livingston indexes tacit assumptions in the more widely familiar proof concerning the relationship between the angles subtended at the centre and at the circumference of a circle. See, also, Knee (1983) who also points to similar tacit assumptions in Euclid's *Elements*.
9. The relevant references are those included in the bibliography.
10. 'Cultural arbitrary' is a term employed by Bourdieu and Passeron (1977).
11. This expression is taken from Eco (1976).
12. These are the components of the linguistic sign in Saussure (1960); expression and content are corresponding (but not synonymous) terms introduced by Hjelmslev (see Eco, 1976).
13. Since the strength of classification may vary, independently, in terms of expression and content (high/low in each case), there are actually four domains. For the purposes of brevity in this chapter, however, I shall refer only to the esoteric and the public.
14. In Vygotsky's (1986) terms, signs (more correctly, perhaps, signifieds) are generally constituted within such practices as 'scientific concepts'. These are contrasted with 'spontaneous concepts' for which meanings are given in use, but not made explicit.
15. There is a third category of textual strategy — 'voice positioning strategies' — but I shall not be concerned with this category in the present chapter.
16. All texts may be understood to construct ideal readers (Eco, 1979); in this case, the ideal reader is described in terms of the language of description.
17. The terms 'icon', 'index' and 'symbol' derive from Peirce (1931–58). However, my use of them is different. In particular, the 'iconic' mode of signification locates the reader, physically, at a viewpoint. Since mathematical objects, such as hexagons, are defined formally, they cannot be signified iconically (a hexagon, in this mathematical sense, is not a visual object), but may be signified indexically (a form of visual signification which is motivated other than by physically locating

Paul Dowling

the reader at a viewpoint). The lack of any esoteric domain definition of 'hexa-gon' in the G text, however, renders invisible the distinction between icon and index. In this case, that is, it is not clear that such mathematical objects cannot be iconized.

18. The exposition preceding these boxes seem to present a bizarre argument: 'Meas-uring angles is not always accurate. You can easily be a few degrees out. Before you draw an accurate shape, it is best to **calculate** the angles' (G2, p. 20). This advice ignores the fact that you cannot measure the angles of a hexagon unless you or somebody else has already drawn one and, furthermore, if 'measuring angles is not always accurate', then it would seem to be an odd method to choose for drawing the objects.

19. There are single page review sections on angle in G1 and in G3, substantially outside the esoteric domain in each case.

20. The teacher's guide for G2 suggests that, as an 'extension', a pie chart scale might be used instead of an angle measurer as a 'slightly different method of construc-tion'. The pie chart scale is a transparent plastic disc marked on a scale from 0 to 100 the incorporation of which operational matrix would necessitate an alteration to both algorithms and would reduce the possibilities for polygon construction insofar as 100 has fewer factors than 360.

21. The notion of an irrational number does not appear explicitly in the Y series. The irrational nature of π is implied by the use of approximations rather than an exact value and by the expression of its decimal expansion to thirty-five places of decimals on what appears to be a very long strip of paper which curls round after the thirty-fifth place (concealing the subsequent digits) and snakes off the edge of the page.

22. Although the generalization is implicit. The final task in the chapter, D4, sug-gests: 'Try drawing regular shapes with more sides. You could use 12 sides, or 15. Then draw a pattern inside them' (G2, p. 25).

23. There is also one esoteric domain task.

24. For example: A 5 cm diameter reel of gold wire has 20 turns of wire on it; 320 cm of wire are needed; is there enough? Using $\pi \approx 3.3$, the answer is 'yes', which is, of course, incorrect.

Acknowledgments

I am heavily indebted to Parin Bahl, Basil Bernstein and Andrew Brown for sustained inspiration and critical engagement throughout the project to which this chapter stands in metonymic relationship.

I am also grateful to Cambridge University Press for supplying the materials used in the analysis and to them and the School Mathematics Project for granting permission to reproduce the pages in Figures 9.2 and 9.3.

References

BERNSTEIN, B. (1971) *Class, Codes and Control Volume 1: Theoretical studies towards a sociology of language*, London, RKP.
BERNSTEIN, B. (1977) *Class, Codes and Control Volume 3: Towards a theory of educational transmissions*, 2nd edition, London, RKP.
BERNSTEIN, B. (1982) 'Codes, modalities and the process of cultural reproduction', in APPLE, M.W. (Ed) *Cultural and Economic Reproduction in Education*, London, RKP.
BERNSTEIN, B. (1985) 'On pedagogic discourse', in RICHARDS, J. (Ed) *Handbook of Theory and Research for the Sociology of Education*, Greenwood Press.

BERNSTEIN, B. (1988) 'On pedagogic discourse: revised', Collected Original Resources in *Education*, 12, 1.

BERNSTEIN, B. (1990) *Class, Codes and Control, Volume* 4, London, RKP.

BERNSTEIN, B. (in press) *Class, Codes and Control, Volume 5.*

BOURDIEU, P. (1977) *Outline of a Theory of Practice*, Cambridge, Cambridge University Press.

BOURDIEU, P. (1984) *Distinction: A Social Critique of the Judgement of Taste*, London, RKP.

BOURDIEU, P. (1990) *The Logic of Practice*, Cambridge, Polity.

BOURDIEU, P. and PASSERON, J.C. (1977) *Reproduction in Education, Society and Culture*, London, Sage.

BRAVERMAN, H. (1974) *Labor and Monopoly Capital: The Degradation of Work in the Twentieth Century*, New York, Monthly Review Press.

BROWN, A.J. and DOWLING, P.C. (1989) *A Critical Alternative to Internationalism and Monoculturalism in Mathematics Education*, Centre for Multicultural Education, Occasional Paper Number 10, London, Institute of Education, University of London, Centre for Multicultural Education, also in GARDENER, R. (Ed) (1992) *An International Dimension in the National Curriculum: an imperative for Britain for 1992 and beyond*, London, Department of International and Comparative Education, Institute of Education, University of London.

BROWN, A.J. and DOWLING, P.C. (1992) ' "Who's Been Restructuring *My* Primary Socialisation?" the impact of school mathematics on domestic space', *Ruling the Margins: problematising parental involvement*, Institute of Education, University of London, September 1992, conference proceedings obtainable from IMPACT project, University of North London.

BROWN, A.J. and DOWLING, P.C. (1993) 'The bearing of school mathematics on domestic space', in MERTTENS, R., MAYERS, D., BROWN, A.J. and VASS, J. (Eds) *Ruling the Margins: problematising parental involvement*, London, IMPACT, University of North London.

DOWLING, P.C. (1989) 'The Contextualising of Mathematics: towards a theoretical map', in *Collected Original Resources in Education*, 13, 2 also in HARRIS, M. (Ed) (1990) *Schools, Mathematics and Work*, Basingstoke, The Falmer Press.

DOWLING, P.C. (1992a) 'Textual production and social activity: A language of description', *Collected Original Resources in Education*, 16, 1.

DOWLING, P.C. (1992b) 'Pedagogic Voices, Pedagogic Messages: a sociological algebra', presented at 'Research into Social Perspectives in Mathematics Education', South Bank University, May 1992 (available from Department of Mathematics, Statistics and Computing, Institute of Education, University of London).

DOWLING, P.C. (1993a) 'A Language for the Sociological Description of Pedagogic Texts with Particular Reference to the Secondary School Mathematics Scheme *SMP 11–16*', PhD thesis, Institute of Education, University of London.

DOWLING, P.C. (1993b) 'Mathematics, Discourse and "Totemism": a language for practice', in The NECC Mathematics Commission, PDME.2: Curriculum Reconstruction for Society in Transition, 2–5 April, 1993, Broederstroom, Pre-conference papers.

DOWLING, P.C. (1993c) 'Theoretical "Totems": A sociological language for educational practice', in JULIE, C., ANGELIS, D. and DAVIS, Z. (Eds) *Political Dimensions of Mathematics Education 2: curriculum reconstruction for society in transition*, Cape Town, Maskew Miller Longman.

DURKHEIM, É. (1984) *The Division of Labour in Society*, Basingstoke, Macmillan.

ECO, U. (1973) 'Social life as a sign system', in ROBEY, D. (Ed) *Structuralism: an introduction*, Oxford, Clarendon.

ECO, U. (1976) *A Theory of Semiotics*, Bloomington, Indiana University Press.

ECO, U. (1979) *The Role of the Reader*, London, Hutchinson.

Paul Dowling

Eco, U. (1984) *Semiotics and the Philosophy of Language*, Basingstoke, Macmillan.

Eco, U. (1990) *The Limits of Interpretation*, Bloomington, Indiana University Press.

Foucault, M. (1965) *Madness and Civilization: A History of Insanity in the Age of Reason*, London, Tavistock.

Foucault, M. (1970) *The Order of Things: An Archaeology of the Human Sciences*, London, Tavistock.

Foucault, M. (1972) *The Archaeology of Knowledge*, London, Tavistock.

Foucault, M. (1973) *The Birth of the Clinic*, London, Tavistock.

Foucault, M. (1977a) 'The political function of the intellectual', *Radical Philosophy*, 17, pp. 12–14.

Foucault, M. (1977b) *Discipline and Punish: The Birth of the Prison*, London, Penguin.

Foucault, M. (1978) *The History of Sexuality: an introduction*, Harmondsworth, Penguin.

Foucault, M. (1980) *Power/Knowledge*, Brighton, Harvester.

Foucault, M. (1981) 'The order of discourse', in Young, R. (Ed) *Untying the Text: a poststructuralist reader*, London, RKP.

Foucault, M. (1982) 'The subject and power', in Dreyfus, H.L., Foucault, M. and Rabinow, P. *Beyond structuralism and hermeneutics*, Brighton, Harvester.

Foucault, M. (1984) *The Use of Pleasure: The History of Sexuality*, 2, Harmondsworth, Penguin.

Foucault, M. (1986) *The Care of the Self: The History of Sexuality*, 3, New York, Vintage.

Gordon, C. (1980) 'Afterword' in Foucault, M. *Power/Knowledge: Selected Interviews and Other Writings, 1972–1977*, Brighton, Harvester.

Hales, M. (1980) *Living Thinkwork: Where Do Labour Processes Come From?* London, CSE Books.

Heidegger, M. (1962) *Being and Time*, London, SCM Press.

Lacan, J. (1977) 'The function of the field of speech and language in psychoanalysis', *Écrits: a selection*, London, Routledge.

Leont'ev, A.N. (1978) *Activity, Consciousness, and Personality*, Englewood Cliffs Prentice-Hall.

Leont'ev, A.N. (1979) 'The problem of activity in psychology' in Wertsch, J.V. (Ed) *The Concept of Activity in Soviet Psychology*, New York, M.E. Sharpe.

Lévi-Strauss, C. (1972) *The Savage Mind (La Pensée Sauvage)*, London, Weidenfeld and Nicholson.

Livingston, E. (1986) *The Ethnomethodological Foundations of Mathematics*, London, RKP.

Luria, A.R. (1976) *Cognitive Development: Its Cultural and Social Foundations*, Cambridge, Harvard University Press.

Matthews, J. (1989) *Tools of Change: New Technology and the Democratisation of Work*, Sydney, Pluto.

Piaget, J. (1972) *Psychology and Epistemology: Towards a Theory of Knowledge*, Harmondsworth, Penguin.

Saussure, F. de. (1960) *Course in General Linguistics*, London, Peter Owen.

Vygotsky, L.S. (1986) *Thought and Language*, Cambridge, Massachusetts MIT Press.

Wittgenstein, L. (1961) *Tractatus Logico-philosophicus*, London, RKP.

Chapter 10

The Dominance of Structure in 'Post-structural' Critiques of Mathematics Education

Jeff Vass

Introduction

It is increasingly recognized (e.g., Walkerdine, 1988; Dowling, 1991) that mathematics education may be viewed as a discourse, and that it works as a system of social representations in as much as the content of any other media can be said to do so, such as advertising, television etc . . . In view of this it makes sense to subject education discourses to the same sort of critical enquiry that other media attract. The basis of this examination is that mathematical activity is to be seen primarily as a social event rather than a cognitive event (in the latter the social becomes known merely as an alteration in cognitive style).

Current theoretical attempts to describe the discourse of mathematics education are undertaken in the context of recent advances away from structuralism. During the 1970s structuralist methods were often employed to examine the 'mechanisms' by which social representations, thought of as circulating messages about identity, gender and class etc., were implicated in systems of ideology. All social practice, it was thought, involved ideological practice. Therefore any social activity seemed to serve as a means of ideological reproduction in addition to achieving the 'notional' objectives of the human agents perpetrating this activity. Structural analyses facilitated much discussion on the basis of much vaunted methodologies which circulated freely among the academic community (especially in anthropology, cultural and literary studies and sociology). But in the 1970s it was felt that the methodologies in circulation were very much still rooted in 1960s structuralism (e.g., Levi-Strauss, 1966; Barthes, 1973). In fact, first attempts at the analysis of social phenomena still depend on methodological developments that started with the linguistic work of Roman Jakobson and which were developed for subsequent use in the analysis of culture by social theorists such as Levi-Strauss.

I believe that structuralism still dominates post-structuralist perspectives. This is to be seen in the view taken of 'discourse' by some contemporary writers. In views which tend towards structuralism will be found an analytical emphasis on 'system' over the 'agents' subjected to the system. While the 'post-structuralist positions' of Foucault, Barthes, Bakhtin and others are behind much current work, ways of providing a structuralist leaning to their theories appear to be sought after, and they are found in abundance. This is partly because structuralism was a potent force during the peak of their careers and much of what they had to say developed on the back of structuralism. This gives us the basis of current contradictions. In what follows I shall focus on the fact that certain aspects of these formative writers have been emphasized over others, particularly to do with how meaning becomes specified in any situation. The specification of meaning is central to any account of how subjects acquire particular identities, including those associated with gender, class and ethnicity. But firstly it is as well to distinguish the sociological implications of the methods by which one might examine, say, the gendering aspects of a social practice.

Methodological Considerations

To examine mathematics as a gender practice, that is to say a form of activity through which gender identities are conferred on, or reinforced in, participants to the activity, might involve either 'correlative' or 'discursive' methods. In the former, which constitutes the majority of studies in education, practices are examined empirically and associations are revealed between 'dimensions' of the practice and differences between the gender roles of participants. Thus, the 'amount of time' a teacher spends with boys as opposed to girls on a particular task becomes a dimension of interest. Other dimensions relate to qualitative differences in linguistic, or cognitive, style etc . . . These correlative, almost 'ethological', studies are important in spotting the phenomena of gender (or class) bias in facets of our culture. However, they start and finish with the already constituted individual in his or her political and civic 'place'. Anyway, it would be pointless to carry out these ethological studies unless one wanted rhetorical ammunition in taking issue with perceived assaults on the rights and privileges of already constituted civic beings who suffer various ignominies which are habitually related to their gender, class or race.

Discursive studies, of which there are now an increasing number within education studies, look at gender and class as 'chronically embedded' features of our culture which traverse the distinctive areas of activity in which human subjects (as opposed to civic individuals) are implicated. Examples of these areas of activity might be teaching, learning, mothering, consuming, entertaining etc . . . Each of these activities is constitutive of social representational forms by, and through, which subjectivity is itself constructed. Here, we are not interested so much simply in the features of culture that we can ethologically associate with already gendered subjects. This ethologizing, effectively, turns the social context into an array of determining factors by which we explain the contents and organization of the behaviour of individuals (Vass and Merttens, 1987; Merttens and Vass, 1989). Discursive studies, by contrast, view the subject not as 'in' a discourse but as 'of' its structure. Subjectivity in this sense implies the primacy of active, discursively managed social forms in which subjects are constructed through particular dynamic involvements. An analogy I find helpful is the following: in English the subject of a sentence is separated from the action as in 'I walk', 'the dog barks' etc. Here the individual is 'located' with respect to the action as the producer or recipient of its effects as related to some context. In inflected languages like Latin the action itself is primary and the subject appears as an inflected quality of the action: *ambulo* (I walk), *latrat canis* (the dog barks). The word dog (*canis*), the subject of barking, appears as merely that which further specifies the third person inflection of the verb to bark (*latrare*). The subject appears as part of the structured differences between verb forms, whereas in English the subject is always distinct and action appears as part of a range of possibilities that can be made contingent on the subject. It seems to me slightly clearer in Latin that the subject of a linguistic event is a dependent feature of verbal structuring: English tends to make the subject *appear* as something anterior or posterior to the event. (I make no assumptions about how Romans thought, rather I am concerned with how the grammar of their language tends to depict the subject of action).

Discourse studies seek to examine the structure of representational forms through which subjectivity is constituted through the inflecting, or structuring, of action. Inflection and structuring imply domains of organized activity beyond the location of the subject. Thus subjects, through their action, are implicated in structuring forces emanating from other locations. I have discussed this issue in more depth elsewhere (Vass, 1993a) in relation to the production of authoritative texts for consumption in teaching contexts such as mathematics education. The issue of 'what lies beyond' the subject outside his/her immediate acts but which nevertheless theoretically has structuring implications for those acts has been a recurrent theme in the social sciences. Before considering how we treat the 'beyond' and its specificatory relation to our present activity I need to provide some background to how specification has been discussed.

Structure and a Chronology of Its Problems

In moving to discursive views of mathematical activity, current approaches have inherited, it seems to me, a number of the problems associated with the revisionist structuralism of the 1970s. The question that must be put to current discursive approaches to mathematics education is to what extent they repeat or develop problems based on earlier theoretical impasses. In broad outline the chronology of these problems may be presented as follows. Structuralism in the 1960s was typified by the application of specific techniques and methods to the analysis of texts and human practices (as in anthropological ethnographies for example). The purpose of these techniques was to describe, and to provide a critique of, the manner in which human agents entered into social relations with one another through acts of 'signification'. Texts were thought of as acts of signification, thus a novel or a poem, or advertisement could be described in its articulation with social relations. The internal meaning of the text consisted of relations between elements that had other relations with aspects of social structure. Thus Barthes (1973) analyses, for example, food products such as steak and chips and argues that the range of meanings associated with their consumption are coextensive with, and dependent on, already existing other social structures and meanings that, for example, distinguish Frenchness from foreignness, masculinity from femininity, and working class from middle class. The technical apparatus which permits such readings of specific texts and practices is built on the linguistic and Saussurean distinction (Saussure, 1974) between *la langue* and *la parole*: that is, language conceived as a fully formed system of established relationships that determine meaning and linguistic structure (*langue*) and individual acts of speech (*parole*). While *langue* worked as a description of a system it was thought to be extendable to other systems of signification whose elements could be isolated and their relationships described: hence 'semiology', or the study of 'sign systems'. Structuralist techniques examine the organization of systems of meaning by mapping elements into relations of opposition and difference. Thus, 'nature' as a meaning gains its specificity by being opposed to 'culture', which is mutually specified by the relation of opposition. Thus we establish a binary pair, culture : nature. We may establish others such as 'male : female'. The denotative specificity of words in acts of signification are said to be dependent on such relationships between elements. Cultural criticism begins when we are in a position to examine connotative structures in signifying practices. A particular society may associate binary pairs such that male: female becomes synonymous with culture : nature. Thus, males are thought of as more 'of culture' and women are identified as 'natural objects'. Signifying practices, and the representational forms of various media, can now be analysed for their 'ideological content' through structuralist analyses of connoted features. From such apparently simple procedures larger critical works could be produced. We can now imagine an entire culture's ideological system, that is its texts and signifying practices, related to its social structure in the form of relations between social roles, distributions of authority and power and so on. *Langue*, as a prototype structure, could be adapted to flesh out the somewhat woolier notions of 'collective representations' which Durkheim (1976) had attempted to use to describe the systems of knowledge societies made use of. Connotative specificity implies the structuring of language beyond individuals (a Durkheimian requirement), and 'beyond' actual contexts of use (a structuralist requirement). More recently, Foucault has been read as if his notion of a system of knowledge (*épistème*), that characterizes particular formations of power and social structure, were an extrapolation of *la langue*. This reading was facilitated by a parallel in Foucault's account of historical change which apparently reflected Saussure's understanding of historical change in language, and, incidently, Levi-Strauss's idea of the historical development of cultures. *Langue* is a set of instantaneous relationships between elements which are subject to change. History is the transformation between one state and the next.

Theoretical and methodological problems with this view of ideological organization began to mount in the 1970s. Foucault's notion of a 'discourse' (e.g., 1973) was a distinct move away from a structural conception of ideological systems. The cavalier application of structuralist methods became to be themselves ideologically suspect from the marxist point of view, partly because individual agents were conspicuous by their absence from the mechanisms by which history happened. Marxism prioritizes the concrete conditions of practice, and thus also of speech and other modes of signification. Abstract collective systems, of which *langue* is the prototype, are dissociated from historically located speakers. *Langue* contains the structure by which acts of speaking are said to derive their organization, yet speakers can only reflect inadequately this dissociated system. Actual historically located activity never seems to reflect the 'ideal speaker-hearer' relationships posed by langue. This criticism of linguistic structuralism is well-known and documented (Coward and Ellis, 1977; Silverman and Torode, 1980). The problem of situated history and social change stimulated attempts at structural marxism (e.g., Althusser, 1976) but fundamental problems surrounding the question of human agency remained (Giddens, 1979). The question hung over the relation between pre-existent formal systems and their relation to human action (Gauld and Shotter, 1977). The notion of discourse seemed to grasp the question of the subject and their historical location. The word discourse appears to emphasize the action over any formalizable system determining it: the word derives from *discurrere*, 'to draw off course' thereby reflecting the contingencies of history rather than the requirements of system. I have explored the notion that discourse theoretically sets limits to our ability to formalize elsewhere (Vass, 1982).

In summary, the attraction of *la langue* as a theoretical and methodological resource in the analysis of human practices is based on its ability to relate any 'element' of practice to any other elements that form part of the same system; and it permits the construction of bridges to other 'connoted systems' of social signification. Methodological problems began to mount and started with the basis of structural analysis. Douglas (1967) argued that the application of Levi-Strauss's techniques to mythical material (conceived as ideological and connoting systems) results in making the form and content of myths arbitrary. Structural specification is meant to take arbitrary elements and combine them thus specifying them. Douglas finds that structural analysis *produces* these elements and then finds them arbitrary. Furthermore, the actual specificity of elements of myths and elements of practice cannot be finally established — it cannot be stated, for example, why a particular binary pair becomes a binary pair: we are missing a theory of history and agency, if not of the subject.

This problem underwent a number of transformations during the marxist phase of structuralism, yet was still a problem for MacCormack and Strathern (1980) in connection with the analysis of gender practices. Empirically and ethnographically practice always appeared to exceed the current possibilities of the 'code' or *la langue*. Structuralists argued that their methods simply allow 'estimates' in the same way that statistics taken from samples allow the estimation of population parameters. That is, one may take a particular text or performance and view it as a partial instance, or an 'estimate', of parameters existing in full, ideally, elsewhere. The image this generates of human practice is that it is always a particular instantiation of a pre-existent code which we cannot fully grasp in its entirety but whose parameters we can have a shadowy grasp of as we engage in practice within the crumpled pleats of history. It was precisely this image that Derrida attacked in *Writing and Difference* (1978). In a number of passages he remarks that the effect of referring to code and to structure and similar notions is to turn history (and practice) into a problem:

> History has always been conceived as the movement of a resumption of history, as a detour between two presences [i.e., two fully formed systems]. But if it is legitimate to suspect this concept of history, there is a risk . . . of falling back into an ahistoricism of a classical type, that is to say, into a determined moment of the history of metaphysics. Such is the algebraic formality of the problem as I see it. More concretely, in the work of Levi-Strauss it must be recognised that the respect for structurality, for the internal originality of the structure, compels a neutralization of time and history. For example, the appearance of a new structure, of an original system, always comes about — and this is the very condition of its structural specificity — by a rupture with its past, its origin, and its cause. (Derrida, 1978, p. 291)

Derrida's analysis (appearing originally in 1967) anticipated most of the issues which came to the fore in the 1970s. The areas to which he wanted our attention to turn were those of history not opposed to structure. He wanted a primacy of *la parole* over *la langue* where the former was not opposed to the latter and where the keywords were to be 'conception, formation, gestation and labour'. The allusion to childbearing is quite explicit since the problem that needs to be addressed is not the structure of presences, nor the structure of outcomes, nor the pattern of results, nor the blueprints of activity, nor the codes of messages but the 'passage' of that which is formless and mute into that which becomes relatively more determined. This has also been a pre-occupation of Shotter (1975; 1984) who emphasizes not the already specified and the already structure but the passage of social relations as activities of *further, never final*, specification. Indeed, one of the central issues of post-structuralism for me is that practices seem to fail to specify. Social identities never seem complete and are always subject to further specification. What critics of social representations of gender, ethnicity and class tend to suggest is that the structures of meaning 'contained within' representations actually specify identities. This view of contemporary social representations is as fatalistic as that which Homer depicts in the *Iliad* and which began speculative philosophical discussion in Ancient Greece. At least the ancient heroes of Homer's epic could choose to accept or reject already specified fate: a reflective capacity denied to us by some modern critics. What they appear to avoid is stating that such specification remains everywhere incomplete, as much at the time of the Trojan war as today.

Discourse, Agency and Specification

We can now begin to restate the problem. If gender and class are produced within historical practices such as those on offer within the discourse of mathematics education then we can approach the problem emphasizing structure or we can emphasize human agency (which is where specification happens). If we emphasize structure then we are likely to proceed by identifying patterns of gender and class messages already situated in the discourse and then we would map the means by which these messages become translated as metaphors into other areas of practice. In other words any mathematical practice may incorporate already coded, already specified messages from other discourses. While this gives us hypotheses concerning the availability of certain messages within a practice it does not give us a theory of reading or of the consumption of those messages. Agents may as well become gendered through mathematics education by magical contagion or association with messages: and this is more or less what Levi-Strauss suggested in his structural analysis of modern mythological systems — connotative specificity is a form of contagion.

To look at the problem from the point of view of agency poses more of a problem. The language available for discussing agency is already hijacked by our need in the vernacular for terms that define action and agency within a language of everyday social accountiblity (Shotter, 1984; Douglas, 1980). Yet we can create plausible stories about action by using analytical methods based on structuralism, and we can follow the form of the argumentation in such work because we already subscribe in our everyday lives to the myth of 'system'. Simply part of what it is to be a member of a social 'order' is precisely to be able to locate, read, place, produce or otherwise isolate and account for elements of action and their outcomes. Knowing how to act in a situation can be made to feel like 'knowing the rules', which in turn can feel like mastery of a system of rules 'beyond' the current context. If I am gendered by encountering a system then not only are we dealing with something which is already pre-structured in terms of its rules and gender messages, but also a system which promises to reveal its composition by analytical means. The consequences of reading human action like this is that neither agency nor discourse are actually required. Where subjectivity is constituted by a system action takes place in accordance with the system. The human 'subject' of the system 'develops' or becomes gendered, ethnicized and classed through a history of transformations of successive 'presences' in the Derridean sense.

Mathematics education, viewed as a discourse, might be seen as a set of 'representational availabilities' where contact and interaction imply gendering and the constitution of subjectivity by acting in accordance with the rules governing its message structure: one's social identity is constructed by being 'on course' in the discourse concerned making use of its available 'rules'. This is to view discourse itself systemically. But my interpretation of the word discourse in the Foucauldian sense, in spite of how Foucault is now read in educational circles, is that discourse means 'off course', a continual movement away from the requirements of system. Pedagogy and, more generally, what Foucault describes as 'disciplinary' activity within culture (Foucault, 1976) are the central features of 'discursive formations' (mathematics education is just such a formation) because discourse at the level of subjects fails to do precisely what system critics see it doing everywhere: it fails to specify. System critics have been too ready to see discursive formations as a set of available resources pre-structured in accordance with established codes. On this view, agency assimilates and then reproduces its structure.

Post-structuralism, as I understand it in this context, involves the abandonment of structural readings which prioritize the system over the speaking subject. To grasp the nettle of what might be involved in doing so means situating ourselves within discourses and confronting the issues of agency and failure of specification and why such things are important not only for social critical activity but also in terms of how we construct pedagogy.

When system/*langue* is prioritized over agency/*parole* teaching and learning become sites of the transmission of structure through coded messages. The activities which this transmission involves result in the location and constitution of subjects within 'subject positions'. Positionality is defined with reference to the production of social identities for 'participants' to discourses. Participants use semiologically loaded resources in the pursuit of their notional activities such as mathematical tasks. The outcome of this is to not only solve problems through the specificatory facilities of language but also to become further specified as subjects in a particular discursive organization of the participants' subjectivities — the discourse of mathematics education clearly specifies social positions and identities for teacher and pupil and may further construct subject positions when parents are made participants to the discourse (see for example Brown and Dowling, 1993). I agree with this description of how the 'texts' of mathematics education produce available positions for human subjects. I do feel, however, that left there the description is inadequate. This sense of inadequacy does not relate to the truthfulness of the description to actual circumstances. I do not propose a 'better model' of the events of mathematics education. I would say that our accounts of social events have an important bearing on how we orientate ourselves in the present. The positioning effect of engaging in any discourse reminds me of Freud's attitude to the unconscious: there is not much we can do about it, it will have its way, we have to make a contract with it. Social positionality theories have a habit of silencing social 'occasionality'. There is the tendency in sociology to absorb the description of an occasion into a description of its positional outcomes for the participants concerned. In this picture social activity becomes everywhere 'finished business'; for a critique of this view of discourse see Billig (1987). That we might need to go beyond positionality theories in our exploration of the discursive quality of mathematics education is suggested at least in the self-dissatisfaction of the original theorists on whom this kind of critical work draws.

I have already mentioned Foucault and his conception of discourse which I see as at odds with the idea of a system of meanings (however heterogeneously structured). Foucault's own analyses take the form of genealogical critiques which situate themselves in a view of history that prioritizes not a system but something more akin to Derrida's prescription for discussing the 'passage' of specification in actualizing discourse: not realizing codes in messages.

The process of actualization places us in the domain of the subject and turns our attention on the consumption of 'meanings' that contexts make available to us. If we return to Roland Barthes at this juncture we might want to note his later sense of inadequacy with the project of describing and analysing systems. He (Barthes, 1982) turns his attention to the problem of consumption and identifies a dimension of the subject's movement within discourse which he previously failed to discuss. In reflecting on the reading of photographs he identifies the field given by semiotic resources as *studium*. *Studium* is what he had always hitherto been concerned with, the field of conventional meanings by which messages are socially coded. But he also identifies *punctum* which is unique to the reader in relation to a particular photograph. In this case something in the photograph, often an unremarkable detail, strikes the reader in a way which disrupts the field of the *studium* making the consumption problematic in some way but certainly attracting or repelling the reader. In his discussion of the consumption of photographs Barthes is exploring the issue of the engagement of subjectivity and the features of reading which 'mark or wound' the subject in some way. The importance of his discussion is that it alerts us to currently over- and under-theorized aspects of discourse: the field of the *studium* (which gets all the critical attention) mobilizes mild interest or boredom and invites the reader into the 'game' of reading and decoding messages. *Punctum* however, refers to unanalysed aspects of socially situated objects and actions which move the subject 'off course'.

For Julia Kristeva (1981) the 'off courseness' of discourse is central to all signifying practices. If we recall the view of discourse as a *langue*-based system, the identity of the subject is relative to discourses that, through the manipulation of the resources they make available, 'fix' the subject into positional relationships. This notion of 'fixity' images the subject as the interstitial point within a nexus of codified significations and was subject to critique in the 1970s (see Coward and Ellis, 1977). Kristeva, with a psychoanalytic background drawing on the work of Lacan, became a source of the psychoanalytic critique of structuralism. Lacan, like

Foucault in different contexts, emphasized the disruption of *dis*course. Kristeva's understanding of the signifying practice, which is what situated discursive activity consists in, is stated succinctly in the following:

> I shall call signifying practice the establishment *and countervailing* of a sign system. Establishing calls for the identity of a speaking subject within a social framework, which he recognises as the basis for that identity. Countervailing the sign system is done by having the subject undergo an unsettling, questionable process; this indirectly challenges the social framework with which he had previously identified . . . [my emphasis] (Kristeva, 1981, p. 18).

Signifying practices contain *both* establishing and countervailing forms of consumption and production of social meaning. I cannot go into Kristeva's post-structural description of language here, but as in Barthes' later work it is centered on *parole* rather than system and is particularly concerned with disruption and lack of structure in the constitution of the subject rather than the abundance of structure we tend to get in semiotic readings.

Countervailing as a dimension of our immersion within discourses needs to be taken seriously. In greater detail elsewhere (Vass, 1993a) I have cited work that theoretically and ethnographically draws attention to our mode of consumption of already structured objects, whether these be market consumables or mathematics texts and pedagogies. Miller's work (1987) on the items of mass consumption dwells on the countervailing tendencies of subjects to 'reappropriate' objects, which otherwise appear to have available semiotic specifications that 'fix' identities. This work might alert us to the idea that the transmission of loaded meanings in the production of gendered or classed subjects is at least not unproblematic, it is certainly not automatic. Minimally, for me, it raises the problem of specification within human action: who specifies what and what specifies whom. Structural descriptions of *la langue* treat the act of speaking (dynamic discursive engagement) as an occasion for realizing a possibility. But it takes an actual occasion for turning the boundaries of possibility into an object for further elaboration. Positional identities are third-person structural descriptions of first and second-person communicational labour. Along with Bilig (1987), Bakhtin (1981) and Shotter (1989) we might want to ask about the actual circumstances of first and second persons 'addressing' each other. While I cannot discuss it here it should be said that these writers find that far from seeing the first and second-person occasion as an event where structural possibility is realized, they see it as the place where subjects produce possibility and make arrangements for 'discursive accidents'.

Reading Mathematics Discourse

While focusing on specific texts and practices within mathematics education we need an approach to situated activity that does pay attention to the construction of social identities, that is critical of the outcomes of such 'formations', and that can theorize the processes involved. Structuralism inserts itself, I suspect, because it lends analytical ease and gives people something to do methodologically.

Walkerdine certainly has important stories to tell us in her analyses of practices and texts. She embraces the critique of structuralism and much of her work depends on a starting point that assumes such a critique. But is it a matter of rhetorical convenience that a leaning towards structure, in the sense of *la langue*, comes across so strongly?:

> What exist are discursive practices which operate according to relations of signification, utilizing different systems of syntagmatic and paradigmatic opposition. School mathematics practices with respect to size discrimination take the discrimination as a focus in a way which is not the case with respect to size in other practices . . . To enter early school mathematics . . . children must become subjects within those discursive practices and recognize the lesson as an example of pedagogic testing discourse with size as the focus. (Walkerdine, 1988, p. 92)

This passage tends to formulate discourse as a system in which children 'become subjects'. But this is at tension with the idea that 'children must . . . recognize' the discourse in its distinctness from others in which they might engage. I feel that the description of the discourse system permits a form of analysis of speech ethnography of a standard structural kind. So, it can be suggested how 'multiple signification of many signs within particular practices demonstrates the way in which participants are positioned and regulated' (*ibid.*: p. 93). I find the following tension in *The Mastery of Reason* that there are numerous occasions in which the theoretical material demands a post-structural view of the agent. Such a view appears to be present but sits together with a methodology that seeks to map 'systems of syntagmatic and paradigmatic opposition' (in the way outlined in the section 'Methodological Considerations' above). Yet the same agents under review need to be able to recognize the difference between two discourses that position and regulate them. Such a recognition is a prime requirement for countervailing activities. It is a recognition of the marginal zones that people occupy as first and second-person interlocutors from where the conditions of possibility are produced (Vass, 1993b). Walkerdine is clearly aware of the theoretical limitations of structuralism and of the kinds of sources, such as psychoanalysis, which provide a countermeasure to its excesses. Yet where such insights enter the field of discussion in *The Mastery of Reason* they take on the structuralist style of the discussion (much like the child described entering the school's system of signification); thus.

> Children's insertion into practices . . . is not totally dependent on 'real life', and their positioning relates also to the imagined through their insertion as subjects within story-telling, the media, and other cultural practices. (*ibid.*, p. 148)

My point is not to deride this important work nor others that similarly have transformed the nature of discussion not only in mathematics education but also in the social sciences generally, but to indicate where post-structuralist insights become positioned and regulated within the field of structuralist writing practices.

References

ALTHUSSER, L. (1976) *Essays in Self-Criticism*, New Left Books.
BAKHTIN, M. (1981) *The Dialogic Imagination*, Austin, Texas University Press.
BARTHES, R. (1973) *Mythologies*, London, Paladin.
BARTHES, R. (1982) *Camera Lucida*, London, Jonathon Cape.
BILLIG, M. (1987) *Arguing and Thinking*, Cambridge, Cambridge University Press.
BROWN, A. and DOWLING, P. (1993) in Merttens *et al.* (1993).
COWARD, R. and ELLIS, J. (1977) *Language and Materialism*, London, RKP.
DERRIDA, J. (1978) *Writing and Difference*, London, RKP.
DOUGLAS, M. (1967) 'The meaning of myth, with special reference to "La Geste d'Asdiwal"', in LEACH, E. (Ed) (1967) *The Structural Study of Myth and Totemism*, ASA Monographs, 5, London, Tavistock.
DOUGLAS, M. (1980) *Evans-Pritchard*, London, Fontana.
DOWLING P.C. (1991) 'Gender, class and subjectivity in mathematics: A critique of Humpty Dumpty', *For the Learning of Mathematics*, 11, 1.
DURKHEIM, E. (1976) *Elementary Forms of Religious Life*, London, RKP.
FOUCAULT, M. (1973) *The Birth of the Clinic*, London, Tavistock.
FOUCAULT, M. (1976) *Discipline and Punish*, Harmondsworth, Penguin.
GAULD, A. and SHOTTER, J. (1977) *Human Action and its Psychological Investigation*, London, RKP.
GIDDENS, A. (1979); *Central Problems in Social Theory*, London, Macmillan.
KRISTEVA, J. (1981) *Desire and Language*, Oxford, Basil Blackwell.
LEVI-STRAUSS, C. (1966) *The Savage Mind*, Weidenfeld and Nicolson.
MACCORMACK, C. and STRATHERN, M. (1980) *Nature, Culture, Gender*, Cambridge, Cambridge University Press.
MERTTENS, R. and VASS, J. (1989) 'Special needs in mathematics', in ROBINSON, O. and THOMAS, G. (1989) *Tackling Learning Difficulties*, London, Hodder and Stoughton.
MERTTENS, R., MAYERS, D., BROWN, A. and VASS, J. (Eds) (1993) *Ruling the Margins: people and practices in parental involvement*, London, The University of North London Press.
MILLER, D. (1987) *Material Culture and Mass Consumption*, Oxford, Basil Blackwell.
SAUSSURE, F. DE (1974) *Course in General Linguistics*, London, Fontana.
SHOTTER, J. (1975) *Images of Man in Psychological Research*, London, Methuen.
SHOTTER, J. (1984) *Social Accountability and Selfhood*, Oxford, Basil Blackwell.
SHOTTER, J. (1989) 'The social construction of "you"', in SHOTTER, J. and GERGEN, K. (Eds) *Texts of Identity*, London, Sage.
SILVERMAN, D. and TORODE, B. (1980) *The Material Word*, London, RKP.
VASS, J. and MERTTENS, R. (1987) 'The cultural mediation and determination of intuitive knowledge and cognitive development', in EGIL, P. and MJAAVATN, E. (Eds) (1988) *Growing into the Modern World*, Trondheim, Trondheim University Press.
VASS, J. (1982) 'Discourse and the Limits of Formalization', Unpublished MSc. Thesis.
VASS, J. (1993a) 'Apprenticeships in the absence of masters: authority and canonical texts in pedagogical communication', in MERTTENS *et al.* (1993) *Ruling the Margins: people and practices in parental involvement*, London, The University of North London Press.
VASS, J. (1993b) 'Marginal dialogues, social positions and inequity in rhetorical resources', in MERTTENS, R. and VASS, J. (Eds) *Parents and Schools — The IMPACT Project*, London, The Falmer Press.
WALKERDINE, V. (1988) *The Mastery of Reason*, London, Routledge.

Chapter 11

Describing the Mathematics You Are Part Of: A Post-structuralist Account of Mathematical Learning

Tony Brown

Where therefore is truth? A mobile army of metaphors, metonymies, anthromorphisms . . . truths are illusions of which one has forgotten that they are illusions. (Nietzsche[1])

Introduction

In recent work within the social sciences and cultural studies there have been moves away from seeing words within a language as being a labelling device to denote pre-existing phenomena. Rather, the very framing consequential to introducing language is the process through which phenomena are brought into existence; the mechanism through which meaning is produced. What does this mean for mathematics and its teaching where we are faced with task of working with symbols produced and exchanged in a social sphere?

Deconstructing Mathematics

The great ideas of mathematics are all culturally derived but have become so embedded within the fabric of our culture that it is hard for us to see them as anything other than givens. Derrida (1967, p. 281) has spoken of the difficulty of deconstructing linguistic structures since there is always a need to use the elements of the structures themselves in dismantling these very structures. For mathematicians it is impossible to deconstruct mathematics without using culturally inherited mathematical tools. Similarly, any 'new' mathematical construction is always made within an inherited language which means that it is always already partially constructed. The culture provides the building blocks and the final building is a function of these. Not only is this true of the 'objective' components of mathematics e.g., '+', '*sine*' or '%', but also there are culturally bound ways of combining them, as in school mathematics, or real-world mathematics, or university research mathematics, or whatever (the architectural styles). We cannot investigate mathematics without being tied into pre-existing styles of categorizing.

Although Derrida himself would chuckle at the term many would regard him as a post-structuralists. A somewhat potted account of how post-structuralism superseded structuralism might be given as follows.[2] Writers like Barthes, Althusser, Foucault, Lacan and Levi-Strauss attempted to develop the linguistic model offered by Saussure into 'a fully fledged "semiology" — that is, a science of signs which goes beneath the surface events of language (*parole*) to investigate a variety of concealed signifying systems (*langue*)' (Urmson and Ree, 1989, p. 311). In Levi-Strauss's work on structural anthropology, for example, there was some belief in a structure (say of a particular society) that could be observed from the outside with some fixed relation between its outward manifestations and its inner workings. The task here was to translate 'the disorder of . . . empirical experience into the order of systematic structures' (*Ibid.*, p. 311). Similarly, for Althusser, '(h)uman individuals were not to be understood as the self-conscious sources of their social life, but rather as "bearers" of a system of social relations which exist prior to and independently of their consciousness and activity' (*Ibid.*, p. 7).

'The post-structuralists (however) rejected the binary oppositions between surface and depth, event and structure, inner and outer, conscious and unconscious as revived forms of metaphysical dualism. They renounced the structuralist quest for a science of signs, celebrating instead the irreducible excesses of language as a multiple play of meaning' (*Ibid.*, p. 311). Such moves resulted in the whole idea of an objective structure being undermined since there could be no agreed relationship as any such view pre-supposed a particular individual perspective. Indeed any supposed meaning itself becomes forever elusive. More importantly however, each individual can only describe the world of which they are part and so there is necessarily a reflexive dimension to any such description. The observer is not so much describing a structure but rather their view of it, and by implication in this they are describing a bit of themselves. By recognizing that mathematics only ever comes to life in human exchanges and that any mathematical expression has been selected for use within such an exchange it follows that mathematical activity also has this reflexive dimension.

Learning About Myself

Within recent writing on mathematics education it is fashionable to reject Platonism yet the consequences of this are not always being fully grasped. A student engaged in a mathematical task will have a particular view of the work he or she is doing and this work would necessarily be described by this student from a personal perspective. Any such description of mathematical phenomena by an individual implies a view of oneself. As an example, at the last ATM conference I was offered an intriguing task. I had to imagine I was a spider positioned somewhere in the room. Other people then had to request information about the shape of things I saw. For instance, from my perspective that table top looked like a trapezium. Gathering together such information my questioners needed to decide where I was. The whole task was about positioning myself in relation to the world around me and it was through this process I got to know aspects of myself through describing my relation with the world of which I was part.

This took place in the 'workshop', a whole room full of practical mathematics equipment. Any task available in this room could be seen in this way, not so much a case of exploring the properties of the things available but rather they could all be seen as devices through which I could find out about myself. Clearly this is not only true of practical maths but also of any representation of any mathematical phenomena. Any act of mathematics can be seen as an act of construction where I simultaneously construct in language mathematical notions and the world around me. Meaning is produced as I get to know my relationships to these things. This process is the source of the post-structuralist notion of the human subject being constructed in language. In this instance the individual subject constructs his or her self in language through describing his or her relations to the world around. Such a view asserts an essential instability in both subject and situation so that there is a need to analyse both, which can be seen as part of each other, as processes. The subject, and the structure in which he or she acts, is asserted, in the ways they are represented in language, through time. This is always subject to change as more things can always be said. These representations are not mere labellings but are instrumental in the construction of subject and structure. It is the very process of signifying in language that brings into being the notions described and these notions then serve in shaping subsequent actions.

I am reminded of a session with Gattegno discussing algebra. He spoke of a young child pointing to a fly on the ceiling. This arm movement meant the fly was by the window, this one meant it was by the light. The child's bodily movements were substitutions for fly positions. I can imagine myself in the ATM workshop making all sorts of other bodily substitutions as I get to know myself in relation to the objects on offer. What can these Dienes blocks tell me about myself, and this tray of polyhedral models? Mathematical education folklore is that these bodily substitutions gradually get replaced by mental substitutions or by movements of the fingers in getting a pen to produce symbols on paper. As I grow older I become initiated into an inherited language of symbols with culturally derived rules for combining these symbols and inherited social practices within which these linguistic practices arise. As I share my thoughts with another person I ask what they can tell me about myself.

I cannot disentangle things independently of my history. For me 'Structure, sign and play in the human sciences' by Derrida (1967) is a marvellous, inspiring but difficult work. I say this as a 37-year-old who was similarly impressed by AS Neill as an 18-year-old, by Freire as a 22-year-old, by Gattegno as a 25-year-old. The person now delivered to Derrida's writing from the 1960s is a historically formed subject who cannot discount his journey there. I use Derrida's writing to help me find out about myself — partly, at least, because it is too difficult to find out what Derrida himself is on about!

If I am presented with a new piece of mathematics I bring to it a whole history of myself. Any construction I make in respect of this new task cannot be independent of this history. Nor can it ignore the circuit of exchange through which I will present any account of this work in the social forum. If I describe a piece of mathematics I am involved in an act of describing a situation of which I am part. I choose the bits that seem important to me. I am describing an extract from my own history, an experience, a process now gathered together in words and symbols. The story becomes in some way fixed as that which it describes carries on moving as the story is told. The story becomes more powerful than that to which it refers. Reality can thus be seen as being asserted through the stories told about it. This slides in to the post-modernist notion, however, (e.g., Zizek 1991, p. 99), that there is always something remaining outside these stories, outside theory, resisting over-arching narratives that account for everything.

Saussure's Linguistics

Post-structuralism of this sort is firmly rooted in the linguistical model developed by Saussure (1966) at the turn of the century. Saussure himself did not write a book — a task he saw as too difficult. The main work credited to him was put together by his students from their lecture notes. It is a largely technical book and is generally disregarded by modern-day linguists. The book nevertheless has provided a framework for many modern writers in other fields. It is also surprisingly clear given the complex nature of the writers who cite him. Saussure's usage and popularization of the terms 'signifier', 'signified' and 'sign' has been particularly influential.

The original formulation of these terms saw the signifier as a sound and the signified as a concept associated with this. The sign was seen as combining these two elements into a wholly mental phenomena. Signs were not seen as having meaning in their own right but rather meaning was seen as being derived from the relationship between signs. This is very different to the naïve notion of a sign which associates a physical symbol with a physical object. Saussure only concerned himself with the relation between signs and did not investigate the way in which they are associated with the physical and social world. Derrida has done most in pursuing this. For him meaning is always in the future, always 'deferred', there is never a closure to a story because this story can always be extended.[3] Any story seen as complete can then be contextualized alongside other stories. This is not unlike Mason's work (1988) in mathematical learning where a quest to find the key result becomes transformed when, after the result is found, it is recognized as merely yet another result alongside others. We can always explore further. The meaning we derive is always contingent. Our understanding is the sense we make of what we have done so far.

The distinction drawn by Saussure between the system of language (*langue*) and its realizations in acts of speech (*parole*) seems highly pertinent here. Mathematics has no reality outside individual acts of mathematics except within Platonism. We are unable to perceive mathematics except through our acts of engagement in it. Whilst there might be some over-arching system of mathematics (analogous to *langue*) we can never survey this holistically in a neutral way. Our performance in mathematics can only ever be judged through our acts of parole. Meaning then cannot be seen as being associated with individual signs within the system. Meaning only emerges as signs are combined in stories that emerge around the activities performed. These stories are never unique since they are necessarily from an individual perspective and are necessarily time-dependent. Walkerdine (1988) speaks of meaning being produced in the process of signifying. I see this as being to do with asserting structures through the use of stories in accounting for mathematical experiences. The language and symbols used shape the developing understanding, and provide the components within this.

Asserting the Linguistic Aspects of Mathematical Activity

In exploring these issues I would like to offer two examples of activities I employ in my own teaching which seek to give primacy to this linguistic production of meaning.

Example 1

As a teacher I have shown Nicolet's animated geometry films to a variety of groups from 11-year-olds to adult. After showing a brief section of film I ask pairs of people to share what they saw using spoken words only. After a few minutes I ask each pair to combine with another pair. Each group of four is then asked to produce a verbal account of what happened on the screen in as much detail as possible. The reality of the event becomes held in this string of words that itself becomes more solid than the memory of an image on the screen.

In an extension of this activity with trainee teachers I ask each group of four to select a 'teacher' who is then asked to leave the room. A second short sequence of film is then shown to the 'pupils' who remain. The teachers are then invited back into the room and are given the task of finding out what the pupils saw, again only through the use of spoken word. They are then required to give a 'lesson' based on what happened on the screen.

Example 2

In another lesson for trainee teachers I give each student a different model made of five centicubes fitted together and say they have been given a 'Pentoid'. However, I hand it to them behind their backs so they are unable to see it. They have to rely on what they can feel with their fingers. One person is asked to describe their model to everyone else as someone records this description on the blackboard. Other students are then asked to say in which ways their own model is similar or different.

The students are then paired and given extra cubes. They are requested to describe their own model (with their eyes closed) so their partner can build a replica. When each pair has made their replicas the original models are collected, without having been seen. The replicas are then gathered together for all to see. The students are then requested to imagine that they are about to telephone a friend in order to describe what a Pentoid is. How would they do this in a one minute call?

In the first activity anyone is able to describe the film using the terms they have available to them. Anyone can describe what they see although such descriptions pre-suppose an intention to be understood by others. The task is very much to do with classifying perception in language. Meaning is brought to the film in the phrasing chosen. The way of structuring the image of the film will be individual but likely to be offered in words from an inherited and (in some ways) shared language. The films may suggest familiar concepts to learned mathematicians but these will not hamper the vision of more naïve viewers. At some level ideas are imposed by the film but the viewer can stress and ignore as he or she chooses according to what he or she sees. The task is more a question of finding the best way of communicating with others. It is difficult to assert a threshold level of achievement on such a task.

Much of this also applies to the second activity where there is a more obvious move towards defining a concept. Whilst one may or may not gather what a Pentoid is the emphasis of the activity is on fitting language to experience, a task of describing one's perspective. The reality of 'pentoid' is held in the words that participants use to describe it. There is little need for an external authority validating work done, since the quest for the correct answer is not the point.

The essential task in both activities is for the students to introduce structures and through this produce meanings in the act of signifying. The purpose is for the students to develop 'signifying practices' which I see as underpinning developing understanding. In stressing the linguistic dimension of mathematics in this way we shift away from emphasizing mathematical activity as being to do with converging to pre-defined and well-known concepts.

Creating Versus Inheriting Mathematics

Recent writings that emphasize the socially constructed nature of mathematics (e.g., Ernest, 1991) tend to hang on to the inherited apparatus of mathematics. Whilst students may be constructing they necessarily do this in the dominant language of the culture. Constructions are always already partly constructed by virtue of the language used in their construction. The cultural derivation of mathematics is essentially a consequence of certain notions being captured in language and being passed down. The base 10 system, Euclidean geometry, algebraic structures are all inventions from the past that have become absorbed in our culture and are among the frameworks we employ when we speak of our world in a mathematical way. They all offer overlays for partitioning what we see but in turn condition what we see. There is nothing natural about them and it would be daft to suppose that they can be discovered as such. They can only be discovered after a fairly comprehensive initiation into the cultural ways of describing the world in language, of which mathematics is necessarily part. So described 'discovery' methods might be seen as being associated with pre-defined products, pre-existing mathematical notions and as such may be seen as being more akin to the older form of structuralism. The relative fixity, in the way in which the mathematical field is partitioned for the purposes of describing it, underplays any linguistic negotiation. The task is to discover the way in which such notions are conventionally described with a particular view of their meaning.

Investigational styles, of the sort that tended to get started in schools in the UK in the 1970s and 1980s (e.g., ATM, 1977), seem different in one important respect. They are not so much about discovery but rather invite the student to introduce and develop structure. The emphasis is not on understanding a particular concept but is more concerned with the produce of conceiving. They have more of a quality of a game. If we set these conditions what can we say? By focusing on the fitting of structures they do offer more scope for linguistic invention (albeit within a borrowed language) than in tasks that are about introducing culturally conventional ways of gathering ideas. They have a creative component which permits the student to assert a more personal identity in the output of this work. 'Investigations' are more concerned with production of both mathematical structures and the linguistic categories associated with them. This is more akin to what I have called post-structuralism. The process of signifying underlying this asserts the centrality of the individual learner in producing the mathematical meaning.

Clearly, however, much mathematical learning is to do with becoming initiated into conventional cultural usage. Mathematics is generally performed in a social sphere and there are definite requirements for participants. So there is a dual task of enabling the student to be conventional in his or her language usage but at the same time inventive in building structures and meaning for themselves.

Conclusion

Mathematics is only ever manifestly represented in acts of symbolic communication and as such offers itself to linguistic analysis. Saussure's work has taught us that meaning is not derived from individual terms but is consequential to the play of differences between successive terms in a particular discourse. For mathematical terms this suggests that there is not an implicit meaning to individual terms as such but meaning is dependent on the individual construction of mathematical expressions. Ultimate meaning, however, to use Derrida's expression, is always deferred. Since we cannot speak of meaning in any absolute sense we always await the final word.

The task for the mathematics teacher is on the one hand to recognize that his or her students need to talk about mathematics in conventional ways. This is to do with learning the language of mathematics and the conventional ways of using it. But, on the other hand, the teacher needs to enable the students to gain experience of linguistic invention towards producing structures and meaning. This latter task is to do with students describing situations of which they are part. Understanding arises through this process of learning to signify, that is, in the attaching of linguistic and symbolic forms to experience.

Notes

1. Originally cited in the 'preface' by Gayatri Spivak to *Of Grammatology* (Derrida, 1976) p. xxii. Also quoted in Easthope and McGowan (1992)
2. Rather more detailed and articulate versions are offered in Coward and Ellis (1977), Urmson and Ree (1989) and Brown (in press).
3. A valuable discussion of Derrida's work and a reprint of the highly complex paper by him, 'Difference', can be found in Easthope and McGowan (1992).

References

ASSOCIATION OF TEACHERS OF MATHEMATICS (1977) *Points of Departure*, Derby, ATM.
BROWN, T. (in press) 'Creating and knowing mathematics through language and experience', *Educational Studies in Mathematics*, Dordrecht, Kluwer, 27, 1.
COWARD, R. and ELLIS, J. (1977) *Language and Materialism*, London, Routledge.
DERRIDA, J. (1967) *Writing and Difference*, Chicago, Chicago University Press.
EASTHOPE, A. and McGOWAN, K. (1992) *A Critical and Cultural Studies Reader*, Buckingham, Open University.
ERNEST, P. (1991) *The Philosophy of Mathematics Education*, London, The Falmer Press.

MASON, J. (1988) 'A delicate shift of attention', *For the Learning of Mathematics*, Montréal, FLM.

SAUSSURE, F. DE (1966) *A Course in General Linguistics*, New York, McGraw Hill.

WALKERDINE, V. (1988) *The Mastery of Reason,* London, Routledge.

URMSON, J. and REE, J. (1989) The *Concise Encyclopedia of Western Philosophy and Philosophers*, London, Unwin and Hyman.

ZIZEK, S. (1991) *For They Know Not What They Do*, London, Verso.

Part 3

The Human Face of Mathematics

The popular image of mathematics is that it is difficult, cold, abstract, and ultra-rational. Even for many persons operating at high levels of competency in numeracy, graphicacy, and computeracy in their professional life this image of mathematics persists (Ernest, 1993). However, like the philosophers in the maverick tradition most contributors to this volume reject this image as unnecessary and mistaken. Most agree with Reuben Hersh's (1988) view of mathematics which has both a front and a back. In the front, the public are served perfect mathematical dishes, like in a fancy restaurant. In the back, the mathematicians cook up new knowledge amid mess, chaos and all the inescapably associated human striving, successes, failures, and displays of ill temper. Rotman (1988) similarly describes mathematics as being like a play, with only a privileged minority being allowed to see behind the scenes.

Instead of the negative image described above, what is needed is for us to show the human face of mathematics more often. Of course, such insights are increasingly widespread. For example, Alvin White founded the Humanistic Mathematics Network and journal to promote the teaching of mathematics, especially in college, as a humanistic discipline. He has just edited a collection of papers promoting this perspective for the Mathematical Association of America (White, 1994).

Each contributor to this section has helped to humanize mathematics through his work. Hao Wang (1974) and Philip J. Davis (Davis and Hersh, 1980) through their well-known contributions to the maverick tradition in the philosophy of mathematics. George G. Joseph (1991) through his important rewriting of the multicultural history of mathematics. Here each presents the human face of mathematics by means of a contrast. Whether it is individual mathematicians, disciplines, or even cultures the contrast helps reaffirm the human setting of mathematics.

References

DAVIS, P.J. and HERSH, R. (1980) *The Mathematical Experience*, Boston, Birkhauser.

ERNEST, P. (1993) 'The popular image of mathematics', *Humanistic Mathematics Network Journal*, 8, pp. 53–5.

HERSH, R. (1988) 'Mathematics has a Front and a Back', Paper presented at Sixth International Congress of Mathematics Education, Budapest, July 27-August 4.

JOSEPH, G.G. (1991) *The Crest of the Peacock*, London, I.B. Tauris.

ROTMAN, B. (1988) 'Towards a semiotics of mathematics', *Semiotica*, 72, 1/2, pp. 1–35.

WANG, H. (1974) *From Mathematics to Philosophy*, London, Routledge.

WHITE, A. (Ed) (1994) *Essays in Humanistic Mathematics*, Washington, DC, Mathematical Association of America.

Chapter 12

Mathematics and Art: Cold Calipers Against Warm Flesh?

Philip J. Davis

The carpenter stretches out a line
He marks it with a pencil
He shapes it with his plane
And marks it with a compass
And makes it into a figure of a man
According to the beauty of man
To be placed in a house.

Isaiah 44:13. (6th Century B.C.)

Introduction

In the fifteenth century, the humanists in Italy played an important role in fostering the rebirth of mathematics. They collected the ancient Greek mathematical texts; they translated them and made them available. In those days, there was hardly a split between the arts and the sciences. The great names in art: Alberti, Brunelleschi, Duerer, Leonardo da Vinci, Michaelangelo had a considerable knowledge of the mathematics and physics of the day. Da Vinci is often regarded as the supreme 'Renaissance man' and a description of his mathematical interests can be found in Veltman's magisterial book. But one might equally well take Leon Battista Alberti (1404–1472), an artist, an architect, a poet, a mathematician, the first person to formulate the principles of linear perspective, as the paradigm of the all-embracing interests and accomplishments of the artists of the age.

This state of integration lasted for, perhaps, a century and a half. Sir Isaiah Berlin (in *The Sciences and the Humanities*) observed that 'the great cleavage between the provinces of the sciences and the humanities was, for the first time, made, or at least revealed, for better or for worse, by Giambattista Vico (1668–1744). Thereby he started a great debate of which the end is not in sight.'

In the past generation, the cleavage has been called the 'two culture crisis' and recent discussions of it have been associated with the names of C.P. Snow (on the part of science) and F.D. Leavis (on the part of the humanities). It is my perception, based on what I've seen in academic life and in the popular media, that the split between the sciences and the humanities is worsening. This is to their detriment and to the detriment of life in general.

Philip J. Davis

As part of a programme of mutual appreciation and reconciliation, it is of importance to arrive at a deeper picture of the interplay between mathematics and art. A full and comprehensive study of the relationship between mathematics and visual art and design has not yet been undertaken. Such a study would be multi-volumed and probably beyond the scope of any one individual. What complicates matters is the split itself; that specialists in art and specialists in mathematics often have rather limited and naive views as to what the important aspects of the other subject are in what is a rather complicated relationship.

To keep the length of this article down, I have deliberately omitted from the article topics related to architecture. The same policy was adopted for computer art, although I have included a bit of discussion of this important subject. As regards to computer art, we are currently in the midst of a great explosion whose end is nowhere in sight and whose impact is not evaluated easily. One can see the trees, but not as yet the forest.

Substantial treatments are available for only a few of the topics inter-relating mathematics and art. As examples: geometry in Egyptian and Greek art, perspective in Renaissance art, the mathematics of perspective and vision, the mathematization of the human figure, ideal beauty via mathematics, the mathematics of tiling, symmetry, the Bauhaus movement and its relation to the philosophy of science, design (both primitive, Islamic, . . .) and its relation to group theory, the mathematical analysis of Escher's work.

The literature of perspective is by itself enormous, written both by art historians and critics and by historians of mathematics. It is my perception that art-critical interpretations in which such terms as 'positioned viewers', 'frames', 'scenographic spaces' are emphasized, would seem incomprehensible or trivial to mathematicians who think in terms of definitions, theorems, proofs and algorithms. On the other hand, computer graphicists or stage designers would probably give the art-critical statements a more appreciative reading.

The purposes of this chapter are threefold: to point out

- that the relationship between art and mathematics is a very rich field for inquiry and speculation;
- that mathematicians who look to this relationship for a reflection of 'deep' traditional or contemporary mathematics are seriously limiting the inquiry; and
- that there is a 'love–hate' relationship between mathematics and art resulting in a history of on-again off-again engagements. The study of this history can cast light on present developments in, say, abstract or computer-assisted art.

Visual or graphical art, out of its very nature, displays features that are geometric. Reciprocally, geometry can be regarded as an abstraction, a distillation, a formalization, an intellectualization of the visual and kinesthetic experience of space. The mutual interaction of the two is profound, often interwoven with other motivations and often perceived only superficially or dimly. Some commentators, e.g., the distinguished mathematician Marston Morse, locate the crux of the interaction on the psychological level: 'The basic affinity between mathematics and the arts is psychological and spiritual, and not metrical or geometrical.' This is an incomplete and unacceptable view of the matter.

Consider, for example, religious art in thirteenth-century France. A superficial reading of Emile Male's classic work *The Gothic Image* will reveal at the very least four types of interpenetration by mathematics: (1) The geometrical arrangements or divisions of the stained glass windows (2) The action or influence of 'sacred arithmetic' (i.e., number mysticism, gematria, etc.) (3) The action of 'sacred mathematics' as regards position, orientation, grouping, symmetry of the images (4) On a totally different meta-level, the personification of the subjects of the medieval quadrivium as female figures representing arithmetic, geometry, astronomy and music.

These types of interaction may be regarded as 'weak' utilizations of mathematics in view, largely, of the subsequent development and concerns of mathematics and the application of some few of them to graphics. A judgment of weakness ignores, for example, the fact that things like numerology or hermetic geometry were once considered to be legitimate applications of mathematics. Nonetheless, weak or strong, produced consciously or intuitively, they are mathematical.

Broadly speaking, if architecture is excluded, the history of western art shows four major engagements with mathematics:

1. the reduction or the conventionalization of the human figure via proportion or other mathematical means;
2. perspective; and
3. dehumanized, de-representationalized artistic productions leaning heavily on geometric constructions or influenced by emerging geometric theories, e.g., non-Euclidean or higher dimensional geometries.

The first concern extends from deep antiquity to somewhat beyond da Vinci. The second comes to great prominence in Renaissance art, while the third begins at the end of the nineteenth century and continuing to the present, ultimately blends with

4. computer-generated, assisted, modulated, or analysed art.

The Mathematization of the Human Figure

I shall first sketch some ups and downs of the mathematizing spirit in depicting the human figure. In the main, I shall follow the presentation of art historians and critics Erwin Panofsky and Sir Kenneth Clark.

Some years ago, I wanted to improve my status as an amateur artist and so I enrolled in a life class. I worked away diligently at my canvas. The instructor came over, looked at what I had accomplished, and shook his head. 'That will never do', he said. Then getting out huge calipers from a storage bin, he gave them to me and said, 'Go over to the model. Measure her. Figure out her proportions, and be guided by your figures.' I was tremendously embarrassed both by my failure and by the suggestion that I measure warm flesh with a pair of cold calipers. However, I did so and I don't now remember whether any improvement resulted in my work.

Here we have a strategy of studio art that goes back at least 2500 years. Here is mathematical modeling in a very literal, hands-on sense. Polykleitos (fifth century BC) who was a sculptor and architect, and who has been called the 'father of Greek anthropometry' (i.e., the measurement of the human figure), once remarked that 'the beautiful comes about little by little through many numbers.' He told his contemporaries that 'from the toes to the last hair on the head, every line was calculated'; that 'Apollo was beautiful because his body conformed to certain laws of proportion and so partook of the divine beauty of mathematics.'

One can distinguish two general approaches to drawing the human figure: the subjective, which may also be called the romantic or the non-rational, and the objective, which may be identified with the geometric or rational. In the objective approach, the human figure is viewed as a purely abstract entity.

Now, one of the basic questions that Panofsky raises (following Alois Riegl) is what is the artistic intent (Kunstwollen) of the artist? Artistic intent, in the sense of these critics embraces both the individual artist and the enveloping artistic *Zeitgeist*. (I know that as a rank amateur, my artistic intent was simply to lay down some paint in a way that would be recognizable as a human form.)

The intent, according to Male, of the art of the Middle Ages was didactic: 'All that was necessary that men should know — the history of the world from the creation, the dogmas of religion, the examples of the saints, the hierarchy of the virtues, the range of the sciences, arts and crafts — all these were taught them by the windows of the church or by the statues in the porch.'

Artistic intent differs from age to age. In the art of ancient Egypt, perhaps 1000 years prior to Polykleitos, the stylized, erect figures evoked the static, timeless eternity of things, and established certain magical realities. The form was all important; the function counted for little. There was rigidity within rectangular grids. The figure was inserted, so to speak, in a uniform rectangular grid or mesh without regard for the underlying bone structure.

In the Periclean age, the Greeks allowed more freedom. The human figure was full of life, movement, and plasticity. They paid some attention to the human bone structure. Architecturally, they observed the foreshortening due to vision and did not build columns with parallel sides. The intent of Greek art was the establishment of an aesthetic ideal, of canons of harmony and beauty. Vitruvius, who wrote on architecture in the first century BC, sought the laws of beauty even as physicists today seek the fundamental laws of particles.

In the medieval period, particularly in Byzantine art, there was a standardization in drawing the heads of saints in terms of a 'three circle' scheme. The thirteenth century architect and artist Villard de Honnecourt drew nudes not from life, not with calipers, but according to an abstract theory of human proportions.

> The divine element in the human body must be expressed through geometry. The Gothic artists could draw animals because this involved no intervening abstraction. They could not draw the nude because it was an idea. An idea that their philosophy of form could not assimilate. (Clark, 1959)

Moving to the High Renaissance, we are all familiar with the picture of da Vinci (1452–1519) of the man fitted into a square and a circle. This was more than a convenient rule. Kenneth Clark observed that

It was the foundation of a whole philosophy. Together with the musical scale of Pythagoras, it was the link between sensation and order, between an organic and a geometric basis for beauty. (*ibid.*)

He says further,

The formalized body of the 'perfect man' became the supreme symbol of European belief. This mystic belief in the perfect form of man . . . persisted surely up to Goethe and sent him on an equally hopeless search for the *Urpflanze* [the basic, primitive botanic forms]. (*ibid.*)

Panofsky asserts that as regards the human figure, some of the artistic intentions in the employment of mathematics have been to establish norms, conventions, constructive relationships, beauty, harmony; also to establish the mystic numerical relationships between the human body and other parts of the cosmos, to see the human body as the microcosm in a macrocosm, and in this way to assert nature's harmonic unity.

Even as the mathematizing tendency flourished, its legitimacy was being questioned. Albrecht Duerer (1471–1528) admired the work of the Italian sculptor Jacopo de' Barbari. But Jacopo had refused to tell Duerer how his figures were composed, 'thus setting up in Duerer's mind the conviction that the classical nude depended on a secret formula . . . guarded by Italian artists in order to surpass their Northern colleagues. In his determination to discover this secret, Duerer began and continued throughout his life the elaborate geometrical analysis of the human figure . . . In common with all Northern artists, he found it difficult to believe that the harmony of the classical nude did not depend on a set of rules, but on a state of mind.'

After 1507, Duerer gave up his geometrical theories and impositions, and took measurements from nature. Duerer remarked: 'There is no man on earth who can give a final judgement on what the most beautiful shape may be. Only God knows.'

By the end of Michelangelo's life (1475–1564), the search was over. In typography, the search persisted well into the 1690s when a commission was set up by the Académie Royale des Sciences to design 'perfect' letters. The search reappeared, in the eighteenth century artist Hogarth's pursuit of a 'line of beauty' and in the nineteenth and twentieth centuries this search was generalized, setting up mathematical criteria for literary as well as visual aesthetics. (Birkhoff, 1933; Stiny and Gips, 1978, and numerous others). It persists today in the field of Computer Aided Geometrical Design (CAGD) where mathematical formulations for 'sweet' lines for auto bodies, etc., are sought.

It should be pointed out that alongside the search for the perfect line, in an age when each artist or his assistant ground his own colour, there was a also a search for the secret formulas for the perfect colours. Of course, given that theories of colour were not mathematized until after Newton, this search for the ideal could not then be translated into the language of mathematics.

What led to the decline of the theory of human proportions? In a word: the rigidity imposed by mathematics was unsuitable for the 'new temperament'. It was an instance of Max Weber's *aperçu* that what supports also restrains. Here is how Panofsky explains the decay. The theory 'was bound to diminish in proportion as the artistic genius began to emphasize the subjective conception of the object in preference to the object itself. In Egyptian art, the theory of proportions meant almost everything because the subject meant almost nothing; it was doomed to sink into insignificance as soon as this relation was reversed. The victory of the subjective principle was prepared . . . by the art of the 15th Century which affirmed the autonomous mobility of the things represented and the autonomous visual experience of the artist as well as the beholder. When, after the revival of "classical antiquity" had spent its momentum, these first concessions to the subjective principle came to be exploited to the full, the role of the theory of human proportions as a branch of art theory was finished.'

The role of mathematics in the theory of human proportions is not a very well-known chapter in the history of mathematics. Today's professional mathematician might say that it involves only measurement and elementary calculations with fractions. Although such calculations were at the outer edge of the knowledge of the average person until perhaps two centuries ago, and although Panofsky devotes rather a bit of space to the computational techniques devised by the famous artists, the professional mathematician would now be bored to tears by this aspect of the topic.

Art school courses in representational art teach the principles of proportion and systems of perspective. Geometric conceptualizations of figures are taught as aids in capturing the form or as a guide to shading and volume representation. Simple geometry is often used as a basis for compositions. Illustrators in the life or botanical sciences take actual measurements on a plant and then scale. Such artists look for geometric forms and patterns: spirals, phyllotaxis, etc. Such studies go up or down in importance as realism itself waxes or wanes in significance and popularity.

To 'counteract' the boredom of the professional mathematician with the perceived mathematical triviality of the topics just mentioned, it would not be amiss to point out that among the mathematizations that are now currently and widely in place in our daily lives, many of them involve operations or concepts that the professional would regard as trivial. Yet, these mathematizations can reorder and shape our lives and our view of the world significantly.

A Few Words on Perspective

A projection may be thought of as a way of transferring or representing the three-dimensional world onto a two-dimensional surface. While numerous schemes for doing this have been known since antiquity, one particular way, known as linear perspective, came into prominence in the fifteenth century, and is one of the major historical marriages of mathematics and art.

The invention (or introduction) of linear perspective has been coupled with the rise of capitalism. (Jay, 1993, p. 57). The mathematician Brian Rotman has recently linked the invention of the vanishing point with the introduction of the number 0 (zero) and with the invention of 'imaginary money' that has no referent to intrinsic value (such as is thought to reside in gold.)

Be all this as it may, what was the artistic intent that led to perspective? Mathematicians had written about optics as early as Euclid (c. 325 BC) Artists prior to the great age of perspective in art (1400–1550) did not employ its principles,

obviously considering it to be of little importance measured against other considerations. Panofsky put forward the thesis that the representation of the visual
world is a matter of artistic or cultural convention and that each historical period
in western civilization had its own kind of 'perspective' that reflected a particular
Weltanschauung. Panofsky's relativistic views have been criticized by numerous
commentators who claim for linear perspective a much more objective status.
Chapter 11 of Edgerton, presents a reconciliation of these views and puts forward
the interesting suggestion that 'linear perspective came about in the early Renaissance not in order to reveal visual "truth" in the purely heuristic sense as meant
by Pirenne, but rather as a means of — literally — squaring what was seen empirically with the traditional medieval belief (stated e.g., in Roger Bacon's *Opus
Majus*) that God spreads His grace through the universe according to the laws of
geometric optics.'

The demands and the stimulus provided by perspective art led to the creation
of projective and descriptive geometry; this occurred several centuries after the
pictorial concern, and by that time, perspective was no longer a major artistic
feature. Projective geometry is alive and well today as a research topic at the
abstract level, and both projective and descriptive geometry feed into graphical
representations via computer. Since standard histories of mathematics (e.g., Boyer
or Kline) have substantial write-ups of the topic, and since there are specialist
mathematical treatments such as Andersen; since also there are extensive treatments from the point of view of art (e.g., Edgerton, Veltman, White, Wright)
I shall say no more about it.

Mannerism

From about 1550 to 1880, mathematics seems to have contributed very little to
art. The extraordinary confluence of art, literature, mathematics, and science, all
seemingly engaged in a common project, fell apart. What led to the collapse of
this wondrous intellectual state; or to put it another way, what lead to the fragmentation of these human activities?

The High Renaissance was followed by the period of Mannerism (late sixteenth century). Though weakened, the mathematical impulse was still at work;
the contribution of mathematics to the art of this period, is rarely treated in
histories of mathematics for the simple reason that it involved no new mathematical material. As opposed to the Renaissance where art and mathematics were
engaged in a mutually supportive development, the contributions of later periods
and up to the present time were applications of pre-existing mathematics. I shall
give the impressions of Fritz Kreidt, a Berlin artist and student of art history with
whom I have had an extensive correspondence.[1] Kreidt wrote me

> In the course of the 16th Century, mathematics does not disappear from
> art like the mysterious dinosaurs, but its role is somewhat diminished and
> obscured. In the period of Mannerism, from about 1530 to 1610, the
> contributions of mathematics seem to be less essential. But they still
> display a rich variety of possibilities and a playful ease in partaking of
> artistic adventures. The role of mathematics in art at this time becomes
> much of what it still is today.

The transition to Mannerism manifests itself most strikingly in a profound change of taste, a collective mood of a feeling of crisis. There is great fatigue with the classical, with harmony and measure, with the ideal. Fascination shifts towards the extreme, the eccentric, the fantastic, the artificial, the strange. The achievements of the previous period are not thrown over, but are viewed in a different light.

One reason for the fading interest in the ideal in art may have been that since numbers and geometry, which have an outward appearance of the ideal, had become linked to the real world, and also had become more accessible, the chase after the ideal lost its metaphysical thrill. Later, when the languages and the procedures of the 'pure' abstract world of mathematics were applied to the 'impure' phenomena of the real world, it became obvious that the ideal had slipped away because it was recognized for what it was: a fiction.

But if the ideal as a subject of scientific-artistic interest vanished, the interest in fictitiousness and an ideal world did not disappear at all; it rather flourished more than ever before: it was the perfect substratum for all the banquets of the gods, the love stories, and all the other mythological material that was so particularly well-suited to pay allegorical tribute, and to heighten the sovereigns' lives and deeds without coming too close to their earthly deficiencies. Where formerly the artist expected an underlying mathematical structure to be the law of the ideal, the law now consisted in indulging the erotic taste of a sovereign (François I: Ecole de Fontainebleau; Rudolph II: The Prague School, Spranger, Heintz, van Aken).

The taste was a new one: distortion becomes a predominant feature of mannerist art. The figures grow ever longer and their heads get ever smaller. They adopt postures in which they appear as twisted as a corkscrew. Astonishingly, this style is by no means an impediment to mathematics; on the contrary, mathematics proved invaluable in contributing to the extravagances of the period. One of the early treasures of the period is Parmigianino's self-portrait in a convex mirror, done in 1523, and is a picture that employs mathematics and optics to produce distortion.

Mannerist taste 'overapplied' perspective to the human figure opening up thereby a new and rich visual field. In 1593, Adriaen de Vries created 'Mercury and Psyche', a sculpted couple entwined in a spiraling movement. In order to demonstrate that this work should be admired from all angles, Jan Muller produced a set of three engravings showing the same sculpture from three points of view. He does the same with a 'Rape of the Sabines', a particularly rewarding subject. But artists' bravura in rendering extreme foreshortening and perspective that were never viewed in life is most dramatically displayed when human figures are depicted hovering in the air, such as occur in Last Judgments, falling angels, Phaeton plunging to the earth, etc.

In this type of perspective exercise, the artist's ambition is not only to render the foreshortened bodies in a masterly fashion which is often emphasized by strong modelling of the volumes, but also, as a proof of his achievement, the suggestion of space with virtually nothing but the figure itself extended in that space. Mannerism also treats the reverse problem of making, so to speak, empty space a subject of representation. In Tintoretto and E1 Greco, we can find vapor and clouds serving only to mark the limits, the construction lines of space and its different planes of depth.

In mural painting, mannerist art sometimes even contradicts 'natural' perspective, i.e., our natural strategies of deciphering real space structures. If at the beginning, the intent of linear perspective was to depict reality in a 'true' fashion, the intent now is deception; artful deception by means of illusion.

In Julio Romano's Palazzo, the visitor has an uncomfortable feeling in passing beneath real horses placed on small pedestals above the doors of the *Sala dei Caballi*, clearly in front of the architectural background, but in fact painted on the same wall. And one even hesitates to enter the *Sala dei Giganti* because of the dismembered fragments of architecture that appear to be falling down from the collapsing ceiling.

In most of these *trompe-l'œils*, the viewer is invited to participate actively in the artist's deception. If the viewer moves, and hence leaves the correct viewing point, he will see through the artist's sophisticated manœuvre, and he will enjoy it even more. There is also the possibility of the reverse: the viewer, assuming the normal viewing position in front of the picture is confronted with an unidentifiable object. However, when the viewer moves to a particular viewing position, he will able to identify the fantastic object. This kind of visual 'play' is known as anamorphosis and Leonardo is one of the first to have employed it. The most famous example of this kind is the skull in Holbein's 'the Ambassadors'.

Mannerism and Ornament

The enjoyment of geometric forms is a basic element of the aesthetic experience. To a large extent, this enjoyment expresses itself in ornament. Geometric ornament may be found in nearly all cultures, going back to archaic civilizations. It is a basic resource of artistic creativity, and it combines with, and draws inspiration from, the organic forms found in nature.

Medieval art, as may be seen from book illuminations, displays enormous variety in its geometrical ornamentation, and, as may be seen e.g., in Celtic art, includes very peculiar combinations of the abstract geometrical and the organic. Nor can the Renaissance artists do without ornament. Their most important contribution to the field is the *grotesque* (i.e., grotto-like), which derives, ultimately, from Pompeian mural painting.

In mannerism, ornament becomes a mania. Ornamental engraving develops into a genre of its own. The output of engravers is utilized, absorbed even, by arts and crafts of all kinds, by gold and silversmiths, by instrument and weapon makers. The grotesque offers a setting for inexhaustible combinatorial fancy. Geometry, frequently appearing as airy architecture, is an important feature of grotesque design. Geometry and its elements of symmetry provide an organizing structure to a world that is otherwise exempt from logic or limitation.

Somewhat more austere and essentially abstract is the *mauresque*, a type of ornament that became fashionable after the publication in 1530 of the designs of

Francesco Pellegrino. The mauresque was inspired by Islamic ornament — as were Leonardo's famous knots — and exhibits a characteristic combination of geometrical and floral elements most often presented in flat, interlacing ribbons.

Toward the 1550s, scroll work, a new type of ornament, becomes a prominent decorative feature. The name derives from its resemblance to cut out leather cartouches of rectangular and semi-circular shapes, interlocked and curled up at their margins, and drawn in seeming relief.

All of these types combine and compete in rampant abundance. *Architectura*, (1593–1598), a work of Wendel Dietterlin, is devoted mainly to decorative elements in architecture, and ornament, largely geometrical, overwhelms the architectonic structures unrestrainedly.

By the second decade of the seventeenth century, the masquerade is over. Artificiality with forms in blown-up abundance have become obsolete, and have given way to a new style, a new taste of measure and moderation. This is the case both in absolutist France as well as in Protestant Netherlands where it emerges as realism.

The Twentieth Century Mathematization of Art

By that time, photography, which gave the illusion of having reproduced the perceptual world with perfect objectivity, was available. It was cheap and began by destroying the livelihood of the miniaturists. Reacting to the development of the daguerreotype, the painter Paul Delaroche (1797–1856) wrote 'From this day on painting is dead.' Not dead, as we know, but seriously altered. For example, as the price of portrait painting was driven up, portraiture as high art did come to an end.

A student of the history of western culture would tell us that as photography prospered and developed into cinema, as painters themselves often worked from photographs and not from natural models, there occurred simultaneously a deheroicization of individual men and women. After World War I it would be difficult, and after World War II almost impossible, to erect in America a public statue either to a specific individual or to a generic virtue such as Wisdom, Justice, Patriotism or Bleeding Humanity in terms of a realistic human figure. The public placement of a such a work of art would have smacked of political or propaganda or of uncritical adulation (e.g., 'Socialist realism'). America has therefore found no need, as the Soviet Union did, to pull down monuments erected after World War II. It had erected very few. We moved into the age of the anti-hero, and the anti-hero could be depicted only with blurred or distorted features or by means of abstract visual statements. Such a frame of mind was served well by mathematics, and stark, anti-heroic, (and paradoxically) pro-humanistic monuments stand in public spaces, rusting, worshipped, ignored, hated, as the case may be, and sometimes the objects of litigation.

The programme of art, mathematized in the service of visual abstraction, had certainly begun by the days of the pointillist Georges Seurat (1859–1891). Seurat, though dealing with landscape and human figures, broke up the canvas into small dots of colour. Seen from a distance, the hundreds of dots, in virtue of the visual phenomenon known as persistence of vision, coalesced into larger figures. When in the 1880s typewriters became commonplace, this kind of image done on the typewriter with letters or blank spaces, was known as typewriter art. In the first generation of computers, typewriter art was automated, and pictures of Washington, Lincoln, Harry Truman etc., were produced in this way. When computer output moved from the typed page to the television or video screen, the whole screen was subdivided into a certain large number, say $1,024 \times 1,024 = 1,048,576$ areas or so-called 'pixels', each of which could be addressed, shaded, coloured or otherwise transformed or manipulated in microseconds by the computer. In a certain sense, this process can be regarded as a computerized and extremely sophisticated version of the children's recreation of 'painting by numbers'. But we are getting ahead of the story.

After the death of Cezanne (1839–1906), cubism erupted in the public consciousness. Cubism (1907) replaced natural forms by geometric surrogates such as the cube, the cylinder, the cone, or the sphere. Some of its practitioners were Braque, Gris and Picasso. Suprematism, associated with the name of Malevich, arrived in 1913. It went further by discarding the human element and simply manipulated circles, squares and triangles of pure colour into what it considered were significant statements. De Stijl, associated with the name of Piet Mondrian, came in 1917, and limited its work to right angles and primary colours. Abstract expressionism sloshed colours around the canvas in a few broad, and often crose stripes. Op art (optical art; a play on the term 'pop' art), was in full swing by 1965. It laid down dense geometric reticulations and called on the irresolution or ambiguities of vision to create vibratory sensations that were sometimes pleasant but more often painful to view for more than a few seconds.

Geometric constructionism (Brancusi, Arp, Pevsner, Naum Gabo, Henry Moore; 1910 to the present) took inspiration from mathematical solids to create sculpted surfaces of clean and sweeping lines or assemblages of stunning geometricity. Of one of these, literary and art critic Herbert Read wrote in 1942: '(The word "creation") is justified only for that absolute lyricism we call "pure poetry", for music, for certain branches of mathematics, and for constructionism in the plastic arts. . . . The art represented by (Naum) Gabo's "Spiral Theme" is the highest point ever reached by the aesthetic tradition of man.'

The work of these schools and of several others not mentioned, are all instances of abstract art. In abstract full denarrativization occurs; while it uses colour, line, form, surface, it creates images having little superficial resemblance to the so-called 'real' perceptual world. The development by the nineteenth-century mathematicians of non-Euclidean and multi-dimensional geometries questioning the uniqueness of the 'real' Euclidean world was exploited by a number of abstract artists who picked up on this ambiguity.

Geometrical art, an extremely important element of the twentieth-century art scene, as mentioned earlier, has been associated with the advance of the technology of photography, as well as with a degradation of the individual politician, clergyman, explorer, etc., as idol or icon. While Man is, at best, a paradox, the visual paradoxes of, say, Magritte, turn heavily on the conflict between what seems possible in the world of two-dimensional representations and what is geometrically possible in the real three-dimensional world. Out of this, viewers may extract whatever spiritual messages they can.

Philip J. Davis

The Bauhaus and Logical Positivism

There is yet another way — a way that is more relevant to the purposes of this chapter — to view the twentieth-century mathematization of art. This was pointed out in a brilliant analysis by Peter Galison that links the Bauhaus to the Wienerkreis (Vienna Circle) of Logical Positivists. The Bauhaus, created in 1919 by the architect Walter Gropius, was a school whose curricular philosophy was to unify the arts, crafts, science, technology and manufacture. Courses were offered along all these lines, and elaborate methodological strategies and philosophical justifications were written and argued. Some of the famous names associated with the Bauhaus are Joseph Albers, Lyonel Feininger, Paul Klee, Wassily Kandinsky, La'szlo' Moholy-Nagy, Mies van der Rohe. In the half century that followed, the Bauhaus, first in Weimar, then in Dessau, Berlin, and finally in Chicago, exerted an enormous influence in art, architecture and design.

In addition to the element of unification, (Moholy-Nagy even spoke of the unification of the whole of life!), there was in Bauhaus philosophy the element of purification or simplification of form and colour. This is expressed clearly by Kandinsky:

> The work in the Bauhaus is synthesis (from fundamental elements of form and color) . . . In both cases the work has to begin with the simplest shapes and progress systematically to more complicated ones. Hence . . . the plane is reduced to three fundamental elements — triangle, square, and circle — and space is reduced to the resulting fundamental space elements — pyramid, cube and sphere. (W. Kandinsky, quoted by Galison, 1990)

It is difficult to scan the pages of Wingler's massive and comprehensive chronicle of the Bauhaus without reaching the conclusion that the mathematizing spirit of the movement was very substantial. The pictures — almost all of them — confirm it, and occasionally the recorded words of the artists. The following are excerpts from a 1926 article by Oskar Schlemmer, artist and director of the Dessau Bauhaus Stage:

> Let's not complain about mechanization, but rather let us delight in mathematics! But not in the kind that one has to sweat out in school but rather in the kind of artistic, metaphysical mathematics that suggests itself by necessity, as in art . . . Novalis writes that 'Mathematics is religion' because it is the ultimate, most refined, and the most delicate. It is only where mathematics deadens the feelings and nips the unconscious in the bud that there are dangers . . . As for myself, I am for the body — mechanical dance, the mathematical dance . . . I hold simplicity to be a great force in which every innovation is rooted . . . Space, when taken as determining the laws of everything that happens with its limits, also determines the gestures of the dancer . . . Out of plane geometry, out of the pursuit of the straight line, the diagonal, the circle and the curve, a stereometry of space evolves, almost of itself, by the moving vertical line of the dancing figure. (Schlemmer, quoted in Wingler, 1969, p. 118)

From the point of view of the professional mathematician, however, the depth of this mathematizing spirit is trifling.

I turn next to the Vienna Circle of Logical Positivists. This was a philosophic movement to promote the unification and the purification of the sciences. Some of the prominent names of the Vienna Circle are Rudolph Carnap, Herbert Feigl, Joseph Frank, Philipp Frank (whose lectures I attended as an undergraduate), Hans Hahn, Otto Neurath, Moritz Schlick. The Vienna Circle attempted to clear out the 'debris of millennia', as Rudolf Carnap put it, from the stables of thought by depriving theology, mysticism, metaphysics, philosophy even, of any meaning. It was thus, paradoxically, a philosophy of anti-philosophy. It attempted to build up a world view on the basis of experience and of logical connectives (if/then, either/or, etc.)

> (Logical positivism) attempts a step-by-step derivation or 'construction' of all concepts from certain fundamental concepts, so that a genealogy of concepts results in which each one has its definite place. It is the main thesis of construction theory that all concepts can in this way be derived from a few fundamental concepts and it is in this respect that (logical positivism) differs from most other ontologies. (Carnap, 1928)

This attempt must surely remind the reader of the *Elements* of Euclid where geometry is built up in this way. The movement also attempted to create simplified, purified and universal verbal and pictorial languages, which would serve across disciplines and across the humanistic and scientific cultures.

Linked by personal friendships, overlapping interests (Joseph Frank was an architect; Carnap and Neurath were both absorbed by architecture), and sympathetic goals, the two groups, one in Germany and the other in Austria until driven out in the mid-1930s by Nazism, supported one another indirectly and directly by letter and by lecture. 'But,' as Peter Galison observed, 'there is another sense in which the two movements were "mutually supporting" . . . Each legitimated the other. For the Bauhaeusler, the Vienna Circle stood for the solid ground of science, the power of technology and the machine age. As such it gave their artistic movement a credence beyond that of taste or style. For the logical positivists, their association with the larger world of modern art certified them as progressive, and identified them with the future in a world in which their philosophical prospects were dim and their ties with traditional philosophy weak.' Abstract sensation and mathematics, then, for the Bauhaus group; logic, mathematics and experience for the Vienna Circle: these became the hallmarks of the two groups if not the personal religion of the zealots within them.

All zealotry ultimately runs itself into the ground by restricting itself increasingly to one principle. The tendency that led ultimately to Albers' oil painting 'Homage to the Square' (1963), was satirized early on. In a 1923 magazine article, biographer Paul Westheim observed,

> In the (traditional) schools of arts and crafts students are plagued with stylizing cabbage leaves from nature, and the Bauhaus people plague themselves with stylizing squares from ideas.
>
> Three days in Weimar and one can never look at a square again for the rest of one's life. Malevich invented the square way back in 1913.

> How lucky he didn't have his invention patented. The ultimate of Bauhaus ideals: the individual square. Talent is a square; genius is an absolute square. The 'Stijl' people have put on a protest exhibition in Jena — they claim to possess the only true squares.

While the children of the Bauhaus have dotted the European and American landscapes with their productions, boredom with its minimalist palette of styles, and the inadequacy of this style to meet the demands of new functions, moved the Bauhaus off the drawing boards and into the chronicles of art.

Similarly, in the 1960s, science and mathematics were perceived as many faceted, whose practices were not stateable let alone formalizable in a few logical principles. While positivist philosophy of science is alive and well as a single element in a variegated totality, it proved an inadequate description of the goals, methods, or the internal criteria of the actual scientific research communities.

The Contribution of Art to Mathematics

The contribution of mathematics to art and design, despite all its ups and downs, has, over the millennia, been substantial; the contribution that has already come from computer graphics and is yet to come, will have a far greater impact than the invention of photography. In this section, I shall not be able to go much beyond a few speculations on the artistic intent of those who come to the craft through computer science.

The principal artistic intent of computer-generated art is, at the moment, to demonstrate the incredible virtuosity of computer graphics with respect to the traditional aspects of line, colour, arrangement, object manipulation, and (which is by no means visible to the observer) the interplay between these aspects and the high-level computer languages that have been devised to effectuate them. One must not neglect to mention animation, for the true visual art form of the general populace is now not the static image, but the moving image as instanced by the cinema, the TV, videos, computer games.

A second intent is to exploit the computational facilities to create objects of mathematical origin whose intricacies are far too difficult to create without computation of contemporary complexity. Lastly, there is the desire to create by visual means 'virtual realities'. Art has always had a goal of *trompe-l'œil*, of the creation of that which does not exist. This goal is now achievable in remarkable ways that were not available using traditional artistic media.

While Panofsky has labelled as 'artistic intent' views such as that the human figure is part of nature's harmonic unity, it might equally well be called art's 'philosophic intent'. The relation between the philosophies of classic Greek art and its philosophy of science is thereby made clear, and Galison's treatment of the Bauhaus/Wienerkreis demonstrates this relationship for the twentieth century. We may speculate as to the philosophic intent of the emerging computer art, and wonder whether and in what way this will relate to newly emerging views on the philosophy of science and mathematics.

In the reverse direction, we may inquire what has been the contribution to mathematics by art. This is harder to describe. There is no documentation as to how the perception of the natural world led five or ten thousand years ago to a proto-mathematics; there is only conjecture. One merely surmises that the necessity to build, the convenience of relevant measurements, and the urge to decorate and to imitate, all led to the development of arithmetic and to the abstraction of formal geometry (in the sense of Euclid) out of physical constructions. If this is the case, it is part of the unrecorded pages of the history of mathematics.

Sir Kenneth Clark has put forward a surmise of a most remarkable sort, one that will surely raise the eyebrows of some historians of mathematics and of art.

It is also arguable that the female body is more plastically rewarding on what, at their first submission, seems to be purely abstract grounds. Since Michelangelo, few artists have shared a Florentine passion for shoulders, knees, and other small knobs of form. They have found it easier to compose harmoniously the larger units of a woman's torso; they have been grateful for its smoother transitions, and above all they have discovered analogies with satisfying geometric forms, the oval, the ellipsoid and the sphere. But may not this argument reverse the order of cause and effect?

Is there, after all, any reason why certain quasi-geometrical shapes should be satisfying except that they are simplified statements of the forms that please us in a woman's body? The recurrent search by writers on the theory of art — Lomazzo, Hogarth, Winckleman — for a 'line of beauty' ends, not inappropriately, in a question mark; and he who pursues it further is soon caught in the sterile fallacy of one cause. A shape, like a word, has innumerable associations that vibrate in the memory, and any attempt to explain it by a single analogy is as futile as the translation of a poem. *But the fact that we can base our argument either way on this unexpected union of sex and geometry, is a proof of how deeply the concept of the nude is linked to our most elementary notions of order and design.* [my emphasis] (Clark, 1959, p. 458)

Moving forward several thousand years, the history of the mathematics of perspective and the impetus it received from art is well documented. Developments of the last generation in mathematical technology, such as Computer Aided Geometric Design (CAGD) and the problems posed by design and production have led to many new and well documented mathematical developments.

The graphical output of digital computers has also led to the notion of 'theorems of visual' type (Davis, 1974, and others). While the eye is able to organize the output along certain lines, formal mathematical analysis is yet unable to predict what the output will be or how it will change as input parameters are changed.

The Ups and Downs of Mathematics and Art

In surveying the past 3500 years of western art even superficially, it becomes clear that the engagement between mathematics and art has been an on-again off-again matter. The conscious employment of mathematical schemes in art can be in conflict with the ideology of the 'free' artist. According to this doctrine, in its most recent and draconic form, the artist declares his independence of all the artistic knowledge, techniques, spirits, intents that went before. There is to be no apprenticeship, no copying. 'Get out there on the canvas and express yourself' was the way one of my teachers of studio art put it.

The mathematization of art requires a reasonable acquaintance with, and acquiescence in, the mathematical discoveries or constructions of the past. Furthermore, there would be many contemporary teachers of art who would agree with Karl Menninger when he wrote of an attitude claiming that 'the cold reason of mathematics has nothing at all to do with art that is born of a hot heart. The artist must look and must not compute or construct. Whenever mathematics invades a work, the artistic spirit dies.' Cold calipers against warm flesh.

On the other hand, what binds often supports. Geometric art, following as it does a geometric pattern or algorithm, allows the mathematics to instruct the artist 'what to do'. The danger is that in so doing, it can become mindless routinization and simply a replacement for individual artistic thought, feeling, impulse or intent.

As indicated, the principal current intersection between mathematics and art occurs in computer-generated art, a field that has only begun to generate a body of criticism or a philosophy. One thing that mathematics, art and literature have shared and suffered in the past two centuries is an intellectual denigration of the visual element either as a source of inspiration or as an end result (another paradox!). In mathematics this has been going on since 1788 when Lagrange announced that mechanics (i.e., statics and dynamics) can be treated by purely analytical means. In literature and art, this tendency, particularly in post-World War II France, has been discussed in depth by Jay in his stimulating *Downcast Eyes*. It is quite possible that computer art, design, and display might be able to turn this tendency around even as the computer is beginning, in mathematics, to end the old established view that truth is synonymous with formal proof.

It is clear that the computer can be much more than an automated paint brush; it can achieve stunning effects, often serendipitously. An example of this is fractals/chaos, a mathematical theory of very recent origin, whose development was spurred, in part, by the unique visual elements that the computer actualized theory produced. These elements are far removed from the basic shapes of traditional Euclidean geometry. The votaries of fractals have found in these elements variously, a mathematical return to the world of biological/geological shapes, a vigorous assertion of the principle of free will, and a limitation of the manipulation and control of nature that reputedly derive from an androcentric science. (On this last point, see Kellert, Chapter 5, who refers to the feminist historian of science E.F. Keller.)

Veltman has written (p. 384) that 'In science, one seeks to establish those relations in which there are no surprises: in art one explores those relationships that are full of surprises.' I believe that one must rephrase the first part by saying that while the universe is full of surprises, the scientist wishes to temper the surprises by placing them within general frameworks. This is the programme of Descartes, and in this respect the programmes of art, science, and mathematics merge.

Computer graphics has revealed many surprises in the arena where the visual meets the mathematical. Despite this, it is by no means clear that computer art represents a revolutionary turn of events and whether it can, of itself, add substantially to the palette of significant forms and artistic intents.

Notes

1. I wish to acknowledge stimulating discussions with Kirsti Andersen, Bianca Iano Davis, Fritz Kreidt, and Anne Morgan Spalter. Through them the points of view of artists and of historians of art were made accessible to me.

    Working in collaboration with Fritz Kreidt, I hope later to be able to put out a small book as an enlarged and fully illustrated version of this chapter.

References

ANDERSEN, K. (1992) *Brook Taylor's Work on Linear Perspective*, New York, Springer Verlag.

ANDERSEN, K. (1993) *Geometrien bag perspektivet*, Koebenhavn, Matematiklaerer-foreningen.

ANDERSEN, K. (to appear) *History of the Mathematical Theory of Perspective from Alberti to Monge*.

ARNHEIM, R. (1992) *To the Rescue of Art: Twenty Six Essays*, Berkeley, University of California Press.

AUPING, M. (Ed) (1989) *Abstraction, Geometry, Painting: Selected Geometric Abstract Painting in America Since 1945*, New York, H.N. Abrams.

BALTRUSAITIS, J. (1955) *Anamorphoses; ou perspectives curieuses*, Paris, O. Perrin.

BANCHOFF, T. (1990) *Beyond the Third Dimension: Geometry, Computer Graphics and Higher Dimensions*, New York, Scientific American Library.

BAXANDALL, M. (1985) *Patterns of Intent: On the Historical Explanation of Pictures*, New Haven, Yale University Press.

BIRKHOFF, G.D. (1933) *Aesthetic Measure*, Cambridge, Harvard University Press.

BOULEAU, C. (1963) *The Painter's Secret Geometry: A Study of Composition in Art*, London, Thames and Hudson.

BOURGOIN, J. (1973) *Arabic Geometrical Patterns and Design*, New York, Dover.

BOYER, C.B. and UTA C.M. (1989) *A History of Mathematics*, 2nd ed., New York, John Wiley.

CARNAP, R. (1928) *Der Logische Aufbau der Welt*, Vienna.

CLARK, SIR K. (1959) *The Nude*, Garden City, Doubleday Anchor.

COLLINGWOOD, R.G. (1958) *The Principles of Art*, Oxford, Oxford University Press.

COY, W. (1985) *Industrieroboten: Zur Archaeologie der zweiten Schoepfung*, Berlin, Rotbuch Verlag.

DABROWSKI, M. (1985) *Contrasts of Form: Geometric Abstract Art, 1910–1980*, New York, Museum of Modern Art.

DAVIS, P.J. (1974) 'Visual geometry, computer graphics and theorems of perceived type', *Proceedings of the Symposium on Applied Mathematics*, 20, pp. 113–27.

DAVIS, P.J. (1993) 'Visual theorems', *Educational Studies in Mathematics*, 24, 4.

DAVIS, W.M. (1979) 'Plato on Egyptian Art', *Journal of Egyptian Archaeology*, pp. 121–27.

DESBOROUGH, V. (1952) *Protogeometric Pottery*, Oxford.

DIETTERLIN, W. (1550–99) *Architectura: The Fantastic Engravings of Wendel Dietterlin*, New York, Dover, 1968.

EDGERTON, S.Y. JR. (1975) *The Renaissance Rediscovery of Linear Perspective*, New York, Basic Books.

EDGERTON, S.Y. JR. (1991) *The Heritage of Giotto's Geometry: Art and Science on the Eve of the Scientific Revolution*, Ithaca, Cornell University Press.

EL-SAID, I. (1976) *Geometric Concepts in Islamic Art*, London, World of Islam Festival.

FARIN, G. (1988) *Curves and Surfaces for Computer Aided Geometrical Design*, New York, Academic Press.

Philip J. Davis

FOMENKO, A.T. (1990) *Mathematical Impressions*, Providence, American Mathematical Society.

GALISON, P. (1990) 'Aufbau/Bauhaus: Logical positivism and architectural modernism', *Critical Inquiry*, 16.

GREGORY, R.L. and GOMBRICH, E.H. (1973) *Illusion in Nature and Art*, London, Duckworth.

GHYKA, M.C. (1977) *The Geometry of Art and Life*, New York, Dover.

GOMBRICH, E.H. (1960) 'Ambiguities in the Third Dimension', *Art and Illusion*, Princeton, University Press, Chapter 8.

GROENEWEGEN-FRANKFORT, H.A. and ASHMOLE, B. (1967) *The Ancient World*, New York, New American Library.

HAGEN, M. (1986) *Varieties of Realism: Geometries of Representational Art*, New York, Cambridge University Press.

HARTMANN, H. and MISLIN, H. (Eds) (1985) *Die Spirale: Im menschlichen Leben und in der Natur; eine interdiziplinaere Schau*, Basel, Birkhauser. (Gewerbemuseum, Basel)

HASKELL, F. (1993) *History and Its Images*, New Haven, Yale University Press.

HELFENSTEIN, J. and VON TAVEL, H.C. (Eds) (1984) *Die Sprache der Geometrie*, Bern, Kunstmuseum.

HENDERSON, L.D. (1983) *The Fourth Dimension and Non-Euclidean Geometry in Modern Art*, Princeton, University Press.

IVINS, W.M. (1946) *Art and Geometry: A Study in Space Intuitions*, Cambridge, Harvard University Press. (Reprinted 1964, New York, Dover.)

JANOWITZ, G.J. (1986) *Leonardo da Vinci, Brunelleschi, Duerer; ihrer Auseinanderung mit der Problematik der Zentral perspektive*, Einhausen, Huebner.

JAY, M. (1993) *Downcast Eyes: The Denigration of Vision in Twentieth-Century French Thought*, Berkeley, University of California Press.

KELLERT, S.H. (1993) *In the Wake of Chaos*, Chicago, University of Chicago Press.

KEMP, M. (1990) *The Science of Art*, New Haven, Yale University Press.

KIELLAND, E.C. (1984) *Geometry in Greek Art: Studied in the Light of Egyptian Methods*, Oslo, Dreyer.

KLEE, P. *Notebooks, vol, 2, the nature of nature (Unendliche Naturgeschichte)*, in SPILLER, J. (Ed) (1964) Woodstock, NY, Overlook Press.

KLINE, M. (1972) *Mathematical Thought from Ancient to Modern Times*, New York, Oxford University Press.

KREIDT, F. Personal Correspondence.

LE CORBUSIER, (1983) *Le Modulor and other buildings and projects*, New York, Garland.

LANGER, S.K. (1957) *Problems of art; ten philosophical lectures*, New York, Scribner.

LEEMAN, F. (1976, 1975) *Hidden Images: Games of Perception, Anamorphistic Art, and Illusion from the Renaissance to the Present*, New York, Original in German: *Anamorphosen*, Koeln, DuMont Schauberg.

MADOFF, S.H. (1986) 'Vestiges and ruins: Ethics and geometric art in the twentieth century', *Arts Magazine*, 61, pp. 32–40.

MARITAIN, J. (1954) 'Creative intuition in art and poetry', Cleveland, *World Publishing*, Chapter 6.

MALE, E. (1958) *Art religieux du XIlle siècle en France*, English language edition: *The Gothic Image*, New York, Harper.

MALINA, F.J. (Ed) (1979) *Visual Art, Mathematics and Computers*, Oxford, Pergamon Press.

MENNINGER, K. (1959) *Mathematik und Kunst*, Goettingen, Vandenhoeck and Ruprecht.

MITCHELL, W.J. (1992) *The Reconfigured Eye: Visual Truth in the Post-Photographic Era*, Cambridge, MIT Press.

MORSE, M. (Summer, 1951) 'Mathematics and the arts', *Yale Review*.

NOVOTNY, F. (1938) *Cezanne und das Ende der wissenschaftlichen Perspektive*, Vienna, Schroll.

PANOFSKY, E. (1955) *Meaning in the Visual Arts*, Garden City, Doubleday.

PANOFSKY, E. (1991) *Perspective as Symbolic Form (Die Perspektive als Symbolische Form)*, Introduction and translation by C.S. WOOD. New York, Zone Books.

PIRENNE, M.H. (1957) *Optics, Painting, and Photography*, London.

ROBBIN, T. (1992) *Fourfield: Computers, Art and the 4th Dimension*, Boston, Little Brown.

ROSE, L. 'Humanist culture and renaissance mathematics', *Studies in the Renaissance*, 20, pp. 46–106.

SCHILLINGER, J. (1948) *The Mathematical Basis of the Arts*, New York, Philosophical Press.

SCHWEITZER, B. (1971) *Greek Geometric Art*, London, Phaidon.

SENECHAL, M. and FLECK, G. (Eds) (1988) *Shaping Space: A Polyhedral Approach*, Boston, Birkhauser.

SHLAIN, L. (1991) *Art and Physics: Parallel Visions in Space, Time and Light*, New York, William Morrow.

STINY, G. and GIPS, J. (1978) *Algorithmic Aesthetics*, Berkeley, University of California Press.

SWETZ, F.J. (Fall, 1993) 'The search for the perfect letter', *Mathematical Connections*, 2, 1, Augusta, Georgia, Augusta College.

TORY, G. (1480–1533) *Champ fleury ou L'art et Science de la Proportion des Lettres* (1529), Cohen, G. (Ed) Paris, Charles Bosse, 1931 (Also Geneva, Slatkine Reprints, 1973.)

UEBEL, T.E. (Ed) (1991) *Rediscovering the forgotten Vienna Circle*, Kluwer Academic, Dordrecht, Boston.

VELTMAN, K.H. and KEELE, K.D. (1986) *Linear Perspective and the Visual Dimensions of Science and Art*, Muenchen, Deutscher Kunstverlag.

WASHBURN, D.K. (Ed) (1983) *Structure and Cognition in Art*, Cambridge University Press.

WASHBURN, D.K. and CROWE, D.W. (1983) *Symmetries of Culture: Theory and Practice of Plane Pattern Analysis*, Seattle, University of Washington Press.

WEYL, H. (1952) *Symmetry*, Princeton, University Press (In German: *Symmetrie*, Basel, Birkhauser, 1955.)

WHITE, J. (1987) *The Birth and Rebirth of Pictorial Space*, Cambridge, Harvard University Press.

WINGLER, H.M. (1969) *The Bauhaus*, Cambridge, MIT Press.

WRIGHT, L. (1983) *Perspective in Perspective*, London, Routledge and Kegan Paul.

YAGLOM, I.M. (1988) *Felix Klein and Sophus Lie: Evolution of the Idea of Symmetry in the Nineteenth Century*, Boston, Birkhauser.

Chapter 13

Skolem and Gödel[1]

Hao Wang

Many logicians would agree that Skolem (1887–1963) and Gödel (1906–1978) are the two greatest logicians of the century. Yet their styles, philosophies, and careers were strikingly different.

Gödel had already published some of his great works and become world famous before he was 25. Skolem, though much respected and appreciated as a mathematician very early, began to publish his important papers only after he was over 30, and his impact grew slowly over the years. Gödel was meticulous in writing for publication and published little after he had reached 45. Skolem wrote informally, often even casually, continuing to publish to the last days of his life.

Gödel was a well-known absolutist and Platonist, who had devoted much effort to studying and writing philosophy. Skolem was inclined to finitism and relativism, and he rarely attempted to offer an articulate presentation of his coherent and fruitful philosophical viewpoint about the nature of mathematics and mathematical activity. Apart from mathematical logic, Gödel made contributions to the philosophy of mathematics and to fundamental physics. Skolem divided his work almost equally between logic and other parts of discrete mathematics, particularly algebra and number theory.

For many years I have been deeply involved in Gödel's work and his life. Even though I was for a long time intensely interested in Skolem's work in logic and made a careful study of it in the 1960s, I have not followed carefully since then the important applications and developments of Skolem's ideas by many logicians. I know very little about Skolem's life and his work in fields other than logic. In my opinion, there is much room for interesting and instructive studies of Skolem's work and his life. One attraction for me in giving the Skolem lecture is the opportunity to learn more about Skolem and about works devoted to the historical and conceptual study of his life and work, as well as of the influences of his thoughts.

Recently I came across Walter P. van Stigt's *Brouwer's Intuitionism*, 1990, in which there is also a fairly extended account of Brouwer's life and general philosophy. I understand that Dirk van Dalen is preparing a full biography of Brouwer. It seems to me that Skolem, in his own way, deserves to be studied in an analogous manner. In particular, Skolem's philosophy of mathematics and his implicit beliefs in the fruitful way to do mathematics represent very well a sound sense shared by many good mathematicians. It is challenging to bring out in an articulate manner what he believed — which he had only communicated informally and fragmentarily.

Last autumn William Boos sent me a typescript of his, written July 1992, entitled *Thoralf Skolem, Hermann Weyl and 'Das Gefühl der Welt als Begrenztes Ganzes'*, (sixty-four pages). Among other things, Boos sketched some of the historical and metaphysical implications of the 'Skolem functions' and tried to relate Skolem's philosophical views to two of his contemporaries: Weyl (1885–1955) and Wittgenstein (1889–1951). (Bernays (1888–1977) was another contemporary.) One surprising reference is to a review by Skolem (signed 'Sk' only) of Weyl's 1910 essay on the definitions of fundamental mathematical concepts (reprinted in Weyl's collected works, volume 1, pp. 299–304): *Jahrbuch der Mathematische Fortschrifte*, volume 41, pp. 89–90. In this connection, Boos asks whether Skolem, already in 1910, embraced the first half but suspended judgment on the second half of Weyl's 'solution' to Richard's paradox in his essay: 'set theory has only to do with countably many relational concepts — not, however, with countably many things or sets.'

In order to facilitate references to the relevant writings by and on Skolem and Gödel, I shall quote primarily from Skolem's *Selected Works in Logic* (briefly, SWL), 1970 and volume 1 of Gödel's *Collected Works* (briefly, CWI), 1986. In particular, I shall generally adopt the abbreviations in the references (pp. 407–59) of the second book.

As I mentioned before, Skolem's work in logic got known and appreciated only gradually. This was in part because logic was at first largely isolated from the principal interests of most mathematicians. In particular, this was true of Skolem's own colleagues, who expected his work in logic to be important only because they regarded him highly as a mathematician. Indeed, as Fenstad reports:

> Skolem's work in logic did not at the time create much interest among his Scandinavian colleagues, and later he indicated that he could not derive much inspiration because his papers remained unread. So from the beginning of the nineteen twenties he turned to more traditional and respectable fields — algebra and number theory. (Skolem, 1970, p. 12)

By the time Gödel began to study logic, Skolem had already published a number of important papers in logic. It is, therefore, not surprising that Gödel did refer to some of these in his early work, although he was not able to read some others which would have been more relevant (see below). On the other hand, even though Gödel had become the leading light in logic from 1930 on, Skolem rarely discussed or further developed Gödel's ideas. This was partly because Skolem was not interested in the internal development of set theory, partly because Gödel's work was often definitive with regard to the immediate problems under consideration but Skolem tended to break new ground in his early work and to deal with simple loose ends in his later work.

Gödel made use of the Skolem normal form in his dissertation (see CWI, p. 77 and p. 109), referring to Skolem 1920 (SWL, pp. 103–36). But for his purpose, Gödel had to retrace the steps of the reduction of every formula to this form to show that each step can be carried out in the initial formal system, to be proved to be complete. In his 1933i, Gödel further reduced the Skolem form to the special case with three initial universal quantifiers only (CWI, p. 323), again referring to Skolem 1920.

From 1932 to 1935, Gödel reviewed five papers by Skolem. Using the abbreviations in CWI (pp. 421–2 and 451–2), these are: Skolem (1931, 1932, 1933, 1933a, 1934) reviewed in Gödel (1932d, 1932n, 1934a, 1934c, 1935), respectively. Of these papers and reviews the most interesting is Skolem 1933a (SWL, pp. 345–54), reviewed in Gödel 1934c (CWI, pp. 379–81): On the impossibility of a complete characterization of the number sequence by means of a finite axiom system.

In addition, three papers by Skolem were discussed extensively by Gödel in the 1960s in his correspondence with Jean van Heijenoort and with me: Skolem, 1922 (SWL, pp. 153–8), 1928 (pp. 189–206), and 1929 (pp. 227–73). The reason is that these papers anticipated at least the mathematical part of Gödel's proof of the completeness of predicate logic, but Gödel had not seen them before he published his proof. There was, therefore, the problem of separating out Gödel's own advance beyond them.

It was probably in 1965 when Professor J.E. Fenstad wrote to invite me to write a survey of Skolem's work in logic, as an introduction to SWL. I accepted the invitation, not only because I valued Skolem's work, but also because I found his free and undogmatic spirit congenial: I felt a strong sympathy with his status as a sort of *outsider* and his tendency to begin from scratch, to find the important in what is simple.

I worked on the project over an extended period, and in September 1967 I sent a draft to Bernays and Gödel for comments and criticisms. As usual, Bernays sent me a number of helpful observations before long. On 7 December Gödel wrote me a long letter, to explain both the relation between Skolem's and his own work on the completeness of predicate logic and his views on the relation between philosophy and the study of logic. — Eventually this correspondence led to a close association between Gödel and me.

Since about 1950 I had been struck by the fact that all the pieces in Gödel's proof of the completeness of predicate logic had been available by 1929 in the work of Skolem (notably his 1922, SWL, pp. 139–42), supplemented by a simple observation of Herbrand's (see the reference to his work under 1.2 on p. 24 of SWL). In my draft I explained this fact and said that Gödel had discovered the theorem independently and given it an attractive treatment.

In his letter of 7 December 1967, Gödel said:

> Thank you very much for sending me your manuscript about Skolem's work. I am sorry for the long delay in my reply. It seems to me that, in some points, you don't represent matters quite correctly. So I wanted to consider carefully what I have to say — You say, in effect, that the completeness theorem is attributed to me only because of my attractive treatment. Perhaps it looks this way, if the situation is viewed from the present state of logic by a superficial observer. The completeness theorem, mathematically, is indeed an almost trivial consequence of Skolem 1922. However, the fact is that, at that time, nobody (including Skolem himself) drew this conclusion (neither from Skolem 1922 nor, as I did, from similar considerations of his own) — This blindness (or prejudice, or whatever you may call it) of logicians is indeed surprising. But I think the explanation is not hard to find. It lies in a widespread lack, at that time, of the required epistemological attitude toward metamathematics and toward nonfinitary reasoning. (Gödel, 1967)

Gödel had not seen Skolem 1922 before the publication of his own proof of the completeness of predicate logic. Indeed, it is now known that Gödel made several unsuccessful attempts to find a copy of Skolem 1922 in 1929 and 1930. If he had seen the paper before publishing his own, he would undoubtedly have cited it and shortened his own paper. It would have become clear that, mathematically, Gödel's proof did not add much to Skolem's work.

This example illustrates a rather general phenomenon with many of Skolem's writings which had often been published initially at places not easily accessible to those who work on related problems. As a result, Skolem did not get the credit he deserved and others had to repeat his work. Another example is what is commonly known as the Zermelo-Fraenkel set theory. As I have elaborated in my survey of Skolem's work (SWL, pp. 35–7), the axiom system should more appropriately be called the Zermelo-Skolem set theory.

There are various discussions of the relation of Gödel's completeness proof to the work of Skolem and Herbrand. On 14 August 1964 Gödel wrote to Heijenoort (see his letter of 1967, p. 510):

As for Skolem, what he could justly claim, but apparently does not claim, is that, in his 1922 paper, he implicitly proved: 'Either A is provable or not-A is satisfiable' [in other words, if A is valid, then A is provable] ('provable' taken in an informal sense). However, since he did not clearly formulate the result (nor, apparently had made it clear to himself), it seems to have remained completely unknown, as follows from the fact that Hilbert and Ackermann 1928 do not mention it in connection with their completeness problem.

In a paper of 1955, Skolem did discuss explicitly the difficulty involved in the notion of arbitrary domains (SWL, p. 582). He asked: 'But what does this really mean? What is the totality of all domains?' He then considered the possibility of using the Löwenheim theorem to simplify the definition of satisfiability by substituting the domain N of natural numbers for arbitrary domains. 'However the formulation of Löwenheim's theorem requires either the notion "domain" in general — or we must formulate the theorem by saying that if not-F is not provable, then F can be satisfied in N.'

Skolem went on to say that (1) without presupposing set theory, the second alternative is the only possible one, and (2) in that case validity can only mean provability in the pure predicate calculus. It seems to follow that the completeness of the calculus is true by definition. Moreover, it is unclear how the reformulated Löwenheim theorem could be proved without first inferring, from the nonprovability of not-F, the existence of some model for F. In short, Skolem appears to be saying in this connection that (a) without presupposing set theory, the completeness question disappears, and (b) even the Löwenheim theorem can only be restated, but not proved (without going through the notion of arbitrary domain or model). In the concluding part of the paragraph, Skolem seems to suggest that different versions of the predicate calculus might make the notion of satisfiability relative to one kind of logic or another. One interpretation of this observation is that he wishes to suspend judgment also between different conceptions of predicate logic, such as the classical in contrast to the intuitionistic.

Apart from my discussion in SWL, the relation between Skolem's work of the completeness proof is considered by Goldfarb, in his papers of 1971 and 1979 (CWI, p. 424), and, more recently, by Dreben and Heijenoort (CWI, pp. 50–6).

In his letter of 7 December 1967 to me, Gödel explains at length how his 'objectivistic conception of mathematics and metamathematics' was fundamental to his work in logic (see Wang, 1974, pp. 8–11), and then concludes by returning to Skolem again:

> Skolem's epistemological views were, in some sense, diametrically opposed to my own. E.g., on p. 29 of his 1929 paper [SWL, p. 253], evidently because of the transfinite character of the completeness question, he tried to *eliminate* it, instead of answering it, using to this end a new definition of logical consequence, whose idea exactly was to *avoid* the concept of mathematical truth. Moreover he was a firm believer in set theoretical relativism and in the sterility of transfinite reasoning for finitary questions (see p. 49 of his paper [SWL, p. 273]). (Gödel, 1967)

There are two problems, on different levels, about Gödel's comments on the relation between Skolem's work and the completeness question. On the local level, Gödel said in his letter that the easy inference from Skolem 1922 to the completeness conclusion 'is definitely non-finitary, and so is any other completeness proof for the predicate calculus'. But Bernays had pointed out in his letter to me at the time that Skolem did not think of the theorems of elementary logic as given in a formal system and, therefore, that the question of full completeness had no meaning for Skolem. Moreover, Skolem did actually use non-finitary reasoning in his early proof of Löwenheim's theorem. In any case, it is clear that Skolem had little interest in the formalization of logic, so that, as Gödel suggested, Skolem implicitly proved an informal version of the completeness theorem in Skolem 1922: if A is valid, then A is provable (by familiar informal reasoning). It is then easy to verify that the actual steps in the informal proof can also be carried out in any familiar formal system for the predicate logic.

The global problem is Gödel's belief that his 'objectivistic conception' is fruitful. This is true with regard to Gödel's own work, as explained in his letter to me. But it does not follow that Skolem's different, more or less finitary, conception of mathematics and meta-mathematics is not fruitful for obtaining (other) results. Indeed, Skolem's various important contributions to logic have demonstrated the fruitfulness of his conception, as much as Gödel's results have demonstrated that of *his*. It seems to me that one can learn, by studying and reflecting on Skolem's work, one fruitful way of doing logic, which is different from Gödel's. That is also one reason why I believe it to be a valuable task to look for an articulate formulation of Skolem's philosophy of mathematics and mathematical activity.

Both Skolem and Gödel are well-known for their results on the limitations of familiar methods in characterizing mathematical concepts such as sets and natural numbers. In 1922, Skolem developed what has since been known as 'Skolem's paradox,' which shows that every thoroughgoing axiomatization of set theory, if consistent, has a countable model. Skolem speaks of 'a relativity of the set-theoretic notions' and goes on to say:

In order to obtain something absolutely uncountable, we would have to have either an absolutely uncountably infinite number of axioms or an axiom that could yield an absolutely uncountable number of first-order propositions. But this would in all cases lead to a circular introduction of higher infinities; that is, *on an axiomatic basis higher infinities exist only in a relative sense.* (Skolem, 1970, p. 144)

In 1929, stimulated by Brouwer's lecture in March, Gödel reflected on 'the inexhaustibility of mathematics' and told Carnap some of his ideas on 23 December 1929, which can be compared with the above quotation. According to Carnap's diary, Gödel said on this occasion:

We admit as legitimate mathematics certain reflections on the grammar of a language that concerns the empirical. If one seeks to formalize such a mathematics, then with each formalization there are problems, which one can understand and express in ordinary language, but cannot express in the given formalized language. It follows (Brouwer) that mathematics is inexhaustible: one must always again draw afresh from the 'fountain of intuition'. There is, therefore, no *characteristica universalis* for the *whole* mathematics, and no decision procedure for the whole mathematics. In each and every *closed language* there are only countably many expressions. The *continuum* appears only in 'the whole of mathematics.' . . . If we have *only one language,* and can only make 'elucidations' about it, then these elucidations are inexhaustible, they always require some new intuition again. (Gödel, 1929)

These observations by Gödel are both more general and less definite than Skolem's discussion. They seem to say that no language, being necessarily countable, could capture fully the continuum.

Gödel's further development of the idea in his famous result, obtained in 1930, shows that also the natural numbers cannot be captured fully by any formal system, either directly or with the help of set theory.

In the last section (SWL, pp. 269–72) of his 1929 paper, Skolem considers a fragment of number theory, and shows that it admits some simple non-standard model by taking a suitable set of polynomials as the natural numbers. In a slightly earlier paper he says (p. 224):

A very probable consequence of this relativism is again that it cannot be possible to *completely* characterize the mathematical concepts; this already holds for the concept of the natural number. Thereby arises the question, whether the unicity or categoricity of mathematics might not be an illusion. Then it would not at all be strange if some problems were unsolvable; they would in fact not be decided by means of the principles which we are able to found them with, and it would not at all be necessary to resort to a new logic, as Brouwer does, in order to see this. (Skolem, 1970)

In 1933 Skolem published his famous result on the concept of natural number, which gives, for any 'axiom system' for the concept, a non-standard model which has the same true (first-order) sentences as its standard model (SWL, pp. 345–66, see also the 1954 lecture, pp. 587–600; compare, for Gödel's reviews, CWI, pp. 376–81 and p. 385). In the 1970s, Gödel said to me that one should not construe this Skolem theorem as establishing the impossibility of fully characterizing the concept of natural number by logic, because we can use the 'theory of concepts', which is also logic but goes beyond set theory in certain ways. I do not fully understand Gödel's ideas, but I think it is interesting to consider the question whether, or in what sense, Skolem's theorem may be said to show the impossibility of capturing natural numbers by *logic*.

My main purpose in this lecture is to select a few quotations from Skolem and propose a few problems, which I find fascinating, for further study. One problem, is the highly non-finitary, non-constructive character of 'Skolem functions', introduced in Skolem 1920. Another problem is the meaning of Skolem's 'relativism'. Skolem's attitude toward set theory is worth considering in the context of the development of set theory and of Skolem's own contribution to it. Among other things, Skolem made several suggestive observations on the continuum hypothesis. It may be argued that he was able to make his particular contributions to the foundations of set theory precisely because he was skeptical toward Cantorian set theory.

As Boos has pointed out in the typescript mentioned above, the Skolem functions are closely related to the tau-symbol (later replaced by the epsilon-symbol), introduced by Hilbert in 1923 to formulate the laws governing quantifiers. For example, in 1929 Skolem quoted with approval Weyl's observation that Hilbert's tau-symbol is a contrived 'divine automat': 'If we had access to such an automat, we would be relieved of all pains; but the belief in its existence is of course the purest nonsense' (SWL, p. 220).

The difference between Skolem's and Hilbert's uses of such an 'automat' is, I believe, the fact that the Skolem functions are employed only hypothetically, to select objects from a domain assumed to exist and to have certain properties — whereas Hilbert uses his 'automat' to represent the very essence of our non-constructive reasoning over infinite ranges, in the sense of the 'actual' infinite.

Skolem's observations on the continuum hypothesis may be viewed as an early conjecture that it is not decidable by the familiar axioms of set theory:

> Since Zermelo's axioms do not determine the domain *B* [the model for them], it is very improbable that all cardinality problems are decidable by means of these axioms. For example, it is quite probable that what is called the continuum problem is not solvable at all on this basis; nothing need be decided about it. (Skolem, 1922, p. 149, note 2)

> [comment on Hilbert's attempt to prove the continuum hypothesis]. It seems in fact that Hilbert wants to uphold the Cantorian views in their old absolutist sense, which seems to me very strange; it is revealing that he has never found it necessary to deal with the relativism, which I proved for every finitistically formulated axiomatization of set theory. (Skolem, 1929, p. 222)

Skolem's skepticism toward Cantorian set theory continued over the years, despite the clarifications in the work of Zermelo, Gödel, and others in the 1930s and the 1940s. For instance, the following two observations indicate that his views did not change between 1915 and 1955:

[conclusion of the paper]. The most important result above is that set-theoretic notions are relative. I had already communicated it to F. Bernstein in Göttingen in the winter of 1915–16 . . . I believed that it was so clear that axiomatization in terms of sets was not a satisfactory ultimate foundation of mathematics that mathematicians would, for the most part, not be very much concerned with it. But in recent times I have seen to my surprise that so many mathematicians think that these axioms of set theory provide the ideal foundation for mathematics; therefore it seemed to me that the time had come to publish a critique. (Skolem, 1922, p. 152)

Is Cantor's set theory still going strong? Sometimes I have had the task to write reviews of articles, where set-theoretical notions and theorems are used without any kind of explanation of what kind of set theory is meant. It is a disagreeable job to write reviews in such cases. One does not know what the author really means. (Skolem, 1955, p. 583)

Apart from incidental philosophical observations in the middle of technical articles, Skolem also wrote a few essays of a philosophical character, usually on the occasion of giving a lecture. Among them are his 1941 (1938) lecture in Zurich (SWL, pp. 455–83), his 1952 (1950) lecture in Cambridge, Massachusetts (pp. 519–28), and his 1958 lecture in Paris (pp. 633–9).

The record of the first lecture includes discussions with Bernays. Bernays observed that things like the 'Skolem paradox' are to be understood as a limitation of the use of formal systems to capture our intuitive mathematical concepts of set and number. Skolem's reply is thus reported in the record: 'Mr. Skolem thinks that one does not have to view the situation from such an angle. In his view, the best way is to refer in each domain of research to an appropriate formalism. This manner of proceeding does not imply any restriction on the possibilities of reasoning, for one has always the liberty of passing to a more extended formalism' (SWL, p. 480).

In the Cambridge lecture, Skolem recommended further developments of predicative set theory (pp. 525–6) and concluded with what he took to be the most important observation. He pointed out that the use of quantifiers is the most difficult thing and proposed to develop mathematics without using them (pp. 526–7):

I think that the fear that mathematics will be crippled by the restriction to the use of only free variables is exaggerated. I am aware that it may look different to mathematicians accustomed to analysis — to the theory of functions say — and those only working in the theory of numbers, but there are certainly many more ways of treating mathematics than we know today.

Now I will not be misunderstood. I am no fanatic, and it is not my intention to condemn the nonfinitistic ideas and methods. But I should like to emphasize that the finitistic development as far as it may be carried out has a very great advantage with regard to clearness and security.

Further there may be good reason to conjecture that it can be carried out very far, if one would make serious attempts in that direction. (Skolem, 1952)

In his Paris lecture, Skolem said that we can prove the consistency of formal systems which use only free variables, by our intuition of mathematical induction, and that 'in the other cases we can adopt the opportunistic standpoint (see my Cambridge lecture, p. 700). My point of view is then that we use formal systems for the development of mathematical ideas' (SWL, p. 634).

This observation seems to involve a change of emphasis from the Cambridge lecture, where he said that 'this standpoint has the unpleasant feature that we can never know when we have finished the foundation of mathematics,' after defining the opportunistic standpoint as follows (SWL, p. 524):

One desires only to have a foundation which makes it possible to develop present-day mathematics, and which is consistent so far as is known yet. Should any contradiction occur, we may try to make such restrictions in the underlying postulates that the deduction of the contradiction proves impossible. This may perhaps be called the opportunistic standpoint. It is a very practical one.

If we put together these observations from 1950 and 1958 by Skolem, we see three components or levels in his position on the study of the foundations of mathematics. First, whenever possible, avoid the use of quantifiers and adhere to the finitistic standpoint. Second, it is desirable to develop further predicative set theory, which, though not as clear as finitary mathematics, is comparatively transparent. Third, adopt the opportunistic standpoint in areas where the first two approaches are insufficient (at present).

Expressed in this way, Skolem's views are not as different from Gödel's views, in the form as they emerged from his conversations with me, as commonly believed. For example, both Gödel and I and indeed most logicians agree that the degree of 'clearness and security' decreases as we move from finitistic mathematics to predicative set theory to classical analysis and then to Cantorian set theory. Moreover, Gödel said to me and I agree with him: which of these theories to prefer depends on how much clarity and certainty one desires. This position seems to agree with the spirit of Skolem's observation in 1950: 'Which one of the different theories shall we prefer? That depends on the desires we have in the foundations of mathematics' (SWL, p. 524).

In my 1958 essay (Eighty years of foundational studies, *Dialectica*, volume 12), I proposed a scheme of replacing the conflict of the different schools on the foundations by a sequential demarcation of things like finitistic, intuitionistic, predicative, and classical mathematics, and suggested that the more instructive study is to clarify the interconnections between these areas: especially a clarification of what natural steps are involved in going from a more transparent domain to a less transparent one. For instance, Gödel's interpretation of intuitionistic arithmetic by a slight extension of finitistic mathematics and his translation of the classical arithmetic into the intuitionistic are striking examples of this enterprise. I have no doubt that Skolem would also find such a programme congenial.

I had only occasional personal contacts with Skolem. In 1954 both he and I took part in a symposium at the International Congress of Mathematicians in Amsterdam. (The proceedings were published in 1955 as a volume entitled *Mathematical Interpretation of Formal Sytems.*) In Autumn 1957 I went to the University of Notre Dame to give a lecture; Skolem came to it and asked a question. In Autumn 1961 I sent to many logicians, for verification and criticisms, copies of a manuscript, which reduces predicate logic, by using the intuitive tool of certain tiling problems, to formulas of the AEA form. Skolem was one of the only two recipients who responded to the request for comments — Dana Scott being the other. My impression from these casual encounters does not contradict Professor Fenstad's evaluation that 'Skolem was very modest and retiring.'

It is quite possible that one would not have learnt more mathematics and philosophy from Skolem through personal contacts than just studying his writings. However that may be, after spending so many hours of my life with his work, it is a special experience to set foot in his home country for the first time and to honour him at his home institution.

Notes

1. This chapter is the text of the 1993 Skolem Lecture, delivered on 19 February 1993 at the University of Oslo.

References

Boos, W. (1992) Thoralf Skolem, Hermann Weyl and 'Das Gefühl der Welt as Begrenztes Ganzes', Unpublished Manuscript.

Gödel, (1986) *Collected Works*, (Ed) Feferman, S., Dawson, J.W., Kleene, S.C., Moore, G.H., Solovay, R.M. and Heijenoort, J. van. New York; Oxford University Press.

Goldfarb, (1979) 'Logic in the twenties: The nature of the quantifier', *Journal of Symbolic Logic*, 44, pp. 351–368.

Skolem, T. (1970) *Selected Works in Logic*, (Ed) Fenstad, J.E., Oslo, Universitetsforlaget.

Wang, H. (1955) *Mathematical Interpretation of Formal Systems*, Proceedings of the Symposium of the International Congress of Mathematicians, Amsterdam.

Wang, H. (1958) 'Eighty years of Foundational Studies', *Dialectica*, 12.

Wang, H. (1993) Skolem Lecture, 19 February, University of Oslo.

Weyl, H. (1910) *Jahrbuch der Mathematische Fortschrifte,*

Chapter 14

Different Ways of Knowing: Contrasting Styles of Argument in Indian and Greek Mathematical Traditions

George Gheverghese Joseph

Introduction

Many of the commonly available books on history of mathematics declare or imply that Indian mathematics, whatever be its other achievements, did not not have any notion of proof. To illustrate, with two examples, the first taken from one of the better known texts on the history of mathematics, Kline (1972) writes:

> There is much good procedure and technical facility, but *no evidence that they (i.e., the Indians) considered proof at all*. They had rules, but apparently no *logical scruples*. Moreover, no general methods or new viewpoints were arrived at in any area of mathematics. It is fairly certain that the Hindus (i.e., the Indians) *did not appreciate the significance of their own contributions*. The few good ideas they had, such as separate symbols for the numbers, were introduced causally with no realisation that they were valuable innovations. They were not *sensitive to mathematical values*. (Kline, 1972, p. 190)

A more recent opinion is that of Lloyd (1990) who writes:

> It would appear that before, in, and after the Sulbasutra [the earliest known evidence of mathematics from India], right down to the modern representatives of that tradition, we are dealing with men who tolerate, on occasion, *rough and ready techniques*. They are in fact interested in practical results and *show no direct concern* with proof procedures as such at all. (Lloyd, 1990, p. 104)

These quotations raise a number of fundamental questions: What is mathematics? How is it created? How is its quality to be assessed? But a more general question is: How do mathematicians produce information about mathematical objects? Underlying all these questions is the issue of proof, often perceived as a litmus test of whether we are 'doing' real mathematics or doing it well.

The first quotation above represents a view point that sees ways of establishing mathematical truths (or what is more commonly know as 'proofs') as being immutable and unchanging. The second quotation is from a text which, while acknowledging the legitimacy of 'informal' proof procedures for confirming or checking a result, requires that a formal proof procedure observes two crucial distinctions: (i) that between the 'practice of proof (of whatever kind) and having an explicit concept corresponding to the practice, a concept that incorporates the condition that need to be met for a proof to be given'. and (ii) that between, 'exact procedures and approximate ones' (Lloyd, 1990, pp. 74–5). On both these criteria, the author concludes that early Indian mathematics did not have 'any explicit notion of what proof is' (Lloyd, 1990, p. 75).

And implied in these quotations is a particular interpretation of the history of early mathematics which has come to be described as Eurocentric and culturally biased. The explosive impact of multiculturalism on academia, especially in the United States and Britain, has called into question the cultural neutrality of such underlying notions of western mathematics as rationalism and abstraction and also inspired recent attempts to bring about a 'decolonization' of the history of mathematics. The reverberations of the multicultural debate seem to have affected professional historians of science in very different ways.[1]

Eurocentrism and Hellenocentrism in Mathematics Histories

A collection of essays, entitled *The Cultures of Ancient Science* appeared in a recent issue of *ISIS* (Volume 83, No. 4, December 1992). The introductory essay claims that there is a 'new direction in the historiography of science consistent with some of the "newer" ideas generated by the philosophy of science and social anthropology of the last hundred years. [This is reflected in] a less ideologically limited, less category-driven approach to sources identified as belonging to science and therefore to its historical development, and [a readiness] to adopt methods in general history that attempt to find a balance between the recognition of the historian's cultural and philosophical contributions — hence the limits on objectivity — and the desire to construct a working model consistent with available knowledge and textual evidence' (Rochberg, *ibid.* , p. 553).[2]

There are two features of Eurocentrism that have aroused interest in recent years: first, a tendency to 'privilege' Greek mathematics over the mathematics of other ancient cultures and second, to adopt a version of mathematics that makes it a creation of the Greeks. Both these features, one suspects, would have puzzled the Greeks who were more than generous in their attribution of the invention of the mathematical sciences to the Egyptians.

To understand Hellonocentrism in science (and mathematics), according to Von Staden (*ISIS*, *ibid.*, p. 582), one should examine critically the 'oft-tacit interpretative deployment of notions of affinity, continuity and origin' — notions which are a complex product of the western search for its identity throughout history and its reaction to the 'other' in more recent times. Affinities are assumed between the ancient Greece and modern West on the basis of shared values relating to 'scientific method' and 'rationality' and an exclusion mechanism that renders a one-to-one mapping between the two cultures. For good measure, this affinity is further emphasized by finding common 'democratic' roots in the sciences of both cultures. Continuity between ancient and modern science (and mathematics) is based on both privileging Greek science over all other ancient sciences but also constructing an unlinear development trajectory that ignores the so-called 'Dark Ages' and continues the link between Greece and modern West. Selectivity cannot be avoided in the history of science for even within the constraints of written and other evidence, the unravelling of historical relationships involves acts of simplification and ommission. What has been missing until recently is an awareness of how an individual historian of science's selection and omission is *culturally conditioned*. And in the case of many western historians of science, the two mutually reinforcing cultural values have been: the perception of ancient Greece as the mainspring of modern culture and western scientific culture as the only lodestar.

The quest for the origins of science is linked with the concerns that arise from the 'affinity' and 'continuity' models of historical interpretation. The search for the origins have generated different acts of 'retrospectivist "genealogical" privileging' (von Staden, *ibid.*, p. 584) in which a number is partly a reaction to the Greek 'miracle' but mainly a reaction to the assumptions, almost universal in the nineteenth and early twentieth centuries that no non-European culture could have been capable of original and seminal discoveries in science and mathematics.[3] It is therefore not surprising that 'many non-Westerners have caught a form of the disease Hellenophilia: they are deluded into believing that the greatest glory an Indian, a Chinese, an Arab, an African scientist can have acquired is that gained by having anticipated either a Greek or a modern Westerner.' (Pingree, *ISIS*, 1992, p. 555). And preceding a recovery from 'a severe sense of cultural inferiority' which is a cause of the disease is the need to tell the true story.

The Nature of Proof

Consider the word 'proof' in the sense that Lakatos (1976, p. 9) uses it to mean a 'thought experiment which suggests a decomposition of the original conjecture into subconjectures or lemmas, thus embedding it in a possibly quite distinct body of knowledge.'

In this broad sense any 'proof' has psychological, social and logical features (Resnick, 1992, pp. 15–17). The psychological task is to convince its readers of its conclusions. The notation and the way in which the argument is formulated, organized, and presented determines whether the proof succeeds at this task. Yet success in convincing an audience does not necessarily mean that the proof is free of error. Proofs make certain claims about mathematical objects.[4] Understanding such claims requires training and the more 'advanced' the mathematics the longer the training required. Nowhere is this training more important than in the comprehension of the logical framework in which the proof is embedded. Therefore, it is important to distinguish between the psychological and logical powers of a proof. A logically impeccable proof could appear obscure and unconvincing because the audience have not acquired through training a satisfactory understanding of the mathematical objects of which the claims are being made in the first place.

It is the third feature of a mathematical proof that is often ignored. Proofs are social and cultural artefacts. They evolve in a particular social and cultural context. And this is important since we might tend to forget that part of finding out how a proof works includes finding out how its intended audience (the author included) come prepared to follow it. This is further complicated by the fact that proofs are context-bound — not only in relation to a proof's language and notation but also its reasoning and data (or the uses to which a mathematical result is put to).

As an illustration, consider the historical development of mathematical analysis. From existing evidence, the beginnings of analysis may be traced to Kerala in South India (Joseph, 1991, pp. 286–94). Between the fourteenth and sixteenth centuries there appeared a number of infinite series and their finite approximations relating to circular and trigonometric functions which predate the work of Newton, Liebniz and Gregory by 200 years. The primary motivation for this work was astronomical computations: the need to calculate as accurately as possible the values of π and the *sine* and *cosine* functions. Demonstrations of these results by Madhava (c.1340–1425) are not completely rigorous by today's standards, but they are nonetheless correct. And these demonstrations may well be chosen for a modern mathematics classroom because the geometric approach is more intuitive. Geometric intuition and logically deductive reasoning formed the basis of 'proofs' both in India and later in Europe. By the end of the nineteenth century, geometry fell out of favour to be replaced by arithmetic and set theory. Thus Bolzano and Dedekind tried to prove that infinite sets exist by arguing that any object of thought can be thought about and thus give rise to a new thought object. Today we reject such proofs and use an axiom of infinity. Beginning with a practical orientation and serving practitioners of the astronomical arts, the subject of analysis by its peculiar logic developed eventually into a highly abstract and rarefied entity for the delectations of primarily the professional mathematician.

The Indian Proofs (or *Upapattis*) of the Pythagorean Theorem[5]

For a period going back to about 2,000 years, a great deal of attention in Indian mathematics was laid on providing what was often referred to as *upapatti* (which may be roughly translated as a 'convincing' demonstration) for every mathematical result. In fact some of these *upapattis* were noted by European scholars of Indian mathematics up to the first half of the nineteenth century. For example, in one of the early English translations (1817) of parts of *Brahma Sputa Siddhanta* of Brahmagupta (b. AD 598) and of *Lilavati* and *Bijaganita of Bhaskaracharya* (b. AD 1114), Colebrook gives in the form of footnotes a number of *upapattis* from commentators and calls them demonstrations. Similarly, Whish (1835) who brought to the attention of a wider public work in Kerala on infinite series for circular and trigonometric functions showed a sample of *upapattis* from a commentary entitled *Yuktibhasa* (c. 1550) which related to the Pythagorean theorem.

One of the main reasons for our lack of comprehension, not merely of the notion of proof, but also of the entire methodology of Indian mathematics, is the scant attention we have so far paid to these commentaries which seem to have played at least as great a role in the exposition of the subject as the original text itself. It is no wonder that mathematicians of the calibre of Bhaskaracharya and Nilakantha (a fifteenth century mathematician/astronomer) wrote not only major original treatises but also erudite commentaries on either their own works or on important works of an earlier period. It is in such commentaries that one finds detailed *upapattis* for results and processes discussed in the original texts as well as more general discussion of the methodological and philosophical issues concerning Indian astronomy and mathematics.

As an illustration, consider the commentaries of Ganesha Daivajna (b. AD 1507) on the works of Bhaskaracharya. According to Ganesha, *ganita* (used both as a generic word to describe the subject of mathematics as well as used in a specialized sense to describe calculation) is mainly of two types: *vykata ganita* and *avyakta ganita*. *Vyaktagnita* (also called *patiganita* or calculations with the board), is that branch of *ganita* which employs clearly laid out procedures or algorithms well-known for general use. This is in contrast to *avyakta ganiti* (also called *bijaganita*) which is distinguished from the first type by including procedures that use indeterminate or unknown quantities in the process of solution. The unknown quantities were referred to by terms such as *yavat tavat* (i.e., 'as much as') and different colours (*varna*) denoted by abbreviations such as *ka* (for *kalaka* or black), *ni* (for *nilaka* or blue), etc., just as in modern algebra unknowns are denoted by symbols *x*, *y*, *z*, . . . etc.

A specific illustration of the use of *upapattis* would be useful. In a chapter on solution of quadratic equation from *Bijaganita*, Bhaskaracharya poses the following problem:

> Say what is the hypotenuse of a plane figure, in which the side and upright are equal to fifteen and twenty? And show the *upapatti* of the received mode of computation

Later he adds:

> The demonstration follows. It is two fold in each case: one geometric (*kshetra*) and the other algebraic (*avyakta*) . . . The algebraic demonstration must be shown to those who do not understand the geometric one. (and vice versa)

Ganesha provides the two *upapattis* which are elaboration of the ones outlined earlier by Bhaskaracharya. These are given *verbatim* (Srinivas, 1987, pp. 6–7), the only change being that we continue to use the Pythagorean triples (15, 20, 25) given in the original example rather than Ganesha's (3, 4, 5).

1. The *Upapatti* for the *Avyakta* Method[6]

Take the hypotenuse as the base and denote it as ya in the figure. Let the *bhuja* and *koti* (the two sides) be 15, 20 respectively. Let the perpendicular to the hypotenuse from the opposite vertex be drawn. This divides the triangle into two triangles which are similar to the original. Now use the rule of proportion. When ya is the hypotenuse the *bhuja* is 15, then when this *bhuja* 15 is the hypotenuse, the *bhuja* which is now the segment of the hypotenuse to the side of the (original) *bhuja* will be 15^2/ya. Again when *ya* is the hypotenuse, the koti is 20, then when the koti 20 is the hypotenuse, the koti which is now the segment of hypotenuse to the side of the (original) koti will be 20^2/ya. Adding the two segments of ya the hypotenuse and equating the sum to (the hypotenuse) *ya* gives ya = 25.

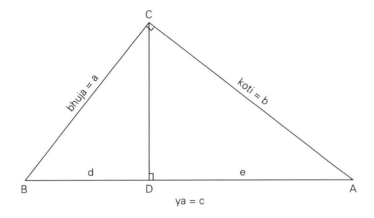

Figure 14.1: *Illustration of the Upapatti for the Avyakta Method*

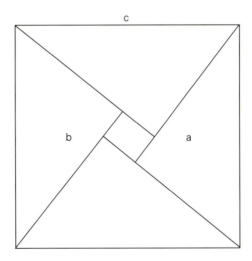

Figure 14.2: *Illustration of the Upapatti for the Kshetragata Method*

Modern notation (See Figure 14.1)

Since   CDB   BDA   CDA are similar
So $a/c = d/a \Rightarrow d = a^2/c$
and $b/c = e/b \Rightarrow e = b^2/c$
Therefore,
$c = (a^2 + b^2)/c \Rightarrow c^2 = a^2 + b^2$
Given $c = 15$ and $b = 20$
Therefore,
$ya = 25 = c = 20^2 + 15^2 = 25$

2.   The *Upapatti* for the Kshetragata Method (See Figure 14.2)[7]

Take four triangles identical to one another and let different *bhujas* rest on different *kotis* to form the square as shown. The interior square has for its side the difference of *bhuja* and *koti*. The area of each triangle is half the product of *bhuja* and *koti* and four times this added to the area of the interior square gives the area of the total figure. This is nothing but the sum of the squares of *bhuja* and *koti*. The square root of that is the side of the (big) square which is nothing but the hypotenuse.

Let ya = c, *bhuja* = a and *koti* + b
$$c^2 = (b - a)^2 + 2ab$$
$$= a^2 + b^2$$

What seems to be all too apparent from this example is that the notion of *upapatti* is significantly different from the notion of proof as understood in the Greek or even the modern traditions in mathematics. Saraswati Amma (1979) sums up the difference in the following way:

> There was an important difference between the Indian proofs and their Greek counterparts. The Indian aim was not to build up an edifice of geometry on a few self-evident axioms, but to convince the intelligent student of the validity of the theorem so that the visual demonstration was quite an accepted form of proof . . . Another characteristic of Indian mathematics makes it differ profoundly from Greek mathematics [is that] knowledge for its own sake did not appeal to the Indian mind. Every discipline (*sastra*) must have a purpose. (Saraswati Amma, 1979, p. 3)

The *upapattis* of Indian mathematics are stated in a precise language, displaying the main steps of the argument and indicating the general principles which are employed. In this sense they are no different from the 'proofs' found in modern mathematics. But what is peculiar to the *upapattis* is that while presenting the argument in an 'informal' manner (which is common in many mathematical discourses today), they make no reference whatsoever to any fixed set of axioms or link the given argument to 'formal deductions' performable from such axioms.

Most of mathematical discourses in Greek as well as modern tradition are carried out with clear reference to some formal deductive system, though the discourse itself might be in the 'informal' modes. More importantly, the ideal view of mathematics in both the Greek and modern traditions is that of a formal deductive system. Their view is that 'real mathematics' is (and ought to be presented) as formal derivations from formally stated axioms. This ideal view of mathematics is intimately linked with yet another major philosophical presupposition of western tradition — that mathematics constitutes a body of infallible or absolute truths. It is this quest for securing absolute certainty to mathematical knowledge which has motivated most of the foundational and philosophical investigations into mathematics and has also shaped the entire course of mathematics in the western tradition right from the Greeks to the contemporary times.

What the *upapattis* of Indian mathematics reveal is that the Indian epistomological position on the nature and validation of mathematical knowledge is very different from that in the western tradition. This is brought out, for instance, by general agreement among the Indian mathematicians as to what a *upapatti* is supposed to achieve. Ganesha declares in his preface to the commentary on Bhaskaracharya's *Lilavati* that:

> Whatever is discussed in the *vyakta* or *avyakta* branches of mathematics without *upapatti* it will not be *nirbhranta* (i.e., free from misunderstanding). It will not acquire any standing in an assembly of scholars mathematicians. The *upapatti* is directly perceivable, like looking in a handy mirror. It is therefore, to elevate the intellect (*buddhi vriddhi*) that I proceed to enunciate the *upapattis*.

As regards the modes of argument which are allowed in the *upapattis* one distinctive feature appears to be that Indian mathematics permitted the use of the method of indirect proof (*reductio ad absurdum*) but only to show the *non-existence* of certain entities.[8] As an illustration, consider the *upapatti* of the result that a negative number has no square root given by Krishna Daivajna (fl. AD 1600).

> A negative number is not a square. Hence how can we evaluate its square root? It may be asked: 'why cannot a negative number be a square? Surely it is not a royal command' . . . Agreed. Let it be stated by you who claim that a negative number is a square as to whose square it is; surely not of a positive number, for the square of a positive number is always positive. Not also a negative number because then also the square will be positive by the same rule. This being the case, we cannot see how the square of a number becomes negative.

In not accepting the method of indirect proof as a valid means for establishing the existence of an entity (which existence is not even in principle establishable via direct means of proof), the Indian mathematicians took what today would be known as the constructivist approach to the issue of mathematical existence. But the Indian philosopher-logician did more than merely disallow certain existence proofs. The general Indian philosophical position is in fact one of completly eliminating from logical discourse all reference to such unlocatable entities whose existence is not even in principle accessible to direct means of verification. This appears to be the position adopted by Indian mathematicians. And 'it is for this reason that many an "existence theorem" (where all that has been proved is that the non-existence of a hypothetical entity is incompatible with the accepted set of postulates) of Greek or modern Western mathematics would not be considered as significant or even meaningful in Indian mathematics' (Srinivas, 1987, p. 12).

Conclusion

The non-recognition of the foundational conceptions and methodologies of non-European mathematical traditions has restricted our understanding of the nature and potentialities of mathematics. Can we seriously believe that we could come to grips with the foundational tensions in modern mathematics without recognizing the deeper culturally determined ideological differences that went into the creation of this mathematics: stress on becoming (dynamic) versus stress on being (static), constructibility versus indirect proof, empiricism versus idealism . . . the polarities are many and hardly ever discussed.

Notes

1. A few personal reflections on some of the reactions to my book *The Crest of the Peacock: Non-European Roots of Mathematics* may be of some relevance in this context. In the midst of many constructive and useful comments have appeared a few that may be put into one or more of the following categories: (i) *Nit-picking pedantry*: 'Dates are wrong . . . transliteration of passages or translation of words not satisfactory . . . etc. (ii) *Injured innocence*: 'Research mathematicians are not interested in history [thank God!] . . . We are all aware of excessive reverence to Greeks and the neglect of others, so what is new? . . . 'An angry anti-Eurocentric voice . . . But isn't anti-Eurocentrism itself Eurocentric?' . . . etc. (iii) *An incomplete story* 'What about the Greeks? Why have they been left out? . . . A multicultural salad bar . . . etc.' (iv) *A question of relevance*: Egyptian numerals or computations taught in the Halls of Montezuma: Are these relevant in learning mathematics? . . . 'Promotes cultural relativism . . . etc. (v) *Is this really mathematics?* 'The book is about calculation more than proof' . . . 'Greek contribution to proof not found elsewhere and there begins mathematics' . . . etc. This chapter addresses the last point.
2. Yet Eurocentrism reigns supreme in certain quarters. To illustrate, the opening paragraph of Abeles (1993, p. 151) reads:

    > Until the development of the calculus, all the methods of calculating π depended on inscribed and circumscribed regular polygons within and about a circle. By doubling the number of sides of a hexagon four times, Archimedes was able to approximate π as 3.1418. His method, however, was slow and cumbersome. The new techniques of the calculus replaced the older geometric methods with analytical functions which are given by integrals of quadratic functions that characterize the curvature of a circle, both Newton and Leibniz calculated approximations for π using series expansions of these functions. Newton used the inverse sine function while Leibniz preferred the inverse tangent function.

    The leap from Archimedes to Newton conveniently ignores the work of the Chinese mathematician, Tsu Chung Chih (c. AD 480) and the Persian mathematician, al-Kashi (AD 1429) who obtained remarkably accurate approximations for π for their time. But more seriously, one searches in vain for even a mention of the Indian work on arctan series approximation for π at least two hundred years earlier than European work in this area.
3. To illustrate, at a conference on the history of science, Crombie, (1950, p. 81) made the following claim: 'It was the Greeks who invented science as we know it, by their assumption of a permanent, uniform, abstract order and laws by means of which the regular changes observed in the world could be explained by deduction, and by their brilliant idea of the generalied use of scientific theory tailored according to the principles of non-contradiction and the empirical test.' Views of this nature have gone hand in hand with specific claims such as the Greeks were the first to 'discover nature', 'practise debate', study irrational numbers (such as the square root of 2) and construct geometrical models in astronomy — claims that are all found in Lloyd (1970, p. 8).
4. The nature of mathematical objects determines how we make contact with them. If mathematical objects are based on the Euclidean ideas of atomistic and an object-oriented view of space (points, lines, planes and solids) this will be in complete

contrast to a Navajo idea of space as neither subdivided nor objectified and where everything is in motion (Bishop, 1990, p. 51). The crucial point is that ideas of proof are culturally created and be understood within that culture, resisting the easy temptation to make crude comparisons across cultures and oppositional ways of deciding between ideas which the quotation from Kline at the beginning clearly typifies.

5. This section owes a heavy debt to Srinivas (1987).
6. A variant of this proof of the so-called Pythagorean theorem using similar triangles may have first appeared in European mathematics in 1685 in Wallis's *Treatise on Angular Sections* ... However, Thabit ibn Qurra (d. AD 901), an Arab mathematician, had produced a generalization of the Pythagorean theorem applicable to all triangles, whether right-angled or not, whose proof also made use of similar triangles. It is a reasonable conjecture that Wallis was aware of Thabit's work. For futher details, see Joseph (1991, pp. 336–7).
7. The geometrical representation above has an uncanny resemblance to that given in the earliest extant Chinese text on astronomy and mathematics, the *Chou Pei Suan Ching* dated around the middle of the first millennium BC. The *upapatti* follows closely the demonstration given by a commentator of the Chinese text, Chao Chung Ching who lived in the third century AD. Possible Chinese influence cannot be ruled out. For further details, see Joseph, 1991, pp. 180–1.
8. If entities are regarded as 'being' or 'non-being', then the existence criteria would require the logic of indirect proof (using the principle of excluded middle). But if entities are regarded as 'accomplished' or 'unaccomplished' then the existence criteria would be constructability. Here we see an important difference between foundational basis of Greek mathematics with its formal logic in which the central principle is the method of indirect proof and that of Indian mathematics with its algorithmic logic and the central principle is that of constructability.

References

ABELES, F.F. (1993) 'Charles L. Dodgson's geometric approach to arctangent relations for Pi', *Historia Mathematica*, 20, pp. 153–9.

APTE, V.G. (Ed) (1937) *Buddhivilasini of Ganesha Daivajna* (2 Vols), Anandasrama Sanskrit Series, 107, Pune.

APTE, V.G. (1939–41) *Siromaniprakasa of Ganesha Daivajna (Grahagnitadyaya)* (2 Vols), Anandasrama Sanskrit Series, 112, Pune.

BISHOP, A.J. (1990) 'Western mathematics: The secret weapon of cultural imperialism', *Race and Class*, 32, pp. 51–65.

COLEBROOK, H.T. (1817) *Algebra with Arithmetic and Mensuration from the Sanscrit of Brahmegupta and Bhascara*, London, John Murray.

DVIVEDE, S. (Ed) (1920) *Bijaganitam Avyaktaganitan with* the commentary *Bijanvankura* by KRISHNA DAIVAJNA, Anandasrama Sanskrit Series, Pune.

JOSEPH, G.G. (1991) *The Crest of the Peacock: Non-European Roots of Mathematics*, London, I.B. Tauris (second edition Penguin books, 1992).

ISIS (1992), 83, 4, December, pp. 557–607.

KLINE, M. (1972) *Mathematical Thought from Ancient to Modern Times*, New York (paperback, 1990), Oxford University Press.

KLINE, M. (1980) *Mathematics The Loss of Certainty*, New York, Oxford University Press.

LAKATOS, I. (1976) *Proofs and Refutations — The Logic of Mathematical Discovery*, Cambridge.

LLOYD, G.E.R. (1970) *Early Greek Science: Thales to Aristotle*, Norton, New York.

LLOYD, G.E.R. (1990) *Demystifying Mentalities*, Cambridge, Cambridge University Press.

RESNICK, M. (1992) 'Aspects of Proof', *Educational Studies in Mathematics*, 24, 4.

SARMA, K.V. (1972) *A History of Kerala School of Hindu Astronomy*, Vishveshvaranand Institute, Hoshiarpur.

SARMA, K.V. (1975) *Lilavathi* of Bhaskaracharya with *Kriyakrmakari* of Sankara and Narayana, V.V.B. Institute of Indological Studies, Hoshiarpur.

SARMA, K.V. (1977) *Tantra Sangraha* of Nilakantha Somayaji and *Yuktidipika* and *Laghuvivriti* of Sankara, V.V.B. Institute of Sanskrit and Indological Studies, Hoshiarpur.

SARASWATI AMMA, T.A. (1963) 'The development of mathematical series in India after Bhaskara II', *Bulletin of the National Institute of Sciences*, 21, pp. 320–42.

SARASWATI AMMA, T.A. (1979) *Geometry in Ancient and Medieval India*, Motilal Banarisidass, Varanasi.

SRINIVAS, M.D. (1987) 'The methodology of Indian mathematics and its contemporary relevance', *PPST*, 12, pp. 1–35.

WHISH, C.M. (1835) 'On the Hindu Quadrature of the Circle and the Infinite Series of the Proportion of the Circumference of the Diameter exhibited in the Four Sastras, the *Tantra Sangraham, Yucti Bhashi Carana Padhata, and Sadratnamala*', Transactions of The Royal Asiatic Society of Great Britain and Ireland, 3, pp. 509–23.

WHITESIDE, D.T. (1960–2) 'Patterns of mathematical thought in the late seventeenth century', *Archive for History of Exact Sciences*, 1, pp. 179–388.

Part 4

The Social Context of Mathematics and Education

Bring out number, weight & measure in a year of dearth

Blake[1]

Women . . . work $^2/_3$ of the world's working hours, earn $^1/_{10}$ of the world's income and own $^1/_{100}$ of the world's property

Shelley[2]

The most frequently recurring theme in this collection is that of the social nature of mathematics. Contrary to traditional epistemology, a number of perspectives including those of the sociology of knowledge, feminist epistemology, critical theory, post-structuralism and post-modernism share the view that knowledge at all stages in its production and acceptance is not only shot through with the values of the social groups and persons involved, but that the very quest for knowledge is preceded and driven by certain social and epistemological interests. This view means that mathematics inescapably brings with it questions of values, social responsibility and social justice, such as the following.[3]

What are the social origins of mathematical knowledge? Whose knowledge is it and in whose interest? What meaning does this have for humankind, and for social change? How can the view that mathematical knowledge is value-laden, and that issues of race and gender have a bearing on epistemology be legitimated philosophically? How can mathematics be reconceptualized to incorporate non-Eurocentric views, and to include the historiography of how and when the Eurocentric view became 'standard'? How has mathematics helped re-orientate the modern worldview in which quality is seen in terms of quantity? How is mathematical knowledge used to understand or obscure political, economic and social issues? What is the relationship between mathematical knowledge and power? How can mathematical knowledge be emancipatory? What does it mean to empower students through mathematics, and how can this be achieved? Can we reconcile learners' concrete ethnomathematical knowledge and the esoteric mathematics that opens the gates of power?

The issue of the social origins and values in mathematics raises two sorts of questions and issues concerning its social responsibility, those of critique and those of redress. A critique of the role of mathematics and mathematical knowledge in society might ask if there is a hidden agenda underlying the popular image of mathematics as difficult, cold, abstract, ultra-rational, important and largely masculine. Through such images it offers access most easily to those feel a sense of ownership of mathematics, the associated values of western culture and the educational system in general. These will often tend to be middle-class, white and male. The image described sustains their social privileges because mathematics acts as a critical filter for entry into higher education and professional occupations, especially so where then sciences and technology are involved.

If it is acknowledged that mathematics serves certain interests in society, and privileges certain groups, there is secondly the issue of social justice and of redressing the balance. How is it possible to achieve the aims of a critical mathematics education, including the empowerment of all individual learners mathematically, irrespective of social background and disadvantage, to facilitate their personal and social development? Does this not necessitate respect for learners and their knowledge and the use of a respectful and dialogical pedagogy? There is also the aim of raising the consciousness of all learners to look critically at the received structures of mathematical knowledge and society; to question them; and to consider more egalitarian and liberating alternatives. In addition, there is the issue of raising awareness of ethnomathematics and the multicultural origins of mathematics, without wanting to condemn any group of learners to a local or 'ghetto' curriculum.

There is a worldwide movement concerned with such issues, and there are several active international associations concerned with women and mathematics and with ethnomathematics, as well as biennial conferences on the Political Dimensions of Mathematics Education. A number of radical academics including Marilyn Frankenstein, Martin Hoffmann and Arthur Powell in the USA have formed the Critical mathematics educators network and newsletter to promote social justice through critical mathematical literacy.

From the perspective of educational and social responsibility the issues raised in this section are undoubtedly the most important in the book. The size of this section ill reflects its import, but a large literature on gender, race, culture and the social critique of mathematics, as well as on critical mathematics education, already exists. See, for example, Burton (1986), Ernest (1989, 1991), Grouws (1992), Julie *et al.* (1993) and Skovsmose (1994), for surveys of research. In addition, the social perspectives of mathematics offered throughout this volume pave the way for a critique. Some earlier chapters, such as that by Walkerdine, complement what is offered here on gender and mathematics. It is also particularly exciting to have contributions from Sal Restivo (1992) and Ubiratan D'Ambrosio (1985), leading contributors to socio-historical and ethnomathematical critiques of mathematics, respectively.

Notes

1. Blake (1790) Plate vii (Trianon Press edition page xviii.)
2. Shelley, N. (1984) Women, Culture and Mathematics. Paper presented at *5th International Conference on Mathematical Education*, Adelaide, 1984. Excerpt reprinted in Carss (1986), 313.
3. Of course a deep commitment to social responsibility and justice through mathematics education frequently coexists with a belief in the objectivity and neutrality of mathematics. But this position makes a radical social critique of mathematics more difficult, to say the least.

References

BLAKE, W. (1970) 'The Marriage of Heaven and Hell', Facsimile edition with text published by Trianon Press, Oxford, 1975.

BURTON, L. (Ed) (1986) *Girls into Maths Can Go*, London, Holt, Rinehart and Winston.

CARSS, M. (Ed) (1986) *Proceedings of the Fifth International Conference on Mathematical Education*, Boston, Birkhauser.

D'AMBROSIO, U. (1985) *Socio-cultural bases for Mathematics Education*, Campinas, Brazil, UNICAMP.

ERNEST, P. (Ed) (1989) *Mathematics Teaching: The State of the Art*, London, The Falmer Press.

ERNEST, P. (1991) *The Philosophy of Mathematics Education*, London, The Falmer Press.

GROUWS, D.A. (Ed) (1992) *Handbook of Research on Mathematics Teaching and Learning*, New York, Macmillan.

JULIE, C., ANGELIS, D. and DAVIS, Z. (Eds) (1993) *Political Dimensions of Mathematics Education: Curriculum Reconstruction for Society in Transition*, Johannesburg, South Africa, Maskew, Miller and Longman.

RESTIVO, S. (1992) *Mathematics in Society and History*, Dordrecht, Kluwer.

SHELLEY, N. (1984) 'Women, Culture and Mathematics', Paper presented at ICME-5 Conference, Adelaide, 1984. Excerpt reprinted on CARSS, M. (Ed) (1986) *Proceedings of the Fifth International Conference on Mathematical Education*, Boston, Birkhauser, 313.

SKOVSMOSE, O. (1994) *Towards a Philosophy of Critical Mathematics Education*, Dordrecht, Kluwer.

Chapter 15

The Social Life of Mathematics[1]

Sal Restivo

Introduction

Mathematicians and philosophers of mathematics have long claimed exclusive jurisdiction over inquiries into the nature of mathematical knowledge. Their inquiries have been based on the following sorts of assumptions: that Platonic and Pythagorean conceptions of mathematics are valid, intelligible, and useful; that mathematical statements transcend the flux of history; that mathematics is a creation of pure thought; and that the secret of mathematical power lies in the formal relations among symbols. The language used to talk about the nature of mathematical knowledge has traditionally been the language of mathematics itself; when other languages (for example, philosophy and logic) have been used, they have been languages highly dependent on, or derived from, mathematics. By contrast, social talk takes priority over technical mathematical talk when we consider mathematics in sociological terms.

Sociological thinking about mathematics has developed inside and outside of the mathematical community. In the social science community, it is manifested in insider, professional sociology. In the mathematical community, the everyday folk sociology of mathematicians became better articulated as mathematical work became better organized and institutional continuity was established beginning in seventeenth-century Europe. Eventually, some mathematicians who were especially self-conscious of the social life of the mathematical community began to write social and even sociological histories of their field (Dirk Struik, for example), or exhibit that self-consciousness in their mathematical programmes (as in the cases of the constructivists, and the group of mathematicians known as N. Bourbaki). It is therefore no longer obvious that technical talk can provide a complete understanding of mathematics.

The decline of Platonic, Pythagorean, formalist, and foundationalist prejudices has opened the door for social talk about mathematics. But the implications and potential of social talk about mathematics have yet to be realized. My task in this chapter is to sketch the implications and potential of thinking and talking about mathematics in sociological terms.

There is a sociological imperative surfacing across a wide range of fields that is changing the way we view ourselves, our world, and mathematical and scientific knowledge. This is not disciplinary imperialism; the sociological imperative is not the same as the discipline or profession of sociology. It is a way of looking at the world that is developing in the context of the modern experience, a mode

209

of thought emerging out of modern social practice. The basis for this Copernican social science revolution lies in three interrelated insights: all talk is social; the person is a social structure; and the intellect (mind, consciousness, cognitive apparatus) is a social structure. These insights are the foundation of a radical sociology of mathematics.

Intellectual Origins of the Sociological Imperative

The programme for a radical sociology of mathematics, in which all talk about mathematics is social talk, begins with Marx's (1956) formulation of the insight that science is a social activity. In order to underline the theme of this chapter, I take the liberty of substituting the term 'mathematical' for 'scientific' in the following quotation:

> Even when I carry out mathematical work, etc., an activity which I can seldom conduct in direct association with other men — I perform a social, because human, act. It is not only the material of my activity — like the language itself which the thinker uses — which is given to me as a social product. My own existence is a social activity. (Marx, 1956, p. 104)

This fundamental statement of the sociological imperative achieves its classical form in the closing pages of Emile Durkheim's *The Elementary Forms of the Religious Life.* Here, Durkheim initiates the transformation of the apparently obvious observations that the mathematician is a social being and that even his/her language is social into a non-obvious sociology of concepts.

Durkheim (1961, p. 485) argues that individualized thoughts can only be understood and explained by attaching them to the social conditions they depend on. Thus, ideas become communicable concepts only when, and to the extent that, they can be and are shared. The laws of thought and logic that George Boole searched for in pure cognitive processes (see the discussion below) are in fact to be found in social life. The apparently purest concepts, logical concepts, take on the appearance of objective and impersonal concepts only to the extent that, and by virtue of, the fact that they are communicable and communicated — that is, only insofar as they are collective representations. All concepts, then, are collective representations and collective elaborations because they are conceived, developed, sustained, and changed through social work in social contexts. In fact, all contexts of human thought and action are social. The next intellectual step is to recognize that 'work', 'context', 'thought', and 'action' are inseparable; concepts, then, are not merely social products, they are constitutively social. This line of thinking leads to the radical conclusion that it is social worlds or communities that think, not individuals. Communities as such do not literally think in some superorganic sense. Rather, individuals are vehicles for expressing the thoughts of communities or 'thought collectives'. Or, to put it another way, minds are social structures (Gumplowicz, 1905, p. 268; Fleck, 1979, p. 39; Mead, 1962).

It is hopeless to suppose that social talk insights could be arrived at or appreciated by people immersed in technical talk. In order to understand and appreciate such insights, one has to enter mathematics as a completely social world rather than a world of forms, signs, symbols, imagination, intuition, and reasoning.

This first step awakens us to 'mathematics worlds', networks of human beings communicating in arenas of conflict and cooperation, domination and subordination. Here we begin to experience mathematics as social practice, and to identify its connections to, and interdependence with, other social practices. Entering mathematics worlds ethnographically reveals the continuity between the social networks of mathematics and the social networks of society as a whole. And it reveals the analogy between cultural production in mathematics and cultural production in all other social activities (Collins, 1985, p. 165; Latour, 1987, p. 174).

The second step in this sequence occurs when we recognize that social talk and technical talk seem to be going on simultaneously and interchangeably. The third step brings technical talk into focus in terms of the natural history, ethnography, and social history of signs, symbols, vehicles of meaning, and imagination (Geertz, 1983, pp. 94–120). The more we participate in the mathematics worlds in which mathematicians 'look, name, listen, and make', the more we find ourselves despiritualizing technical talk. The final step in comprehending the sociological imperative occurs when we realize at last and at least in principle that technical talk is social talk.

Mathematical knowledge is not simply a 'parade of syntactic variations', a set of 'structural transformations', or 'concatenations of pure form'. The more we immerse ourselves ethnographically in mathematics worlds, the more we are impressed by the universality of the sociological imperative. Mathematical forms or objects increasingly come to be seen as sensibilities, collective formations, and worldviews. The foundations of mathematics are not located in logic or systems of axioms but rather in social life. Mathematical forms or objects embody mathematics worlds. They contain the social history of their construction. They are produced in and by mathematics worlds. It is, in the end, mathematics worlds, not individual mathematicians, that manufacture mathematics (Becker, 1982).

Our liberation from transcendental, supernatural, and idealist visions and forces begins when the sociological imperative captures religion from the theologists and believers and unmasks it; it becomes final (for this stage of human history) when that same imperative takes mind and intellect out of the hands of the philosophers and psychologists. It is in this context of inquiry that the larger agenda of the sociology of mathematics becomes apparent. Durkheim set this agenda when he linked his sociological study of religion to a programme for the sociological study of logical concepts. The first full expression of this agenda occurs in Oswald Spengler's *The Decline of the West*.

Spengler on Numbers and Culture

In one of the earliest announcements of a 'new sociology of science', David Bloor (1976, p. 95) mentions Oswald Spengler as one of the few writers who challenges the self-evident 'fact' that mathematics is universal and invariant. But Bloor says little more about Spengler's (1926) chapter on 'Numbers and Culture' in *The Decline of the West* than that it is 'lengthy and fascinating, if sometimes obscure'. Length and obscurity are apparently two of the reasons Spengler has been ignored as a seminal contributor to our understanding of mathematics. He is also considered too conservative, and even a fascist sympathizer and ideologue, by some intellectuals and scholars and thus unworthy of serious consideration as a thinker.

But Spengler was not a fascist, and certainly no more conservative or nationalistic than other scholars and intellectuals who have earned widespread respect in the research community (Max Weber, for example). And the interesting affinities between Spengler and Wittgenstein, and in fact Spengler's influence on this central figure in the pantheon of modern philosophy, are only now beginning to come to light. Of special interest in this respect is their common, and widely over-looked ethical agenda. But it is their common vision of an anthropology of mathematics that is of immediate interest.

There can be little doubt that part of the reason for the resistance to Spengler is that unlike other writers who have challenged the central values of western culture (including Wittgenstein), Spengler is harder to address as a reasonable and recognizable opponent or ally. Contradictions and paradoxes in his work aside, he does not really want to play the games of modern science, culture, and philosophy. Those who do want to play these games cannot really 'use' Spengler, even when they somehow can appreciate him. Bloor is a case in point. Whatever his admiration for, and indebtedness to, Spengler, in the end Bloor's sociology of mathematics is grounded in a defense of modern (western) science and modern (western) culture. Spengler's analysis does not assign a privileged status to western culture or western science. It is also important to recognize the significance of the priority he assigns to numbers. The first substantive chapter in Volume 1, Chapter 2, is on numbers and culture, and it identifies mathematics as a key focus of Spengler's analysis of culture. Since I have discussed Spengler's views at length elsewhere (Restivo, 1983, pp. 161–75), I will be very brief in identifying the central tenets of his theory.

Number, according to Spengler, is 'the symbol of causal necessity'. It is the sign of a completed (mechanical) demarcation; and with God and naming, it is a resource for exercising the will to 'power over the world'. Because Spengler conceives of cultures as incommensurable (although he allows for the progressive transformation of one culture into another), he argues that mathematical events and accomplishments should not be viewed as stages in the development of a universal, world 'mathematics'. A certain type of mathematical thought is associated with each Culture — Indian, Chinese, Babylonian-Egyptian, Arabian-Islamic, Greek (classical), and western. The two major cultures in Spengler's scheme, classical and western, are associated, respectively, with number as magnitude (as the essence of visible, tangible units) and number as relations (with function as the nexus of relations; the abstract validity of this sort of number is self-contained). Spengler's theory of mathematics yields a weak and a strong sociology of mathematics. The weak form is the one that students of mathematics worlds who have accepted the validity and utility of social talk about mathematics find more or less reasonable. It simply draws attention to the variety of mathematical traditions across and within cultures. The strong form implies the sociological imperative — the idea that mathematical objects are constitutively social.

The Weak Sociology of Mathematics

The weak form of Spengler's theory is illustrated by the alternative mathematics discussed by Wittgenstein and Bloor (these are not, in fact, alternatives to modern mathematics but rather culturally distinct forms of mathematics), and by specific mathematical traditions (European, sub-Saharan, Chinese, etc.). The study of these traditions produces stories about the 'mathematics of survival', sociocultural bases for the rise and fall of mathematical communities, ethno-mathematics, the social realities behind the myths of the Greek and Arabic-Islamic 'miracles', and the organizational revolution in European mathematics and science from the seventeenth century on. The episodic history of Indian mathematics can thus be shown to be related to, among other factors, the fragmented decentralization of Indian culture, and the caste system. 'Golden Ages' in ancient Greece, the Arabic-Islamic world between 700 and 1,200, seventeenth-century Japan, T'ang China, and elsewhere can be causally linked to social and commercial revolutions. And the centripetal social forces that kept mercantile and intellectual activities under the control of the central bureaucracy in China can be shown to be among the causes of China's failure to undergo an autochthonous 'scientific revolution'.

The differences between and within mathematical traditions do not necessarily signify incommensurability. They are compatible with the concept of the long-run development or evolution of a 'universal' or 'world' mathematics. But the strong form of Spengler's theory — that mathematics are reflections of and themselves worldviews — is another story.

Basic Principles of the Strong Sociology of Mathematics

There is no ready, intelligible exhibit of the strong form of Spengler's theory of numbers and culture, that is, an example that would persuade a majority of mathematicians and students of mathematics studies that indeed it is possible to describe and explain the content of the 'exact sciences' in sociological terms. But there are signposts on the road to such an exhibit. Some of these signposts are ingredients of the sociological imperative; some of them are the results of the still very slim body of research in the sociology and social history of mathematics. Based on these signposts, we can begin to anticipate telling a story about mathematics in terms of the strong form of Spengler's theory. The story might begin as follows.

Mathematical workers use tools, machines, techniques, and skills to transform raw materials into finished products. They work in mathematical 'knowledge factories' as small as individuals and as large as research centres and worldwide networks. But whether the factory is an individual or a centre, it is always part of a larger network of human, material, and symbolic resources and interactions; and it is always itself a social structure. Mathematical workers produce mathematical objects, such as theorems, points, numerals, functions, and the integers. They work with two general classes of raw materials. One is the class of all things, events, and processes in human experience that can be 'mathematized' (excluding mathematical objects). The second is the class of all mathematical objects. Mathematical workers work primarily or exclusively with raw materials of the first class. Mathematicians and especially pure mathematicians work primarily or exclusively with raw materials of the second class. The more specialized and organized mathematical work becomes, the greater the extent of overlap, interpenetration, and substitutability among mathematical objects, raw materials, machines, and tools. The longer the generational continuity in a specialized mathematics world, the more abstract the products of mathematical work will become.

As specialization increases and levels of abstraction increase, the material and social origins of mathematical work and products become increasingly obscure. In fact what happens is an intensified form of cultural growth. Cultural activity builds new symbolic layers on the material grounds of everyday life. The greater the level of cultural growth, the greater the distance between the material grounds of everyday life and the symbolic grounds of everyday life. Increasingly, people work on, and respond to, the higher symbolic levels. Imagine the case now in which a mathematical worker is freed from the necessity of hunting and gathering or shopping and paying taxes, and set to work on the purest, most refined mathematical objects produced by his/her predecessors. Under such conditions, the idea that pure mental activity (perhaps still aided by pencil and paper — already a great concession for the Platonist!) is the source of mathematical objects becomes increasingly prominent and plausible. Workers forget their history as creators in the social and material world, and the history of their ancestors working with pebbles, ropes, tracts of land, altars, and wine barrels. Or, because they do not have the language for recording social facts, ignorance rather than failed memory fosters purist conclusions. The analogy with religious ideas, concepts, and thoughts is direct and was probably first recognized by Durkheim. In Spengler, this idea achieves an explicit and profound expression.

Specialization, professionalization, and bureaucratization are aspects of the organizational and institutional history of modern mathematics. These processes occurred in earlier mathematics traditions but their scope, scale, and continuity in modern times are unparalleled. Their effect is to generate closure in mathematics worlds. As closure increases, the boundaries separating mathematics worlds from each other and from other social words thicken and become increasingly impenetrable. Specialized languages, symbols, and notations are some of the things that thicken the boundaries around mathematics worlds.

Ultimately, in theory, if the process I have sketched goes on unchecked a completely closed system emerges. This is technically impossible. But as closure becomes more extreme, the mathematics world (like any social world) becomes stagnant, then begins to deteriorate, and eventually disintegrates.

Some degree of closure facilitates innovation and progressive change; extreme closure inhibits them. The advantages of closure therefore must be balanced against the advantages of openness, that is, the exchange of information with other social worlds. Specifically, the danger for the social system of pure mathematics is that it will be cut off from the stimulus of external problems. If pure mathematicians have to rely entirely on their own cultural resources, their capacity for generating innovative, creative problems and solutions will progressively deteriorate. As a consequence, the results of pure mathematical work will become less and less applicable to problems in other social worlds.

The closure cycle reinforces the community's integrity; the opening cycle energizes it with inputs and challenges from other social worlds. The interaction of insider and outsider sociologies of mathematics, mathematical and non-mathematical ideas, and pure and applied mathematics are all aspects of the opening cycle that are necessary for creative, innovative changes in mathematical ideas and in the organization of math worlds.

The Social Life of Pure Mathematics

Pure mathematics is grounded in, and constituted out of, social and material resources (Restivo, 1990). The idea that pure mathematics is a product of some type of unmediated cognitive process is based on the difficulty of discovering the link between the thinking individual, social life, and the material world. It is just this discovery that is being slowly constructed on the foundations of the works of Durkheim, Spengler, Wittgenstein, and others. Establishing this link involves in part recognizing that symbols and notations are actually 'material', and that they are worked with in the same ways and with the same kinds of rules that govern the way we work with pebbles, bricks, and other 'hard' objects.

George Boole's (1958/1854) attempt to discover the 'laws of thought' failed because he did not understand the social and material bases of categorical propositions. Categorical propositions are actually high-level abstractions constructed out of 'real-world' experiences, grounded in the generational continuity of teacher–student and researcher–researcher chains which get reflected and expressed in chains of inductive inferences. The 'self-evidence' of such propositions arises not from their hypothesized status as 'laws of thought' but from their actual status as generalizations based on generations of human experience condensed into symbolic forms.

In the case of meta-mathematics, problems, symbols, and meanings that seem to be products of pure intellect and of arbitrary and playful creativity are in fact objects constructed in a highly rarified but nonetheless social world. Increasingly abstract ideas are generated as new generations take the products of older generations as the resources and tools for their own productive activities; still higher orders of abstraction are generated when mathematicians reflect on the foundations of abstract systems, and self-consciously begin to create whole mathematical worlds.

We can watch this process of moving up levels of abstraction from the 'primitive' ground or frame of everyday life in Boole's discussion of the 'special law', $x^2 = x$. He begins by proposing in an abstract and formal way a realm of number in which there are two symbols, 0 and 1. They are both subject to the special law. This leads him to describe an algebra in which the symbols x, y, z, and c 'admit indifferently of the values 0 and 1, and of these values alone'. Now where does that 'special law' come from? Boole actually constructs it on the basis of a 'class' perspective grounded in 'real world' examples such as 'white things' (x), 'sheep' (y), and 'white sheep' (xy). This establishes that $xy = yx$. He also gets $x^2 = 1$ by interpreting 'good, good men' to be the equivalent of 'good men'. In the case of $xy = yx$, he argues that since the combination of two literal symbols, xy, expresses that class of objects to which the names or qualities x and y represent are both applicable, it follows that 'if the two symbols have exactly the same signification, their combination expresses no more than either of the symbols taken alone would do'. Thus, $xy = x$; and since y has the same meaning as x, $xx = x$.

Finally, by adopting the notation of common algebra, Boole arrives at $x^2 = x$. We are now back in a world in which it is possible to make ordinary language statements such as 'good, good men', and mathematical statements such as $1^2 = 1$. A careful review of Boole's procedure shows that far from creating a 'weird' notation out of thin air, he simply describes a pristine 'everyday' world in which only 0s and 1s exist. This is a rarified world indeed, but it is one in which the rules that govern the behaviour of 0s and 1s are similar to the ones that govern the behaviour of material objects in the everyday material world. Symbols and notations are simply higher-order materials which we work with the same way and under the same sorts of constraints that apply to 'hard' materials. (Eventually, Boole interprets 0 and 1 in logic as, respectively, nothing and universe).

It is interesting that there is a tendency for philosophers of mathematics and meta-mathematicians to reproduce a largely discredited naïve realism to 'explain' the process of operating on old abstractions and creating new ones. Kleene (1971), for example, writes:

> Metamathematics must study the formal system as a system of symbols, etc. which are considered wholly objectively. This means simply that those symbols, etc. are themselves the ultimate objects, and are not being used to refer to something other than themselves. The metamathematician looks at them, not through and beyond them; thus they are objects without interpretation or meaning. (Kleene, 1971, p. 63)

This process stylizes the idea of objective science. But without a sociological theory of intellect and knowledge, it is impossible to see that the same reasons for abandoning naïve realism in physical science are relevant in the case of the so-called exact sciences.

Some mathematicians and philosophers of mathematics have recognized that abstraction has something to do with iteration (Restivo, 1992, pp. 150–3). They have expressed this recognition in such ideas as 'second generation abstract models', and 'algebras constructed upon algebras'. An important instance of invoking the iteration principle is Richard Dedekind's (1956, p. 529) demand that 'arithmetic shall be developed out of itself'. One could even claim that mathematics in general is an iterative activity. Sociologically, iteration is the social activity of unbroken chains of mathematical workers, that is, generational continuity.

As generational continuity is extended and closure proceeds in a mathematical community, mathematicians work more and more in and less and less out of their mathematics worlds. As a result, their experiences become progressively more difficult to ground and discuss in terms of generally familiar everyday world experiences. The worlds they leave behind are pictured worlds, landscapes of identifiable things. Mathematics worlds are worlds of specialized symbols and notations. This is the social and material foundation of so-called 'pictureless' mathematics. But mathematical experiences in highly specialized mathematics worlds are not literally pictureless. The resources being manipulated and imagined in mathematics worlds are so highly refined that they are not picturable in terms of everyday reality; the referents for mathematical objects are increasingly mathematical objects and not objects from the everyday world. Since closure is never perfect, some degree of everyday picturing does occur even in the most abstract mathematical work; and in any case everyday pictures are almost inevitably produced as mathematicians move back and forth between mathematics and other social worlds. At the same time, new picturing experiences and processes lead to the development of new pictures, mathematics world pictures. During the period that these pictures are being socially constructed (that is, while mathematicians are learning to interpret or 'see' or 'picture' objects in their mathematics worlds), mathematical experience in its more abstract moments will necessarily appear pictureless.

The Manufacture of Proofs

In 1928, G.H. Hardy wrote:

> There is strictly speaking no such thing as mathematical proof; . . . we can, in the last analysis, do nothing but point: . . . proofs are what Littlewood and I call gas, rhetorical flourishes designed to affect psychology, pictures on the board in lectures, devices to stimulate the imagination of pupils. (Kline, 1980, p. 314)

Some years later, the mathematician R.L. Wilder argued that a proof is merely a way of 'testing the products of our intuition . . .'

> Obviously, we don't possess and probably will never possess, any standard of proof that is independent of time, the thing to be proved, or the person or school of thought using it. And under these conditions, the sensible thing to do seems to be to admit that there is no such thing, generally, as absolute truth [proof] in mathematics, whatever the public may think. (Kline, 1980, p. 314)

And Whitehead himself argued against grounding philosophic thought in the exact statements of special sciences; from the viewpoint of the advance of thought, exactness and logic are 'fakes' (Kline, 1980, p. 315).

The End of Epistemology and Philosophy of Mathematics

The sociological imperative is having an impact on the work of mathematicians and philosophers who utilize the vocabularies of psychology, culture, empiricism, and pragmatism. But there is some resistance to giving full expression to that imperative. Take, for example, Philip Kitcher's (1983) views on the nature of mathematical knowledge. Kitcher, as an empiricist epistemologist of mathematics, constructs a 'rational' explanation of beliefs and knowledge that brings psychology into the philosophy of mathematics, but in its psychologistic form. But psychologism cannot carry the burden of his attack on the apriorists unless it is recognized for what it is — a truncated sociology and anthropology. Kitcher seems to realize this at some level. He understands that knowledge has to be explained in terms of communities of knowers, and that stories about knowledge can be told in ways that reveal how knowledge is acquired, transmitted, and extended. This is the only story Kitcher can tell; but he is intent on making his story confirm rationality and well-founded reasoning in mathematics.

Rationality and well-founded reasoning cannot be separated from social action and culture. Where it appears that we have effected such a separation it will turn out that we have simply isolated mathematical work as a socio-cultural system, and told a sociologically impoverished story of how that system works. The extent to which mathematics is an autonomous social system will vary from time to time and place to place, and so then will the extent to which an empiricist epistemologist can construct a rational explanation for mathematics. 'Rational' refers to the rules governing a relatively well-organized social activity. Taking the sociological turn means recognizing that 'rational' is synonymous with 'social' and 'cultural' as an explanatory account. Kitcher can save the rationality of mathematics only by showing (as he does very nicely) that mathematics is a more or less institutionally autonomous activity. But this makes his 'rational' account 'nothing more' than a social and cultural account. He misses this point in great part because he thinks primarily in psychologistic terms. As soon as we replace psychologism with the sociological imperative, rationality (as a privileged explanatory strategy) and epistemology (as a philosophical psychologistic theory of knowledge) are nullified.

The same situation is characteristic of philosophical treatments of knowledge and perception in general which are half-conscious of the sociological imperative but repress its full power. Richard Rorty's (1979) pragmatism starts out as a strategy for extinguishing epistemology; but in the end, Rorty 'westernizes' (or better, 'americanizes') epistemology (this a reflection of the power of pragmatism as an 'American philosophy') and gives it a reprieve. He explicitly restricts moral concern to 'the conversation of the West'. On the brink of a radical social construction conjecture on the nature of knowledge, he is restrained by (1) his stress on the ideal of polite conversation and his failure to deal with the more militant and violent forms of social practice in science and in culture in general, (2) his western bias, manifested in his intellectual and cultural debts, (3) his Kuhnian conception of the relationship between hermeneutics ('revolutionary inquiry') and epistemology ('normal inquiry') which is prescriptive, an obstruction to critical studies of inquiry, and the coup that saves epistemology, and (4) his focus on an asociological conception of justification. Patrick Heelan (1983) also shackles a potentially liberating contextualist theory (this time of perceptual knowledge) by talking about worlds belonging to the western community even while he implicates himself in the project of the 'redemption' of science from its Babylonian captivity in the West.

And finally, I recall Bloor in this context, and his strong programme which helped set the stage for the study of mathematics by the new sociologists of science. He dilutes the sociological imperative with a normative commitment to western culture and western science.

Given so much westernism in philosophy, I have to wonder about the extent to which pilosophers such as the ones I have been discussing are ideologues of cultural orthodoxy and prevailing patterns of authority. The reality of these sorts of ideological chains is exhibited in the ways in which philosophers, pressured by empirical and ethnographic research to see that Platonism and apriorism (along with God) are dead, reach out adaptively for social construction. Their failures are tributes to the professionalization process in philosophy and its grounding in psychologism. This is all relevant for an appreciation of the significance of the sociological imperative in mathematics studies because mathematics is 'the queen of the sciences', the jewel in the crown of western science. The protective, awe-inspired, worshipful study of mathematics is thus understandable — readily as a defence or appreciation of western culture, less readily as a vestigial homage to the western God. In either case we are closer to theology than to sociology of mathematics.

Conclusion: Values and the Sociological Imperative

Mathematics worlds are social worlds. But what kinds of social worlds are they? How do they fit into the larger cultural scheme of things? Whose interests do mathematics worlds serve? What kinds of human beings inhabit mathematics worlds? What sorts of values do mathematics worlds create and sustain? In his description and defence of 'the sociological imagination' (a form of the sociological imperative) C. Wright Mills (1961) drew attention to the relationship between personal troubles and public issues, the intersection between biography and history in society, and questions about social structure, the place of societies in history, and the varieties of men and women who have prevailed and are coming to prevail in society. If we approach mathematics worlds from this standpoint, the questions we ask will be very different from those that philosophers, historians, and sociologists usually ask. The questions I have posed elsewhere concerning science worlds in general apply to mathematics worlds too (Restivo, 1988):

> . . . what do scientists produce, and how do they produce it; what resources do they use and use up; what material by-products and wastes do they produce; what good is what they produce, in what social contexts is it valued, and who values it; what costs, risks, and benefits does scientific work lead to for individuals, communities, classes, societies, and the ecological foundations of social life . . . What is the relationship between scientists and various publics, clients, audiences, patrons; how do scientists relate to each other, their families and friends, their colleagues in other walks of life; what is their relationship as workers to the owners of the means of scientific production; what are their self-images, and how do they fit into the communities they live in; what are their goals, visions, and motives? (Restivo, 1988, p. 218)

These questions are relevant to the study of mathematics worlds because they help us to recover the social worlds that get progressively excised in the process of producing and finally presenting (and re-presenting) mathematical objects.

Explaining the 'content' of mathematics is not a matter of constructing a simple causal link between a mathematical object such as a theorem and a social structure. It is rather a matter of unpacking the social histories and social worlds embodied in objects such as theorems. Mathematical objects are and must be treated literally as objects, things that are produced by, manufactured by social beings. There is no reason that an object such as a theorem should be treated any differently than a sculpture, a teapot, or a skyscraper. Only alienated and alienating social worlds could give rise to the idea that mathematical objects are independent, free-standing creations, and that the essence of mathematics is realized in technical talk. Notations and symbols are tools, materials, and in general resources that are socially constructed around social interests and oriented to social goals. They take their meaning from the history of their construction and usage, the ways they are used in the present, the consequences of their usage inside and outside of mathematics, and the network of ideas that they are part of. The sociological imperative, especially when informed by the sociological imagination, is a tool for dealienation and for uncovering the images and values of workers and social worlds in mathematics.

Note

1. This is a slightly edited version of a paper originally published (1988) in *Philosophica* 42, 2, pp. 5–20. An expanded version of that article was published as Chapter 13 in S. Restivo, J.P. van Bendegem, and R. Fischer, (Eds) (1993) *Math Worlds*, New York, SUNY Press.

References

BECKER, H. (1982) *Art Worlds*, Berkeley, University of California Press.

BLOOR, D. (1976) *Knowledge and Social Imagery*, London, Routledge and Kegan Paul.

BOOLE, G. (1985/1854) *The Laws of Thought*, New York, Dover.

COLLINS, H. (1985) *Changing Order*, Beverly Hills, Sage.

DEDEKIND, R. (1956) Irrational number', in NEWMAN, J.R. (Ed) *The World of Mathematics*, 1. New York, Simon and Schuster, pp. 528–36.

DURKHEIM, E. (1961) *The Elementary Forms of the Religious Life*, New York, Collier Books.

FLECK, L. (1979/1935) *Genesis and Development of a Scientific Fact*, Chicago, University of Chicago Press.

GEERTZ, C. (1983) *Local Knowledge*, New York, Basic Books.

GUMPLOWICZ, L. (1905) *Grundrisse der Soziologie*, Vienna, Manz.

HEELAN, P. (1983) *Space-Perception and the Philosophy of Science*, Berkeley, University of California Press.

KITCHER, P. (1983) *The Nature of Mathematical Knowledge*, New York, Oxford University Press.

KLEENE, S. (1971) *Introduction to Metamathematics*, Amsterdam, Wolters-Nordhoff, Groningen, and North-Holland.

KLINE, M. (1980) *Mathematics, The Loss of Certainty*, Oxford, Oxford University Press.

LATOUR, B. (1987) *Science in Action*, Cambridge, MA, Harvard University Press.

MARX, K. (1956) *Economic and Philosophic Manuscripts of 1844*, Moscow, Foreign Languages Publishing House.

MEAD, G. (1962/1934) *Mind, Self, & Society*, Chicago, University of Chicago Press.

MILLS, C.W. (1961) *The Sociological Imagination*, New York, Grove Press.

RESTIVO, S. (1983) *Social Relations of Physics, Mysticism, and Mathematics*. Dordrecht, D. Reidel.

RESTIVO, S. (1988) 'Modern science as a social problem', *Social Problems*, 35, pp. 206–25.

RESTIVO, S. (1990) 'The social roots of pure mathematics', in GIERYN, T. and COZZENS, S. (Eds) *Theories of Science in Society*, Bloomington, Indiana University Press, pp. 120–43.

RESTIVO, S. (1992) *Mathematics in Society and History*, Dordrecht, Kluwer.

RORTY, R. (1979) *Philosophy and the Mirror of Nature*, Princeton, Princeton University Press.

SPENGLER, O. (1926) *The Decline of the West*, 1. New York.

Chapter 16

Research in Gender and Mathematics Education: The Production of Difference

Mairéad Dunne and Jayne Johnston

Introduction

Our aim in this short chapter is to take a 'critical' look at the area of gender research in mathematics education. In doing so we are particularly interested in considering what it is that constitutes gender in this research. Our critical position is informed by feminist philosophers, educational researchers and methodologists (see for example Grosz, 1990; Harding, 1986, 1991; Lather, 1991, 1992) and we have also drawn on the work of Habermas (1972) as it has been applied to education by Grundy (1987).

We look first at the contribution of feminists to issues of research. By problematizing research processes many methodological questions are raised, bringing into contention traditions of research which have previously been taken on uncritically. We outline some of the methodological implications raised through the development of feminist and critical positions and the critique of positivism. We then review some of the research into gender and mathematics education in reference to our previous work, in which we identified strands within this research (Dunne and Johnston, 1992 and Johnston and Dunne, 1991, in press). In these earlier papers we adopted a critical stance informed by Habermas (1972) and feminist theorists to examine the methodologies of this research.

In our final section we maintain this critical position in an exploration of the use of the gender construct within the reviewed research. We look at gender as a production through the construction of difference in social practices. In the process of this review and in cognisance of feminist and critical positions we begin to reconceptualize the construct of gender, which has significant implications for the development of research into gender and mathematics education.

The Feminist Contribution

As stated above, our concern here is in considering how recent feminist and critical research can inform the work that is being done into issues of gender in mathematics education. Since gender is the focus of this work there are clear associations with the general feminist research. It seems to us however that these associations are often underplayed in this research, compared to the associations with mainstream mathematics education.

Feminist researchers have made a major contribution in their critique of positivist research methodologies through emphasizing power relations (see for example, Harding, 1986, 1991; Lather, 1991, 1992; Ramazanoglu, 1992; Roberts, 1981; Stanley, 1990; Stanley and Wise, 1983). At the heart of this feminist critique the politics of the claims to objectivity of the scientific tradition are explicitly addressed. The power relations which constitute the construction and legitimation of knowledge as a social practice are central. Lather makes this point with respect to the contribution of feminist educational research to the demise of positivism:

> Like all the sciences, educational research is increasingly construed as a value-constituted and value-constituting enterprise, no more outside the power/knowledge nexus than any other human creation . . . Educational research, then, reflects and contributes to the multi-sited demise of positivism and the growing acknowledgement of social inquiry as value laden. Feminist research in education is both shaped by and a shaper of such a conjunction. (Lather, 1992, p. 91)

The work of feminists provides critical analyses of areas of knowledge, particularly those associated with science or drawing upon its methods, by raising questions of power. These include the hierarchical positioning of knowledge as disciplines, the processes of legitimation within these disciplines and considerations of whose interests are being met. Such questions would seem crucial in tackling issues of inequity in school mathematics, but are rarely asked. The powerful position that mathematics holds as a discipline inevitably remains inviolate in the gender and school mathematics research, where the implicit message seems to be that all will be well once sufficient (but clearly not all) girls have access to the power and privileges of mathematics.

What is implied by the feminist position that we have sketched here is that a consideration of issues of inequity, and particularly of gender relations, requires an engagement in research methodologies which render all aspects of the research process problematic. Not only are the foundations of the traditional disciplines being questioned, but so too are the very processes by which research is carried out. The scope for critique is immense and is itself problematic. Thus, as stated above, we will confine our focus to the construction of gender. However, before exploring the implications of the questions raised within feminist research we will briefly discuss our previous review of research into gender and mathematics education.

A Brief Overview of the Research

In previous papers (Dunne and Johnston, 1992 and Johnston and Dunne, 1991, in press) we have reviewed research into gender and mathematics and science education with the explicit intention of foregrounding the political nature of the research process. We summarized the research by identifying three dominant strands. By describing and characterizing the purposes and methods of each of these strands, we explored their relationship to Habermas' educational interests (1972), and the conceptualization of gender within each.

Habermas identifies three 'knowledge constitutive interests', technical, practical and emancipatory. Although this framework did not arise directly from educational considerations it provides an analytic tool for describing research and its relationship to particular philosophical positions. Grundy (1987) applies Habermas' framework to education. She describes these three interests in the following way:

These interests constitute the three types of science by which knowledge is generated and organized in our society. These three ways of knowing are empirical-analytic, historical-hermeneutic and critical. (Grundy, 1987, p. 10)

The power of Habermas' schema as an analytic tool stems from the position of critique which explicitly constitutes the third interest. For our purposes, this interest may be understood as a position of critique which centres on the absence of an explicit recognition of the politics of knowledge constitution in the technical and practical positions. Lather (1992) also makes use of Habermas' framework, applying it more generally in her discussion of research methodologies and extending it by suggesting a fourth position relating it to post-structuralism.

In our review of the research into gender and mathematics and science education, the first strand we described was concerned with finding and documenting sex differences using quantitative methods. This research focuses upon differences in achievement or participation, for example, through gathering statistics to compare the enrolments of females and males in science and mathematics courses (Dekkers *et al.*, 1986; Doron, 1991; Jones, 1991; Lock, 1992; Megaw, 1991; Reilly and Morton, 1991). Research in the second strand that we identified attempts to find explanations for the apparent differences between the sexes by appealing to biology. These investigations assume that there are differences in aptitudes between boys and girls which have innate causes, and attempt to isolate the nature of these differences (for example Gray, 1981; Sherman, 1983; Smith, 1964).

In Habermas' terms both these strands are located within technical interests, which Lather (1992) associates with positivism. The research methodology assumes the authenticity of the gender categories used, the reliability of scientific methods to accurately describe the differences and hence, the neutrality of the knowledge produced. Research that falls within the technical interests is predicated on the assumption that the environment can be described, and is predictable and ultimately controllable. What counts as knowledge is thus not open to question, it is revealed through observation and can be verified through experimentation.

Social explanations for gender differences constitute the third strand of research which we have described. This strand includes studies which link students' perceptions and attitudes to a masculine image of science and mathematics; the influence of teacher attitudes and practices; and the influence of sex-stereotyping in the home and family (Ethington, 1992; Fennema and Leder, 1990; Kelly, 1987; Leder, 1974, 1976, 1982; Murphy, 1991; Sjoberg and Imsen, 1988). A search for ways of changing the existing situation has given rise to research that can broadly be described as interventionist (GEMS, 1990; Kelly *et al.*, 1987; Whyte, 1985). Some projects have concentrated on changing the girls by attempting to change their learning characteristics to match more closely those of the boys or to change the basis on which they make choices. Another set of strategies has concentrated on altering the curriculum to make it more gender inclusive (Barnes, 1991; McClintock, 1988). Yet others suggest that changes in the learning environment or the school organization, such as the implementation of single-sex classes, may have an impact (Barnes, Plaister and Thomas, 1984; Burton, 1986, 1989, 1990; GAMAST, 1988).

We locate this strand in Habermas' practical interest. Much of the research is qualitative in nature, drawing upon interpretive, naturalistic and hermeneutic methods. While these research methodologies recognize the importance of context and setting in the mediation of meaning, it is assumed that the product of the research will adequately describe the research site in terms of its social processes and the understandings constructed. The aim of this research is to describe as accurately as possible the 'reality' of the mathematics learning environment for girls and boys. The position of the researcher in the practical interests is assumed to be neutralized by the methods used just as it is in the technical interests. As Stanley and Wise (1983) have noted:

> 'Naturalism' is essentially 'dishonest', in the sense that it too denies the involvement, the contaminating and disturbing presence, of the researcher. Here too, just as in conventionally positivist research, we necessarily look at events *through* the researcher; but, in spite of this, such research is presented to us in such a way as to deny this, to suggest that what we have instead is 'truth'. (Stanley and Wise, 1983, p. 160)

Our contention then, is that the majority of research we have considered deals with the issues of gender within either the technical or the practical interests. As outlined earlier in our consideration of the feminist contribution to research, we suggest that the methodological implications of Habermas' critical position provide a more powerful position for development of research in this field. Indeed there is some research that has considered gender issues in mathematics education both more critically and more broadly. For example the work of Walkerdine and colleagues (see Walden and Walkerdine 1982, 1985; Walkerdine 1984, 1989) has drawn on feminist and critical theories in researching the position of girls in primary and secondary mathematics classrooms. It is significant that this work is part of a broader critique of the influence of psychology in education, and that a central concern is to understand the role of education in the construction of gender.

Through a critical analysis, the social and political contexts which circumscribe the production of knowledge are made explicit and are recognized for the constitutive role they play in the production and validation of that knowledge. This is the case for both the arena which is being researched and for what counts as research. In our previous papers we explored general methodological implications of this critical position in relation to the processes used in gender and mathematics education research. In this chapter we focus particularly on the constitutive role of research in the production of gender.

The Construction of Gender

Central to our critical position is the view that knowledge is produced through social practices, that is, knowledge is constructed rather than found. In terms of the research which is the focus of this chapter the knowledge produced is dependent upon how the research question is conceived as well as the processes of the research.

Returning to the research which we have associated with Habermas' technical interests, that is, research which is largely positivist in methodology, the gender categories are considered to be discrete and natural. The assumption is that these categories and their differences pre-date the situation being described in the research. They are part of the 'natural order' and outside the influence of the social. As such they are certainly outside the influence of the researcher who aims to 'accurately' describe the research site in terms of these categories. The purpose of the research is to reveal the differences, which are the logical consequences of the existence of the gender categories, by the use of sufficiently objective research methods. Thus the differences described are considered to be reflections of innate characteristics of the members of each category.

Research in our third strand, which we have associated with Habermas' practical interests, acknowledges the biological basis for the construction of gender categories but places emphasis upon the role of social practices in constituting the differences. It is both biology and interactions in the social environment which produce the gendered individual. Interpretive research in this field describes the site by looking for differences in the experiences and interactions of females and males. The assumption is that the differences that have been observed characterize the members of each category. In effect the experiences that have been observed and described assume the position of essential gender characteristics.

As with technical interests the researcher's position is seen as separate from the research site. In the technical interests this is a fact of scientific (or neo-scientific) research methods. Within the practical interests the potential for contamination is acknowledged but the researchers' position is apparently neutralized through the application of appropriate methods, such as triangulation or verbatim accounts of interviews. The power and privilege accorded to the researcher's account in such a position is thus not recognized.

Statements arise from this research which are taken to represent the 'truth' about girls, boys and mathematics. These include such statements as 'girls prefer collaborative learning environments', 'girls need opportunities to use their language skills', 'girls prefer to share and support each other in tackling mathematical problems', 'boys perform better in competitive situations than girls', 'girls need encouragement to build their confidence and self esteem'. A change in the situation, then, requires either girls to have experiences that compensate for their deficiencies (e.g., playing with spatial toys, encouraging assertive behaviour, helping them to make better choices), or for the mathematics learning environment to be altered to compensate for the learning styles of girls (e.g., group work, writing in mathematics, emphasizing the 'humane' applications of mathematics). In seeking to affirm the experiences of girls in school mathematics gendered oppositions are noted (or in our terms are constructed) and these provide the explanations for interventions. Thus social constructs such as collaboration and competition, dependence and independence, compliance and aggression, are inscribed upon the original biological divisions and are assumed to be characteristics of individuals in each category. The social and biological are conflated in the production of 'essential' characteristics.

What must be recognized here is that the oppositions that are constructed and the interventions developed from them are constitutive of gender, they produce and reproduce the categories that they are assuming to describe. Ironically in this production, the relationship that this work is seeking to challenge, the dominance of the masculine over the feminine, is reproduced by these oppositions. Girls as collaborative (in terms of prefered work mode), dependent (on each other and the teacher) and compliant (to the demands of the classroom, the curriculum and the researcher) are differentiated from boys who are competitive, independent and aggressive. But in terms of mathematics it is competition, independence and aggression that are valued. The male side of the opposition is defined positively and treated as the norm. Success in mathematics demands such attributes. The female side of the opposition is thus negatively positioned in relation to this norm and to school mathematics. It is this point which is exemplified in Walkerdine's work.

Grosz (1990) warns of the limitations of the views of gender that we have described as typifying our original strands of research:

> . . . in claiming that women's current social roles and positions are the effects of their essence, nature, biology, or universal social position, these theories are guilty of rendering such roles and positions unalterable, necessary, and thus of providing them with a powerful political justification.
> . . . they are necessarily ahistorical; they confuse social relations with fixed attributes; they see fixed attributes as inherent limitations to social change; . . . (Grosz, 1990, p. 335)

Such positions are unlikely to produce significant change, and worse, may be used to justify a lack of change. The essentialisms that Grosz describes stem from inadequate conceptions of social relations. Almost all the research we have described here presumes the autonomy of the actions of individual human subjects in considering or describing the research context. The research that we have described as technical has no conception of the social. The focus of the research is upon groups of individuals who share common characteristics, in this case their sex, and on describing how those groups perform under certain conditions. Any conception of an interaction between those conditions (e.g., achievement in school mathematics) and the gender categories under investigation is not possible.

The research that we have described as practical considers the influence of the social in terms of the interaction of each individual with the learning environment. Constructs used to describe social interaction become defining attributes of gender categories and change is only possible if the individuals, in this case girls, adjust their attributes or their choices (Willis, 1992).

From the critical position the emphasis on social relations rather than a delineation of fixed attributes is highly significant. It transforms gender research from descriptions based on static categories to a consideration of the social dynamic (Connell, 1987). As outlined in the critiques above, this dynamic is a manifestation of power relationships which are realized through the construction of differences. Gender, then, must be conceptualized in ways in which the construction of difference within the contingencies of a specific context are made explicit. In considering it as a dualistic and hierarchical relation, produced and reproduced by social practices, it cannot be conceived of as pre-given, either by biological or social means.

Conclusion

That there is 'an issue' about gender and school mathematics is now widely accepted although the conception of what the problem is has changed (Willis, 1989). These conceptions range from the view that gender differences in mathematical performance and participation are 'only natural', to a position that the psychological explanations of innate capacities is required, to considerations of the conditions under which girls choose not to participate in mathematics. In this chapter we have considered what it is that each of these strands of research has taken as the object of its research, that is, what it is that constitutes gender. We have done so from the critical position, drawing on feminist and non-feminist work that explicitly foregrounds the political nature of knowledge constitution.

Assuming a 'critical' position is not uncommon in social research today. In educational research the term has been applied broadly to philosophical and methodological positions which emphasize the political nature of schooling, usually addressing social inequities constructed around gender, class and racial differences. Stressing that no knowledge is politically neutral, that all institutions are ideologically bound, critical research aims to problematize the institutional foundations of knowledge and to make explicit the investments in power which constitute those foundations.

Our consideration of the role of research in the construction of gender categories is one attempt to problematize the foundations of the research process. For research into gender and mathematics a critical perspective demands that the categories used to delimit the construct of 'gender' are explicitly addressed in terms of their construction. An acknowledgment of social processes in the construction of gender is not sufficient. What is required is an engagement with the dynamics of this construction: the production and reproduction of this dualistic relation in and through social practices. Research from the practical and technical interests is predicated upon fixed categories as if these precede the research process. From our critical position the focus shifts to the production of categories, both in the social practices that constitute the empirical site and in the processes of framing and undertaking the research.

But this is not enough. A critical research position must also consider (and deconstruct) the privilege that access to mathematics confers on its 'chosen few', to understand its 'gate-keeping' role in relation to further education and future careers, and consider this in the production and reproduction of hierarchical gender (and class and race) relations. What constitutes mathematics, what counts as valued mathematical knowledge, how things came to be this way and how they are sustained are critical questions. Such questions foreground relations between power and knowledge that exemplify the critical position.

References

BARNES, M. (1991) *Investigating Change: An Introduction to Calculus for Australian Schools*, Melbourne, Curriculum Corporation.

BARNES, M., PLAISTER, R. and THOMAS, A. (1984) *Girls Count in Mathematics and Science: A Handbook for Teachers*, Darlinghurst, NSW, GAMA.

BURTON, L. (Ed) (1986) *Girls into Maths Can Go*, London, Holt, Rinehart and Winston.

BURTON, L. (1989) 'The cultural role of mathematics education in the future', in BISHOP, A., KEITAL, C. and GERDES, P. (Eds) *Mathematics, Education and Society, Document Series 35*, Paris, UNESCO.

BURTON, L. (Ed) (1990) *Gender and Mathematics. An International Perspective*, London, Cassell.

CONNELL, R.W. (1987) *Gender and Power*, Cambridge, Polity Press.

DEKKERS, J., DE LAETER, J.R. and MALONE, J.A. (1986) *Upper Secondary School Science and Mathematics Enrolment Patterns in Australia, 1970–1985*, Perth, Western Australia, Curtin University of Technology.

DORON, R. (1991) 'Gender similarities and dissimilarities in prediction of academic achievements by psychometric tests among Israeli practical engineers', in RENNIE, L.J. *et al.* (Eds) *Action for Equity: The Second Decade. Contributions to the Sixth International GASAT Conference*, July 1991, Melbourne Australia, pp. 544–52.

DUNNE, M. and JOHNSTON, J. (1992) 'An awareness of epistemological assumptions: the case of gender studies', *International Journal of Science Education*, 14, 5, pp. 515–26.

ETHINGTON, C.A. (1992) 'Gender differences in a psychological model of mathematics achievement', *Journal for Research in Mathematics Education*, 23, 2. pp. 166–81.

FENNEMA, E. and LEDER, G. (1990) *Mathematics and Gender*, New York, Teachers College Press.

GAMAST (1988) *Girls and Maths and Science Teaching. Professional Development Manual*, Canberra, Curriculum, Development Centre.

GEMS (1990) *Canberra, Curriculum Development Centre*, 1, pp. 1–5.

GRAY, J.A. (1981) 'A biological basis for the sex differences in achievement in science', in KELLY, A. (Ed) *The Missing Half: Girls and Science Education*, Manchester, Manchester University Press.

GROSZ, E. (1990) 'Conclusion: A note on essentialism and difference', in GUNEW, S. (Ed) *Feminist Knowledge. Critique and Construct*, London, Routledge.

GRUNDY, S. (1987) *Curriculum: Product or Praxis*, London, The Falmer Press.

HABERMAS, J. (1972) *Knowledge and Human Interests*, 2nd edition, London, Heinemann.

HARDING, S. (1986) *The Science Question in Feminism*, Milton Keynes, Open University Press.

HARDING, S. (1991) *Whose Science? Whose Knowledge?*, Milton Keynes, Open University Press.

JOHNSTON, J. and DUNNE, M. (1991) 'Gender, Mathematics and Science: Evading the Issues or Confronting New Questions', A paper presented at the American Educational Research Association. Chicago, April.

JOHNSTON, J. and DUNNE, M. (in press) 'Revealing Assumptions: Gender Issues in Mathematics and Science Education', in PARKER, L.H., RENNIE, L.J. and FRASER, B.J. (Eds) *Gender, Science and mathematics: Shortening the Shadow*,

JONES, M.G. (1991) 'Competitive science: gender differences in the physical and biological sciences', in RENNIE, L.J. *et al.* (Eds) *Action for Equity: The Second Decade. Contributions to the Sixth International GASAT Conference*, July 1991, Melbourne, Australia, pp. 261–69.

KELLY, A. (1987) 'Why girls don't do science', in KELLY, A. (Ed) *Science for Girls?*, Milton Keynes, Open University Press.

KELLY, A., WHYTE, J. and SMAIL, B. (1987) 'Girls into science and technology: final report', in KELLY, A. (Ed) *Science for Girls?*, Milton Keynes, Open University Press.

LATHER, P. (1991) *Getting Smart*, London, Routledge.

LATHER, P. (1992) 'Critical frames in educational research: Feminist and post-structural perspectives', *Theory into Practice*, 31, 2, pp. 87–99.

LEDER, G.C. (1974) 'Sex differences in mathematics: Problem appeal as a function of problem context', *Journal for Educational Research*, 67, 8, pp. 351–53.

LEDER, G.C. (1976) 'Contextual setting and mathematical performance', *Australian Mathematics Teacher*, 3, 4, pp. 119–27; 32, 5, pp. 165–73.

LEDER, G.C. (1982) 'Mathematics achievement and fear of success', *Journal for Research in Mathematics Education*, 13, 2, pp. 124–35.

LOCK, R. (1992) 'Gender and practical skill performance in science', *Journal of Research in Science Teaching*, 29, 3, pp. 227–41.

MCCLINTOCK COLLECTIVE (1988) *Getting into Gear. Gender Inclusive Teaching Strategies in Science*, Canberra, Curriculum Development Centre.

MEGAW, W.J. (1991) 'Gender distribution in the world's physics departments', in RENNIE, L.J. *et al.* (Eds) *Action for Equity: The Second Decade. Contributions to the Sixth International GASAT Conference*, July 1991, Melbourne, Australia pp. 604–12.

MURPHY, P. (1991) 'Gender differences in pupils' reactions to practical work', in WOOLNOUGH, B. (Ed) *Practical Science*, Milton Keynes, Open University Press.

RAMAZANOGLU, C. (1992) 'On feminist methodology: male reason versus female empowerment', *Sociology*, 26, 2, pp. 207–12, May.

REILLY, B. and MORTON, M. (1991) 'Performance in a nationwide mathematics examination at tertiary entrance level', in RENNIE, L.J. *et al.* (Eds) *Action for Equity: The Second Decade. Contributions to the Sixth International GASAT Conference*, July 1991, Melbourne Australia. pp. 301–09.

ROBERTS, H. (Ed) (1981) *Doing Feminist Research*, London, Routledge.

SHERMAN, J. (1983) 'Girls talk about mathematics and their future: A partial replication', *Psychology of Women Quarterly*, 7, pp. 338–42.

SJOBERG, S. and IMSEN, G. (1988) 'Gender and science education 1,' in FENSHAM, P. (Ed) *Development and Dilemmas in Science Education*, London, The Falmer Press.

SMITH, I. (1964) *Spatial ability: Its Education and Social Significance*, San Diego, Robert P. Knapp.

STANLEY, L. (1990) *Feminist Praxis*, London, Routledge.

STANLEY, L. and WISE, S. (1983) *Breaking Out: Feminist Consciousness and Feminist Research*. London, RKP.

WALDEN, R. and WALKERDINE, V. (1982) *Girls and Mathematics: The Early Years*, Bedford Way Papers 8, London, Heinemann.

WALDEN, R. and WALKERDINE, V. (1985) *Girls and Mathematics: From Primary to Secondary Schooling*, Bedford Way Papers 24, London, Heinemann.

WALKERDINE, V. (1984) 'Developmental psychology and the child centred pedagogy: the insertion of Piaget into early education', in HENRIQUES, J. *et al.* *Changing the Subject: Psychology, Social Regulation and Subjectivity*, London, Methuen.

WALKERDINE, V. *et al.* (1989) *Counting Girls Out*, London, Virago Press.

WILLIS, S. (1989) 'Real Girls Don't Do Maths', *The Construction of Privilege*, Geelong, Deakin University Press.

WILLIS, S. (1992) 'Gender Reform Through School Mathematics', Working Paper IOWME Study Group, ICME 7, Québec, August.

WHYTE, J. (1985) 'Girl friendly science and girl friendly school', in WHYTE, J. *et al.* (Eds) *Girl Friendly Schooling*, London, Methuen.

Chapter 17

Ethnomathematics, the Nature of Mathematics and Mathematics Education

Ubiratan D'Ambrosio

A Motivation for Ethnomathematics

Much has been said about the universality of mathematics. This concept of universality seems to become harder to sustain as recent research, mainly carried out by anthropologists, shows evidence of practices which are typically mathematical such as observing, counting, ordering, sorting, measuring, and weighing, plus attitudes and reflections which have clearly a logical structure, techniques of inferring and criteria of validity, which are carried on differently according with both natural and cultural environments. This encourages further research on the evolution of mathematical concepts and practices within a cultural and anthropological framework. We feel this has been done only to a very limited, and we might say timid, extent. On the other hand, there is a reasonable amount of literature on this by anthropologists and psychologists. To recognize a bridge between those and historians of culture and of mathematics is an important step towards identifying different modes of thought which lead to different forms of mathematics, which we may call ethnomathematics.

In Anton Dimitriu's extensive *History of Logic*, he briefly describes Indian and Chinese logic merely as background for his general historical study of the logic which originated from Greek thought. For example, we know from other sources that the concept of 'number one' is itself quite a different concept in the Nyaya-Vaisesika epistemology: 'number one is eternal in eternal substances, whereas two, etc. are always non-eternal' and from this follows an arithmetic (see Pooter, 1977, p. 119) Practically, nothing is known about the logic underlying the Inca treatment of numbers which, from what is known through the study of the 'quipus', represents a mixed qualitative-quantitative language (Ascher, 1988). The concept of experience, or the experimental method, is something else that must be discussed.

There has been much research on ethnoastronomy, ethnobotany, ethno-chemistry and so on. Particularly, ethnomethodology is of growing importance in general sociology. Although less recognized than these arbitrarily compartmentalized fields of research, Ethnomathematics seems to be the appropriate approach when we want to pursue global ideals. Clearly, to talk about 'ethno-specialties' sounds contradictory. Indeed, Ethnomathematics directly challenges Descartes' prescription for acquiring knowledge: 'second, to divide each of the difficulties which I was examining in as many parts as possible and necessary for better solve them' (Descartes, 1973). This challenge may be regarded as a first step towards Ethnomathematics. Other steps that have been and surely will be developed in the 'Programme Ethnomathematics' will hopefully lead to something else than an alternative method, since it is related to another conception of man and of nature and consequently of society. There is implicit in it a visionary look into the future of humanity. Much inspiration for this was drawn from the words of Bertrand Russell and Albert Einstein 'We appeal, as human beings, to human beings: Remember your humanity, and forget the rest. If you can do so, the way lies open to a new Paradise; if you cannot, there lies before you the risk of universal death.'[1]

Mathematics in a Global Viewpoint

Many of the reactions I have received to the last paragraph above are of surprise and even astonishment. What does mathematics have to do with these visionary looks? Of course, the successive deformations of history and philosophy of mathematics throughout history have led to reactions of this kind.

These remarks invite us to look into the history and philosophy of mathematics in a broader context, so as to incorporate other possible forms of knowledge of natural phenomena. But we go further on these considerations in saying that this is more than a mere academic exercise, since its implications for pedagogy are clear, mainly if we refer to recent advances in cognitive science, which show how strongly culture and cognition are related. Although for a long time there have been indications of a close connection between cognitive mechanisms and cultural environments, a reductionist tendency, which goes back to Descartes and to a certain extent has grown in parallel to the development of science, imply culture-free cognitive models.

Let us look briefly into some aspects of science through history, mainly from the point of view of its transmission and institutionalization. We need some sort of periodization for this overview, which corresponds, to a certain extent, to major turns in the socio-cultural composition of western history. We disregard, at this moment and for this purpose, considerations of other cultures and civilizations. For reasons which we shall not discuss in this chapter, practices of scientific and mathematical nature, such as sorting, classifying , counting, measuring, which are performed in different cultural settings, acquired, developed and transmitted through generations, appears universally as the earliest structured form of knowledge. It is recorded in all civilizations, before other forms of understanding and explaining the world had been structured. For this reason, we use in what follows the word 'mathematics' in the *latu sensu*. Although we agree that the word 'mathematics' as a discipline is relatively new, going back only to the fourteenth century, to refer to mathematics when looking into the history of ideas seems quite appropriate and we have to understand that the discipline was not clearly defined in all the known cultures. Even the Greek and Arabic uses of it are somewhat vague, not to say the Latin.

The Programme Ethnomathematics

The research programme ethnomathematics must be interpreted in the broad sense of scientific knowledge in general. We use programme in the general sense given by I. Lakatos. In coining the word ethnomathematics we incurred, intentionally, in an etymological abuse: *ethno* stands for culture or cultural roots, *mathema* is the Greek root for explaining, understanding, learning, dealing with reality, *tics* is a modified form of *techné*, which stands for arts, techniques or modes. Thus *ethno mathema tics* stands for distinct modes of explaining and coping with reality in different cultural and environmental settings.

Although the idea of examining the strong links of science and mathematics with the socio-cultural and natural environment has been going on for some time, these links have always been faced as a less fundamental way than the inner organization of theories themselves. Science and mathematics have been considered, with some timid exceptions seen mainly in some elementary curricula, as context-free.

Ethno-mathematics includes the work of anthropologists since the beginning of the century and more recently of psychologists and sociologists who have recognized different ways of counting and measuring, even of classifying and of inferring in distinct native cultures all over the world. Clearly, to consider mathematics of native cultures is germane to our programme ethnomathematics. It is so that some people, including myself in my early writings, call ethnomathematics the mathematics of other cultures. For example, a most important book on ethno-mathematics by Marcia Ascher, deals with mathematical ideas in non-literate cultures (Ascher, 1991). Our programme ethnomathematics includes all these approaches and indeed rely on this more focused research.

Pedagogical Implications

Current research in mathematical education leads to increasing evidence that cognitive power, learning capabilities and attitudes towards learning are enhanced by keeping the learning ambiance related to cultural background. There is also evidence that socio-political dimensions create learning barriers which affect particularly children from deprived minorities. At the same time it is recognized that outside the school environment the performance of these children, lower achievers in schools, is successful. The same is true with adults. It is well documented that children and adults can perform 'mathematically' well in their out-of-school environment — counting, measuring, solving problems and drawing conclusions using the arts or techniques [*tics*] of explaining, understanding, coping with their environment [*mathema*] that they have learned in their cultural setting [*ethno*]. These practices have been generated or learned by their ancestors, transmitted through generations, modified through a process of cultural dynamics and learned by them in a more casual, less formal way. It is a patrimonial knowledge of their cultural group. It is the ethnomathematics of the group.

This socio-cultural behaviour has been identified in rural and urban communities, in workers performing specific duties, in several populational groups, both in industrial nations and in so-called less developed countries, in native communities. Particularly interesting is the ethnomathematics of researchers in different fields. They develop their own jargon, even special codes and symbols; they relax or modify conveniently rules to satisfy their modes of work, in a sense to conform to their modes of thought, and they generate, organize and even transmit this 'mathematics', which in most cases is even denied mathematical status by the mathematical establishment. The history of mathematics abounds of examples and in recent times we mention distributions and fuzzsets among others. But this is not less true, as far as jargons, codes and styles of reasoning are concerned, even among different subjects of academic mathematics.

All these facts are research topics of the programme ethnomathematics. Essentially, the programme ethnomathematics is the study of the generation, organization, transmission and dissemination and use of these jargons, codes, styles of reasoning, practices, results and methods.

These steps, from the generation through the progress of knowledge, in particular of mathematical knowledge, are the result of a complex conjunction of factors. Among them we recognize practices resulting from immediate need, relations with other practices and critical reflection, hence theorization over those practices, curiosity and some sort of intrinsic cultural interest. Increasingly, as mankind progresses, cultural dynamics plays a fundamental role among these factors. Of course, there has been not much doubt that these factors produce *ad hoc* knowledge. The main issue in the programme ethnomathematics is the passage from *ad hoc* knowledge to methods and theories, and from theories how does one proceed to invention as the result of creativity? Considering research in the history and philosophy of mathematics nowadays we see much convergence with our proposal. These questions are germane to any investigations of the nature of mathematical knowledge, both from the historical viewpoint as well as from exciting questions related to mathematical progress and education. Where do mathematical ideas come from, how are they organized? How does mathematical knowledge advance? Do these ideas have anything to do with the broad environment, be it socio-cultural or natural?

Historical Bases for Ethnomathematics

To understand the programme ethnomathematics it is first of all necessary to accept the fact that mathematics is a construct of the human mind. It is knowledge generated by human beings and organized in a certain intellectual framework which is recognized by its practitioners as mathematics. Let us not attempt to define mathematics. The breadth of the domain of mathematics is seen in the subject classification of MR/ZM, as well in the recent published Volume II of the AMS Centennial Publications: *Mathematics into the Twenty-first Century*. Although some trace the history of mathematics back to Classical Antiquity, the characteristics of current mathematics are easier to recognize after the seventeenth Century. Indeed, it is difficult to isolate and sometimes even recognize mathematics from other forms of knowledge and for the general cultural effervescence of the Middle Ages in various distinct cultures. Looking into the Roman times and to other cultures of the period, there are many practices, modes of thought and theories which have many characteristics of what we now label mathematics but which would not be called mathematics nowadays. This is true also in many pieces of Greek and Islamic mathematics.

Let us look back into the Greeks and ask what they would call mathematics. What is the origin of the word? Etymology tells us that *mathema* or *mathemata* is essentially explanation, understanding. Although the Greeks never used the word 'mathematics' in the sense we today attribute to a form of knowledge which we call Greek mathematics, they were, as everyone else, trying to explain to understand, and, in fact, to cope. Explaining, understanding, coping with what? As it is proper of human nature, explaining, understanding, coping with the socio-cultural and natural environment. This has been the driving force behind human behaviour since the early ages of our species. And of course, done in different ways in distinct environments. To distinguish the close relation of these *tics* of *mathema* in the distinct environments we introduced the prefix *ethno*. Thus I have coined the word 'ethnomathematics' to mean the arts or techniques developed by different cultures to explain, to understand, to cope with their environments. It is possible that the term ethnomathematics was used before, although I have not seen it before. Ethnobotany, ethnopsychiatry, ethnomethodology and several others of a similar nature have been in use for some time in a sense similar to the less general concept of ethnomathematics, referring to the respective practices of native populations.

The Opportunity of the Programme Ethnomathematics

We face nowadays profound transformations in the world order established since the historical episode of the discoveries, 500 years ago. The discoveries were followed by conquest and then colonization and finally the imperial order, with obvious economic objectives and also to extend the benefits of civilization, as expressed by the racial, material, and cultural superiority of the Europan racial stock, concentrated in *circa* 10 million square kilometres to the rest of mankind, spread over *circa* 120 million square kilometres over the planet. The origin of this cultural superiority was focused on the mediterranean, mainly Greek philosophy, with special mention to mathematics. It allowed for the material development through science and technology, and Charles Darwin came with the scientific explanation for racial superiority. The imperial order was consolidated in the turn of the century and supported by an umbilical cultural history developed since the early nineteenth century. Particularly, this affects our vision of mathematics and of science in general. Although variants such as an externalist history have been proposed, their umbilical characteristics are always dominating.

A close look into both the urban environment of modern cities and the rural communities opens up an important fissure in the tranquil imperial explanation. Mainly looking into communities founded by immigrants in the Americas — as it is the case of most of the USA, of Argentina, Brazil and many areas of Latin America, where we find practically no presence of native culture, but much evidence of the struggle of Europeans and Africans to compatibilize their modes of explanation and their ways of doing and knowing to the new environment. This analysis has much in common with what nowadays we call technology transfer affecting the so-called Third World countries. Although not explicitly studied, culture transfer is a major problem. It was not explicitly studied because one sees culture detached from the natural environment. Hence, no surprise that mathematicians get surprised when we include mathematics in these remarks. After all, mathematics is universal — this means transcend cultural barriers, and how can we see in natural factors in mathematics! So, no point in concerns about mathematical trasfer. It makes sense to adapt a corn hybrid or to find the most appropriate vehicle for desert travelling. But trying to relate culture, and mainly mathematics to the environment . . . it is nonsense! So, reflections on mathematics continues to be umbilical!

Modern theories of cognition support the necessity of looking for broader attitudes towards mathematics. Cognition and culture are indeed closely related and there is not much hope of reaching creative power without cultural roots. The interdisciplinarian atmosphere was a good ground to realize these connections. A careful comparison enticed me to look into the history of mathematics, initially Greeks, Romans, Hebrews and Arabs, focusing in the aspects of cultural dynamics which were clearly noticeable in my early experience in Mali and in Latin America and the categories of analysis I had been using (see D'Ambrosio, 1991). For example, concepts of time and space, features associated with form, such as colour, and mythical associations with concepts of mathematics and of truth, as well as modes of property and production.

Another Look into the History of Mathematics

The main strategy asks for a different interpretation of classical antiquity, and limitations of sources have been an obstacle. Indeed, this is the main obstacle in the research when we move into other cultures. The difficulties of looking into cultures which were less successful in resisting the dominating cultures, such as for example the Amazonian indians, are enormous. Above all it is difficult to access their registered memories. The register, which certainly exists, follows different techniques. To ignore these techniques and to claim that these cultures lack memory of these cultures has been the main tool of the dominating culture to impose itself to the culture which was dominated. Elimination of the memory of the conquered by the conqueror is normally facilitated by the lack of cultural self-esteem.

Thus, ethno-mathematics offers not only a broader view of mathematics, embracing practices and methods related to a variety of cultural environments and normally left aside, but also a more comprehensive, contextualized perception of the processes of generating, organizing, trasmitting and disseminating mathematics throughout the history of Mankind. Through the valorization of the history of different cultures there is a greater opportunity of generating cultural self-esteem, which is a key factor in opening the way for individuals to reach their full creative power.

Up to Plato, our sources rely on his accounts and our main reference for the beginning growth of mathematics points to two clearly distinct branches: what we might call 'scholarly mathematics', which was incorporated in the ideal education of Greeks, and another one, which we may call 'practical' mathematics, reserved mainly for manual workers. Since the Egyptians there was a reserved space for mathematical practices which was taught to workers. This is carried on to the Greeks and Plato clearly distinguishes that 'all these studies [ciphering and arithmetic, measurements, relations of planetary orbits] into their minute details is not for the masses but for a selected few', and 'we should induce those who are to share the highest functions of State to enter upon that study of calculation and hold it, . . . not for the purpose of buying and selling, as if they were preparing to be merchants or hucksters.' (Plato, in Hamilton and Cairns, 1966). This distinction between scholarly and practical mathematics, reserved for different social classes, was adopted by the Romans through the *trivium* and *quadrivium* and through a practical training for labourers. In the Middle Ages we begin to see a convergence of both forms, scholarly and practical, in one direction. That is, practical mathematics begins to use some ideas of scholarly mathematics, firstly in the field of geometry. Practical geometry becomes a subject in itself in the Middle Ages. In fact, these are early steps towards engineering science, through artisanal work. The approximation of practical to theoretical geometry is done after the translation from the Arabic of Euclid's *Elements* by Adelard of Bath (early twelfth century). Dominicus Gomdissalinus, in his classification of sciences, says that 'it would be disgraceful for someone to exercise any art and not know what it is, and what subject matter it has, and the other things that are premised of it' (see Victor, 1979, p. 8). With respect to ciphering and counting, change started to take place with the introduction of Arabic numerals. *Liber Abacci*, written in 1202 by Leonardo de Pisa, the Fibonacci, is probably the first to present practical and theoretical aspects of arithmetic in a mixed way.

The next step in our periodization is the Renaissance, where a new labour structure in the domain of architecture took place with the appearance of technical drawing. This became accessible to bricklayers, and the description of machinery was illustrated thanks to the emergence of drawing. This allowed techniques to be reproduced by people other than the inventors. In painting, schools became more efficient, and treatises began to be available. The approximation of scholars to the general public is clear and scholars, who started to use vernacular for their scholarly works, sometimes wrote in a non-technical language and in a style accessible to non-scholars. The best known examples are Galileo and Newton's 'Optik'.

The approximation of practical science and mathematics to scholarly science and mathematics took an increasing pace in the industrial era, not only for the reason of the necessity of dealing with increasingly complex machinery and instructional manuals, but also for social reasons. Exclusively scholarly training would not suffice for the children of an aristocracy which had to be prepared to keep its social and economic predominance in a new order. The approximation of scholarly and practical science and mathematics begins to enter the school systems, if we may call school system the pedagogical practices of those ages.

Finally, we reach a last step in this rough periodization by attaining the twentieth century and the widespread concept of mass education. More urgently than in Plato, the question of *what* science and mathematics should be taught in the systems of mass education, that is, taught to every one, was then posed. For those in power, it must be the science and the mathematics that keep the economic and social structure remaining with the aristocracy. Of course, this requires a better training of all subjects for them to be able to consume in the increasing level of sophistication offered. At the same time, it was essential to prepare the elites to assume effective management of the productive sector, as advocated by Plato. In the case of mathematics, this gave place to a 'scholarly practical' mathematics which we call from now on in this book 'academic mathematics', i.e., the mathematics which is taught and learned in schools. In contraposition, we will use the word ethnomathematics for the mathematics that is practised among identifiable cultural groups, such as national-tribal societies, children of a certain age bracket, labour groups, professional classes and so on.

This is equally true with science in general. Much of the practices such as curing, plant growing, and divination fit in the category of ethnoscience, as contraposed to 'academic science'. This depends largely on focuses of interest and motivation and on certain codes and jargons which do not belong to the realm of academic science and mathematics. We go even further in these concepts of ethnomathematics and ethnoscience to include much of the mathematics and physics which are currently practised by engineers, mainly calculus, which do not respond to the standards of rigour and formalism developed in academic courses. As an example, the Sylvanus Thompson approach to calculus may better fit into this category of ethnomathematics. Masons and well diggers and shack raisers in slums are examples of practitioners of ethnomathematics and ethnoscience.

Of course, this concept asks for a broader interpretation of what science and mathematics are. Now we include as science and mathematics, other than the Platonic ciphering and arithmetic, mensuration and relations of planetary orbits, also the capabilities of observing, classifying, ordering, inferring, and modelling and the use of tools and instruments. This is a very broad range of human activities, throughout history, which has been expropriated by the scholarly establishment, formalized and codified and incorporated into what we call academic science and mathematics. But these activities are still performed, in a manner much closer to the original practitioners and are alive in culturally identified groups and constitute routines in their daily practices.

Again on Pedagogical Practices

We would like to insist on both the broad conceptualization of what science is and which allows us to identify several practices which are essentially scientific in their nature. And also we presuppose a board concept of ethno, which includes groups which are culturally identified through their jargons, codes, symbols, myths and even specific ways of reasoning and inferring. Of course, this comes into a concept of culture which is the result of a hierarchization of behaviour, from individual behaviour through social behaviour and leading to cultural behaviour.

This relies on a holistic model of individual behaviour based on the cycle . . . reality → individual → action → reality . . . which we have studied elsewhere (D'Ambrosio, 1988). We simply assume reality in a broad sense, both natural, material, social and psycho-emotional. Now, we observe that the links are possible through mechanisms of information, including both sensorial and memory (genetic and acquired) systems, which produce stimuli in the individual. Through a mechanism of reification, these stimuli give origin to strategies (based on codes and models), which generate action. Action impacts upon reality by introducing facti into this reality, both artifacts and 'mentifacts'. We have introduced this neologism to mean all the results of intellectual action which are not material, such as ideas, concepts, theories, reflections and thoughts. These are added to reality in the broad sense mentioned above, and clearly modify it. The concept of reification has been used by the socio-biologists as 'the mental activity in which hazily perceived and relatively intangible phenomena, such as complex arrays of objects or activities, are given a factitiously concrete form, simplified and labelled with words or other symbols.' We assume this to be the basic mechanism through which strategies for action are defined. This action, be it through artifacts or mentifacts, modifies reality, which in turn produces additional information which, through this reificative process, modifies or generates new strategies for action and so on. This ceaseless cycle is the basis for the theoretical framework upon which we base our ethnoscience concept.

Individual behaviour in certain ways which are homogenized through mechanisms such as education, build up into societal behaviour, which in turn generate what we call culture. This allows for the concept of culture as the strategy for societal action. Now the mechanism of reification which is characteristic of human behaviour, is replaced by *communication*, while information, which impacts upon an individual, is replaced by history, which has its effects on society as a whole. We will not go deeper into this theoretical framework for the concept of culture (see D'Ambrosio, 1990).

As we have mentioned above, culture manifests itself through jargons, codes, symbols and ways of reasoning and inferring. Associated with these we have practices such as ciphering and counting, measuring, observing, classifying, ordering, inferring, modelling, modes of explanation and experimental inference and so on, which are identified with scientific thought and which are the primary *tics* in the ethnomathematics approach.

Methodological Issues

The basic question then posed is the following: How 'theoretical' can ethnomathematics be? It has been long recognized that scientific practices, as those mentioned in the end of the previous paragraph, are known to several culturally differentiated groups, and when we say 'known' we mean these are practised in a way which is substantially different from the western or academic ways of doing them. This is commonly seen in the research of anthropologists and, even before ethnography had been recognized as a science, by travellers all over the world. The interest has been drawn mainly as curiosity or as a source of anthropological concern of learning about the way natives think. We go a step further in trying to find an underlying structure of inquiry into these practices, which are commonly classified as *ad hoc* practices.

In other words we have to pose the following questions:

- How do we pass from *observations and ad hoc practices* and solution of simple problems to *experimentation and methods*?
- How do we pass from experimentation and methods to *reflections and abstractions*?
- How do we proceed to *theories and inventions*?

It seems, through the study of the history of science, that these have been steps in the building-up of scientific theories. Research programmes in the history of science are essentially based on these four steps and the three questions of passage.

The main issue is then a methodological one, and it lies in the concept of history in itself, in particular of history of science. We have to agree with the initial sentence in Bellone's excellent book on the second scientific revolution: 'There is a temptation hidden in the pages of the History of Science — the temptation to derive birth and death of theories, the formalization and growth of concepts, from a scheme (either logical or philosophical) always valid and everywhere applicable ... Instead of dealing with real problems, history would then become a learned review of edifying tales for the benefit of one philosophical school or another.' (Bellone, 1980, p. 1). This permeates the analysis of popular practices such as ethnomathematics, depriving it of any history. As a consequence, it is deprived of the status of being a form of knowledge.

Conclusion

It is appropriate, at this point, to make a few considerations about what science is nowadays, regarded as a large-scale professional activity. As we have already mentioned, it developed into this current situation only since early nineteenth century. Although scientists communicated among themselves and scientific periodicals, meetings and associations were known, the activities of the scientists did not receive reward as such. It came more as the result of patronage. Universities were little concerned about preparing scientists or training individuals for scientific work. Only in the nineteenth century to be a scientist began to be regarded as a professional activity. As Derek Gjertsen points out in his recent book on 'Science and Philosophy: Past and Present' a scientist is a new concept (Gjertsen, 1989). According to him, the term was used for the first time by William Whewell in 1840. A quick look into the history of science confirms this. Specialists, professionals in doing science as their occupation and paid for such, with the expectation to produce something defined in advance, appear in the middle of the last century, with the growth of the 'scientific' society. Before that, they — individuals looking for scientific explanations and modes of doing — were all philosophers. And out of this change, the differentiation of science into scientific fields and the appearance of specialists became unavoidable. The training of scientists, now professionals with specific qualifications, was done in specific subjects, in universities or similar institutions, and mechanisms to qualify them for professional activities were developed. And standards of evaluation of credentials were developed. Knowledge, in particular scientific knowledge, was granted status which allowed to bestow upon individuals the required credentials for their professional activity. This same knowledge, practised in many strata of society, at different levels of sophistication and depth, was expropriated by those who would have the responsibility and power for professional accreditation. The building up of a power structure based on knowledge was thus completed.

We may cite as an example, in the case of mathematics, the parallel development of scientific discipline outside the established and accepted model of the profession. The example is the discovery of Dirac's delta function, which only about twenty years after being in full use among physicists, was expropriated and became a mathematical subject, structured as the 'Theory of Distribution'. This is part of the internal dynamics of knowledge *vis-à-vis* of society.

There is unquestionably a time lag between the appearance of new ideas in mathematics outside the circle of practitioners and the recognition of these ideas as 'theorizable' into mathematics, with the appropriate codes of the discipline, until the expropriation of the idea and its formalization as mathematics. During this period of time the idea was to put into use and practice. This is an example of what we call ethnomathematics in its broadest sense. Eventually, it becomes mathematics in the style or mode of thought recognized as such. In many cases, it never gets into this formalization, and the practice continues restricted to the culturally differentiated group which originated it. A mechanism of schooling replaces these practices by other equivalent practices which have been expropriated in its original form and returns in a codified version, accessible only to those initiated, i.e., accepted in the power structure. The same is true of scientific knowledge in general.

We claim a status for those practices. Paraphrasing the terminology of T.S. Kuhn, they are not 'normal science'. Very unlikely it will generate a 'revolutionary science' in the Kuhnian terminology. They will keep its life, evolve as a result of societal change, but the new forms will simply replace the former ones, which go into oblivion. The cumulative character of this form of knowledge cannot be recognized, and its status as a scientific discipline becomes questionable. The internal revolutions in these practices, which result from societal changes as a whole, are not sufficiently linked in the Kuhnian concept of 'normality'. There is no sense in talking about 'normal ethnoscience'. Thus the claim of historical development, which is the spine of a body of knowledge structured as a discipline, is not recognizable and as a consequence, ethnomathematics is simply not recognized as a structured body of knowledge, but rather as a set of *ad hoc* practices.

It is the purpose of our research programme to identify ethnomathematics as a structured body of knowledge. For this, it is essential to follow the three steps described above, and later develop methodological alternatives.

As it stands now, we are in the stage of collecting examples and data on practices of culturally differentiated groups which are identifiable as scientific and mathematical practices, hence ethnomathematics, and trying to link those practices in patterns of reasoning, as modes of thought. Both from cognitive theory and from cultural anthropology we hope to trace the origin of those practices. This way we may reach a systematic organization of these practices into a body of knowledge.

For effective research in this field, are required not only an intense experience in science, but also investigative and research methods to absorb and understand knowledge in the broad sense. This clearly requires quite difficult anthropological research in the sciences, a field as yet poorly cultivated. Together with social history of science, which aims at understanding the mutual influence of sociocultural, economic and political factors in the development of science, an anthropological history of science, if we may coin a name for this specialty, are topics which we feel are essential research themes not as a mere academic exercise in itself, as they have been drawing interest, but as the underlying ground which we can understand, in a relevant way, for the evolution of scientific knowledge.

History of science acquires also a more global, clearly holistic approach, not only by the consideration of methods, objectives and contents of scientific knowledge in solidarity, but mainly by the incorporation of the results of anthropological findings into it. This is quite different from what has frequently and mistakenly been done, which is to analyse each of these components individually. This has many implications for research priorities in the history of science and has obviously a counterpart in the development of science itself. Clearly, the distinction between science and technology has to be interpreted in a different way. What has been labelled as science, or we might emphasize pure science, and continues to be such, is the natural result of the evolution of the discipline within a social, economical and cultural atmosphere, which cannot be disengaged of the main expectations of a certain historical moment. For example, in talking about mathematics, we must not disregard the fact that L. Kroenecker (the famous mathematician who said 'God created the integers — the rest is the work of men'), K. Marx, and Charles Darwin, were contemporaries. Pure mathematics as opposed to applied mathematics, a distinction highly artificial and ideologically dangerous, came into use at about that time, with obvious political and philosophical undertones. Clearly, to revise research priorities in such a way as to incorporate national development priorities to scientific practices, which in the end generates university research, is a most difficult thing to do. This problem leads naturally to a closing theme for this chapter, which is the relation of science and ideology.

Ideology is implicit in dressing, housing, titles and naturally in the forms of thought, including the inherent logic of structured knowledge. Of course, science results from some logic which underlies the ideological roots of western civilization. We have assumed, throughout this chapter, a broad conceptualization of science, which allows for looking into common practices which are apparently unstructured forms of knowledge. This results from a concept of culture which is the result of hierarchization of behaviour, from individual through social behaviour and leading to cultural behaviour. This depends on a model of individual behaviour based on the ceaseless cycle . . . reality → individual → action → reality . . . The conceptualization of science which derives from this model allows for the inclusion of what might be considered marginal practices of a scientific nature, and which we have called ethnomathematics. Of course, these common practices are impregnated with ideological overtones which are deeply rooted in the cultural texture of the group of practitioners. The full understanding of these ideological overtones is an essential component of the 'Programme Ethnomathematics.'

Notes

1. These are the last phrases of *The Russell-Einstein Manifest*, endorsed in 9 July 1955 by many scientists in a meeting in the Canadian town of Pugwash.

References

ANTON, D. (1977) *History of Logic*, Abacus Press.

ASCHER, H. (1991) *Ethnomathematics. A Multicultural View of Mathematical Ideas*, Pacific grove, Brooks/Cole Publishing Company.

ASCHER, M. and ASCHER, R. (1988) *Code of the Quipu*, Ann Arbor, MI, University of Michigan Press.

BELLONE, E. (1980) *A World on Paper*, Cambridge, The MIT Press.

D'AMBROSIO, U. (1988) *Da Realidade ä Ação: Reflexões sobre Educação (e) Matemática*, 2 edição, São Paulo, Summus Editorial.

D'AMBROSIO, U. (1990) *Etnomatemätica. Arte ou Técnica de Explicar e Conhecer*, São Paulo, Editora Atica.

D'AMBROSIO, U. (1991) *Several Dimensions of Science Education*, CIDE/REDUC, Santiago de Chile.

DESCARTES, R. (1973) *Discurso do Método* Coleção 'Os Pensadores', Abril S/A Cultural e Industrial, São Paulo (Original edition 1641).

GJERSTEN, D. (1989) *Science and Philosophy. Past and present*, Penguin Books.

PLATO, *The Complete Dialogues*, in HAMILTON, E. and CAIRNS, H. (Eds) (1966) Bollinger Series, New York, Pantheon Books (Laws VII, p. 818, and Republic VII, p. 525b.)

POOTER, K.H. (Ed) (1977) *Indian Metaphysics and Epistemology*, Encyclopedia of Indian Philosophies, Princeton NJ Princeton University Press.

VICTOR, S.K. (Ed) (1979) *Artis Cuiuslibet Consummatis* (unknown author), in *Practical Geometry in the High Middle Ages*, The American Philosophical Society, Philadelphia.

Notes on Contributors

David Bloor is a reader in the Science Studies Unit of the Department of Sociology at the University of Edinburgh, Scotland.

Tony Brown is a senior lecturer in mathematics education at the Manchester Metropolitan University, England.

Philip J. Davis is emeritus professor of applied mathematics at Brown University, Providence, Rhode Island, USA.

Mairéad Dunne is a researcher at the School of Education, University of Birmingham, England.

Ubiratan D'Ambrosio is professor of mathematics at the University of Campinas, Sao Paulo, Brazil.

Paul Dowling is a lecturer at the Institute of Education, University of London, England.

Paul Ernest is reader in mathematics education in the School of Education at the University of Exeter, England.

Jeff Evans is a principal lecturer in statistics at Middlesex University, London, England.

Reuben Hersh is professor in the Department of Mathematics at the University of New Mexico, Albuquerque, USA.

David W. Jardine is a professor in the Faculty of Education at the University of Calgary, Alberta, Canada.

Jayne Johnston is a mathematics education specialist at the Ministry of Education, Western Australia.

George Gheverghese Joseph is a senior lecturer in the Faculty of Economic and Social Studies at the University of Manchester, England.

Sal Restivo is professor of sociology and science studies in the Department of Science and Technology Studies at Rensselaer Polytechnic Institute, Troy, New York, USA.

Brian Rotman took early retirement from the Department of Mathematics at the University of Bristol, England, and is now a freelance writer and consultant based in Memphis, USA.

Anna Tsatsaroni is a researcher in the Department of Primary Education, University of Patras, Greece.

Thomas Tymoczko is professor in the Department of Philosophy at Smith College, Northampton, Massachusetts, USA.

Jeff Vass is a lecturer in education in the Faculty of Humanities and Teacher Education, University of North London, England.

Valerie Walkerdine is professor in the Department of Media and Communications, Goldsmiths' College, University of London, England.

Hao Wang is professor in the Department of Philosophy at the Rockefeller University, New York, USA.

Index

2 + 2 = 4: sociological character of 21–31